CHRISTIAN BEGINNINGS

Word and Community
from Jesus
to Post-Apostolic Times

CHRISTIAN BEGINNINGS

Word and Community from Jesus to Post-Apostolic Times

Jürgen Becker, Editor

Translated by
Annemarie S. Kidder
and Reinhard Krauss

Westminster/John Knox Press
Louisville, Kentucky

Book design by Drew Stevens

Published by Westminster/John Knox Press
Louisville, Kentucky

This book is printed on acid-free paper that meets the American National Standards Institute Z39.48 standard. ∞

PRINTED IN THE UNITED STATES OF AMERICA
9 8 7 6 5 4 3 2 1

Library of Congress Cataloging-in-Publication Data

Anfänge des Christentums. English.
    Christian beginnings / Jürgen Becker, editor : translated by
Annemarie S. Kidder and Reinhard Krauss.
        p.   cm.
Translation of: Die Anfänge des Christentums.
Includes bibliographical references.
ISBN 0-664-25195-1 (pbk. : alk. paper)

    1. Bible. N.T.—History of contemporary events.   2. Bible. N.T.—
History of Biblical events.   3. Bible. N.T.—Criticism,
interpretation, etc.   4. Church history—Primitive and early church,
ca. 30-600.   I. Becker, Jürgen, 1934–   .   II. Title.
BS2407.A5413   1993
225.9'5—dc20   93-9308

Contents

Preface*   7
Introduction   Jürgen Becker*   9

I. Jesus

1. Jesus of Nazareth   Christoph Burchard*   15

II. The First Generation of Early Christianity

2. The Oldest Jewish-Christian Community   Carsten Colpe*   75
3. The Circle of Stephen and Its Mission   Karl Löning*   103
4. Paul and His Churches   Jürgen Becker**   132

III. The Post-Apostolic Period

5. The Synoptic Evangelists and Their Communities
   John K. Riches   213
6. Post-Pauline Christianity and Pagan Society
   Peter Lampe and Ulrich Luz*   242
7. Apocalyptic Currents   Ulrich B. Müller*   281
8. Johannine Christianity   C. K. Barrett   330

Contributors   359

*Translated by Annemarie S. Kidder
**Translated by Reinhard Krauss

Preface

The present volume is an international and ecumenical cooperative work. Though written as part of one common inquiry, each contribution is the responsibility of its author. One may doubt whether it is at all possible at this time for a single author to respond to this inquiry with a comprehensive presentation of early Christianity. Still, the question of how early Christianity is intertwined with antiquity on such levels as governmental institutions, social reality, culture, and religious phenomena focuses on an important aspect of early Christianity. This aspect cannot be neglected if New Testament studies are not to lose sight of the concrete historical dimension of early Christianity.

In recent years individual studies have increasingly pointed to this dimension. Important details have emerged, but much remains unexplained. Quite a few things will forever remain in the shadows of history. This is due in part to the sources themselves, which offer only indirect information concerning the present inquiry. They were not written to quench this thirst for information. Nevertheless, the time seems right not only to make an attempt in a cooperative work to advance research in individual aspects but also to present a general overview of the connections between early Christianity and the Hellenistic-Roman world.

Naturally, each author has his own overall concept when writing his contribution. Also, individual phenomena may be evaluated differently in particular instances. That is consciously accepted in the bargain. For the authors agree that the reader will still recognize a large current of common understanding. Differences of perception that are not swept under the carpet are a good reflection of the present state of research, and they provide an incentive to look further for the truth.

This book was originally conceived as the first volume of the church history series "Christentum und Gesellschaft" (Christianity and Society). When the series was discontinued, the manuscript of this volume was basically complete. This course of events explains why one of the editors of the discontinued series, H. Gülzow, has played an important role in the development of this volume both in the conceptual part and in the selection of authors.

Finally, the reader needs to know that only those abbreviations have been used that can be easily identified or are listed in S. Schwertner's *Theologische Realenzyklopädie* "Abkürzungsverzeichnis" (Berlin, 1976) or in *Die Religion in Geschichte und Gegenwart* (Tübingen, 1957–65).*

Jürgen Becker

*In the present English edition the abbreviations are generally those used in the *Journal of Biblical Literature*.

Introduction

Jürgen Becker

In the ancient world Christianity's country of origin belonged to the barbaric territories. After Alexander the Great had passed through the land also, it became more or less caught up in the widespread process of Hellenization; also during the time of the Diadochi (Alexander's successors), it became a bone of contention between the Ptolemies and the Seleucids, between Egypt and Syria. The area became part of the Pax Romana shortly before the start of the Augustan era: in 63 B.C. Julius Caesar came to the country. The long period of peace under Herod the Great was due to Augustus's benevolence. Augustus inherited Judea in 6 B.C. and turned it into an imperial province. Therefore Pontius Pilate probably represented Roman authority between A.D. 26 and 36. In the remaining parts of Herod's kingdom, Augustus installed Herod's sons as procurators—Jesus' procurator, for example, was Herod Antipas for the region of Galilee. Since Augustus achieved a provisional peace with the Parthians in the East, the securing of the empire's borders shifted to the north, where Caesar had already established the Danube and the Rhine as natural borders. Thus, Palestine held little interest during Jesus' time and during the early beginning of Christianity. For centuries people had been using the country as a trade corridor between Egypt and Syria. It was known as the homeland of the Jews, who adhered to a special, exclusive, monotheistic religion, and could be found in almost all parts of the empire.

The beginnings of Christianity were limited to the country of origin only during Jesus' lifetime. He and his circle of disciples remained centered in Palestine in more than a geographical sense. They certainly did not have a worldwide mission in mind. It seems that with Jesus' crucifixion (probably around A.D. 30), his brief public appearance was interrupted and termi-

9

nated in the same manner as that of many other contemporary prophets who are mentioned by Josephus; the Romans wiped them out in order to keep peace in the land. However, Josephus does not mention Jesus; neither do Roman sources, which do not take note of Christianity until Nero persecuted Christians in the imperial capital (Tacitus).

Jesus' death and the Easter visions form the first decisive caesura in the earliest history of Christianity. Jesus' God continued to be proclaimed as the Father of Jesus Christ; the proclaimer of the approaching kingdom of God became the One proclaimed, the Lord of the world, in whose name people soon missionized outside Palestine—first in Syria and in Asia Minor, then in Macedonia and Greece, and at the same time also in North Africa, in Rome, etc. It was mainly in the cities of the Roman Empire that Christian congregations now emerged. Within one generation, Christianity became firmly rooted in almost all the larger cities of the Mediterranean area. In this, of course, Paul played the major role. His Gentile-Christian churches, forming independently outside the network of synagogues, shaped the post-Easter image of Christendom in such a way that slowly but surely Jewish Christianity (related to synagogues) became a Christian minority.

With the death of the apostles and the great missionaries of the first generation around A.D. 60, we find a second caesura in the early history of Christianity. It coincides roughly with the end of the Julian-Claudian dynasty, which marks one of the most peaceful periods within the Roman Empire from the time of Augustus to Nero and thus provides favorable conditions for the spread of Christianity. World traffic and world trade flourished; language and culture became standardized. Also, a religious syncretism provided the general preparation for an openness to a new religion. Now, after the first generation had passed, Christianity no longer viewed itself as an integral part of early Christian origins but looked back on the beginnings of Christianity as a given spiritual heritage. Now Christianity had a history of precedents that went back farther than the current Christian generation. People looked back to these past origins as the great and normative time. The fathers had passed away; children and grandchildren preserved the heritage but felt rather small by comparison. It was not new departures but consolidation that defined the tasks of the time. The imminent expectation of the Parousia was fading. The almost breathtaking dynamic in the development of Christology had slowed; ethics, with a tendency toward independence, became the new topic of general importance and was responsible for the judgment at the time that Christianity was becoming legalistic. Once led by the Spirit, churches were now on their way to an ecclesiastical structure in which the first offices were taking shape and were linked with the preservation of tradition and doctrine. In the antagonism between Jewish and Gentile Christians, Jewish Christianity was ultimately put on the defensive, mainly because Judaism lost its spiritual center with the insurrection of the Zealots and the resulting destruction of Jerusalem by Titus (A.D. 70/71). The innovations of this period are the first Christian "heresies": The "struggle against heretics" had begun.

This postapostolic period was no longer a Christianity without literature. In the first generation Paul was the great exception with the legacy of his letters; in the postapostolic period—also called the age of emerging Catholicism—literary production experiences its first flowering. Apart from the genuine Pauline letters, almost all New Testament writings originate during this period, as do those of the so-called apostolic fathers. In Luke-Acts, for the first time, we encounter an attempt to deal with the history of Christianity as a theme in itself. Typical of its time, this double work is governed by a comprehensive concept of salvation history. The placing of Christianity into the course of world history at large, signaled by the Lukan world-historical synchronicities, and the programmatic presentation of religious history—for example, in the Areopagos speech (Acts 17)—are signs of the new awareness. This period—and with it early Christianity in general—concludes with the transition to Christian apologetics; it is marked by Hadrian's renewed conquest of Jerusalem at the end of the Bar-Kokhba revolt (A.D. 132–35) and by the first Gnostic systems, now accessible in literary form (Nag Hammadi), according to which the Gnostic milieu had already been developing for at least one generation as a nonliterary intellectual climate. Hadrian was the last Roman emperor to guide the destiny of the empire contemporaneous to early Christianity. After Nero, first the Flavian dynasty (from Vespasian to Domitian) and then the first adoptive emperors directed the politics of Rome in parallel with the history of Christianity.

Hence, we can identify three periods in early Christian history: the time of Jesus, the generation of the apostles (the first early Christian generation), and the postapostolic period, a time of transition that would eventually evolve into the early Catholic church (second and third early Christian generations). This division determines the organization of the present work and sketches the outline of the task at hand. While each of the three periods has its own makeup, the interconnections of early Christianity with the ancient world have to be indicated separately for each period.

I

Jesus

1

Jesus of Nazareth

Christoph Burchard

a) Background

(*1*) *The sources.* Like most people in antiquity, Jesus of Nazareth did not leave anything behind that can be seen. Also, he did not write or dictate anything. No eyewitness or listener speaks directly to us. By and large, we know Jesus through the influence he had on people. He won disciples and followers among his compatriots, who then formed, together with Jesus, what today is often called the Jesus movement, and who, after Jesus' death, more or less carried on his cause in Palestine and soon also outside of it. In other words, we know of Jesus through the history of primitive Christianity.

Part of this history is the fact that a tradition formed based on Jesus' words, deeds, and fate, and that this tradition was used to minister in his name, to embark on missions, and to direct and regulate one's personal life and thought. According to most scholars, the Jesus tradition remained oral for several decades, namely, in a way that Jesus' stories and sayings were passed on by individuals or groups. Only slowly did fixed themes or subject complexes emerge, organized by geographic-historical aspects, and books attempting to include all of Jesus' life were certainly published as early as in the sixties of the first century A.D. Of these, for the most part, only the four Gospels of Matthew, Mark, Luke, and John have been preserved. These books are our main source of the Jesus tradition, especially the first three, which run parallel to each other and are therefore called the Synoptic Gospels.

However, primitive Christianity did not simply live off the Jesus tradition and propagate it. It could also be influenced by Jesus in those aspects where it does not explicitly mention him. We know of the life and thought of primitive Christianity from early Christian literature, mainly those writings that were joined in the course of the second century and later received the name *New Testament*. The oldest and, apart from the Gospels, most important part of the New Testament is the corpus of letters written by the apostle Paul during the fifties of the first century to Christian communities founded by him (except for the first): Romans, 1 and 2 Corinthians, Galatians, Philippians, 1 Thessalonians, Philemon. (The rest of the letters "of Paul" were probably written by his students or by their students in turn.) Paul is the oldest Christian we know from self-testimony.

Overall, one has to do the same with Jesus as with people whose works are preserved, together with their heritage, and this also applies, by the way, to primitive Christianity: one improves the situation of the sources by looking at the history of the period. Whatever else Jesus was, he was a Jew from Galilee, and the Jesus movement was, at least in its beginnings, Galilean Jewish or, at any rate, Palestinian Jewish. We know of Jesus' environment from contemporary writings, including those used at the time such as the Old Testament, which, of course, did not yet have that name. In addition, we have archeology and geography. Since over the past years both sciences have oriented themselves more toward regional and social history, they now yield more information on country life and that of ordinary people. Especially Galilee has benefited from this reorientation, since very few monuments have remained.

Hence, one has access to Jesus in two ways: first, by the history of primitive Christianity, insofar as it can be understood as the history of Jesus' influence; and second, the history of Palestine, insofar as it was the place of Jesus' ministry. In both instances, history is understood in a comprehensive way—from the affairs of the government and the state to the affairs of everyday life, from head to toe. The points of access complement each other and sometimes overlap. Both Jesus and the beginnings of early Christianity are part of the history of Judaism in Palestine.

That means, of course, that one can gain access to Jesus only by detours and even then not to the whole person. One cannot write a biography of Jesus. Neither his height nor the color of his eyes is told. His development, his personality, and his inner life can hardly be grasped. What we can understand, in addition to many details, is (1) the temporal and local framework of his public ministry, which ended with his death, (2) his goal and the typical traits of his actions, and (3) his influence.

After all, opinions about what Jesus was really like must differ, even among people working with the same presuppositions, sharing the same interests, and employing the same methods. Ultimately, the reason lies with Jesus himself. He wanted to be born into the present, not into the future.

(2) *Palestine during Jesus' time.* The period in which Jesus lived cannot be limited to the years when he was alive. History flowed more slowly in antiquity than it does today, especially in border areas of the Roman Empire, to which Palestine had belonged since 63 B.C., as well as among people like the Jews, who kept their distance from the superpowers, and above all in rural areas such as Galilee.

The death of Herod the Great (40–4 B.C.) was a turning point, especially in a political sense. Though Herod was a loyal vassal of the emperor Augustus (31 B.C. to A.D.14), he was independent in internal affairs and had ruled almost all of Palestine and some areas in the East, Northeast, and beyond in the manner of a Hellenistic despot. That much territory had been governed only by David and Solomon (tenth century B.C.), and they were Herod's models. Of Herod's possibly one-and-a-quarter million subjects, about one million were Jews; of the latter, between two hundred thousand and three hundred thousand lived in Galilee; the rest were mainly in Judea, Idumea, and Perea. The mother tongue of most of them was probably Aramaic, yet many also spoke Greek. Hebrew was the language of Holy Scripture (which therefore had to be translated during worship), also of scholars and lawyers, yet not of the common people. In addition, one finds Greek-speaking Jews in the land ("Greco-Palestinians"), some of whom had returned from the Diaspora or were descendants of those who had returned.

When Herod died, the country was divided among his three sons. Archelaus (4 B.C. to A.D. 6) received Judea, Samaria, and Idumea; Herod Antipas (4 B.C. to A.D. 39) received Galilee and Perea; and Philip (4 B.C. to A.D. 34) received the Golan and other areas in the Northeast. In A.D. 6, the Romans dethroned Archelaus because of his mismanagement, and the area became a Roman province led by a governor, who resided in Caesarea by the sea. When Jesus came on the scene in the late twenties, Antipas, Jesus' ruler, and Philip had been firmly in power for more than a generation, though in a manner more bearable than that of their father. The governor of Judea had changed several times; during Jesus' time Pontius Pilate held the office (A.D. 26–36). The governors tried to follow the political plan Augustus had established for governing the provinces: peace and order, securing of the borders as far as they were external borders of the empire, timely soliciting of the not exactly low taxes without sucking the country dry (cf. *e*, 8 below), and generally protective treatment of the people living in the provinces. It should be clear, however, that Pilate was a harsh and insensitive man.

Judaism in Palestine was hardly affected by the outside either culturally or religiously. It kept to itself, though on the inside it was anything but uniform. Both aspects were probably the result of the internal conflicts of Maccabean times (second century B.C.). At that time, people had repelled an attempt forcibly to integrate the Jerusalem temple and the entire Jewish tradition into the large culture of Hellenism (see also *e*, 7 below), which had become international since Alexander the Great (356–323 B.C.). Yet the older assumption that Hellenism never reached Jewish Palestine at all is wrong. In many ways Palestine had prevailed against the cultural super-power only in its own mind (M. Hengel).

The world in which Jesus lived did not change fundamentally until the first Jewish war (A.D. 66–73). The temple—the place that "God will choose . . . to put his name" (Deut. 12:5) and where God indeed resided in the eyes of simple people, this worldwide center of Judaism—was destroyed in A.D. 70 and never rebuilt; the cult that provided atonement for Israel stopped, since the leading priests had died during the war. Judaism in Palestine lost what was left of political independence, together with the last traditional governing organ, the Sanhedrin in Jerusalem, a kind of senate with the high priest at the top. Judaism lost the holy city and Judea, the population of which was killed, sold into slavery, or driven out. It took the remaining populated areas decades to reorganize themselves, especially Galilee. The leadership in this project was taken on by the only group of Judea's leading class that had not lost its role and had not become completely decimated: the scribes. These scholars formed the type of "rabbinic" Judaism that prevailed in Palestine and beyond and incorporated or expelled all other forms that had survived the war. Most of what holds true up to then for Palestine holds true also for the first decades of the first century, although this cannot be proved for that particular period.

b) The Origin and Education of Jesus and His Followers

(1) *Jesus*. From antiquity's viewpoint, the Jesus of the Jesus tradition was a man in his best years: He was a *tektōn* (construction worker, carpenter, or wheelwright?) by profession yet did not work as one; he was without family, grew up speaking Aramaic, could read and perhaps also write, and understood at least some Hebrew, perhaps even some Greek. Jesus knew the Holy

Scriptures and had a theological education, even if not a professional one. He was a good speaker, fluent in traditional sayings, who created parables that became world literature; the Aramaic Lord's Prayer even rhymed. It is hard to say how familiar Jesus was with more recent Jewish history. He certainly knew no less of non-Jewish history and culture than any other Palestinian who kept his or her eyes open. For Jesus, however, the names Plato and Thucydides, Cicero and Virgil probably had no meaning.

One can only guess who and what shaped Jesus. He came from a village. He was born under Herod the Great (d. 4 B.C.), although the location in Bethlehem south of Jerusalem is doubtful (Matt. 2:1; Luke 2:1–7). He probably grew up in the Galilean Nazareth as the oldest child of a large family. When Jesus entered his public ministry, his mother Mary, his brothers James, Joses, Judas, Simon, and some sisters (Mark 6:3) were still alive. Their names are classically biblical; Jesus himself is named after Moses' successor, Joshua (Heb. *Jehoshua*, abbreviated "Jeshua" or "Jeshu"). Jesus' father Joseph was also a *tektōn*, perhaps not only in the small town of Nazareth. Only six kilometers north of Nazareth is Sepphoris, just beyond a series of hills (from which one can see the Mediterranean Sea). After 4 B.C., people could find work there. The Romans had destroyed the city when, after the death of Herod the Great, Palestine boiled over with rebellion, so that Antipas, who had chosen the city as his seat, had to rebuild it. Between A.D. 17 and 22, Antipas founded Tiberias by Lake Gennesaret (Sea of Galilee) as the new capital of Galilee. There also workers were needed. It is possible that Joseph's family had land. We do not know about the family's financial and social status in the village. If it is true that the family had lineage from David (Rom. 1:3; Matt. 1:1–17; Hegesippus in Eusebius, *Hist. Eccl.* 3.20.1–6), it meant neither gentility nor wealth, nor that the family assumed that one of its members was called to greatness. Jesus' public ministry apparently seemed odd to his family (Mark 3:21; 3:31–35 par.). Later, the members of Jesus' family became Christians (Acts 1:14; 1 Cor. 9:5). Soon after Easter, James headed the Jerusalem congregation (Gal. 1:19; 2:1–10, 12; Acts 21:18) and in A.D. 62 became a martyr (Josephus *Antiquitates* 20.200). There is no reason to doubt that Jesus had a religious upbringing both at home and in the synagogue. We only know of one certain influence on him decades later: John the Baptist (see *b*, 3 below). Until then, Jesus may have managed as a manual worker, which obviously does not exclude reflection, and he may have been in both Nazareth and Sepphoris, or he may have traveled. This could explain why he apparently never married.

(2) *The disciples.* We know even less about the background of the disciples (see *d*, 1 below). Mainly "the Twelve" are known by name: Simon the
son of John, whom Jesus called Cephas or Peter (the "rock"), and his
brother Andrew, James the son of Zebedee and his brother John, both
called Sons of Thunder, Philip, Bartholomew, Matthew, Thomas, James
the son of Alphaeus, Thaddaeus, Simon the Cananaean (the Zealot), Judas Iscariot (Mark 3:16–19 par.; some names differ in the parallels). In
addition, there are Levi the son of Alphaeus (Mark 2:14 par.), Nathanael
(John 1:45–51), Joseph, called both Barsabbas and then Justus, and Mat-
thias (Acts 1:15–26); perhaps also Cleopas (Luke 24:18), Aristion, and an
elder by the name of John (probably called thus later; see Hegesippus in
Eusebius, *Hist. Eccl.* 3.39.4).

Judas Iscariot was possibly from Kerioth in southern Judea; the others
may have been Galileans. James and John came probably from Capernaum,
a fishing village with only a few thousand inhabitants, a synagogue, a military post, and a border checkpoint on the northwest shore of Lake Gennesaret. Although Peter, Andrew, and Philip came from Bethsaida, four
kilometers east of Capernaum across the Jordan River in the area of Herod
Philip, Peter was married in Capernaum (Mark 1:30). Andrew appears to
have lived there also. Peter, James (Acts 12:1ff.), and John played a role in
Jerusalem congregation after Easter. This fact may be related to their common place of origin.

The names Andrew, Philip (named, perhaps, after the country's ruler),
Cleopas, Aristion, and possibly also Simon (in spite of the name's similarity to Simeon) sound Greek; Bartholomew ("Son of Ptolemy") and Thaddaeus (from Theodotos, perhaps) sound Aramaic, yet in their present form
have again a Hellenized sound: are they Greco-Palestinians?

Peter, Andrew, John, and James were fishermen, Levi a tax collector,
though perhaps only an employee, since he sat where payments were made.
John and James worked with their father side-by-side with day laborers;
Peter (and perhaps also Andrew) worked with his father-in-law. Peter is
also the only one reported to be married; no children are mentioned at all.
It is certainly no accident that we hear of nobody leaving his own business
or farm and especially of no farmer at all. The calling of the rich young man
was unsuccessful (Mark 10:17–22).

If the surname of the second Simon means that he was a Zealot or
thought like a Zealot (see *c*, 9 below), he would be the only one whose
religious connection we know. In addition, however, some of Jesus' later
followers were drawn to John the Baptist, as Jesus himself was.

Perhaps we may generalize. The typical disciple came from a border area on the northern shore of Lake Gennesaret and thus possibly knew already some of the other disciples before meeting Jesus. This disciple possibly knew both Aramaic and Greek. He was probably not a farmer, at least not a landowner or tenant. Still young, or perhaps for other reasons, he was not yet fully established, though he had settled. The disciple's family was at most in the class of local notables but certainly not in the small upper class that, in Galilee as in other comparable regions, controlled power, money, and presumably culture and life-style. (This class was most often found in the few larger cities.) The disciple tended to be not older but younger than Jesus, was single rather than married, and had no children. He was not religious enough to have acquired a sobriquet, yet he was interested enough to have been baptized by John the Baptist. (Concerning women in the group of disciples, see d, 1a below.)

(3) *The decisive influence: John the Baptist.* John the Baptist played an important role in the development of Jesus and of some of Jesus' disciples. Otherwise we would not know much about John the Baptist. Apart from Josephus (*Antiquitates* 18.116–19), the only rich sources are the Gospels. Here, of course, John's beginnings are legendary (Luke 1, 3), and everything is given a Christian coloring: John is the preparer of the way. And that is just what he wanted to be, but not for someone else.

(a) *Origin and aim of John the Baptist.* John was apparently from Judea, though from the country. He was a priest, into which status one had to be born, just as one had to be born a Levite, the lower servant of the cult. The functions of both priest and Levite were almost exclusively reserved for the temple. However, only a few of the priestly and Levite families lived in Jerusalem; the rest were scattered around Jewish Palestine, including Galilee. Twice a year, the men of these families eligible for service moved to the holy city for a week of duty. Whether John ever served and what he did with his remaining time, we do not know. When he entered the limelight of history, he was active as a prophet on the east bank of the lower Jordan River, probably not far from Jericho, though still in Perea. There, he proclaimed the end time, called all Israel to repent, and baptized willing people in the river. Later, he possibly did so farther north also (John 3:23). At least the first spot was close to a route used by many pilgrims to Jerusalem. John appeared perhaps in A.D. 28 (Luke 3:1ff.) and was active at most for a few years. Then, still during Jesus' ministry according to Mark 6:14–29, Herod Antipas had him arrested and executed. John's place of ministry is called "in the wilderness" (Mark 1.4), a fitting place for camel's hair, locusts, and wild honey. This was not asceticism—at least not primarily—but the symbolism of salvation history to make clear that the hour had come. Just as the people of the exodus in their time had entered from the wilderness into the holy land by crossing through the Jordan, now those baptized were standing on the border between the sinful present and the time of salvation. John himself may have used the quotation from Isaiah about a voice crying in the wilderness (Isa. 40:3), which the Gospels apply to John (Mark 1:3). The Essenes also had used this quotation and applied it to themselves (1QS 8.14). Symbolism related to the exodus was not uncommon among people who consciously anticipated the turn of history.

There were many such people, especially since the Maccabean period (when the book of Daniel was written), although they did not form one united movement and had varying expectations as to what the turn of history would actually bring. In addition, people were probably quite ready to become agitated over eschatological issues and be moved either to political actions or to religious activities and rituals, which were to prepare for the end or accelerate it. What is curious about John is his radicalism: judgment day is close at hand; all of Israel will be judged; only immediate repentance and purification will help (Mark 1:4; Luke 3:7–9 par.). It is unlikely that John had a person in mind when he said, "One who is more powerful than I is coming after me. . . . He will baptize you with the Holy Spirit and fire" (Matt. 3:11–12); presumably he was thinking of a heavenly creature, God himself or, more likely, an authorized angel of judgment—perhaps the Son of man (see c, 8 below). Possibly John viewed himself as the earthly counterpart of the one to come. John's word of judgment foreshadowed the voice of the last judgment; his baptism foreshadowed baptism by the Spirit. The one to come would ratify both. Since John's baptism guaranteed that, it was almost a sacrament.

Nevertheless, John not only pronounced quick judgment on the earthly lives of those he baptized, but also gave instructions for the short remaining time. According to Josephus (*Antiquitates* 18.117), John taught virtue, namely, righteousness and piety. These were, of course, the two main themes of Greek ethics; Josephus characterizes John here not as an individual but as type: a teacher, not a politician. What it was that John demanded in particular is uncertain. Apparently, fasting (Mark 2:18–19) and certain prayers (Luke 11:1) were part of it. John's reproach of Antipas's second marriage to Herodias, his sister-in-law (Mark 6:17ff.) seems to be based on Lev. 18:16—it was a forbidden marriage between relatives. Hence, John was concerned with the Torah at least in this case, which, furthermore, posed a problem also to Jesus and others (see *e*, 1 below). It remains doubt-ful whether the sermon in Luke 3:10–14 comes from John.

As a whole, John's theological perspective and his background are un-clear because of a lack of sources. What kind of crime was it that caused all Jews to be lost? Israel was the only one of all nations that God had chosen for an eternal covenant; to Israel God had given the Torah as a constitution and the temple as a place of atonement. Were these no longer effective (J. Becker)? What would happen after the one to come arrived? Would those baptized continue to live on earth after the others had burned to death, or would they live someplace else, and how? Where does the expec-tation of the one to come originate, and what is the source of John's bap-tism, without which there probably would be no Christian baptism either? According to Josephus, baptism was to consecrate the body once righteous-ness had cleansed the soul, so that baptism was only valid with that proviso (*Antiquitates* 18.117). Yet was baptism especially developed for the eternal preservation of the body? Was it a sublimation of the cleansings through which the priests and Levites had to keep themselves purified and holy, and without which no layperson, either, could enter the Holy of Holies? Or did baptism represent a symbolic passing through the Jordan in analogy to Is-rael's entering the Promised Land (Josh. 3; cf. 1 Cor. 10:1–2)? Or was it both?

The response to John's preaching must have been considerable and transregional, even though we cannot quantify it. John appears to have had disciples (Mark 2:18 par.; 6:29 par.; Luke 7:18 par.; John 1:35–51; 3:25), who stayed with him at least for a time and helped in the baptisms. Overall, he did not organize his disciples, which is understandable, since he fully expected the imminent arrival of the end time. Still, his influence was great. Otherwise Antipas would probably not have arrested his critic.

(*b*) *Jesus and John the Baptist.* Jesus had John baptize him; it is the first religious statement we have of Jesus. According to the Synoptic Gospels, it was only that and nothing else. Jesus went to Galilee at the time John was arrested; only then did Jesus start preaching—of his own accord—and col-lecting disciples (Mark 1:14–20 par.). According to the Fourth Gospel, Jesus was discovered by John in Judea and became part of John's disciples, as Peter, Andrew, Philip, and Nathanael had earlier. Jesus then went out on his own, taking these disciples of John's with him without causing a great break, and continued baptizing at first (John 1:29–51; 3:22–30; 4:1–2). That does not look like pure invention. It is possible that the Jesus move-ment indeed began with a secession among John's disciples in Judea, that the group then went back to its homeland in Galilee, perhaps because the Baptist had been arrested, and that there Jesus made a new start.

If that is true, the time Jesus and some of his disciples spent with John was a preliminary stage before their own activity and possibly the only specific orientation they received. It is possible that they even owed the Baptist everything they knew beyond what attentive visitors of the synagogue knew. Yet this did not make them theologians. The Jesus movement was composed of laypeople. Nevertheless, at least Jesus must have found his own calling beyond what he was offered. One may ask whether his calling took shape in a call experience (Mark 1:9–13), but we cannot answer.

(c) *John's disciples after John's death?* There are several indications that after the Baptist's death, John's disciples carried on and formed groups that venerated John as a savior figure, groups that were perceived as competition by Christians and perhaps were just that. The stories about John in Luke 1 may have originated at this point; John 1:6–8, 15, 19–28; 3:22–30 could be read as polemics against John's disciples, and Acts 19:1–7 could be interpreted as a report that a group of John's disciples had been accepted into the church. Later Christian literature tells about John's disciples somewhat more than we find in the New Testament, yet only about the original disciples. Many scholars presume that the Johannine movement was absorbed by the Mandaean sect, which still has a few members in Iraq; in the extensive literature of this sect, John is highly esteemed.

All of this can be interpreted as proof that John's disciples carried on after John's death, assuming that they indeed existed, but it is insufficient to establish the fact. Josephus reassures us that at the end of the first century A.D., the Baptist was still remembered positively even by Jews. Yet in Josephus's opinion, as one who should know, John is not a founder of faith communities but an educator of the people. Therefore, it remains questionable whether a Johannine movement existed after John's death, and if so, whether it survived the first century. We only know of one group for certain that venerated the Baptist: the Jesus movement and early Christianity.

c) The Aim of Jesus and His Disciples

(1) *The legacy of the Baptist.* Jesus not only had kind memories of the Baptist, but he also built on him. Like John, Jesus was convinced that God was on the verge of completing the covenant with Israel with a final judgment and eternal salvation. Like John, Jesus viewed himself as the last messenger God had sent to the people. Like John, Jesus called for repen-

tance and gave instructions. Like John, Jesus was active full-time and accompanied by his disciples. But Jesus did not continue what John did. Jesus felt that although the events predicted by John had not taken place yet, judgment and salvation were already under way through his own activity. The Baptist did not foresee such immediacy. At most, John had left a period of waiting between his activity and the end time. Hence, Jesus neither assumed John's role nor fulfilled something John had announced. Jesus did something new and different. Therefore, some of the similarities he shared with John are in fact differences. Even though Jesus, like John, announced some future event or even some person that was to come, he could base this announcement on experience. Thus, the present received new meaning, and the future promised a continuation, not merely a radical, new beginning. Like John, Jesus also called on people to repent, but it was not his first word to all. He gave up baptizing: he had more to offer than John did with his water baptism. Yet Jesus did not declare water baptism invalid. It is possible that John's success contributed to Jesus' even greater success. Before John, all of Israel was lost. Now, at least those that had asked to be baptized were saved. For Jesus, the Baptist remained the greatest person that had lived so far (Luke 7:28 par.). It may be true that Jesus declared John to be the returning Elijah (Mark 9:11–13 par.) who, it was hoped, would admonish and correct Israel before the end time. John had indeed done so, but as the forerunner of Jesus. This historical effect, by the way, was actually against John's own declared intention. One does not always remember that the Baptist did not influence only Jesus and his disciples but also many other people whom Jesus addressed later on. Jesus could presuppose their familiarity with John, and without John's preparatory work they might have received Jesus differently.

(2) *The coming of the kingdom of God.* The new thing Jesus envisioned and for which he fought until his death can be formulated as the coming of the kingdom of God. This phrase contains a term that Jesus himself used.

The term *kingdom of God* goes back via *regnum dei* to the Greek *he basileia tou theou* and presumably to the Aramaic *malekhutha delaha*. It is the term Jesus used. (According to Matthew, it is almost always the kingdom of heaven; however, that might be an assimilation to a Jewish expression that became predominant only after Jesus' death.) The term means, in literal translation, the kingly rule of God. Many people prefer this use, since it does not carry the connotation of state and nation but rather that of an active, personal rule, which is the actual meaning. Naturally, antiquity's sources also call the rule of Alexander, Augustus, or Herod a *basileia*, but there is no danger that anyone today might translate the word as kingly rule. In addition, the word denotes a certain space, defined by the scope of sovereign power and not by national borders that have been secured by international law or by a nation's settlement of territory. (Moreover, *imperium* and *provincia* also originally denoted power and only secondarily territories.) After all, Jesus' *malekhutha* and the Greek *basileia* are definitely positive words, as opposed to *rule*, which has a negative connotation today. For that reason, we might as well stay with *kingdom of God*, since we will have to explain either way.

Nevertheless, Jesus used the phrase *kingdom of God* much less than one should expect, assuming that the tradition is representative. The related words are missing: God is not called king, God's status and nature are not kingly, and God's ruling is not a "royalizing" (though English does not have such a verb form, both Greek and Aramaic do). Only very rarely does Jesus depict God as king, and he does not give his own ethical instructions in the name of the king. That does not mean, of course, the incorrectness of the almost unanimous view that Jesus called the main thrust of his message the kingly rule of God. This view is also supported by the fact that, apart from the Jesus tradition, primitive Christianity did not use this phrase very often or build on it theologically. (In Paul's case, for example, the phrase corresponds in many respects to the "righteousness of God.") Yet Jesus expressed what he intended to convey to many other words and images. Jesus did not even attempt a consistent use of linguistic terms and images; no one did in his time, and it certainly would not have been easy. Of course, consistency as a basic precept is helpful when talking *about* Jesus. Since *kingly rule* is at least a characteristic phrase of Jesus and somewhat a fixed expression, we can use it as a starting point. I will use *kingly rule of God* where Jesus appears to have done so also, and I will use *kingdom of God* as a generic term for the completion of the covenant, in which God acts in one way—but only in one—especially as king.

It was a common concept of long-standing tradition during Jesus' time that the God of Israel was the king of the chosen people and as such also the king of all peoples, though this concept was only one among others. It involved less the idea of a world mover or a ruler over Israel in all current matters than a sovereign helper, standing above all human authorities, a protector and merciful judge, who rewards the good, punishes the wicked, helps the weak, and therefore can demand honor and obedience. For that reason God acts especially then in kingly fashion when rescuing Israel from its enemies, thus bringing honor to God's own name, now or in the future and forever; in this way he is also king of the entire world (Isa. 52:7–10; Zech. 14:9, 16–17; *Pss. Sol.* 2; 5; 17; *As. Mos.* 10; *T. Dan.* 5.10–13; cf. *Joseph and Aseneth* 16.16; 19:5, 8). This idea can be expressed by the establishment of a kingly rule without implying that God had not been the king all along. To say that God is or becomes king, hence, does not simply transpose a political term into some other context; rather, it remains a political statement. The only two differences are that God's kingly rule can do what human kings cannot, for example, conquering the devil (*As. Mos.* 10.1), and that God's rule demands not only outward submission but also hearts.

Still, the future hopes at Jesus' time did not particularly focus on God's kingdom. It may not mean much that the abstract term *kingdom of God* does not often occur in the texts dealing with the future and is never accompanied by the verb meaning "to come" (only the new aeon, the time of salvation, "comes"; the Messiah and the kingly rule of God are "revealed"); the term is also rare in the Old Testament. Hence, the subject itself is not frequently mentioned. Nevertheless, even in Jesus' time, pleas similar to the Lord's Prayer were contained in the Quaddic prayer and were recited during synagogue worship: "Praised and worshiped be his great name in all the earth, which he has created according to his will. Quickly and soon, he will establish his kingly rule during your lifetime, in your days, and during the lifetimes of all belonging to the house of Israel." This one text would then represent many actual usages. Moreover, no particular school or group during Jesus' time seems to have talked much of God's kingly rule in the end time; apparently, neither did the Baptist. It was only one of many possible ways of expressing an aspect of God's eschatological activity (O. Camponovo), namely, in such a way that it appeared as the completion of what God had done so far. Hence, the topic may be common as the content of prayer but not as an object of reflective thought. Never prior to Jesus' time was the topic the nucleus or even catchword for a certain concept of the end time. This very fact could have made the term *kingdom of God* attractive, especially to someone who intended to say something new.

(3) *The kingly rule of God that has come near and is yet to come.* When trying to envision what God's kingly rule in particular is and does, based on the Jesus tradition as far as it appears representative of Jesus himself, one finds the following examples. God's kingly rule indirectly drives out demons in the way Jesus does it: "If it is by the finger of God that I cast out demons, then the ⌊kingly rule⌋ of God has come to you" (Luke 11:20 par.).

One might extend that to all the miracles Jesus performed (see d, 2b below). The kingly rule of God makes the poor rich, the hungry full, and the
sad joyful, thus offering all of them a new status: "Blessed are you who are
poor, for yours is the [kingly rule] of God. Blessed are you who are hungry
now, for you will be filled. Blessed are you who weep now; for you will
laugh" (Luke 6:20–21 par.). The Beatitudes do not mean that the poor will
get nothing to eat and will not laugh; conversely, the hungry and the sad
will also partake of the kingly rule: They too will rule under and with the
King, God. Similarly, in regard to children: "Let the little children come to
me; do not stop them; for it is to such as these that the [kingly rule] of God
belongs. Truly, I tell you, whoever does not receive the [kingly rule] of God
as a little child will never enter it" (Mark 10:14–15 par.). The kingly rule
also remits debts: "Father, hallowed be your name. Your [kingly rule] come.
Give us each day our daily bread. And forgive us our sins, for we ourselves
forgive everyone indebted to us. And do not bring us to the time of trial"
(Luke 11:2–4 par.). Under the kingly rule of God, people from all over the
world, and thus the Gentiles, are invited to eat with the Jewish patriarchs,
and the former subjects of God are threatened with exclusion: "I tell you,
many will come from east and west and will eat with Abraham and Isaac
and Jacob in the [kingly rule] of heaven, while the heirs of the [kingly rule]
will be thrown into the outer darkness, where there will be weeping and
gnashing of teeth" (Matt. 8:11–12 par.).

All of this is not meant figuratively but literally. The poor are indeed
poor rascals (those without income and assets, not those with low income);
they are not poor sinners (yet the kingly rule also has something for them).
The concept of king corresponds here with both the traditional and the
first-century ideal of the king who is a helper in need and benefactor, not
administrator of affairs. It corresponds with tradition also in so far as
the above sentences do not understand God's kingly rule as God's rule in
the course of time but as comprehensive and permanent changes. Since the
king is God, even demons are vanquished, and these particular poor are
helped (not simply poor people in general); they not only receive alms but
are also exalted. Since some interpreters feel that the kingly rule of God
means God is king, the most important change would then be that this
distant majesty now comes near. However, that does not seem to be the
case. The kingly rule of God is now, with Jesus (see c, 7 below), and in the
future (see c, 8) induced by messengers.

Whatever the kingly rule of God does, it is in part already reality, in part
still promise. The kingly rule of God both has arrived (the Jesus tradition

uses here "come to you," as in Luke 11:20 par., and "come near," e.g., in Mark 1:15 par.) and is yet to arrive. It has arrived in the form of miracles and the granting of status; in individual acts, hence "to you" (Luke 11:20), meaning those experiencing these acts or those hearing about them; and among those who were already "heirs of the [kingly rule]," namely, Israel (Matt. 8:12 par.; yet cf. *c*, 5 below). The kingly rule of God will come fully and finally—so that people will be "in" it (only in future-related statements does the phrase "in the kingly rule of God" appear)—and to all people.

Nevertheless, the kingly rule of God does not come in such a way that what has arrived will expand and perfect itself. One might understand the parable of the mustard seed in that way (Mark 4:30–32 par.). However, the parable implies not an organized development but a jump: the little seed vanishes in the ground and, after a time, becomes a "tree" that quickly shoots up. If, indeed, the poor participate in the reign and the Gentiles eat with Abraham, Isaac, and Jacob, then not only must the earthly social order be reversed, but also the separation between heaven and earth must be overcome (see *c*, 8 below). The meaning of the future kingly rule of God for the individual is basically not different from that of the present kingly rule; still, the former is different enough not to be within the reach of human beings, not even of Jesus (see *c*, 7 below). People can only ask for it to arrive. That is also true for those who are already under the kingly rule. Also the saved are to pray the Lord's Prayer, as Jesus himself probably did too.

The concept remains consistent, but apparently not the expression. It was normal in the environment of antiquity for a king to need time or take time to validate his reign everywhere and fully, to proclaim his reign at first and express it by various means before implementing it completely. However, Jesus talked of the present kingly rule of God as if nothing else was to follow and of the rule to come as if it had not yet arrived. How to explain that is a perpetual problem of scholars. Some have tried to absolve Jesus of one of the two phrases, but we cannot do that. Or one has been played down vis-à-vis the other. The fact that the kingly rule had arrived would mean that the rule yet to come had already come or that its signs would be evident; but that could have been said anyway. The fact that the kingly rule is coming must mean that what has arrived is to endure forever or, existentially speaking, that God meets people halfway and takes time for them; however, the coming probably refers to a future event that has not yet taken place. Hence, we must still explain why Jesus could tell the same people that the kingly rule of God had arrived with them *and* that it was yet to come.

One might explain it biographically. Jesus called mainly his miracles the kingly rule that had arrived. He must have discovered his charismatic gift sometime while with John or later. With the imminent expectation of the end time, produced by John, Jesus could easily interpret his miracles as fully valid events of the end time, not just as preparatory ones. John did not perform such miracles or predict them. Since Jesus' miracles were acts of salvation with the help of God, who precisely as savior was king, one might say appropriately: here the eschatological kingly rule of God was taking place. Yet it is an open question where Jesus got the phrase—perhaps from a prayer (see above). It was consistent of him to say that the kingly rule had come near, not that it had come: the miracles could not have been all there was to it. The comprehensive happening yet to come could hardly have been called anything other than the kingly rule of God. But Jesus left it at the traditional verb *to come*, also used by John, even though it no longer fit (something like "to be completed" would have been better). Yet that can be explained: Jesus' main interest was not in what was yet to come. The expectation of the end time was not his own but John's. Still, he had discovered that the kingly rule of God had come near, and it left him partially speechless.

As already stated, the kingly rule of God was not everything for Jesus. What else there was will be arranged according to various aspects in the following sections.

(4) *The God of the kingdom.* It is for reasons of content that Jesus did not use any king-related vocabulary except for the kingly rule of God. Among Jesus' parables are quite a number that deal with God's eschatological action, mostly as this action relates to the present and as it is often explicitly tied to God's kingly rule in the Gospels. However, when God appears in these parables as a person, only once is God a king with officials (Matt. 18:23–34); otherwise God is a landowner with tenants or day laborers (Mark 12:1–11 par.; Matt. 20:1–16; Luke 15:11–32; 16:1–8?), a master (Luke 14:16–24 par.), a man with money (Matt. 25:14–30 par.), a farmer (Matt. 21:28–32), a shepherd (Matt. 18:12–14 par.), a judge (Luke 18:1–8), perhaps even a housewife (Luke 13:20–21; 15:8–10). Likewise, a Hellenistic king is the richest man in the country, a great landowner, the highest judge (but not a "househusband"), and the smaller he is, the more direct is his rule. In this respect, the parables do not deny God's kingly rule. Nevertheless, Jesus does not seem to be thinking even of a minor king,

which his own ruler was, though without title. A king was also a com-
mander (cf. Luke 14:31–32—yet not ordained by God), an architect, a
benefactor, but we find none of that in the parables. Jesus finds the best
material for comparison in the landowner, who provides in a patriarchally
generous way for his family and people, who demands of everyone what is
required, yet who also accepts a lost son when he remorsefully returns.

It is consistent that in the parables (Matt. 21:28–32; Luke 15:11–32)
and outside them (e.g., Luke 6:36 par.; 12:30 par.), Jesus spoke explicitly of
God as "Father" and also that the prayer asking for the coming of God's
kingly rule says "Father" and not "king" (Luke 11:1–4). In Jesus' time, the
father was the ruler of the house, as the king was ruler of the state, and even
a king can be called father. (When Augustus called himself *pater patriae*, it
was not meant in a casual way; it meant, rather, that the residents in the
kingdom were his clientele: he provided for them, but they were obliged to
him.) Jesus, however, did not use the father of the country but the father of
the family as his metaphor for God, and he stressed God's kindness. By the
way, the term *father* as a form of address in Jewish prayer was not particularly common. The fact that Jesus used it must be connected with his experience of God. It was the same experience that in a different context he
called the kingly rule of God that had come near, except that the latter
phrase was apparently inadequate.

Yet Jesus did not portray God in familial terms. The Father did not cease
to be Lord of Israel and of all creation. It is certain that Jesus did not
particularly focus on the fact that God created the sun, the moon, and the
stars, ruled cosmic forces, and guided the history of the world. Instead,
Jesus emphasized that God gave life and continued to maintain it (Matt.
5:45; 6:26–30). The God that was Lord of history played no role for Jesus,
not even as the director of Israel's history of salvation.

(5) *The citizens of the kingdom of God.* Jesus did not call the people for
whom the kingdom of God had arrived, and would arrive, its citizens. If
citizens are responsible and socially apt members of a nation directing all
power, the kingdom of God has no citizens. Wherever God rules, all power
issues from God. On the other hand, even an authoritarian state like the
Roman Empire had citizens, though only a few of them existed outside of
Italy. Hence, the word *citizen* can signify not only the native owners of state
power, who by force of their own decision place someone above themselves,
but also the favored and privileged subjects of an absolute ruler. The people
under God's rule are certainly not subjects, much less slaves. When considering the parables, one might call them the family of God or housemates

(cf. Eph. 2:19; 1 Tim. 3:15). Yet the kingdom of God is more than a house or an estate. For that reason, the term *citizen of the kingdom of God* is a possible name for a member of this kingdom.

According to Jesus, apparently anybody could become a citizen. The citizenship of the kingdom of God is viewed in a universal sense. Nationality, social status, demon possession, disease, minority do not exclude; neither do moral defects. Also the angels are part of the future kingdom of God. Demons and devils remain excluded. Naturally, the entire citizenry is not gathered all at once. Jesus addressed Palestinian Jews (see *d*, 2 below). Non-Jews asking him for help were apparently not refused, but that was all. For the Jews in the Diaspora and the rest of the people outside Palestine, Jesus did nothing directly. These people would be incorporated later into the kingdom by God himself (see *c*, 8 below).

On the other hand, Jesus viewed no one as a kingdom citizen by birth, except for Abraham, Isaac, and Jacob; one had to become one. Primarily the chosen people of Israel were destined for the kingdom, which was the reason why Jesus remained at first among his people; still, this election did not guarantee citizenship in the kingdom. According to general opinion, Jesus made the right to citizenship dependent on a personal decision for his message or even for his own person: repentance and conversion. It is assumed that Jesus thereby "individualized" a person's relationship with God in a way previously unknown in Israel's religion. However, God's rule came and comes to people much as the Romans came to Judea in A.D. 6, yet purely as liberation, solace, and bestowal of status. God's rule did not offer freedom of decision but created faits accomplis. Whoever became a deliberate follower of Jesus made a decision not in view of God's rule but under it. Whoever explicitly rejected Jesus became, strictly speaking, a rebel.

Nevertheless, Jesus probably regarded not only the people deciding for him as citizens of God's kingdom. He does not seem to have pushed for as many individual decisions as possible (see *d*, 2 below). At least, he did not develop a particular form to express them: He had given up baptism. He did not found an organization one might join (see *f* below). Jesus probably acknowledged as citizens of the kingdom those who accepted the fact that the kingly rule of God had come near to them and who acted accordingly. In antiquity's view, that could also mean that "salvation has come to this house," that the head of the family had received Jesus (Luke 19:9). One did not absolutely have to meet Jesus personally (see *d*, 2a below), perhaps not even indirectly. An honest follower of the Baptist was certainly also a citizen of the kingdom, even if for some reason he or she had never heard of Jesus.

Therefore, Jesus cannot have made citizenship under God's rule dependent on a personal tie with himself or even on something like faith in him.
Such ties existed even beyond the circle of disciples. But citizenship in the
kingdom of God went further. It is primarily the miracle stories that mention faith. Faith means to attribute to Jesus the miracles he wrought by the
finger of God as an expression of the kingdom of God that has come near.
Whenever Jesus himself mentions citizenship, it is in this sense.

Not every Jew was automatically a citizen in the kingdom of God. Those
who rejected the Baptist's call for repentance and continued in that view,
as well as those who rejected Jesus, also rejected the kingdom of God. The
same is true of those who first accepted but later denied or did not act
accordingly (see c, 8).

(6) *The ordering of life in the kingdom of God.* A large part of the Jesus
tradition tells directly or indirectly how a person is to live. The material
varies from proverb-like wisdom sayings ("The laborer deserves to be paid";
Luke 10:7 par.) to general admonitions ("Do to others as you would have
them do to you"; Luke 6:31 par.) and concrete injunctions and prohibitions ("Love your enemies"—Luke 6:35 par.; "Do not swear at all"—
Matt. 5:34; "When you pray, say: . . ."—Luke 11:2), including the Ten
Commandments and legally binding basic precepts ("What God has
joined together, let no one separate"—Mark 10:9 par.). A number of parables, likewise, teach directly or indirectly how to live (e.g., the good Samaritan in Luke 10:29–37). In addition, tradition reports Jesus' exemplary
behavior (e.g., especially in the passion story). All of these I shall call injunctions of Jesus. Some of these injunctions are only for the disciples (see
d, 1a below). The majority are intended for all and for life in the present;
whether life has to be regulated in the future kingdom of God is doubtful
(see c, 8 below).

Through his injunctions Jesus wanted to express God's will, not his own
ethical insights or decrees of the citizens of the kingdom of God. Even
where he passed on traditional or personal life experiences, they were experiences of the life that God had given. After all, the main focus is harmony
with God, not a fulfilled life or social justice, though the latter two are to
flow from the former; overall, God wants to benefit the person. For a Jew,
God's will was none other than the Torah, which was formulated even
before creation and used as a blueprint of the world. The Torah had been
formally decreed by Moses on Mount Sinai and handed over to Israel as a
charter of God's covenant. Attached was the task of teaching it to all nations and henceforth interpreting it, since it had already been written down

in the five books of Moses, also called Torah, and was unchangeable. Did Jesus want to interpret the Torah with his injunctions, or did he go beyond that? If so, where, how far, and by what authority? These questions are debated more than anything else in studies of Jesus. One reason is that only a few of Jesus' injunctions are explicitly derived from the written Torah or at least refer to it. It was no different in Jesus' environment. What was considered the Torah was not simply the written sentences; some were not valid at all because they were clearly out of date. The legally binding Torah was the interpretation that had developed, though by no means uniformly, and which was by no means related formally to the written Torah in every sentence. Besides, long before Jesus' time, the entire wisdom tradition of Israel had already been forged into Torah in general (Sir. 24; Bar. 3:9–4:4). What counts is (1) that some injunctions of Jesus fit only with difficulty or not at all into the framework of what we know of the Torah concept at the time, (2) that Jesus is supposed to have criticized Moses (Mark 10:1–12 par.), (3) that he was reproached for offenses against the Torah (see *f* below), and also perhaps (4) that he did not discuss but, instead, sovereignly ordered or forbade. One can interpret that to mean that in particular instances Jesus consciously revoked the Torah or expanded it. That could mean that he sensed some other access to the will of God, one that ignored the Torah, or that he claimed basic authority over the Torah, so that even where he left the Torah in force, he had the last word, or even that he viewed his injunctions as the new eschatological Torah, substituting it for the old traditional one.

It is likely that Jesus occasionally made injunctions that contradicted the written Torah or the generally accepted interpretation, even though no Torah passage is unambiguous. Yet one has to wonder whether, in doing so, he intended to contradict the Torah. The fact that he was accused of it does not mean much: that was a common argument among people involved in Torah debates. And even if he revoked individual Torah precepts, other people did that too, without thereby placing their own authority above that of the Torah as a whole. It is reasonable to imagine that Jesus did just that, though one would have to find a reason for it. The reason might well have been the kingly rule of God that has come near. However, though Jesus used the kingly rule of God as a way to motivate people to action (see *c*, 8 below), he hardly based his injunctions on it—certainly none of those that could have been intended as critical of the Torah. That is also true for the few basic statements about the Torah that are attributed to Jesus (Matt. 5:17–20; Mark 12:28–34). Besides, both passages say that the Torah is valid. If the second passage summarizes the ethical content (as we might call it) of the Torah in the two commandments concerning love of God and neighbor (which, by the way, correspond to the two basic duties of Hellenistic ethics, piety and justice—cf. *b,* 3a above), then it is not because all other individual commandments have been superseded by these two, but because these two are developed in the Torah. Hence, the Torah probably remained for Jesus what it was or should have been for Israel all along.

That does not mean that Jesus simply inculcated "the" Torah. Jesus did not even touch on many aspects of the Torah, and no single area of life was treated by him completely. The reason for that is probably not that the traditional injunctions are the remnants of a complete presentation of the Torah or the beginnings of one never completed. Instead, Jesus, like others, has mainly incorporated into injunctions what was important to him or what he wanted treated differently. He was able to do so since the Torah was, of course, already there; it was valid in all those points he did not address. Nothing suggests that Jesus would have condoned painting God, not circumcising male babies, not paying the tithe to the priests, eating milk and meat together, or assaulting, deceiving, and denouncing people. That is also true in cases where he no longer backs the Torah. Hence, the injunctions are not yet the "ethics" of Jesus; his ethics also includes everything else that was Torah to him (for that reason the term "ethics of the kingdom of God" is not appropriate). Nevertheless, these injunctions are the characteristic part of it (for details, see *e* below).

Not all the injunctions are new. Many of them are found in the world of the Jews or have their beginnings there. This world is the old homeland of ethical culture. Jesus' profile emerges in his choice, emphasis, *and* innovation. What is true for the Torah as a whole is true for Jesus' injunctions: one is to do them and not fail to do them, not even where Jesus was strict. He was not strict at all points (see *e* below). He did not ask for any superhuman effort. For that reason his injunctions do not focus on heroic acts of repentance, which were to force the coming of God's kingdom (in this sense A. Schweitzer spoke of "interim ethics"). On the contrary, his injunctions presupposed the kingly rule of God and tried to be in harmony with it (see *e,* 9 below).

(7) *Jesus as representative of the kingdom of God.* Probably with good reason, the Jesus tradition depicts one individual, Jesus, with disciples and followers, not a group in which one was outstanding. Whatever Jesus attempted appeared to him and his environment as his own affair, regardless

of who might have contributed to its formation. For that reason we must examine Jesus' role.

According to a common view, Jesus preached or proclaimed the kingdom of God. His miracles, injunctions, and behavior (and ultimately his death) support this view or are related to it. For that reason books on Jesus often incorporate in their titles Jesus' preaching or proclamation, or at least mention it in the subtitles. Jesus easily emerges as a kind of archetypal pastor endowed with charismatic gifts. However, Jesus did not proclaim the kingly rule of God that "has come to you"; he implemented it, just as a Roman official implemented Augustus's direct rule over Judea in A.D. 6. He needed words for this, as well as to explain what he was doing. While statements like "Come out of him," "Take up your bed and walk," "Your sins are forgiven," and "Blessed are the poor" are performative sentences, the clause "if it is by the finger of God that I cast out demons" is commentary; neither the one nor the other is proclamation. Jesus could only *talk* about the coming kingdom of God; he had to *call* for repentance and give injunctions *orally*—apart from illustrative actions (see *d*, 2b below). One might call that preaching, especially since the kingly rule of God that had come near was always the focus, whether expressed or not. Still, we do not know how much Jesus' forms of speech contained what we call preaching today (see *d*, 2b below).

It is difficult to put into one concept what Jesus wanted to be. Apparently, not even he tried to do so. He did not view himself in the traditional role of an eschatological God-man; whether anyone called him Messiah even before his death is another question. Besides, not all of Jesus' contemporaries were waiting for the Messiah, and those who did had different expectations. The Messiah could be a warrior-like prince from the house of David, but he could also have prophetic-charismatic traits. At any rate, Jesus viewed himself and was viewed by others as a prophet (Mark 6:15 par.; 8:27-28; Luke 11:49-51; 13:34-35 par.). Also, a prophet was expected to perform miracles and give injunctions, both of which characterized Jesus (see *g*, 4 below). As a prophet, Jesus must have known that he possessed the Holy Spirit. Though this is not reliably reported, one can still infer it. Nevertheless, the term *prophet* denotes merely a type, even if we add charismatic or eschatological attributes in order to distinguish him from other prophetic figures, such as the Baptist. What was special about Jesus was that he implemented God's rule as far as possible under earthly conditions and announced the rule to come. For that reason one can call him the representative of the kingdom of God (H. Merklein), even if that smacks of business jargon. He had no peers, and no one like him was to come after him. Of course, he remained someone with a commission, one who was no more God himself than Pontius Pilate was the emperor. And his commission, at first, probably covered only his earthly life (see c, 8 below).

(8) *The future of the kingdom of God.* What was supposed to come if God fulfilled the second petition of the Lord's Prayer, and what thereafter? What Jesus had to say on that under the catchword *kingly rule of God* is very brief (see c, 2 above). Beyond that, tradition provides a series of individual concepts, which for the most part are traditional. Jesus apparently did not use particular apocalyptic revelations. The dead are raised (all or only the just?), the last judgment takes place, Israel is restored to a people of twelve tribes, possibly with a new temple as its center (see g, 2 below), the Gentiles are also called, and then comes eternal life or eternal condemnation. However, Jesus does not seem to have clarified in detail—perhaps not even to himself—how all of that was to take place and how it was related. In general, his contemporaries did not do it either (nor do biblically knowledgeable Christians today). Also in Jewish literature, complete scenarios are very rare.

Whatever it was Jesus envisioned, it apparently was to perpetuate his own activity, as happened later after his death (see g, 4 below). Jesus did not anticipate the disciples' carrying on, and especially not a mission extending beyond Palestine. An "interim" between Jesus' time and the arrival of the kingdom of God was not foreseen, not even indirectly by means of conditions that had to become reality first. An interim, however, is not necessarily precluded. Perhaps, a reversal from above to below would take place, a sudden one. It is clear that if Jesus indeed announced meteorological and political portents such as an eclipse of the sun or a war (e.g., Mark 13:7-8 par.), he cannot have meant a long time. An eschatological holy war, as expected by the Qumran community, is not mentioned by Jesus. Like Jesus and his disciples, people will work on the kingdom of God here and now, not later. The future kingdom is not built but prayed for.

Apparently, the future kingdom, like the present one, is envisioned mainly in personal terms, except that the future one includes the Jewish Diaspora and the rest of humanity. It remains unclear whether animal and inanimate creation will also be affected, restored, or even replaced by a new heaven and a new earth; the last point probably does not apply. Besides, it seems that Jesus had nothing at all to criticize about what we call nature (Matt. 5:45; Luke 12:22-31). But he did about people. Therefore, they must go to court, both Jews and Gentiles, both the living and the dead. They are judged on their behavior, especially their social behavior. The criteria are not superior deeds. As far as criteria can be determined, they appear as reasons for exclusion (cf. the Ten Commandments in Mark 10:17–22; the sayings about entering the kingdom of God, e.g., Mark 10:15 par.; 10:23 par.; etc.; cf. also 1 Cor. 6:9–10; Gal. 5:19–21; Matt. 25:31–46). Jesus presumably meant that the court will inquire of people's neighborly love and judge those who intentionally violated this kind of love. Also wealth that is counterproductive to society is a criterion (see *e*, 5 below). One finds no specific mention of historical misdeeds. In contrast to Jewish apocalyptic accounts and the Revelation to John, the Jesus tradition did not especially threaten to judge the leading rulers or their areas of influence—not even the Romans. Still, nothing good is in store for them. When the kingdom of God comes, they will no longer be rulers.

The followers of Jesus will also be judged by one more criterion: loyalty to Jesus under trying conditions. It is for these and not for all people or for everyday life (see *c*, 5 above) that the statement is intended: "Everyone who acknowledges me before others, the Son of Man also will acknowledge before the angels of God; but, whoever denies me before others will be denied before the angels of God" (Luke 12:8–9 par.).

On the other hand, the followers of Jesus (or all people?) may hope to be rewarded by the court. The reward is probably not acquittal, but something more. Protestant interpreters like to call it the reward of grace. Yet it was already grace that God chose the person or accepted the person under God's rule. If people live up to this rule, they deserve a reward—not as pay for delivered moral merchandise but as gratitude for loyal services, on which even God insists. For that reason, the reward is prorated. It is unclear, however, what this reward is, perhaps various ranks within the kingdom of God (Matt. 5:18–19; Luke 7:28 par.).

It appears that Jesus treated what follows judgment with even greater reticence than judgment itself. The condemned simply go to hell. The others live on, probably forever, though not as fluttering spirits. Those within the Jewish biblical tradition do not imagine a person without some sort of body. Identity will be preserved. Besides Abraham, Isaac, and Jacob, the Queen of Sheba will be present, because she acknowledged Solomon's wisdom; so will the people of Nineveh, because they repented (Luke 11:31–32), and, of course, John the Baptist, Jesus himself, and his disciples. One can only guess where they might live, and how. Since there is supposed to be a new temple, perhaps they will live on (the re-created?) earth. In the temple worship will have to take place, but what kind? One will eat and drink (Matt. 8:11–12; Mark 14:25 par.), yet where does the food grow, and who produces it? Marriage, of course, will no longer exist; instead, people "are like the angels in heaven" (Mark 12:25 par.). If it is true that Jesus promised the Twelve that they would "judge" the tribes of Israel (Matt. 19:28 par.), and if that means "rule" (it can also mean "judge on judgment day"), then even eternal life has dimensions related to the state. However, nothing points to the idea that David's kingdom, supposedly eternal according to Nathan's prophecy (2 Sam. 7:12–16), would be restored, as many of Jesus' contemporaries hoped (e.g., *Ps. Sol.* 17; 1QSa. 2.11–22; Rom. 1:3–4; Luke 1:32; Acts 2:22–36; 15:13–18).

What is the future like for the "representative" of the kingdom of God? Does he participate at all when it comes? The answer depends greatly on how one views the Son of man—literally, "the son of humanity"—of whom many of the traditional Jesus sayings speak. These sayings are often divided into three groups: (1) The Son of man now does, has, or is something (e.g., Mark 2:28 par.; Luke 9:58 par.); (2) he will suffer and rise from the dead (e.g., Mark 8:31 par.); (3) he will do something at the end of days, especially in the judgment (e.g., Luke 12:8–9 par.). In all cases, the Son of man is thought to be Jesus himself. Since within primitive Christianity the term *Son of man* occurs almost exclusively in the Jesus tradition and here only in Jesus sayings, it is likely to have come from Jesus. In Aramaic, however, he must have spoken of *baränasch* or *baränascha*. Although the word *bar* means "son" and the word *änasch(a)* "person," the entire phrase does not mean "son of [one] person," but "human being, person, humankind." There are mainly two ways in which to interpret the phrase from Jesus' standpoint: as "a person [like you and me], I myself, I" (e.g., G. Vermes) or as the name of an eschatological figure for whom the term *Son of man* has become standard (e.g., W. G. Kümmel). Still, one cannot clearly prove that "I" is philologically possible. Also, it is not uncontested that Judaism during Jesus' time indeed expected a figure named "human being" or "son of man"; however, Daniel 7; *1 Enoch* 37–71; and other traces in apocalyptic literature offer support. This figure is a mysterious heavenly person, functioning as judge or advocate on the day of judgment and thereafter perhaps as ruler. The figure is called "a human being" because of its appearance (Dan. 7:13); the name is an incognito rather than a description of a function or nature. It certainly was not a common expectation and was probably only one element of a concept, not a concept itself.

Still, Jesus could have absorbed this element. But how? The "human being" is only called that but is not one; rather, it is a kind of archangel, by nature or as an ancient figure transposed into heaven. It would have been unprecedented for anyone during the first century A.D. to say that he was or would be the Son of man. Of course, Jesus could still have said that, though not without explanation. The Son-of-man sayings, however, sound quite natural. The explanation might be that it was primitive Christianity that first identified Jesus as the Son of man; 1 Enoch (70–71) does something similar with the biblical Enoch (Gen. 5:24). But one could also imagine that Jesus announced this heavenly figure. Nothing speaks against the assumption that Jesus wanted to be the representative of the kingdom of God on earth; the Son of man is no earthly being. Then Jesus would not have expected to participate actively in the final events; instead, he would have viewed himself as the earthly figure parallel to the Son of man, provided the above-mentioned passage in Luke 12:8–9 comes from him: whatever a person did to Jesus on earth would be evaluated and judged by the Son of man as if the Son of man were Jesus himself. This parallelism recalls the relationship in which John the Baptist saw himself with the one to come who would baptize with the Spirit and fire (see b, 3a above). It would make sense that after Easter, Christians easily assumed Jesus had meant himself when prophesying about the Son of man. (That would then have been the beginning of the hope concerning his Parousia, his descent from heaven at the end of days.) Also, the term *Son of man* became a name for Jesus from the very start. The reason that this term occurs only in Jesus' sayings may be the incognito aspect. Jesus himself could use the term, for it did not (yet) refer to him. After Easter, the incognito was removed, and the "human being" had a name. In addition, *Son of man* was not as useful a title as *Messiah, Christ, Lord,* or *Son of God;* the concept was not widespread, and the mere expression was prone to misunderstandings.

Another question is what role Jesus envisioned for himself in eternal life. If the twelve tribes of Israel were to reign, as assumed earlier, then Jesus as their master would have to be above them as prince or viceroy of Israel. It is logical to assume that the representative of the kingdom of God will not be placed on the lowest rung in the future kingdom. However, tradition says nothing about that, and Jesus must not have drawn all the conclusions he could have drawn.

(9) *The kingdom of God's nearness to earth.* The kingdom of God that Jesus promoted was also a political matter, provided that *political* means related to the formation of civil affairs. The kingly action of God, which Jesus saw as being under way, was intended for God's chosen people. Thus,

Jesus did not envision a future with blessed individuals or an eternal religious community, but Israel together with the Gentiles in their perfected social state. Of course, one should not measure the political quality of this state by a modern democratic legal and bureaucratic system, which explicitly defines itself not in terms of living under God's grace but as a nonreligious citizens group that does not even consider its constitution as final. From antiquity's viewpoint, no state could exist without religion, and the idea that God or a representative ruled this state was anything but absurd. Every Hellenistic ruler since Alexander enshrined himself in an aura of world perfection. Through Augustus, this aura was inherent in the entire Roman empire. The founder of the principality was celebrated as savior; a new golden age had begun, and the world been rejuvenated.

Nevertheless, the common view that Jesus wanted to act only in a religious sense is well founded. He did not politicize, even on what is now called the grassroots level. Certainly, Jesus acted with social awareness and asked the same of others. But he did not demand a change of social conditions, either by popular initiatives or revolt at the bottom, or by justice and reform at the top—as necessary as the latter may have been. In Galilee as elsewhere, a small, rich upper class lived off the many others, who could just barely manage. The agricultural system was unhealthy. Because of debt and because farms were small but liabilities great, free farmers easily became the tenants of large landowners or even had to become day laborers. Most people had just enough for subsistence; others not even that. Jesus did not remark on that explicitly. In contrast to John the Baptist, Jesus did not criticize the ruler directly. He did not mention the Romans at all. Still, Jesus was not much impressed by the rulers of his time (Mark 10:42 par.; Luke 7:25 par.), though that is a general observation and not a political analysis. He called Antipas a reed shaken by the wind (Luke 7:24 par.) and a fox—and that, according to tradition, in response to a death threat (Luke 13:32).

Jesus' imminent expectation of the end time cannot be the only reason he might have viewed political engagement or at least criticism as meaningless. The Baptist had the same expectation when he took on Antipas. The reason was also that the kingdom of God, regarded as a communal affair, lacks some present and future dimensions. It appears to be made for people who have hunger, leprosy, and little money, but apparently no nationalistic needs; for people oppressed by demons but not by foreign soldiers; for people whose affairs of marriage, inheritance, and taxes have to be regulated, but not their city or state administration; for people who need forgiveness for their sins but not for their wars of conquest or wrong religious policies. If the kingdom of God is, indeed, to be the ultimate social order of humanity, politics is not the only aspect missing. Culture is too, since this order no longer holds cultural requirements. The blind see, the lame walk, the lepers become clean, and the poor hear the gospel (Luke 7:22 par.). At the return of the prodigal son, people danced (Luke 15:25). Tradition does not say that the illiterate will read, ignoramuses learn poems, simpletons examine the secrets of creation, and farmers take up painting. The kingdom of God is not an empire but a village.

The more one sees Jesus' Palestinian environment as immersed in social conflict and political upheaval, the more one will perceive that—from the viewpoint of daily politics—what Jesus intended is moderate. It could be debated whether throughout the first century a united sociopolitical resistance movement, later named the Zealot movement after one of its centers during the Jewish war, existed (e.g., M. Hengel) or did not exist (e.g., S. Freyne). At any rate, the conditions within Judaism, which was both socially and politically divided, were not stable and harmonious at the time of Jesus. One might then regard Jesus' attitude either as realism or as reactionism—and perhaps pointedly so: Jesus and his disciples become counteragitators to the Zealots, in league with the ruling class (H. Kreissig). The latter view cannot be supported by the Jesus tradition. Many assume, however, that Jesus was against the Zealots, or against Zealot ideas if Zealots no longer existed. It appears to me, however, that the political characteristic of Jesus' concept of the kingdom of God is born not from the rejection of another concept but from a natural Galilean perspective. Galilee had disappeared from history after the demise of Israel's northern kingdom in 722 B.C., and it was ruled by foreigners, yet never in conjunction with any other Jewish territory. Not until c. 100 B.C. did the Hasmonians integrate the land into a Jewish state. Yet even then it did not participate in history but instead became its object—and not a very important one at that. In Antipas it had its own ruler, but Antipas was no Galilean, and Galilee had not elected him. If one has never made history, one need not expect much if given the opportunity. Also, it is not certain that the Galileans were very intent on Israel's national rebirth. The people would continue to have their center in Jerusalem, and Galilee would continue to lie halfway between there and the Diaspora. Concerning culture, one may doubt whether Galilee even missed it. It stands to reason that especially a Galilean prophet would expect salvation not from human activities, not even from a Messiah of the house of David, but from God; that this prophet's hope was not Israel's reunification in peace and liberty and possibly world rule, but another worldly temple community that included the just among the Gentiles; and that this prophet viewed eternal life as still the simple life, but without illness and hunger.

Nevertheless, the kingdom of God is not provincial but fundamental. For that reason, it could be universal. If Jesus had pictured a theocracy, it would not have long survived the transition to other times and places. Galilee is everywhere. Yet Galilee does not cover all aspects of life. And so, as the Jesus movement survived Jesus and began to spread, the kingdom of God had to be enlarged.

d) The Jesus Movement in Galilee

According to the Synoptic Gospels (see *a*, 1a above), Jesus, together with his disciples, pursued his goal first in Galilee and then in Jerusalem.

(1) *Jesus and his group of disciples*

(*a*) *Composition and purpose.* The beginning and later nucleus of the group was formed probably by those who had been disciples of the Baptist and who, together with Jesus, had become independent (see *b*, 3b above). Whether they were disciples of Jesus already at this point is unclear. It is possible that Jesus did not make them his followers until Galilee (Mark 1:16–20 par.). Then he probably called other disciples on his own. Yet people approached him, too. The majority of them were probably young men who were somehow free and unattached (see *b*, 2 above). It is likely that there were more than just those known to us by name, but the group apparently remained manageable (cf. Acts 1:15). It is uncertain whether women were part of the group. Female disciples might have been Mary Magdalene, "from whom seven demons had gone out"; Joanna, the wife of Chuza, a steward of Herod (Antipas); Susanna; Mary, the mother of James the Younger and of Joses; Salome (Luke 8:2–3; Mark 15:40–41, 47 par.; 16:1 par.; Luke 24:10); and the unnamed mother of James and John (Matt. 20:20–21; 27:56). Mary Magdalene (named after Magdala, a fishing village ten kilometers southwest of Capernaum) was a Galilean, and the others probably also. Joanna was probably part of the upper class; her husband may have been all kinds of things as a steward, but he certainly would not have been mentioned had he been only a fairly minor official. She and others apparently had money (Luke 8:3). The others may have come from the same circles as the disciples, since two of the women are the mothers of disciples. Of course, tradition never calls these women female disciples (the word appears in the New Testament only in Acts 9:36). Some appear once as fellow travelers in Galilee (Luke 8:2–3); the rest appear in the reports of the crucifixion and the Easter event. It might mean that these women joined the group of disciples as late as on the journey to Jerusalem. Their function may have been "to serve" or to give financial support (Luke 8:3). The fact that Mary Magdalene, the one mentioned most frequently, is recalled as the one who had demons exorcised (which never happened to a disciple) and that two women are identified through their sons probably means that the women did not have the same status as the men. That they are even mentioned at all remains remarkable enough. Though not female disciples, they were not mere maidservants either.

This group is often called the circle of disciples. Today, however, *circle* means a number of people meeting at regular intervals for a certain purpose. The disciples did more than that. They are the original reference for what the Jesus tradition calls discipleship (Mark 8:34 par. and similar passages). They were literally followers: they lived with Jesus, though perhaps not continuously, and went where he went. This meant leaving their families, homes, and workplaces (Mark 1:16–20 par.; 10:25 par.; Luke 9:57–62 par.; 14:26 par.); it also meant accepting criticism for doing so. Discipleship even superseded the Torah command to bury one's dead father (Luke 9:59–60 par.). A married person like Peter, however, did not have to send his wife away, since that was explicitly forbidden by Jesus (see *e*, 1 below); on the other hand, we do not know whether he took her with him, as he did later as a missionary (1 Cor. 9:5). It is possible that the disciples were to live in abstinence (Matt. 19:12). The community of Jesus (cf. Mark 3:33–35 par.) replaced the abandoned or suspended family relations. Life together, however, was not to be lived for its own sake: the disciples were coworkers with Jesus (see *d*, 2a below).

(b) *Inside the group of disciples.* Since discipleship meant following, Jesus dominated. Yet it is not the case that he was the only one issuing commands and disposing of matters; after all, at least some of his disciples were no longer adolescents when joining the group. Among themselves, the disciples were to be equal and to serve each other (Mark 10:41–45 par.; Matt. 23:8–12), which perhaps did not happen without conflict (Mark 10:35–45 par.). In addition, at least Peter had a special position.

We do not know exactly how the group lived together. Nothing is reported on common meals, conferences, the study of scripture, worship, and prayers; only that Jesus himself withdrew for prayer (e.g., Mark 1:35 par.). If the Lord's Prayer was at first intended for the disciples (Luke 11:1), then it was probably a part of regular daily prayers: three times a day, every Jewish man was to pray, in addition to reciting the Shema mornings and evenings (Deut. 6:4-9; 11:13-21; Num. 15:37-41). Jesus trained the disciples for their tasks (see below, cf. also *e*, 4). It remains questionable whether he gave them formal instruction beyond that and whether a part of this was esoteric, that is, matters he did not mention in public (R. Riesner).

It remains also questionable whether within the group of disciples Jesus nominated "the Twelve" with Peter at the top (see *f*, 2 above)—and if so, to what end—or whether the Twelve formed later, possibly on account of the Easter visions (cf. 1 Cor. 15:3-5). The number twelve must be related to the twelve tribes of Israel and more precisely to Israel's rebirth in the end time, since the ten and a half tribes of the northern kingdom, overthrown in 722 B.C., were considered lost or at least did not live in Palestine. If Jesus himself chose the Twelve, then it was not for the purpose of limiting his followers to this group at some point. It may be true that he chose them as messengers (see *d*, 2a below), thus making his intentions clear. That would accord with the idea that the disciples were to rule the twelve tribes in the everlasting life (see *c*, 8 above).

(c) *Sustenance*. It appears that Jesus and the disciples did not work or have a fixed residence during their public ministry. Since none of them was wealthy, the group must have lived on invitations and donations; begging by the group is not reported. Though Judas may indeed have "had the common purse" and from it doled out alms (John 13:29), the group did not constantly live from hand to mouth. However, it is possible that the money bag was only procured for the journey to Jerusalem, where the group did not know anyone. In any case, almsgiving, a religious obligation, is mentioned only in this passage. One may argue whether this kind of "itinerant radicalism" was a freely chosen sacrifice of normal life (G. Theissen) or an escape from intolerable hardship (L. Schottroff and W. Stegemann). It probably depended. Hardly any disciple was well-to-do, and even an indigent disciple had renounced something by leaving parents, a wife, or a roof over his head. At any rate, Jesus interpreted their sacrifice in a religious manner; otherwise it would have been parasitism. It meant radically trusting in God, who would feed a person just as he feeds the ravens (Luke 12:22-31 par.), and being grateful for whatever came along. Not all of Jesus' followers were to live this way, only those ministering for the kingdom of God; they could expect a reward for their work (see *c*, 8 above).

That reward was apparently enough to live on, and the surrounding world accepted it. The Pharisees seem to have complained that Jesus' group did not obey the purification laws and, in contrast to John the Baptist, did not fast regularly. Fasting is hardly possible when one relies on hospitality. Yet Jesus regarded his conduct as correct and not just unavoidable. He rejected the Pharisaic purification ideal as a matter of principle (see *e*, 6 below). He viewed fasting, which is a ritual of repentance and mourning, as untimely: the time had come to celebrate (Mark 2:18–22 par.). It seems that Jesus actually celebrated at times and was criticized for it: "For John the Baptist has come eating not bread and drinking no wine, and you say, 'He is a demon'; the Son of Man has come eating and drinking, and you say, 'Look, a glutton and drunkard, a friend of tax collectors and sinners!' Nevertheless, wisdom is vindicated by all her children" (Luke 7:33–35 par.).

Saying that the Baptist was demon-possessed is defamation. Saying that Jesus ate and drank too much smacks of exaggeration. According to tradition, Jesus had indeed been invited to banquets (Luke 7:36–50; 14). He was reproached for having contact with "tax collectors and sinners" on other occasions also (Mark 2:16–17). Tax collectors (Greek *telōnēs*, "tax buyers") in Galilee were probably local small-business people who held land contracts for levying indirect taxes on such things as roads, bridges, and trade, and who collected them at a profit; whether they were also responsible for direct taxes (cf. *e*, 8 below), or whether Antipas collected these through his officials, is not certain. Incidentally, employees of tax collectors were also called that. Tax collectors were considered greedy and dishonest, but hardly as henchmen of the Romans, at least not in Galilee. "Sinners" were common people who notoriously or by vocation violated the Torah or who had this reputation among strict thinkers. Since the quoted Jesus saying deals with food and drink, tax collectors and sinners were probably Jesus' hosts and had a higher standard of living than Jesus. There were such tax collectors, and even sinners can be well imagined among the notables. They did not have to be despisers of the Torah; they could also have been liberals, who deviated from standard morality. It may have been a matter of survival that the group of disciples not decline such invitations. Nevertheless, opportunism was not their motive, especially since criticism could be anticipated. Jesus made it clear for whom the kingdom of God was intended, and he perhaps even demonstrated it (see *d*, 2b below). Overall, one should not think that Jesus and his disciples nourished themselves mainly at the banquets of individuals of doubtful repute. Bread and fish eaten with honorable people was simply not noteworthy.

(2) *The ministry of Jesus and of his disciples in Galilee*

(a) *Places and routes.* The Galilee of Antipas was small: 35–40 kilometers wide between Lake Gennesaret and the eastern edge of the coastal plain on the Mediterranean Sea, 50–55 kilometers long between the edge of the Plain of Jezreel and the area of Gishala, with 1600 square kilometers (625 square miles); its 200,000 to 300,000 inhabitants were mainly Jews. The country is divided into the hilly lower Galilee (300–600 meters in altitude) and the mountainous upper Galilee (600–1200 meters in altitude). The border runs from the northern tip of Lake Gennesaret westward, with a gentle curve to the north. One might view the lake (an ellipse of 20 by 11 kilometers, running north and south, 200 meters below sea level: geologically, a basin in the Jordan valley) and its western shore as a separate, third part of the land. To the south lies Samaria, which was part of the province Judea during Jesus' time. Overall, Galilee was surrounded by Hellenistic city-states, which were self-governed within the province of Syria. Those to the southeast and east formed a loose federation, the Decapolis. Jews lived in all states as more or less strong minorities.

In contrast to John the Baptist, Jesus and his disciples did not limit their ministry to one place. Tradition describes them as mobile and even mentions various names of Galilean villages. The most frequent is Capernaum (see *b*, 2 above); then come further towns along the northern shore of Lake Gennesaret, westward to Gennesaret, and eastward to Bethsaida and into the area (not into the city) of Gadara, which was already part of the Decapolis. Also Corazin, two kilometers north of Capernaum, is mentioned, yet only in one Jesus saying (see *f* below). Also, Jesus was presumably in Cana, Nazareth, and Nain in the middle part of lower Galilee, in the general area of the Decapolis (but not in its cities), in the areas of Tyre and Sidon, stretching in the north from upper Galilee inland, and in the area of Caesaraea Philippi, Philip's capital, a good forty kilometers northeast of the lake. The indications of the areas as a whole must mean simply the Jordan valley north of the lake. In what sequence Jesus was where, if he was there, and whether he was on a continuous journey or traveled out from Capernaum, can no longer be said for certain. The only cities of Galilee, Sepphoris and Tiberias, are missing from the report; so are the city-like Magdala, the western part of lower Galilee, all of upper Galilee, and of course the cities outside Galilee.

It is possible that the preserved Jesus tradition originated mainly in the villages it mentions by name, or that the tradition's reporters had great interest in these places. If the reported picture is correct, however, what would that mean? Jesus apparently started his ministry on the northern shore of the lake, perhaps because several of his first disciples were from there, and especially in Capernaum, because Peter had a house there (or perhaps his in-laws did). This home could have been at first the center of the Jesus movement and then remained as a base. In a small village a non-working group of disciples would have been hardly able to form and survive. Concerning his journeys, Jesus probably did not simply drift along, nor was he driven—say, by Antipas's people—into continuous flight (H. Kraft), at least not basically. In the first case, it is difficult to see—in the second, impossible—why upper Galilee does not play a role in the Jesus tradition. That means that Jesus probably journeyed for the most part in order to reach people—Jews, that is: the kingdom of God "is coming." Yet in this case one would expect greater mobility. It appears that Jesus did not see the need personally to be everywhere with the finger of God and his proclamation. On the contrary, he avoided certain villages and areas, the cities in general even when he entered their district, and upper Galilee. That can be explained, though not by a single point. The Galilean cities were Helle-nized, the others did not belong to Galilee, and upper Galilee was hilly and remote. Yet do these reasons fit a representative of God's kingdom if he was mobile at all? Perhaps the whole question is based to a degree on an optical illusion. First, it could be that Jesus limited himself in principle to the northern shore of the lake and that he went elsewhere only for a special reason or occasion. Then he would have been stationary in the larger sense. Second, one has to ask whether the frequent mention of Jesus' ministry under open sky and outside the villages must be taken seriously, and whether one must conclude from this that Jesus, though avoiding towns, did not avoid people. Perhaps it was his way of being "in the desert." It could explain, at least in part, why the tradition contains so few place names. Third and probably most important, according to the Synoptic Gospels, Jesus—though not from the very beginning—sent out disciples in pairs to be messengers and do somewhere else what he himself did. Only his instructions are reported, not their execution (Mark 6:7–13 par.; Luke 10:1–20 par.). The details are uncertain, since the tradition was apparently used to regulate the primitive Christian missions and was, in turn, influ-enced by this. It is also unclear whether the sending-out was a one-time occurrence or was repeated. The sending-out was possibly Jesus' attempt not to intensify efforts where he had already laid the groundwork, but to cover new territory instead. The idea was not to send certain disciples to certain places but to send them on a journey. Where they were received, they were to heal and to proclaim the kingdom of God; where they were not, they were to go on with a cursing gesture. At any rate, they were probably told to return in the end.

If that is true, then Jesus—always aware of the coming kingdom—probably did not minister at random in Galilee but followed a set plan. The idea was not to confront each Galilean Jew with the kingdom of God but to reach Galilee at large, without having to cover every single area.

(b) *Forms of ministry.* Jesus (the name includes his coministering disciples) talked to and with the people in Galilee, performed miracles and symbolic actions, and also influenced people through his conduct, at times in demonstrative fashion. Whether he formally forgave sins is a disputed question. Jesus ministered in synagogues, in private homes, and in open air. We can no longer say how he connected his forms of ministry and in what proportions, how much time he spent ministering, and whether he learned from experience (cf. *f* below). One could easily imagine that Jesus, as later also the early Christian mission, used especially the work-free Sabbath day. Mark reports one Sabbath incident (Mark 1:21–38), but was it representative?

Concerning his talks, Jesus gave public speeches and had private conversations (but were they also pastoral in nature?); when questioned, he explained his intentions and defended them against criticism. He clarified the present kingdom of God (see *c*, 7 above), announced the future kingdom, called for repentance where it was needed, and gave authoritative instructions. His method of argumentation would be worth examining; the Holy Scriptures played a role (at least their content, for Jesus probably did not own a copy of them), theological tradition, and also experience in life, but apparently not history and personal visions (cf. Luke 10:18, however). Jesus was not a class-conscious or morality preacher. Though general words about this "evil generation" are reported (e.g., Luke 11:29–32 par.), Jesus apparently did not focus on its vices, nor did he probe anyone's individual conscience.

It is hard to say how Jesus connected the content and form of speeches or whether certain ones were reserved for special occasions. Did Jesus have a preaching pattern? On the Sabbath in the synagogue, did he use a Bible passage as his point of departure, as Luke once reports (Luke 4:16–20)? We have no speech of Jesus or of someone in his immediate environment that could give a clear picture. It is possible that he held more private conversations than speeches, and perhaps for that reason mainly his stories and sayings were preserved.

It seems that Jesus' listeners were people of every gender, age, and occupation, though notables probably more likely in the synagogue or their own homes. Still, Jesus never seems to have solicited listeners. He went to the synagogue, where one existed, or he went where he could be heard, addressed, or invited. Normally, people came to him. It is also reported that he withdrew at times (e.g., Mark 1:35 par.), which may be true. Apparently, he was not always available to everybody.

The miracles Jesus performed are still called miracles today, and justly so. They were occurrences that both Jesus and those involved experienced with astonishment as the effects of God's power, not as successful medical treatment by a layperson. Such things were a part of the ancient world, though they were not everyday events. As such, they remain historical realities, even if they cannot be explained by natural science. These occurrences have as much or as little to do with the natural course of things as love has with internal secretion. Of course, the miracles were not unambiguous. What Jesus viewed as God's kingly rule was to others an act of the devil (see f below). One cannot doubt that Jesus cured the possessed, the blind, the deaf, the mute, those with skin disease, and the lame, and that these exorcisms and healings were considered miracles. Yet it is questionable that also resurrections of the dead (Mark 5:21–43 par.?; Luke 7:11–17; John 11), a calming of the storm (Mark 4:35–41 par.), or a feeding of the multitudes (Mark 6:33–44 par.) were viewed as miracles. At any rate, most miracles were services to help people. Mere demonstrations of Jesus' power to work miracles or miracles performed to help himself or as punishment apparently did not occur.

Accordingly, Jesus did not generally stage miracles but reacted to emergencies, both when asked and when not. How often? The Gospels may be correct in saying that the masses sometimes crowded around (e.g., Mark 1:32–34 par.). Still, one can hardly imagine that miracles were an everyday occurrence. This assumption could be supported by the fact that during the presumably short last days in Jerusalem, no miracles are reported, unless Jesus restrained himself here on purpose. Besides, one finds hints that once in a while the miracles of Jesus (Mark 6:5 par.) and his disciples (Mark 9:14–29 par.) failed. News of the miracles must have traveled quickly, but it is doubtful that Jesus encouraged its spread (Mark 5:19–20 par.). Probably neither Jesus nor the disciples participating in his ministry were themselves a part of the recounting of the miracles: the reported stories do not mention the kingdom of God in the least. Besides, Jesus did not need to recount miracles: he performed them. A charismatic movement did not evolve from them: the miracles were Jesus' affair, though they were probably imitated (Mark 9:38 par.).

Symbolic actions are telling gestures or pantomime, performed once or repeatedly. In a larger sense, demonstrative habits can be part of them. Such actions were also known from biblical prophets (e.g., Isa. 8:1–4; 20; Ezek. 4–5; Hos. 1). John the Baptist had lived symbolically in the desert (see b, 3a above). Jesus ate symbolically with tax collectors and sinners (see d, 1c above). Symbolic actions of Jesus were probably his intentional healings on the Sabbath (see e, 7 below), the nomination of the Twelve (see d, 1b above), possibly some instances where he forgave sins, later on in Jerusalem the cleansing of the temple, and perhaps two gestures during the last meal with his disciples (see f, 4 below).

If it is true that Jesus refused to settle an argument over inheritance (Luke 12:13–15), he could have been confused with a scribe, but he did not intend to be.

e) The General Social Instructions

Basic observations have already been made about Jesus' instructions and the particularities relating only to the disciples (see c, 7; d, 1). Here, we will make a few additional points regarding instructions that go beyond the circle of disciples, namely, those addressing human coexistence. Not all of Jesus' instructions are included here, but there are enough to suggest an emphasis.

The general social instructions were not addressed to the members of a new social group that Jesus was organizing but to Israel, which was already organized. Since Jesus intended his instructions to say what the Torah meant in each particular situation, they naturally shared the universal validity of the Torah (see c, 7 above). Here Jesus was hardly concerned either in general (see c, 9 above) or in particular with what we now call structures, such as the synagogue or the village community. One finds no word about the ordering of worship or almsgiving. Jesus' starting point was the behavior of the individual, yet with various emphases then leading to various structures.

(1) Divorce law. To begin with the most obvious, Jesus prohibited divorce and possibly also remarriage after divorce, including marriage of a single man with a divorcee. Primitive Christianity followed Jesus' example, thus setting itself apart from the rest of the world. The cases mentioning this prohibition all show traces of previous usage, thus primarily confirming

the so-called constitutional status of the prohibition (1 Cor. 7:10–11; Mark 10:1–12 par.; Luke 16:18 par.; Matt. 5:32). Not by coincidence, this law is part of the small aggregate of the Jesus tradition explicitly used by Paul. Yet Paul probably does not quote but only renders the gist of the matter: "To the married I give this command—not I but the Lord—that the wife should not separate from her husband (but if she does separate, let her remain unmarried or else be reconciled to her husband), and that the husband should not divorce his wife" (1 Cor. 7:10–11). The next verse, however, shows that Paul considered this law valid only within the congregation. That, too, could go back to Jesus in the sense that initially the prohibition of divorce had validity only where the Torah had legislative authority. On the other hand, the idea of a woman asking for divorce does not seem to fit Jesus' time, neither does the fact that it is mentioned first.

Judaism permitted (and still permits) dissolving a marriage, which even then was as a rule a monogamous union. Marriage and divorce were affairs of civil law; governmental or religious organs were not even involved in the task of registering. By her marriage a woman passed, in exchange for a sum of money (in a marriage of purchase), from the authority of the father, or a substitute such as a male relative, to the authority of her husband. Before and after marriage, the woman was legally in the same kind of bondage as slaves and children. (Of course, that does not yet fully describe the relationship between marriage partners and the woman's role in the house.)

Related to this situation is the fact that a husband committed adultery only if another married woman was involved; betraying his wife with an unmarried woman was not considered adultery, though not morally proper either, even if in literature it often sounds that way. In practice, divorce was possible only as a "dismissal" by the husband and, according to the then prevalent legal interpretation, as many times as desired. The husband had to dismiss an adulterous wife, but the adulterer was not allowed to marry her. The woman thus dismissed had the right to a divorce certificate, which freed her for remarriage, and a fixed divorce settlement, as stated in the marital contract. In general, the woman could not defend herself. Divorce and its legal format are neither commanded nor prohibited in the writings of the Torah; they are presupposed. The Torah only prohibits remarrying one's divorced wife if she has remarried in the meantime (Deut. 24:1–4).

By his divorce prohibition then, Jesus reinforced the Torah in its traditional interpretation and did not abolish it. He only invalidated certain precepts. The duty of dismissal in case of adultery may not have been one of them; Matthew seems to affirm it (Matt. 5:32; 19:9), but this could have been a later accommodation to prevalent Jewish law.

According to Mark 10:1–12, Jesus explained the prohibition of divorce by connecting two sentences of the Torah's creation account. Since God created man *and* woman together (Gen. 1:27), they become inseparably "one flesh" when marrying (2:24). Jesus also explained the divorce proceedings of the Torah given by Moses (Deut. 24:1–4) as a contingency rule, which when applied does not dissolve the marriage. It is not certain whether Jesus really argued this way. But he must have believed that a marriage was indissoluble, since he said that divorcees violated the sixth commandment if they remarry. A man also violates this law, though indirectly, even if his second wife has never been married, because his dismissal pushes his first wife into remarriage (Mark 10:11 par.).

Still, regardless of whether Jesus declared the prohibitions of divorce and remarriage as creation precepts or based these prohibitions on the sixth commandment, the question remains: Why? Substantiation is not cause. Jesus was not a scholar of scripture prompted to new ideas by the study of the Torah. The matter has to be connected with the kingdom of God. If Jesus indeed used the creation story, then perhaps it was in the following way. Since the kingdom of God has arrived, God's original will becomes governing law; or since in the future kingdom people will no longer marry (see *c,* 8 above), no man shall dismiss his wife from the bond ordained by creation. However, the connection could also be less direct. There was already a long-standing tendency to reinforce marital laws and complicate divorce and the remarriage of divorcees (Mal. 2:14–16; *Jub.* 20; 33; 41; Sir. 7:26; CD 4.20–21, where Gen. 1:27 is also mentioned; John the Baptist), so as to keep Israel pure and the cult intact (priests were never allowed to marry divorcees; Lev. 21:7). The kingly rule of God could have prompted Jesus to push this tendency to the extreme.

The prohibition of divorce could represent the woman's protection from unwanted dismissal but also an obstacle to a desired one; likewise, the prohibition of marriage to a divorced woman could appear as social harshness. It is hard to say what the effects of the divorce prohibition were in Jesus' environment, since we know far too little about divorce procedure, the ratio of women to men, and opportunities for single and divorced people. Since almost any reason was sufficient for divorce, it is sometimes assumed that Jesus' contemporaries changed wives at will and thus that Jesus had eradicated a rampant social ill. In reality, however, divorce in small towns was fraught with consequences and thus rare, occurring mainly in the upper class. In Galilee, then, the divorce prohibition, insofar as it was accepted, changed conditions less than awareness. (In a major Hellenistic city such as Corinth, things were different later on.) Those viewing divorce laws as a male privilege now had to change their thinking. Those simply trying to avoid divorce now knew that this was in accordance with divine law. Those regarding the divorce practices of the upper class as too lax now found confirmation. The remarriage prohibition after a divorce must have demanded abstinence of all divorcees; Jesus would hardly have approved of free love.

(2) *The status of women, children, and slaves.* Without having in mind equal rights as such, Jesus said and did various things that improved the status of the Jewish woman. Women were not free either socially or religiously. They had no voice in public. During synagogue worship women were not allowed to read from the Torah or speak; in the temple they were only allowed into the women's court. Women did not need to recite the daily prayers and the Shema (see d, 1b above)—this was not a privilege but a blemish. More easily than men, they became unclean as, for example, during menstruation and childbirth (see e, 6 below). On all these matters no saying of Jesus is reported, but there is also none that degrades women. Whatever Jesus said in favor of women was said indirectly in his instructions to men. Yet we should not overestimate the divorce prohibition (see e, 1 above). It did not abolish marriage based on purchase and the patriarchal marital order. Still, it at least revoked a male privilege and protected the woman from having her status lowered below that of a wife, which would have legally separated her from her children. There is also the fact that Jesus called it adultery even when a husband was tempted to seduce another married woman (Matt. 5:27–30). Yet most important is Jesus' treatment of women. Women were healed by him; they were among his listeners, his partners in dialogue, his hosts (Luke 10:38–42), his followers, and at least on the fringe of his group of disciples (see d, 1a above).

Only a little is reported about Jesus and children. No healing of a child is found; Jairus' daughter was twelve (Mark 5:42), which made her almost or just barely eligible for marriage. Yet Jesus accepted children (Mark 10:13–16) and ordered people to care for them (Mark 9:37 par.), since the kingly rule of God also came to children and did not exclude them. Apparently, Jesus did not give much thought to what became of a child in the afterlife.

Jesus not only did not criticize slavery but also compared a person's relationship to God and others with slavery (e.g., Luke 12:42–46 par.; Mark 10:42–45 par.). One slave healing is reported, if the servant of the centurion in Capernaum was a slave (Matt. 8:5–13 par.), yet none describing Jesus' encountering a slave. Presumably, not many slaves lived in rural Galilee; where seasonal work prevailed, as in farming, day laborers were cheaper. Slaves were certainly not excluded from the kingdom of God. Yet nothing says that the future kingdom would eliminate slavery. Apparently, Jesus did not especially consider slavery a social problem. Actually, slaves were not among the poorest of the poor. Much worse off were day laborers, who worked only temporarily, the permanently unemployed, and the chronically ill.

(3) *Behavior toward the ostracized and ill-famed.* No explicit instructions are reported for acceptance of the ostracized and ill-famed, yet Jesus certainly did just that and defended such behavior. Among the ostracized were the tax collectors and sinners. One tax collector was called as a disciple (see *b,* 2 above); with others Jesus ate (Mark 2:15–17 par.; Luke 7:31–35 par.), just as he did with sinners (see *d,* 1c above). Jesus reportedly forgave the sins of a prostitute (Luke 7:36–50). Yet these were not the only ones Jesus cared for. Lepers were forced to live in isolation and were considered under punishment; according to tradition, Jesus healed several of them (Mark 1:40–45 par.; Luke 17:11–19; cf. Luke 7:22 par.), including a Samaritan, who as such was already ill-famed. Samaritans, though worshiping the God of Israel, were considered heretics, since they worshiped on Mount Gerizim near Nablus and accepted only the Torah as Holy Scripture. Jesus probably did not minister in Samaria, except perhaps when traveling through, though he did not exclude the Samaritans. The reason that Jesus did not exclude them is explained by the story of the Samaritan who, in contrast to a priest and a Levite, helped the victim of a robbery—most likely a Jew—and even paid for his recovery (Luke 10:30–37). This story confirms, incidentally, that for Jesus it was not a question of laissez-faire. He praised the Samaritan because he fulfilled the commandment of neighborly love (Lev. 19:18). Leprosy was healed, sins were forgiven, and the chief tax collector Zacchaeus promised to pay back any excesses (Luke 19:8). Jesus ignored both ostracism and ill-fame, not because he considered them unfounded but because he wanted to remove their basis.

(4) *Humanitarianism.* According to tradition, Jesus commanded care for one's old parents (Mark 7:10–13 par.), almsgiving (Matt. 6:2–4; Mark 10:17–21 par.; 12:41–44 par.), care for the hungry, the naked, strangers, the sick, and prisoners (Matt. 25:31–46), and perhaps also the adoption of orphans (Mark 9:37 par.). All these were traditional Jewish virtues (cf. Tobit 4), which were presumably in Jesus' spirit even if the tradition does

not go back to him. More characteristic, apparently, were instructions aimed at resolving conflict: not being angry and insulting but reconciling (Matt. 5:21–26); not judging but forgiving (Matt. 7:1–5 par.; 18:21–35); not defending oneself should a ruffian attack, a creditor seize the outer garment, or soldiers demand services, but preventing a chain of violence and counterviolence through intentional compliance, treating enemies (not bad neighbors but persecutors) as human beings through kindness and intercession (Luke 6:27–36 par.). Also the prohibition of taking an oath was probably intended to reduce conflict; it did not apply to the oath of service or testimony but to everyday imprecations and curses imploring God as witness or avenger. Yet it may not have come from Jesus; the version of James 5:12, reportedly not stemming from Jesus, seems older than Matt. 5:33–37. Also, the prohibition was not as new as is sometimes suggested.

All of these injunctions could be summarized in the command to love one's neighbor or in the Golden Rule (a nonbiblical but widespread maxim in and outside of Judaism) as, for example, Matthew has done (7:12), but we must consider another aspect. Certainly, one ought to help and encourage a person suffering physical hardship; just as clearly, however, one ought to strive for peace through the conscious, visible effort of putting one's personal interests second.

(5) *Wealth as social obligation.* Jesus denounced wealth and commanded its owner to give it up. He did not have in mind here the few superrich with their political, economic, and cultural influence—possibly because he did not reach these people—but the wealthy in his surroundings. For Jesus wealth was everything going beyond a survival minimum and promoting profit ("storing up treasures," Matt. 6:19–21 par.), business expansion (Luke 14:18–19?), a leisurely life without work (Luke 12:16–21), and luxuries (Luke 16:19–31).

Jesus probably asked only the disciples to give up all possessions (Mark 10:17–22), perhaps not always and only down to a minimum, so they still could sustain themselves. Peter, it seems, kept his house in Capernaum (if it was his). Those that were not disciples could have a flock of sheep (Luke 15:4–6 par.). The widow's giving her last coin is commended but not commanded (Mark 12:41–44 par.). The life-style of a landowner with festive clothing and a fatted calf in reserve is not offensive (Luke 15:11–32). Jesus did not intend to redistribute or socialize the means of production. What he demanded was paying day laborers not by the number of hours they worked but by the minimum needed for survival (Matt. 20:1–16), paying back what was gained by fraud (Luke 19:8), not pressuring debtors (Matt.

18:23–34), and supporting the poor who are unable to work (Mark 10:17–22 par.). The rich person who gives will receive his or her reward in the life to come, just like all others (see *c*, 8 above). The one storing and amassing riches worships not God but mammon (Luke 16:13 par.) and will go to hell (Luke 16:19–31). Jesus had no false hopes: the future of the rich was dim (Mark 10:25 par.).

(6) *Ritual purity.* Purity laws were a vast territory in the world of Jesus. They seem foreign to us, at least by that name. Uncleanness was commonplace and sometimes unavoidable. Things such as corpses, forbidden foods, semen, menstruation, childbirth, leprosy, Gentiles, and their merchandise and food made one unclean (Lev. 11–15; Num. 19; Deut. 14). Uncleanness complicated some social contacts and above all prevented one from participating in the cult: it precluded the holiness required for temple worship. Uncleanness could be related to sin yet was not a sin in itself; on the contrary, it could even result through obedience to the Torah (burying the dead was a religious obligation and a good work, though it made one unclean). For that reason uncleanness did not have to be forgiven or atoned for, though it had to be ritually removed—at the latest when one wanted to participate in the temple cult. We find Jesus' remarks on the subject only in a passage dealing with food, and these are polemical remarks. Apparently Jesus opposed measures such as the rinsing of farm products and giving a tenth, just in case one had not done so earlier (Mark 7:1–8 par.; Luke 11:39–42 par.), as a guarantee for pure food. He intended this for the Pharisees, a movement of laypeople whose ideal was to live as unblemished in their daily lives as the priests did in the temple. Apparently Jesus did not prohibit such behavior (Luke 18:9–14), yet he denied that it was commanded. According to the letter of the Torah, he was right.

Jesus' saying concerning food is rather famous: "There is nothing outside a person that by going in can defile, but the things that come out are what defile" (Mark 7:15 par.). The words seem to say that Jesus thinks that no food whatsoever could make one unclean, especially when we read the following verses (17–23). It has been concluded from these words that Jesus abolished the Torah on these points (Lev. 11; Deut. 14:3–21) and only focused on moral uncleanness and indeed that he basically abolished the distinction between sacred and profane, the consequences of which shook the foundation of not only the Jewish but also the ancient cult in general. However, it is hard to imagine that Jesus would have permitted people to eat pork or crabmeat simply because these foods remained mere externals, even when swallowed—certainly not with a saying like Mark

7:15. Spoken from one Jew to another, the saying could only have referred to foods the Torah did not positively forbid eating. In any case, the saying does not deny uncleanness altogether (leprosy and corpses do not go inside the person; during menstruation uncleanness occurs from within) and thus invalidate the cult (besides, see g, 2 below). If Mark 7:15 comes from Jesus and not, for example, from primitive Christianity (cf. 1 Cor. 10:23–33; 1 Tim. 4:4), then Jesus did not demand food laws intensifying the Torah but purity of heart—nothing new, by the way. The distinction between sacred and profane is not abandoned. On the contrary, citizens of the kingdom of God are supposed to be holy. It is no coincidence that later on Paul regarded his Gentile-Christian churches as sanctified vessels, whose members' holiness had to be maintained through certain moral commandments (1 Thess. 4:1–8).

It is a different matter that Jesus may have allowed his disciples to neglect the food commandments when sent out on a journey (Luke 10:7). That, together with his rejection of Pharisaic purity laws, could explain why at least a part of Jewish Christianity was in favor of the Jews' eating with Gentiles in Christian churches or even felt they were obliged to do so (Gal. 2:11–14; Acts 10–11).

(7) *Healing on the Sabbath.* For centuries the public day of rest demanded by the third commandment (Ex. 20:8–11; Deut. 5:12–15) had been considered a primary sign of Israel's election among other peoples, and the commandment itself was a centerpiece of the Torah. During Jesus' time the Sabbath was uncontested in both Palestine and the Diaspora. Jews kept the Sabbath, and others knew it as a Jewish characteristic and respected it, partly with sincerity, partly with sarcasm, calling Jews lazy. Keeping the Sabbath meant abstaining from work and attending worship in the synagogue or in the temple in Jerusalem, where more sacrifices took place on the Sabbath than on any other day. It also meant clean dress and good eating, possibly with guests, but the food had to be prepared the day before.

It seems that Jesus neither promoted the Sabbath with its worship in the synagogue (Galileans could only participate in the temple cult when on a pilgrimage or other journey) nor refrained in principle from keeping it. There are stories of Jesus defending certain of his and his disciples' actions on the Sabbath, namely, plucking heads of grain (Mark 2:23–28 par.) and performing healings (Mark 3:1–6 par.; Luke 13:10–17; 14:1–6; John 5:1–18; 9). One could debate whether Jesus had words about the Sabbath only in such situations or whether the stories were embellished with sayings reported at a later point. At any rate, Jesus healed on the Sabbath and sometimes in a demonstrative way. As long as he healed only by his words, it was not considered work. Even the grain-plucking is consistent with a group living off donations. If the material providing the Sabbath stories is representative of Jesus' behavior, then Jesus did not intend to have charity supersede the commanded rest from work and certainly not the third commandment in general. It is a question of actions in which the kingly rule of God is at work (see c, 3 above) and of the sustenance of the group proclaiming this rule. Jesus apparently saw such actions as permissible on the Sabbath. Therefore, his instructions concerning the Sabbath are no longer part of the general rules but of the rules of discipleship, and that is where they are most appropriate (see d, la and e, 6 toward the end).

Jesus' words on the Sabbath seem to have far-reaching implications, especially when he says: "The sabbath was made for humankind, and not humankind for the sabbath" (Mark 2:27 par.). This sentence, however, is a Jewish teaching, possibly going back to experiences during the Maccabean period (1 Macc. 2:31–41). It meant that Sabbath rest did not need to be kept if it could lead to self-destruction. But the teaching does not mean that only the things that do not hinder the well-being of a person remain valid in the Sabbath command, and it can hardly mean that for Jesus either, if he used it. If the sentence did not strictly mean that the kingdom of God had arrived for humanity's sake and hence could be implemented on the Sabbath, then it meant at least that help in situations of need was generously permitted on the Sabbath. The Essenes, for example, limited such help to situations where one's life was in danger (CD 11:16–17).

(8) *Taxes for Rome.* According to Mark 12:13–17 par., Jesus considered it permissible to pay taxes to Rome. Taxed were land and what the land produced (land tax), as well as one's assets, including one's able body (head tax). The land tax affected mainly farmers; the head tax, nonagricultural activities. Taxes were not considered rerouted costs of communal affairs but contributions subsidizing the ruler, a mixture of tribute and protection money. The ruler himself and the state-bearing upper class, in the case of Rome its Roman citizens, were free (cf. Matt. 17:25–26). The question, "Is it lawful to pay taxes to the emperor, or not? Should we pay them?" (Mark 12:14–15), concerned, during Jesus' time, only the Jews directly, because only they lived in a Roman province; and it concerned them only as to whether one should continue paying the taxes one had been paying for the past thirty years, specifically the head tax, and if one did not pay, whether one not only owed Rome money but also had renounced one's obedience as a subject. It was not an economic question. Since A.D. 6, the

Romans had been doing little else but rerouting the taxes paid previously to Archelaus (see *a*, 2 above) into the imperial treasury, and if the emperor no longer levied taxes, then a Jewish ruler would. The question was theological in nature with political overtones—or vice versa. It was a ticklish question, the way it was posed to Jesus. He is explicitly addressed as a teacher of the word of God (v. 14). Whoever basically justified the tax on theological grounds (and not simply on the governing circumstances) could be denounced as a traitor (as early as A.D. 6, critical scholars and priests had declared the emperor's tax irreconcilable with God's rule over Israel); whoever rejected the tax was a rebel. As basis for decision, those asking had to show a denarius and confirm that the emperor was depicted on it, probably in order to reveal their true selves: they acknowledged the emperor and had the appropriate tax money in their pockets. Hence, the famous saying, "Give to the emperor the things that are the emperor's and to God the things that are God's" (v. 17), means in the first half that from A follows B: if one allows oneself to be governed by the emperor, one should also pay taxes to the emperor. The second half does not move the altar next to the throne. The parallel structure here should not be misinterpreted; emperor and God are not rulers of equal rank. It is possible that already the second part of the question indicates the double answer and its meaning: "Should we pay them or should we not?" (v. 15). The answer is both: pay taxes but no more than that. The rest must go to God—in the fullest sense of what is described in the Torah (and this hardly means only sacrifices and the annual temple tax).

The story is reported because early Christianity could use it; taxes were not uncontroversial (cf. Rom. 13:6–7). Yet one could very well imagine that Jesus indeed judged in the way reported. Then he would have accepted, like most of his Jewish contemporaries, the provincial status of Judea, under which the Jews could, nevertheless, live according to their own laws. However, in contrast to Josephus later, Jesus did not justify Roman rule with a historical-theological interpretation. Paying taxes to the emperor is permissible. This permission does not have a positive connotation. To say that Jesus affirmed tax obligations is almost an exaggeration. But Jesus certainly did not permit a person to let the ruling authority take away "things that are God's."

(9) *The ethical aim.* When we try to formulate in both content and form a concept of all that has been said, things become difficult. Love of neighbor is a possibility. Yet it is hard to see how the divorce prohibition and taxes would relate to that. What about extreme strictness in Torah matters?

With the divorce prohibition and love of enemies, Jesus demanded more than his contemporaries; concerning cultic purity, keeping the Sabbath, and dealing with tax collectors and sinners, he demanded less than many others. One might say that in many of his social instructions a common tendency is at work: to break down social, status-related, and moral barriers through charity and mercy; to resolve private conflicts through compliance and a readiness to forgive. To say it differently, Jesus' social instructions are not directed at the general moral stabilization or renewal of his fellow human beings in their dealings with each other; instead, they are directed at integration. He was probably not concerned with everybody's participation in social life and the just distribution of the gross national product; instead, he was concerned with the integrity of Israel, whose King was in the process of rescuing it. Nevertheless, this social integrity expressed itself in a certain humane social form. Israel's integrity meant its holiness since it was, after all, the nation chosen by God. Although *holy* and related words hardly occur in the Jesus tradition, there is an occurrence in the Lord's Prayer. God's name is hallowed not only by keeping it holy or by not pronouncing it (which was no longer done in Jesus' time), but also and above all by the holiness of God's worshipers. If it is true that the Lord's Prayer had to be prayed daily, then the ethical goal of Jesus and his followers must have been this personal holiness.

f) Acceptance and Conflict in Galilee

According to the Gospels, multitudes gathered in Galilee and vicinity to hear Jesus speak (Mark 3:7-12 par. and elsewhere). That may be exaggerated but not untrue. Neither miracles nor sermons were an everyday occurrence in Galilee. A person like Jesus had to draw attention, even if only because he interrupted everyday life in the country. Many people may have seen him more than once. It is not unlikely that at least all of Galilee heard of him.

Jesus managed to gather a group of disciples and shape them in such a way that they continued where he left off, even though they had not been prepared to do so. Next to the disciples, he had local followers, whom he could visit; yet the two most famous, Mary and Martha, may not be from Galilee (Luke 10:38-42; John 11:1-12:11). It is hard to guess how many consciously accepted Jesus and tried to live according to his instructions, and how many were among his followers: perhaps quite a few. Not even a contemporary could have told exactly. Apparently, no Jesus groups formed or were intended. There are no baptisms, no official acts, and no attendees at gatherings to tally. For that reason, it remains uncertain which social class, gender, and age group Jesus and his disciples affected. Most certainly, they appealed to their own social group (see *b*, 1–2 above) and also to farmers (the parables are mainly agricultural in topic). Jesus probably also reached local notables such as the large farmers, the overseers of synagogues, and the scribes, but higher than that, only a few (Luke 8:3?). He himself may not have counted numbers either, if it is true that he did not insist on a personal following except for his disciples (see *c*, 5 above). Then, it is true what Jesus supposedly said about an exorcist using Jesus' name without being his disciple: "Whoever is not against us is for us" (Mark 9:40 par.). That means all of Galilee, minus those that were against Jesus.

There were probably people against Jesus from the very beginning. Some may have been against him out of indifference; others may have had reasons. Jesus performs miracles because he is in league with the devil (Mark 3:22–30 par.); he forgives sins without assuring proper repentance first (Mark 2:1–12 par.); he himself lacks the seriousness of repentance since he eats with tax collectors and sinners (see *d*, lc above); he is not concerned with kosher food (*e*, 6); he does not keep the Sabbath properly (*e*, 7). Whether mainly the Pharisees were against Jesus, as the Gospels assert, remains debated. It seems likely that a distinct resistance issued from people with deep convictions. Yet it may be the wishful thinking of modern Protestantism that "especially the pious," and possibly all of them, rejected Jesus.

Without doubt, Jesus sometimes felt that he was not welcome (e.g., Mark 6:1–6 par.). It is possible that already in Galilee some wished him dead, including perhaps Antipas (Luke 13:31–33). Serious private or official accusations are rather doubtful. The conflict leading to Jesus' death did not develop until Jerusalem (see *g*, 3 below). His adversaries there were neither Galileans nor Pharisees, and they did not condemn what he had done in Galilee, although their judgment was probably influenced by what they knew.

Another question is whether Jesus' rejection increased the longer he ministered in Galilee and finally came to a climax. In support of this view, one can mention the laments about the unrepentant cities of Chorazin, Bethsaida, and Capernaum; these places were a center or the main center of Jesus' ministry (Luke 10:13–15 par.). Yet they must have been neither Jesus' last words concerning the three places nor indicative of all Galilee.

The question is whether they are indeed Jesus' words. They might also have resulted from the animosity toward Christians after Easter. In no way do the words admit failure: they only reiterate an instruction to the disciples in case their ministry meets with rejection (see *d, 2* above).

g) The Close of Jesus' Ministry in Jerusalem

(1) *The aim of the journey to Jerusalem.* The ministry of Jesus ended with his journey—on foot, of course, and accompanied by his disciples and followers—to Jerusalem, where he was executed. Since he died during a Passover feast, the external context must have been a Passover pilgrimage. If it was not the first Passover journey during his ministry (as the Gospel of John says), it still differed from the others. Apparently, Jesus had no intention of returning. According to the Synoptic Gospels, Jesus went to Jerusalem only to be killed and raised; he had explained his intention several times and in detail in the so-called passion prophecies (Mark 8:31 par. and elsewhere). Hence, from a certain point on, Jesus made sure that he could suffer the very thing that for Paul, for example, and for the primitive Christian tradition in which he stood, replaced the present kingly rule of God as the truly salvific aspect of Jesus' earthly ministry (1 Cor. 15:3–5). Such a view finds support in Jesus himself (see *g, 4* below), yet the way the Gospels tell it is rather unlikely. What Jesus effected in Galilee as a representative of the kingdom of God was salvific without his death and resurrection. It is unlikely that from the very start Jesus foresaw his destiny as a prerequisite for salvation and simply kept quiet about it, even though the Gospels assume just that. Then Jesus would have presumably known at one point that his ministry demanded his death in Jerusalem; the basis for this insight could only have been negative experiences in Galilee. We can only guess what they might have been. Perhaps because the promised kingdom had not come (A. Schweitzer) or because Jesus' ministry had reached a crisis when all Israel rejected him (F. Mussner), Jesus realized that God expected him to give his life as an atoning sacrifice. However, Jesus was in no hurry to meet this expectation (see *c, 8* above), and it is not certain that all Israel rejected him. And what if Israel did reject him? If Jesus considered himself a prophet (see *c, 7* above), he did not need to be surprised by rejection. Still, why did he go to Jerusalem? Whatever conclusions Jesus may have drawn from his ministry in Galilee, they are not sufficient to motivate his subsequent primary wish to die in Jerusalem.

It is more likely that Jesus went to Jerusalem because he had finished his ministry in Galilee, with whatever success, and wanted to continue his work in the South. Of course, he only went to Jerusalem and remained there; it was probably not his death that prevented further travels. It seems, instead, as if on the occasion of the feast, Jesus wanted to reach the entire region and even all of Israel. According to the Torah, all Jewish men were to visit Jerusalem for the three annual pilgrim feasts (the other two were Pentecost and the feast of Booths in the fall; Deut. 16:16–17). To the individual, the precept was only recommended, not binding. However, at least for the Passover tens of thousands came, often with their families (cf. Luke 2:41–51). It would be reasonable to assume, at least from a Galilean perspective, that Jesus wanted to do here all at once what he had had to do in Galilee village by village.

If that is the case, the journey to Jerusalem was not only intended to perpetuate Jesus' ministry but to conclude it—the last act of the representative of the kingdom of God before the future kingdom. It is likely that Jesus was prepared for a violent death, perhaps even before Jerusalem. John the Baptist had been executed. According to tradition, prophets had always died a violent death. However, these prophets' deaths were not a basic salvation event. In fact, for those responsible it was the very opposite.

(2) *Jesus' ministry in Jerusalem.* Whether Jesus stayed in Jerusalem for exactly the five days the church calendar indicates is not told by tradition, but it was probably not much longer than that. It seems that he stayed (with the disciples, perhaps) in Bethany, about three kilometers east of Jerusalem, not in the crowded city. He was in Jerusalem only during the day and according to tradition either in the temple district, which was the goal of pilgrims, or outside the walls. He spoke in public and debated. Miracles apparently no longer occurred. Jesus' effect must have been immense; otherwise, he probably would have survived (see g, 3 below).

One can assume that Jesus stayed within the temple district because he had an audience there. Hardly any larger places existed in the city. Synagogues in Jerusalem were probably scarce and had only been formed by immigrant groups (cf. Acts 6:9); true residents of Jerusalem and pilgrims came to the temple district with its courts and buildings. (The temple itself was not a meeting place, and only priests on duty were allowed to enter it.) Speaking in the temple was not the only thing Jesus wanted. One can glean that from the tradition of his entry into Jerusalem, in reality into the temple district, and from his so-called cleansing of the temple (Mark 11:1–17 par.) and his predictions against the temple, especially the so-called temple saying (Mark 14:58 par.; John 2:18–22; Acts 6:13–14; cf. Mark 13:2 par.).

Jesus' cleansing of the temple must have been limited; otherwise, the security guards or the Roman garrison, situated in the Antonia fortress at the northwest corner of the temple district, would have intercepted it. Hence, Jesus' cleansing was not an act of revolt but a symbolic action intended to illustrate a characteristic of the future kingdom of God. By this action Jesus hardly wanted to say that the cult was no longer to be held in the temple; to say that, Jesus would have had to do something to the temple rather than only drive out dealers and money changers (one needed Tyrian currency for paying the temple tax) from the temple area or the adjacent buildings. By the way, the Isaiah saying concerning a "house of prayer for all nations" (Isa. 56:7), probably placed in Jesus' mouth (Mark 11:17 par.), refers to a cultic place that could be visited also by Gentiles in earlier days, not to a place purged of the cult. Also a symbolic destruction of the temple does not seem a good interpretation of Jesus' action. Thus, it must have been a symbolic cleansing: in the kingdom of God the temple district will no longer be desecrated because people haggle there over the price of sacrificial items or exchange rates or, in case the dealers and money changers were part of the temple staff, because the temple's services were too expensive (cf. Zech. 14:21).

Of course, Jesus also announced that the temple would be destroyed first and rebuilt after three days. That is what the temple saying expresses; even though its reported versions all differ, this announcement seems to be its main thrust. By destruction Jesus probably did not mean an unavoidable razing before new construction, but a form of punishment. Jesus had not said anything of this sort about Galilean synagogues. Do we find here again a Galilean perspective? Did Galileans perceive more strongly the difference between religious purpose and technical business traffic, which was chaotic during pilgrim festivities? Did they perceive Herod's reconstruction, which had turned the district into a jewel of Hellenistic architecture in 20/19 B.C., as too worldly? Be that as it may, Jesus probably had no such historic catastrophe in mind as the one that occurred forty years later, but rather a supernatural one involving the arrival of the kingdom of God and with it a wonderful new construction—nothing that could not be anticipated (Jub. 1.17; 11QS 29.8–18; 1 Enoch 90.28–29; Sib. Or. 5.422).

If it is true that Jesus wanted to bring his ministry to its goal in Jerusalem, then that was it for the moment. He probably could do no more than announce the imminent reconstruction of the temple, where God was present as nowhere else, and underline it with symbolic action.

(3) *Jesus' trial and execution.* Jesus' ministry in Jerusalem led to his trial and death. Tradition is more detailed here than on any other event in Jesus' life (Mark 14–15 par.), yet tradition's literary form is highly stylized and theologically overcharged. For that reason much remains in the dark. Besides, we do not know enough about current legal practice, especially that of Jews. It is clear that Jewish authorities cooperated with Pontius Pilate, who, as always during festivals, had come to Jerusalem with his security troops; it is not clear who these authorities were and how they cooperated.

It seems that in the night before Good Friday in Gethsemane, an olive plantation in the Kidron Valley east of Jerusalem, the Jewish side had Jesus, and only him, arrested from the closest circle of disciples, after the group had eaten supper together in the city earlier. Treason may have been necessary to find the location. The place may support the assumption that it was the night following the Passover feast: this night had to be spent within a one-mile radius of Jerusalem. Then, too, the supper was the typical Passover meal, as the Synoptic Gospels describe it.

It is uncertain whether the Sanhedrin or another authority conspired against Jesus or at least deliberated about him—and if so, with what result—or whether Jesus was only to be held for an indictment before the governor on Friday morning, as a means of public deterrence. Otherwise, one could have done away with him clandestinely. In public trials, only the governor could carry out a verdict. It is a much-debated question whether the Jewish judiciary could not only pronounce a verdict but also execute it—two different functions. It certainly could do so according to its own precepts, since the appropriate Torah rules were in effect; according to the Roman understanding, however, they were pushed aside by the higher authority of the governor. If the governor was far away or his post not filled, things were different. To condemn Jesus to death with the governor present (it would have had to be by stoning, by the way) would have been at least unwise; to execute him, a crime.

One can only guess the reasons on the Jewish side. It was not punishable to promote eschatological hopes, to pronounce doom on the temple or proclaim a new one, to present oneself as a representative of the kingdom of God or even as Messiah, thereby, enthralling the people. A violation of the law could have been based, perhaps, on the Torah regulations concerning false prophets (Deut. 13:1–5) or blasphemy (Lev. 24:16; Num. 15:30). Many scholars assume that either one or the other happened. Yet it was probably much simpler than that. Jesus' ministry prompted fears of unrest, which were all the more serious since they would provoke Roman interven-

tion. Pilate was not known for sensitivity. Up to now, no unrest had occurred, yet one anticipated even more dramatic things of Jesus, perhaps
because people knew what his charisma had done in Galilee. Connected
with this may be the fact that only Jesus was arrested. If one intended to see
Jesus brought before Pilate from the very beginning, one probably did not
seriously try to base the indictment on a violation of Jewish law. Before
Pilate, anyway, the indictment was "King of the Jews." It is hard to say
whether the phrase contains an allusion to the kingly rule of God. Pilate
could only interpret it to mean that one individual purported to be the king
of a Judea or an Israel that was no longer to be a Roman province. Hence,
the indictment implied revolt or at least attempted revolt. The governor of
the province condemned Jesus to death by crucifixion and had him executed immediately, as was usual, probably northwest of the former city
where today stands the Church of the Holy Sepulchre.

The Romans crucified mainly major criminals, slaves, and provincials.
The punishment was considered typically Roman (though the history of
Jewish law also contains a few crucifixions), abominable, and cruel. The
condemned was tied to a mainly T-shaped beam cross—rarely nailed to
it—and died usually hours or days later with circulatory failure. Often the
body remained on the cross as a deterrent. Jesus died in the afternoon and
was buried before dusk, as the Torah (Deut. 21:22–23), the approaching
Sabbath, and custom demanded.

Jesus was executed because Jerusalem's city council or some of its members feared that he would cause unrest, prompting the Romans to act. He
did not die because his relationship to the Torah and to Israel was such
that Torah-believing Jews saw no other choice. Neither did he die because
of "the" Jews, although it may be true that the crowd screamed, "Crucify!"
when Jesus stood before Pilate. Responsible for Jesus' death was the city's
administration, which in turn was responsible to the governor in matters of
peace and quiet in the city. Without this situation, into which Jesus, of
course, consciously entered, he might have remained unharmed. Since the
situation existed, the steps on the Jewish side were understandable if also
not unavoidable. Pilate judged harshly, yet within the boundaries of his
authority. Execution was, indeed, permissible as a preventive measure for
order. Jesus did not receive justice, yet his execution did not violate the
legal system at the time.

(4) *Jesus' death from his own viewpoint.* Once in Jerusalem, Jesus probably realized fairly soon that his life was in danger. If the tradition concerning Judas' betrayal is true, he also knew that he was to be eliminated, but he

must not have known how. Presumably, he could have fled. Instead, he accepted his death. He had commanded his disciples to acknowledge him when persecuted, or they would be punished by their loss of eternal life. That was now also true for him. We do not know how difficult things were for him. Yet his behavior corresponded to that during his ministry. Jesus had done all he had intended to do in Jerusalem. He did not foresee a task connected with the future kingdom of God that would require his staying alive. If he thought of himself as a prophet, the violent end he endured without protest did not diminish his ministry; it only confirmed it. Still, he did not simply remain quiet on his fate as a prophet; he interpreted it as an event that would bring salvation to others.

One can gather such an interpretation of Jesus mainly from the so-called installation report of the Lord's Supper (1 Cor. 11:23–25 par.; Luke 22:15–20; Mark 14:22–25 par.; Matt. 26:26–29). This report mentions two statements Jesus used for commenting on the bread (here, as elsewhere, the actual meal; the rest is interpretation) and a cup, while he performed two rites that were part of any formal Jewish meal (also of the Passover meal): namely, when he, like the father of a house, first pronounced the blessing over the bread, broke it, and distributed it, and when at the close, again after a blessing, he passed a cup.

Apparently, the installation report does not intend to record Jesus' last evening meal with his disciples but instruct what the early Christian Lord's Supper offers. Already the two oldest versions (1 Cor. 11:23–25 and Mark 14:22–25), though fairly uniform on the general thrust of Jesus' action, differ in the details of Jesus' two statements. In addition, Mark's comment on the cup is longer: Jesus not only says what the cup "is" but also explains that he will drink wine again only after God's kingly rule has come. For that reason, some conclude that we no longer are able to know what Jesus did and said about the bread and the cup during the Last Supper, if it took place at all. Still, the primitive Christian Lord's Supper can probably be best explained by relating it to the actual happening described in the installation report, and since important people like Peter were present, the report is in substance probably no less authentic than other Jesus traditions. Jesus' interpretation of the bread and the cup matches the Jewish custom of interpreting the Passover meal during Passover (matzos, lamb roast, bitter herbs, and fruit sauce; cf. Ex. 12:26–27; 13:8), even though Jesus' words do not seem to refer to the feast celebrating the deliverance from Egypt. On the other hand, it makes sense that the details of the Passover meal do not appear in the installation report; they do not occur in reports of the early

Christian Lord's Supper either. Hence, Jesus explained during the Last Supper what his death meant positively and in such a way that the remaining disciples ritually repeated Jesus' interpretation in the context of a meal.

It may have been like this: With the words, "This is my body," Jesus first turned the breaking of bread into a symbolic gesture of his death, which he thus announced (at the supper there were no matzos but the standard flat cakes, which were torn). Then, at the end of the meal, he took a full cup (it must have contained red wine, as was customary at the Passover meal) as a sign of his shed blood (not of bloodshed) and explained for whom and for what he would give his life. Realistically, that must mean that he summarized what he had said during the meal. According to the installation report, Jesus' blood was to seal a covenant. Many consider this the interpretation of primitive Christianity. Even if that is not the case, questions remain. Why a blood covenant with the disciples? Was this the promised new covenant of God with Israel (Jer. 31:31–34; cf. Ex. 24:8)? What was its intended effect? Covenant or not, one can probably interpret the meaning of the words concerning the cup in two ways: atonement or community. At any rate, the drinking of the cup means that the disciples not only were told but also received something. If Jesus intended to atone for something by his death, then it was hardly the sins of the disciples and of those already citizens of God's kingdom (they possibly needed forgiveness for various things they had done, but not such dramatic atonement). Then Jesus must have meant the people he had not reached, perhaps the Gentiles included, or specifically those who had killed him, and perhaps those who had previously rejected him. Thus, the disciples at the table would have represented all these groups. However, it would be too much to say that Jesus saw all Israel in the state of sin only because Jewish officials had plotted his death and that he, therefore, wanted to die for Israel. At any rate, if Jesus wanted to bring atonement by his death, then this atonement was, after the miracles and many other things, the last event to represent the kingdom of God before its ultimate manifestation, and no more than that. Yet if Jesus' death was to establish community among people, then it would most likely do so among the disciples. His death would not separate him from them. In other words, everything Jesus had done and been so far was still valid.

Tradition does not report that during the Last Supper (or before) in Jerusalem, Jesus even so much as mentioned anyone's death but his own. Perhaps because no one else had to die but him. On the other hand, it appears that the disciples were really in no danger. Hence, it may be true that on the night he was betrayed, Jesus prepared the disciples only for his death. Then the supper was a farewell meal. The representative of the kingdom of God had fulfilled his duty.

Hardly twenty-four hours later, Jesus died on the cross and was buried, as many assume, on Friday, 8 April A.D. 30. Some women followers looked on; the disciples were in hiding. Nothing else happened. The kingdom of God had not yet come.

Bibliography

Cultural Environment

Alföldy, Géza. *Römische Sozialgeschichte.* 1975.

Baumbach, Günther. *Jesus von Nazareth im Lichte der jüdischen Gruppenbildung.* 1971.

Becker, Jürgen. *Johannes der Täufer und Jesus von Nazareth.* 1972.

Bösen, Willibald. *Galiläa als Lebensraum und Wirkungsfeld Jesus.* 1985.

Camponovo, Odo. *Königtum, Königsherrschaft und Reich Gottes in den frühjüdischen Schriften.* 1984.

Freyne, Seán. *Galilee from Alexander the Great to Hadrian.* 1980.

Hengel, Martin. *Die Zeloten: Untersuchungen zur jüdischen Freiheitsbewegung in der Zeit von Herodes I. bis 70 n. Chr.* 1961; 2nd ed., 1976.

———. *Judentum und Hellenismus: Studien zu ihrer Begegnung unter besonderer Berücksichtigung Palästinas bis zur Mitte des 2. Jh. v. Chr.* 1969; 2nd ed., 1973.

Jeremias, Joachim. *Jerusalem zur Zeit Jesu.* 3rd ed., 1962.

Kippenberg, Hans G., and Gerd A. Wewers, eds. *Textbuch zur neutestamentlichen Zeitgeschichte.* 1979.

Kopp, Clemens. *Die heiligen Stätten der Evangelien.* 1959; 2nd ed., 1964.

Kreissig, Heinz. *Die sozialen Zusammenhänge des judäischen Krieges.* 1970.

Leipoldt, Johannes, and Walter Grundmann, eds. *Umwelt des Urchristentums.* Vol. 1, *Darstellung des neutestamentlichen Zeitalters* (1965); vol. 2, *Texte zum neutestamentlichen Zeitalter* (1967); vol. 3, *Bilder zum neutestamentlichen Zeitalter* (1966).

Lohse, Eduard. *Umwelt des Neuen Testaments.* 1971; 6th ed., 1983.

Maier, Johann. *Geschichte der jüdischen Religion.* 1972.

Meyers, Eric M., and James F. Strange. *Archaeology, the Rabbis and Early Christianity.* 1981.

Neusner, Jacob. *Judaism in the Beginning of Christianity.* 1984.

Rostovtzeff, Michael. *Gesellschaft und Wirtschaft im römischen Kaiserreich.* 1929.

———. *Gesellschafts- und Wirtschaftsgeschichte der hellenistischen Welt.* 1955–56.

Schalit, Abraham. *König Herodes.* 1969.

Schürer, Emil. *Geschichte des Jüdischen Volkes im Zeitalter Jesu Christi.* 1901–11; reprints, 1964, 1973.

Jesus

Berger, Klaus. *Die Gesetzesauslegung Jesu.* Vol. 1. 1972.

———. *Die Auferstehung des Propheten und die Erhöhung des Menschensohnes.* 1976.

Blinzler, Josef. *Der Prozess Jesu.* 4th ed., 1969.

Bornkamm, Günther. *Jesus von Nazareth.* 1956; 13th ed., 1983.

Bultmann, Rudolf. *Jesus.* 1926; reprint, 1983.

Goppelt, Leonhardt. *Theologie des Neuen Testaments.* Vol. 1, *Jesu Wirken in seiner theologischen Bedeutung.* 1975; 3rd ed., 1978; reprint, 1985.

Hengel, Martin. *War Jesus Revolutionär?* 1970.

Holtz, Traugott. *Jesus aus Nazareth.* 1979.

Jeremias, Joachim. *Neutestamentliche Theologie.* Vol. 1, *Die Verkündigung Jesu.* 1971; 3rd ed., 1978.

Kertelge, Harl, ed. *Rückfrage nach Jesus.* 1974.

Kraft, Heinrich. *Die Entstehung des Christentums.* 1981.

Kümmel, Werner Georg. *Jesus der Menschensohn?* 1984.

———. *Dreissig Jahre Jesusforschung (1950–1980).* 1985.

Machovec, Milan. *Jesus für Atheisten.* 1972; 5th ed., 1977.

Merklein, Helmut. *Jesu Botschaft von der Gottesherrschaft.* 1983.

Mussner, Franz. "Gab es eine 'galiläische Krise'?" In *Orientierung an Jesus,* edited by Paul Hoffmann et al., 238–52. 1973.

Oberlinner, Lorenz. *Todeserwartung und Todesgewissheit Jesu.* 1980.

Perrin, Norman. *Rediscovering the Teaching of Jesus.* New York, Harper & Row, 1967.

Riesner, Rainer. *Jesus als Lehrer.* 1981. 2nd ed., 1984.

Sanders, Ed P. *Jesus and Judaism.* 1985.

Schottroff, Luise, and Wolfgang Stegemann. *Jesus von Nazareth: Hoffnung der Armen.* 1978. 2nd ed., 1981.

Schrage, Wolfgang. *Ethik des Neuen Testaments.* 1982.

Schweitzer, Albert. *Geschichte der Leben-Jesu-Forschung.* 1913. Reprint, 1984.

Smith, Morton. *Jesus the Magician*. San Francisco: Harper & Row, 1978.

Theissen, Gerd. *Urchristliche Wundergeschichten*. 1974.

———. *Studien zur Soziologie des Urchristentums*. 1979. 2nd ed., 1983.

Thyen, Hartwig. *Studien zur Sündenvergebung im neuen Testament und seinen alttestamentlichen und jüdischen Voraussetzungen*. 1970.

Trautmann, Maria. *Zeichenhafte Handlungen Jesu*. 1980.

Vermes, Geza. *Jesus the Jew*. 1973.

Weder, Hans. *Die Gleichnisse Jesu als Metaphern*. 1978. 3rd ed., 1984.

Yoder, John H. *The Politics of Jesus*. Eerdmans, 1972.

Zeller, Dieter. *Die weisheitlichen Mahnsprüche bei den Synoptikern*. 1977.

My gratitude for help and advice goes to Renate Kirchhoff, Helga Wolf, and Michael Hoffmann.

II

The First Generation
of Early Christianity

2

The Oldest Jewish-Christian Community

Carsten Colpe

Preliminary remarks. The term *Jewish Christian* (*ity*) is academic language and never a translation of words or phrases in the sources. It can be understood as a genitive, as an adjective, or as a compound-noun construction. One can also find a threefold meaning in the history of interpretation, though not exactly the same. Between the term's first and second understandings lies its objective definition as Christians of Jewish origin, who themselves keep observing the law and remain as such in the evolving church at large. Thus, in the eighteenth century Thomas Morgan spoke of the "Nazarene Jew," and John Toland of "Jewish Christianity." The second interpretation of the term matches fairly closely the objective definition: Christians who, regardless of their origin, continue to think along Jewish theological lines. This view emerged in the nineteenth century in the work of Wilhelm Martin Leberecht de Wette and is at present elaborated in great detail by Jean Daniélou. From the second understanding to the third, all the way to the ultimate fixation on a compound noun, ranges the definition that the term describes believers who were both Jewish and Christian, became a separate party, were not accepted by the church at large, and hence suffered their own particular group destiny. One finds such a definition in fragments in Johann Salomo Semler's work of the second half of the eighteenth century; it was explored two generations later by Ferdinand Christian Baur. At the present, mainly the studies of Hans Joachim Schoeps are devoted to this definition. The following survey deals exclusively with this third type of Jewish Christians. Only this type existed at first.

a) The Organization of a Jewish Minority as "Nazaraeans"

(1) *Ecstatic motivations.* There is no doubt that Jewish Christianity originated historically with pneumatic experiences after Jesus' death. A portrayal of the oldest congregation has to begin with these events.

"The kingdom of God had not yet arrived" (cf. chapter 1). That is how Jesus' followers had to interpret his crucifixion. With the execution, however, the hope of God's kingdom had not been eradicated also. In the remaining future hope, the "not yet" retained a certain tension with the "already" and thereby left all possibilities open for people to respond in a certain situation to a certain event and its consequences.

In order to understand—if not explain—which of these possibilities actually became reality, we have available several hermeneutic presuppositions; among them are those that spanned the range of interpretation even back then. The statements vary from short phrases and interpretative sayings to detailed narratives and allow for a variety of conclusions as to what actually took place. In this way they exclude any individualized, exclusive reconstruction and suggest instead that everything may have happened at once, which goes beyond an acceptance of death uncomforted by hope and a forgetting that surrenders to destiny—not only in the group as a whole but also in individuals. Only thus is the conclusion most likely reached that visions, voices, glossolalia, and raptures may have been closely related— even interrelated—and that their individual themes in the reports present themselves as a consequence of time- and space-related boundaries, so that when reporting these, a certain narrative order had to be maintained. This complexity of what was experienced permits us to speak of an ecstatic basic disposition of those left behind by Jesus, even though there may be definitions of ecstasy much too narrow to allow for a debate on the characteristics of these experiences.

Next to the ecstatic complexity, the reports reflect a second element: interpretations that this ecstatic complexity received because during its development it was bound to a religiocultural frame of reference. This frame consisted of biblical-Jewish tradition, which would have to influence any interpretation here: only with the interpretations, not just with the mere trances, does the shock receive meaning—a shock initially experienced on account of Jesus' death by those who had distanced themselves from the old aeon and saw themselves at the beginning of the new one. The new interpretation was such that it was perceived as one offered or received by revelation, not as one intentionally or autonomously produced. The interpretations could consist mainly in "words" a person received, in a commission with which a messenger was dispatched, or in the content of a calling.

"Managing" such affairs is not a spontaneous reaction but can only start shortly after the prompting event. The spontaneous reaction to the execution was the departure of apparently all men and perhaps some women to Galilee (see below). That is where the Jesus movement had developed. Hence, one went there from a place where such development had apparently no chance of proceeding. Thus the new orientations began in Galilee. These consisted of visions, connected at the same time with instructions, which were equivalent to earliest interpretations. These interpretations, in turn, represented the basis for later interpretations, which had a large treasury of connecting points based on Israel's tradition: the exaltations of Enoch (from Genesis 5:24 to the *Enoch* books) and of Elijah (from 2 Kings 2:11 to the Elijah apocalypses) from their earthly lives, temporal raptures of Ezra (4 Ezra 14:9, 49–50) and of Baruch (*2 Apoc. Bar.* 13.3 etc.) in order to bring news from heaven, ascensions after death (in some books reported of Moses, Isaiah, and some rabbis), resurrections of martyrs (from 2 Macc. to Rev. 11), and outpourings of the Spirit of God (from Joel 3 to the large pilgrim festivals). The first instructions demanded that the men return to Jerusalem (see below); the interpretation included here said that there— and not in Galilee—the kingdom of God would manifest itself. In most reports on the pneumatic experiences, where remaining Jews argued about Jesus' disappearance from their midst in differing ways, one finds a paradigm for the fact that the proven models of historicogenetic and yet to be developed historicopsychological interpretations are not applicable.

If one tries to take in one direction or another the path between the factual occurrence and the reports in their detail, which contain the interpretation of the former and on which we rely, one finds a phenomenological evidence of sorts, consisting of a line that leads from the most compact to the most detailed. One should not necessarily assume the psychological necessity of this line: what stands developed here at the end could easily appear to a narrative-oriented person as the original report, and what stands at the beginning could appear to an intuitionist as late-developing symbolism. Where things are this close together, one no longer can prove an earlier or later part.

Probably the densest report is the interpretation of spacial exaltation, where the body of the person tied to the cross on the floor is raised as the cross is brought to a vertical position; the interpretation of this report is one of a qualified exaltation, that is, exaltation into a dignified position that allows the practice of a new kind of rule. Based on this view are John 3:14 and the relatively numerous citations of Psalm 110:1 regarding Jesus' fate after death. A first degree of development occurs on account of the world view: Heaven is "above"; being exalted into heaven means ascension. Thus, exaltation is viewed as ascension—at first, directly from the cross (still in Justin, *1 Apol.* 41.4; *Dial.* 73.1). Then the time element of an event prompts a second degree of development: only a living person can ascend into heaven; if he was killed, he must have come back to life (Rom. 6:9-10; 14:9; Rev. 1:18; 2:8; 1 Pet. 3:18). Then ruling from the heavens over those living on earth required a connection by which the latter could perceive the heavenly power, and that is the Spirit. Each of these three stations can now be extended in a thematically separate way. Jesus' return to life is first extended to visions that can be seen by believers (1 Cor. 15:5-7 etc.); then it is made concrete from God's angle as the raising of Jesus (Rom. 6:9; Mark 16:6; Matt. 28:6-7) and from Jesus' angle as his resurrection (1 Thess. 4:14). All that leads finally to the consequence that Jesus' grave in Jerusalem was found empty by the women that had not accompanied the others returning to Galilee—and only by them! (Mark 16:1-8). Because of unbelief and criticism, one had to continue embellishing this story in popular ways (from Matt. 28:2-5 to *Gos. Pet.* 9-11 or 34-46). The ascension is reported as both a replay of the resurrection and a prelude to the outpouring of the Spirit. It does not carry the independent weight of the events preceding and following it; yet it concludes in less illustrative fashion the Gospel of Luke (24:50-53) and the added ending of Mark's Gospel (16:19-20) and introduces—with more imaginative tools—the book of Acts (1:4-11). The thematization of the Spirit's outpouring offered, and still offers, the fewest problems, since the environment at the time was full of ecstatic phenomena.

For the transposing of these phenomena to later calendar time, according to which people lived, there were patterns available. That the resurrection took place on the third day after the execution—counting that day as the first—is based on an interpretative element that was in the air, so to speak, in various ways. Jesus had spoken in enigmatic words of a perfection on the third day (Luke 13:32); Hosea 6:2 had always been connected with the resurrection of the dead; a popular belief—most easily grasped today, incidentally, in the old Iranian Hadokt Nask—tells of a three-day lingering of the liberated soul with the body before departing. The number forty, which was supposed to limit the number of days between the execution and the ascension (Acts 1:3), was also quite popular in apocalyptic literature, yet it also had become a piece of cultural tradition as the symbolic number for the duration of an exemplary work. The seven weeks between resurrection and the outpouring of the Spirit coincided with those spanning between the Passover and the feast of Weeks (Pentecost).

From there it was only a natural step to interpret this scandalous event not only as the salvation of the few gathered in Jerusalem but as the salvation of all (the "many"); it was also natural to say that this very interpretation formed the content of a message the small community of faith owed to the whole wide world from now on. Already the one whom the disciples saw in Galilee had no longer sent them back to Jerusalem but out into the world and to other peoples (Matt. 28:18-20).

The details of the events can only be identified in fragments, though still in retraceable order. The fact that the male disciples went to Galilee after Jesus' death can be concluded from the instructions given to the women by the empty grave. They were instructed to tell the men and especially Peter to go to Galilee, where they would see Jesus (Mark 16:7). This report legitimizes a posteriori an event that had apparently already happened. An escape during Jesus' arrest preceded this event (Mark 14:50-51). According to all three passion narratives, Jesus is on the cross all by himself. The women—"the acquaintances" in Luke 23:49 is a reference to Psalm 38:11—stand apart and look on from a distance; the men are not there at all. The application of Zech. 13:7 to this event (Mark 14:27-29 par.) hints at a cowardly flight from the city, especially since Peter at first opposes it out of guilt. By the grave, Jesus appears only to the two Marys and the Zebedee mother Salome; in Galilee, only to the men. It is possible that there was soon felt a need to blur this remarkable difference in behavior. According to Luke 24:6-7, the men are not in Galilee but remained in Jerusalem, and they discard the women's message as prattle; according to Luke 24:49, the men are even instructed to stay in the city. Nevertheless, even Luke knows only the women as the first witnesses of Jesus' death and of the empty grave and hence could testify indirectly to the men's departure to Galilee—perhaps with the exception of Peter, if Luke 24:12 is original. Only in the Gospel of John is the annotation finished and unambiguous. According to John 20, not only Mary Magdalene but also Peter and "the other disciple"—John, perhaps—are by the grave, and Jesus appears not only to Mary but also to the gathered male disciples in Jerusalem.

Perhaps, the retouching was so easy because the stay in Galilee was indeed only one episode among many. Paul, who renders the historically most reliable report of earliest apostolic tradition, enumerates Jesus' appearances as to Peter, the Twelve (male disciples), more than five hundred brothers (no sisters) all at once, Jesus' brother James (1 Cor. 15:5-7), and himself (v. 8). Paul does not indicate the location, yet he cannot mean Jerusalem, where not even he himself had been called. In a rather natural way, the addition to the Gospel of John (ch. 21) reports that Jesus was seen in Galilee by the disciples, including Peter. Apparently, it was no longer crucial to presuppose the departure of all to Galilee, since meanwhile Peter's role as head of the Jerusalem congregation had become more important than the place of his calling, which apparently occurred at the Sea of Tiberias (Sea of Galilee).

The historic picture of primitive Christianity at the end of the first century, according to Acts 1-12, indicates furthermore that the community of those left by Jesus actually formed in Jerusalem and included again some women, Jesus' relatives (though not his father), one replacing the departed Judas Iscariot among the Twelve, and—as we can only assume—some of the five hundred. This contradicts the idea that a second primitive congregation existed, namely, in Galilee; yet it supports the idea that from there followers returned to Jerusalem once again. Since common sense would oppose this action, it could have been prompted only by a faith decision based on an instruction, the content of which resulted from the interpretation of the appearances in Galilee.

Apart from what is glimpsed in later tradition in the form of a small chain of facts, the vision of the ascension as an independent ecstatic motivation moves into the background. The end of the Gospel of Luke, which shortens the events around the Galilean episode, has the ascension occur directly after the resurrection—Jesus' appearance to the disciples (Luke 24:36-49) is the prelude—thus emphasizing the interpretation that it occurred in Jerusalem and confirming the resurrection there as final. The beginning of Acts, on the other hand, places forty days in between. By doing so, it does not yet reflect a Christian calendar, it already shows such an accumulation of Christian tradition that one no longer could find a "situation in the life of Jesus," as one had in the meantime grown used to seeing. Everything else Jesus could have said only after his resurrection. In terms of content, it must have been what entered the newer layers of the Gospels and is called today, for example, "post-Easter sayings of Jesus," not the interpretation Gnostics later infused into the forty days. Of course, the Gospel authors are not inclined to distinguish between the words of the earthly and the risen Jesus; Luke only says in summary that during these forty days, Jesus continued to talk "about the kingdom of God" (Acts 1:3).

Accordingly, one can no longer establish more exact connections with the Gospel traditions. The fact that a short proclamation on Jesus' part after the resurrection is reported at all thus becomes all the more important. However, the ascension does not suggest a historical starting point for the development of a community, not even as a relatively easy-to-date pneumatic or ecstatic group experience.

It is a different matter with the event that took place one day and seven weeks after the Passover feast; the Greek word for "fiftieth" (day) becomes *Pentecost* in English. Here, the Jewish calendar dictated the feast of Weeks (Heb. *hag sabueot*), and as a "feast [of conclusions] of the [wheat] harvest" (Heb. *hag haq-qasir*) it has a place firmly allocated by nature. Long ago the feast had become the second of three great pilgrims feasts, for which numerous Jews came from the Diaspora to Jerusalem; in addition, it was replete with salvation-historical symbolic meanings. Although their two most important meanings, the sealing of the covenant and the giving of the law, became clearer only later with the rabbis, there existed sufficient indications that both symbols were celebrated in connection with the feast of Weeks already in pre-Christian times. How the "articulation" of God's law—not comparable with the human voice—was perceived then has been described, for example, by Philo of Alexandria:

> This newly created voice, however, stirred God's power by mere breathing, increasing the former and making it resound everywhere; and it made the end even clearer in sound than the beginning by calling forth in each person's soul another and far more powerful sound than the one perceived by the ear. That is so since the physical ability to hear, by nature slower [than the ear of the Spirit], remains calm until it is touched by air and moved to motion; the ear of the Spirit saturated by God, however, rushes at great speed even ahead of speech (*Decal.* 35).

Interpreted historicopsychologically, the above is a description of ecstatic role behavior that includes audition and perhaps—if one presupposes that speaking, indeed, follows the Spirit's ear rushing ahead—also glossolalia. All roles, even the ecstatic ones, can be adopted; and glossolalia is a phenomenon that can still in our time be anthropologically examined and linguistically analyzed. Something of that nature must have happened at the feast of Weeks in the year 30 (cf. chapter 1).

The participants were probably the one hundred twenty persons mentioned in Acts 1:15, in addition to the pilgrims, who had come to the feast of Weeks from about fifteen different countries where Diaspora communities existed. Among them were also proselytes (Acts 2:11). In everyday life the worshipers spoke the languages of their host countries. It is likely that the ecstatic communication took place between these two groups. The fact that the sound sequences heard by the pilgrims were devoid of proper articulation and structure is also expressed by the reported misunderstanding of the uninvolved who suspect that these sounds represent the moderate beginnings of alcoholic excesses (Acts 2:13). Yet the participants and reporters can perceive and preserve the occurrence, because of their given cultural frame of reference, only in an articulated and structured fashion; this is different from the scholar of glossolalia who is mainly concentrating on phonetics, voice levels, intonations, and similar things. The interpretation of the event taking place during the feast of Weeks is that the foreign worshipers utter sound sequences both Judeans and Galileans can understand (2:11); it must have led to the conclusion already at any early stage that the latter were also speaking in these languages (2:4)—apparently with the basic intention of showing that this revelation at the feast was meant for *all* Jews.

The concrete explanation of the event's meaning, however, occurred by proclaimed interpretation, which must have taken place at first in public— and that meant in front of the temple. The decisive comments both before and after the Pentecost event are placed in Peter's mouth. Without doubt, he was the leading figure in the newly formed group of Jews. It is no coincidence that he is named the first visionary in the oldest kerygma; hence, also the later resurrection reports confirm his leading role (see above). As soon as the interpretations had reached the point where the Spirit's messages no longer merely clarified God's law or made it the new reality but instead reconstituted the people of God, Peter was needed to be their first representative.

(2) *The first institutionalized forms and the formation of parties.* Ecstatic experiences in Jerusalem took place also later on (Acts 7:55–57), and they were to continue in Paul's ministry (Acts 18:9–10; 22:17–21) and in some of his churches. Yet the first common experience in Jerusalem had an initiating character and can thus be compared with the first seeing of the risen One in Galilee. Just as only in this vision did the actual calling take place and as ensuing visions were mainly intended to remove doubts, now the Pentecost event became constitutive for the formation of a new group among Jerusalem's Jews. Thereby, the self-understanding of Jesus' followers

turned into a status whose newness was qualitatively different from the one the resurrection had produced. That is exemplified by the comparison of what happened before versus what happened after the "Spirit" experience; the internal facts of evidence indicate at the same time that Acts 1–2 intends a chronologically correct description—which indeed is correct—while in what follows ("one day" [3:1]; "during those days" [6:1]; undated individual stories) Acts is not thus concerned and therefore does not allow a chronological reconstruction.

One might already call the reconstitution of the Twelve instigated by Peter (Acts 1:15–26) a form of institutionalization, yet it still had an eschatologically symbolic character, for it was meaningful only if, as according to Jesus, the twelve tribes of Israel were to be fully represented at the arrival of the kingdom of God. However, the necessity resulting from the end of the Pentecost experience was fully characterized by a rationalization of the fact that things had become normal again, as occurs whenever and wherever reconstruction occurs, especially after an unfulfilled prophecy. And an unfulfilled prophecy had indeed occurred: the new aeon with its ensuing collapse of the world had not come; life continued as before. Hence, the institutionalized forms that now followed were not oriented toward the world's coming to an end but toward a continuation of the present aeon. From this viewpoint, on the one hand, Pentecost still represented an eschatological event. This view is confirmed by the interpretation of Joel 2:28–32 (Hebrew: 3:1–5), which must be considered as having been actually proclaimed in public, since the passage is still reported in Acts 2:17–21—a text, already written during "the time of the church": if the church's birth into the world had been constructed based on its ecclesiology, the report would certainly be quite different. From the viewpoint of institutions, on the other hand, Pentecost was also the introduction of circumstances that were to turn the eschatological community henceforth into an entity subject to social conditions; this view is expressed in the fact, for example, that what had empowered the visitors at the feast of Weeks was already called "Holy Spirit" (2:4)—the same Holy Spirit that the church would later know as their guide through the apostles.

The most important new institutionalization was the introduction of baptism, which included the conferral of the Holy Spirit by a laying on of hands. It is possible that with it were connected also the affirmation that one's sins were forgiven and possibly exorcism "in Jesus' name." The faith rationale for this rite was probably that Jesus had been baptized by John. The most compact interpretation of baptism, comparable to the interpretation of the crucifixion as an exaltation in John 3:14, occurs when Jesus' burial and resurrection are joined as in Col. 2:12 and in Rom. 6:3–4, for example, with an expanded ethical interpretation on Paul's part. It is possible that this most compact interpretation, reduced to formulas, was also the oldest interpretation and was presented to the baptized, along with their symbolic inclusion in Jesus' death, as well as in the destiny of his resurrection; the gift of the Spirit was naturally included here. This interpretation could have been developed later into multifaceted baptismal formulas. The interrelatedness between such an interpretation and the act of baptism would become rather clear if one envisioned this act as a ritual immersing and reemerging. Whatever the case may be, the church insisted most definitely on the connection between baptism and the gift of the Spirit, or the act of baptism and the laying on of hands, and it administered the latter when it had been omitted at an earlier point (Acts 8:16–17). This act was both an admission into the church and an initiation into its faith.

Such rites were common at the time, of course, differing in their particular meaning from case to case. There were those who cleansed themselves daily in the residential areas by the larger rivers, including the Jordan, with the first cleansing rite perhaps symbolizing initiation. And there were closed groups whose constitutions included a highly valued unique initiation act—e.g., in some mystery religions in Hellenistic areas and perhaps also among John's disciples—or where the "baptism" of initiation was repeated in the form of various cleansings and baths, for example, among the Essenes and Elcesaites. Closely related to the baptism of the new Jerusalem church is the baptism of proselytes, yet it is not certain when the latter originated. The view that such customs in the new Jewish church aided the development of a ritual acceptance procedure that evolved into a sacrament does not preclude the fact that this sacrament had its own particular christological significance. The two meanings are simply related to each other like form and content.

The congregation's acceptance of the first larger number of "souls" or "people"—hence, men and women—had already occurred through baptism (Acts 2:41). The number three thousand does not have to be exact, but it certainly indicates only a small percentage of Jerusalem's population, estimated between thirty thousand and fifty-five thousand, and an even smaller percentage of pilgrims coming to the feast, estimated between one hundred thousand and one hundred twenty-five thousand. Still, it is uncertain whether the Twelve and the small core group of one hundred twenty were initiated by baptism.

The second important institutionalization was the Lord's day (called that in Rev. 1:10), probably equivalent to the celebration of the Lord's Supper. The Lord's day was set for the day after the Sabbath (Acts 20:7); the former was celebrated by the new church, of course, along with the latter in the synagogue and in the temple—though here under certain limitations. Henceforth, the group had to reassure itself of its new identity through weekly celebrations in remembrance of Jesus' resurrection, even though its worship in the synagogues and the temple was already distinctive; Matt. 28:1 presupposes that already, including the day. If one views as given the drastic closeness between death and the new life in Jesus, as is also possible in baptism, then the breaking of bread (Acts 2:42; 20:7), as a symbolizing of Jesus' bodily death especially in relation to the day of resurrection, appears as meaningful from the start—regardless of the character Jesus' last meal with the disciples may have had. Yet much had to happen to turn the Lord's day into "Sunday" (*dies solis*), the Lord's Supper into the sacramental Eucharist, and the celebration of the one in the other into a liturgically designed worship service; still, their beginnings were very early.

While baptism and the Lord's day with the Lord's Supper became and remained required for the entire new church, the third institutionalization probably indicates a split. This form has entered common Christian thought as the diaconate and is described in Acts 6:1–6 as caring for widows (one will have to view *diakonia* in v. 1 in this larger sense) and as table service (with the verb *diakonein* in v. 2—possibly caring for the poor). A description of the function or title of the office of "deacon" is not found in the passage. It was by necessity that a community of faith, no longer apocalyptic in orientation but pneumatic and disposed to face conflict with the outside world, could no longer be satisfied with the mere eschatological institution of the Twelve but had to find other forms of social organization instead.

Offices comparable to these now becoming necessary already existed in the synagogue and in the Qumran community. While the offices of the synagogue involved merely liturgical functions, those of the Qumran community, especially the office of the *maskil,* bear a striking resemblance to that of a Christian deacon of later times. The Greek cult religions were farther removed not only geographically but also sociologically, since the benevolent component of the "deacon" function is missing here. In addition, one finds in the world of Semitic language the institution of the *marzeah.* These were cult communities founded to establish a connection with their patron god by assembling for a common meal. We know of these

communities from the places and times of the old Ugarit (second century
B.C.), the old Aramaean (fifth century B.C.), the Nabateans (first century
A.D.), and the Palmyreans (between A.D. 29 and 273). The Palmyrean
sources reveal a close resemblance of the *marzeah* with the Hellenistic *thiasos*; the former was mentioned by both Gentiles (Lucianus *Peregr. Morte*
11; Celsus in Origines *Cels.* 3.23) and Christians (Euseb. *Hist. Eccl.*
1.3.12; 10.1.8) when seeking to describe the church by some comparison.
The Palmyrean cultic table fellowship included priests and common men,
sometimes perhaps also women. A leader, the *rab marzeah*, was in charge of
liturgy, provisions for the members, and divination. Helpers were responsible for, among other things, procuring the food, preparing the sacred communal meals, waiting on tables, entertaining members during the meal, and
clearing the tables afterwards. Two inscriptions dating from the third century confirm that the leader and the helpers formed a staff of seven.

The priestly character of the *Marzeah* cult guild, which still portrays the
lowest helpers as proper cult officials and does not distinguish diaconal from
leadership activities, would also explain why the tasks of the Jerusalem
Seven are anything but secondary and seem to compete directly with the
tasks of the Twelve, who apparently wanted to delegate the diaconate's
tasks to the Seven. That is at least what can be gathered about the function
of the two men of whom more than usual is reported. Stephen performs
signs and wonders and interprets scripture in such a new way that he is
martyred. Philip is, according to Acts 21:8, one of the Seven (here without
the title, as elsewhere "the Twelve") and is called "the evangelist"; he carries the new teaching to Samaria, converts the magician Simon and an Ethiopian court official (ch. 8), and coministers with four prophetically gifted
sisters (21:9). In light of the teaching and word power of these two "deacons," one is tempted to look ahead in time when an archdeacon was entitled to put his hand over the bishop's mouth if the latter was in the process
of proclaiming a heresy (Sozomen H. E. 4.28.6 = GCS 50.185.17–18).

At the same time, the new institution shows a split. It is hardly a coincidence that the seven men all have purely Greek names. Whatever their
tasks may have been, they are to serve only one group, the so-called Hellenists. By that can only be meant Greek-speaking Jews, of whom some
were residents of Jerusalem and some had moved there during the Passover
and Pentecost feast or shortly thereafter. The "Hebrews," by whom the
Greek-speaking Jews felt neglected, were Jews who spoke Aramaic in everyday life and Hebrew during temple worship. The difference in languages
was certainly a handicap in the life of common people, and it could have

been quite acute, especially, in regard to caring for the widows, yet it should not have been a problem among the "Hebrews." For that reason, it is superfluous to ask whether the Seven ministered on behalf of the entire church or whether they represented the interests of their own Hellenistic group.

Nevertheless, one finds various tendencies. Here a group aware of its unbroken continuity regarding Israel's history visits the temple daily as a group (Acts 2:46)—in 2:14–36 this group's ideology is placed in Peter's mouth. There a group with a historically progressive relationship to the law of Moses wants, in the end time in which it believes it lives, to let God dwell everywhere and not only in a building constructed by human hands—this is the gist of a speech attributed to Stephen (7:1–53). One need not consider the second group's ideology as a continuation of the Qumran or Essene community's temple criticism; it could also have evolved as a consequence of Hellenistic-Jewish circumstances.

(3) *The Sociology of the Nazaraeans.* The following factual analysis, as imprecise as it may be in its particularities, warrants giving the community a common academic name. It will have to be more specific than the ambiguous "Jewish Christians" and most of the nineteen self-designations we know from our sources; however, it will have to be more general than "Ebionites," coined by Irenaeus in the second century (*Adv. Haer.* 1.26.2; 3.15.1; 3.21.1; 4.33.4; 5.1.3). It is most reasonable to start with a Jesus attributive such as we have, for example, in Acts 24:5 with the "sect of the *Nazoraioi*," a name outsiders probably gave Jesus' followers, since Jesus was called by Judeans a "Nazoraean." This name serves as a variant of "Nazarene," which denotes in unambiguous fashion the Jesus coming from Nazareth and thus would not be appropriate for his disciples. Other variants in the sources and among scholars are the derivatives *nazir*, "the one [especially] sanctified [by God]"; *neser*, "the root"; and *nasar*, "observing [baptismal rites]." For that reason it may be best to use *Nazaraei*, since this Latin form is removed from other connotations and leaves etymological problems behind (Jerome Commentary on Isa. 40:9–10 and on Ezek. 6:13).

When Luke subordinates the Seven (see 2 above) to the Twelve and has the latter even lay hands on the former—thereby, of course, unveiling a ministry not merely limited to charity but going far beyond—he thus becomes the first to attest to a factual and ideological circumstance, as will happen over and over again later on. First comes plurality of groups with their individual opinions; later on unity is desired and projected back into the beginnings.

At the same time, the connections of these two groups to each other—even subbranches existed; see below—must have been even stronger than the separating factors. One can draw this conclusion from the mere fact that the Gospels are written only in Greek. The translation—and thus the recording and expansion—of the narrated pieces, which the Gospel writers had later in the form of longer or shorter interconnected pieces, can only have originated gradually in a congregation with bilingual members, in which people speaking one language communicated with those speaking another on a social level other than that of service, hence, by transgressing the boundaries between groups. It is possible that one translated from the oral Aramaic into both the verbal and the written forms of Greek; yet it is also possible that one or the other text was initially recorded in Aramaic or Hebrew. This last assumption would support the common thesis that in these languages were not only sources of the four ultimately canonized Gospels but also other completed Jewish-Christian gospels. Also participating in the redaction of the traditional material were certainly a few Pharisees and scribes, whose interpretation of the Hebrew Bible and the Septuagint took a new direction. Nevertheless, factual sociological conclusions from preredaction Gospel stages—for example, from the Christologies of Son of man, Son of God, or son of David regarding certain bearers of tradition—are no longer possible, since doctrines carry signs of origin at best only in their early beginnings but are soon interchangeable and no longer reflect their original developmental tendencies, not even dialectically.

Peter's interpretation of the Spirit event at the feast of Weeks, which he characterized as Jesus' pouring out the Holy Spirit that he had received from God (Acts 2:33), may have had the same publicity as the ecstasy of the participants, which bystanders had well observed. After that, however, the new message of the Nazaraeans tended to travel from house to house, even though Acts also stylizes this event as great public sermons, especially by Peter and the Zebedee John. If several wanted to listen, they had to gather on the upper floor of a private home—probably no house had another floor on top of that—where there was more privacy. Hence, the meetings cannot have been larger than a clay-covered ceiling made of wooden beams and straw could carry (Acts 1:13; in other cities 9:37; 20:8). One cannot imagine a room that could have held the entire congregation; thus, the Lord's day and the Lord's Supper celebrations probably took place in several houses at once. In a city of at the most fifty-five thousand inhabitants, news traveled fast; after all, people dwelling near public buildings lived fairly close together and even closer when their number nearly tripled during pilgrim festivals: one could cross town in half an hour and never be alone. The members of the congregation, including the Greek-speaking ones, continued to attend their synagogues and work in their occupations. These were mainly manual trades—about twenty of them existed—as well as positions in the temple, work in tourism, in street and sewer sanitation, on surrounding farms, and, not least of all, in commerce. In most occupational groups there were Pharisees. Women participated mainly as helpers in various trades, but purely women's occupations seem to have existed only in service to other women. Most of those having come from Galilee were apparently able to continue working at their trades. The texts do not tell to which trade the fishermen from Lake Gennesaret switched. It is not impossible that men such as Peter and John were supported by the congregation.

The Nazaraean community was stabilized by individual house (*oikos*) churches, at times perhaps by common neighborhood agreements. There may also have been numerous possibilities for men to meet according to the model of existing or traditionally known fellowships and possibly to organize themselves formally, for even before the Hellenistic era, and then especially in it, no social form was peculiar to one country or people. The *marzeah* community, for example, was already known to Amos (6:7) and Jeremiah (16:5). The *haburah* had communal structures and was known both without any detailed offices and with those of *nazir* or Pharisee. Such communities functioned as multipliers, since what the men received there and learned they passed on to their homes, families, and possibly servants.

The enthusiasm of the Nazaraean community was perpetuated, not diminished, by the awareness of the Holy Spirit's inspiration, renewed on every Lord's day. Occasionally, this enthusiasm may have been magically charged, as is typical also of other groups that carry the claim of their own absoluteness to the extreme. Members of such groups internalized the collective consciousness, which can firmly develop under such conditions. In case someone withdraws from this process or refuses involvement, two things can happen: if the individual is stronger, the magic integrity of the group breaks; if the group is stronger, the individualist goes under. In such circumstances, "social death" can become a physical one, whatever the medical diagnosis may be. The group can even reconstitute its integrity and power through murder. Josephus's reports (*Bello* 2.143) and the Qumran Rule of the Community (1QS 7 1–2, 16–17, 24–25; 8.22–23; 9.1) presuppose such a magically directed socialization among the Essenes; its preservation is ritualized in the form of excommunication, which can lead to death in consequence of the group consciousness remaining compulsively active within the individual and of the initial vows connected with it—or this process can be stopped by revoking the previous excommunication. In Acts 5:1–11 a report documents without embellishment the still unritualized earliest form of such a procedure in the Nazaraean community. A man named Ananias has opposed the power of the collective claim—it is secondary here what this claim was and hence what the substance of the man's opposition was—and Peter makes this magical breach become reality by naming it. Ananias falls down dead. Peter did not pronounce a verdict or perform a punishing miracle; he did not excommunicate or execute the first case of church discipline. The death of the arriving wife, Sapphira, is likewise not induced by any of these means but by a kind of magical repetition.

The murder of Stephen (Acts 7:56–60) is probably on the border line between such an archaic occurrence and blatant lynch law. The murder did not occur based on the Sanhedrin's verdict since the Sanhedrin had to surrender the right to pronounce capital punishment to the Roman government; also, in this case it did not see itself in a position to pronounce the verdict to execute: Stephen had not pronounced God's name (*Sanh.* 7.5; procedure: ch. 6). Also, the event is not the prelude to a "persecution of Christians." A young man by the name of Saul was not involved here. Later he will uninhibitedly discuss his persecution of the *ekklesia* (Gal. 1:13–14), but that was in other places. As a point of distinction between Stephen and his enemies emerges not simply Jesus' name but Jesus' claim concerning the preliminary nature of the temple and Moses' law (6:14). It was the latter point that the temple visitors and the members of the four Hellenistic synagogues, arguing with Stephen (Acts 6:9), must have viewed as the breach of their collective identity. Their identity apparently could be restored only by a burst of hatred on their part, which was cathartic for the synagogue members but deadly for Stephen.

Nevertheless, there was a unifying basis that proved its strength whenever no stifling exceptional situations prevailed, such as acute differences in language and culture or a compulsion of loyalties, and this was the collectiveness of possessions (Acts 2:44–47; 4:32–37). Through the ideal picture of this that Luke draws—its basic coloration stems both from Jewish prophecies about the future disappearance of poverty (here from Deut. 15:4 yet repeatedly from then on) and from the Greek community ideal (from Plato *Crit.* 121a; *Polit.* 421, 424a, 451–2, 464; to Jamblichus *Vita Pyth.* 30.168)—we see a reality in which eschatological indifference to possessions, an active demonstration of one's spiritual poverty before God, individual neighborly love, and organized social welfare are ambiguously mixed. This social structure is not a form of "communism" if one means by it the communal possession of the means of production, for the private property of the Nazaraeans, from which a profit is realized and distributed, is maintained (in distinction to the Essenes). Also, this social structure is not a form of "egalitarianism," since everyone receives according to need. Finally, this social structure is not a form of "collectivism," since there was neither communal production nor central administration of communally produced income. If one must use a modern sociological term, one may speak here of a "consumer cooperative"—yet with the absolute restriction that participation was voluntary (5:4) and the relationship between supply and demand was not regulated by contract. It is also possible that the example of important benefactors—only the Cypriot Barnabas and the local Ananias (4:36; 5:1–2) are mentioned by name—has established standards, by which the individual again and again, yet differently from case to case, is oriented toward the members' mutual obligation to support each other financially. Hence, the alternative Peter gave Ananias to give either nothing or everything (Acts 5:3–4) does not result from the practice of redistribution as such but from a quite differently motivated, zealous feeling of community. Only in this connection—original in this exceptional instance—does the ethical content of a consumer cooperative turn into a rationalization of the pressure under whose magical power two church members who withheld something must die.

Just as ambiguous is the position and (self-)evaluation of the poor. For we find here not only people who concretely benefited from the consumer cooperative but also those who represented the Nazaraean community in its basic nature. The "poor" (Gal. 2:10) "among the saints" (Rom. 15:26) in Jerusalem whom Paul remembers and for whom he wants to collect money, have been understood as applying to themselves the Jewish view of the *ebionim*, who as the destitute and oppressed feel especially close to God, and the word *poor* has been regarded as the original self-designation of the first congregation in Jerusalem; it is also on this basis that we need to interpret the parallel self-designation "the saints." Since with the beginning of the Jewish war against the Romans (see *b*, 3 below), this congregation migrated to the land east of the Jordan and since Jerome called the Christians still living there in the fourth century *ebionaei* or *ebionitas*, and Epiphanius called them *ebionaioi* (*Panar.* 30.2.7) and explicitly related them to the poverty of the primitive church (*Panar.* 30.17.2), a reliable conclusion concerning the first Jerusalem congregation seemed to result; yet the relationship between titular designation, actual economic situation, and "spiritual poverty" remains unclear. However, Luke, who for good reason is called the "evangelist of the poor" and certainly would not have missed such a name for the congregation, does not use the word *ptochos* in his book of Acts; and Hegesipp, who appears to strive for completeness when enumerating various names of sects (in Euseb. *Hist. Eccl.* 3.32.6; 4.22.4–5), also remains silent here. Hence, the poor for whom Paul collects (1 Cor. 16:2; 2 Cor. 8:13–14; 9:12) are most likely people who experienced material hardship. There may have been several reasons for that: economic and financial difficulties, which could be experienced by anybody; the difficulty of Galileans with mainly village-related occupations who had to find work in a city like Jerusalem; the famine mentioned in Acts 11:27–28 (according to Josephus Ant. 20.101, probably in A.D. 46/48) even made worse by a Sabbath year without yield (A.D. 47/48); and the eschatological renunciation of possessions, which a core group led by a strong eschatological expectation, seems to have endured easier than others oriented toward ways of the world. It is possible that the former were the "poor among the saints," yet they were not the church at large. Besides, neither poverty nor wealth alone determined one's membership in a certain social class; other contributing factors were involved. And although material poverty made it easier for the "spiritually poor" to practice their piety—as long as it did not become absolutely unbearable—it was not the one and only prerequisite. Finally, it is possible for outsiders to become confused in their descriptions of groups; the groups' names can wander, and the groups' identities commonly have a more irregular history than is presupposed in the Ebionite thesis.

b) History of the Nazaraeans up to the Jewish-Roman War

(1) *From eschatological gathering to theocratic governing* is the first notable phase in the Nazaraeans' development. The expulsion of Stephen's followers by Hellenists falls into this period, when it was most likely to occur because of the political constellation in A.D. 36 (more on that in chapter 3). It is important in this connection that within the momentous difference between two church concepts developing here, a remarkable parallel remained between the Nazaraeans inside and outside Jerusalem. The parallel was that neither of the orientations wanted to discard eschatology programmatically, yet both were forced to do so by normative force. Those

expelled from Jerusalem must have called people everywhere to an eschatological return to Zion, a return for which they had opted earlier when they
settled in Jerusalem. In no other way could they have endured the unavoidable cognitive dissonance evolving between a faithful expectation of God's
rule and the experience of everyday life far from where that rule was revealed. That the Samaritans developed this idea first was to be expected.
After all, the Samaritans were constituted based on the Torah, just as were
the Nazaraeans in Jerusalem, and the point was to restore this state in light
of the disrepute the former had reaped from the latter. In the course of
mission—we might call it that, though members were not yet sent out—
one would then have turned from maintaining the group's eschatology to
surrendering it. Yet also among those still remaining with the temple in
Jerusalem, normative forces must have effected changes, but here the forces
were of a different nature. One might best describe these changes as those
turning a community brought together by the expectation of an immediate
Parousia into a church united by its social structures (the Greek *ekklesia*
means both).

That makes sense, especially in regard to leadership. The eschatological
institutionalization process (see *a*, 1 above) had been Peter's work. He led
the congregation for God and was thus God's theocratic representative. As
such, he could only be a single individual. If one wants to draw later parallels for what comes next—they are offered especially by the history of Islam
in its beginnings and at the present—the formation of the Jerusalem congregation is like a constitution developed shortly after a revolution. Even
such a constitution can still be theocratic, and indeed it is, if the just and
those led by justice guard its observance. These guardians are not determined or elected by the congregation but are called by God and recognized
as such by the congregation. If such a recognition does not occur by majority approval, the entire life of the congregation is upset or crippled; this
state is all the more unbearable, the more one moves away from the eschatological event or from the revolutionary impulse. In order to prevent such
a case when necessary, one can either acknowledge several theocratic representatives or one can see the gift of the eschatological prophet, who is no
longer eschatological, as being at work in one of his relatives.

The Nazaraeans in Jerusalem decided, initially, for the first option. After
Peter, they had only two other men in mind who, with him, could form a
theocratic governing committee; these were the sons of Zebedee. Women
had no chance in such cases, and also in this instance the status quo was to
override the women's prominence, which they had gained by staying nearby

during Jesus' execution and by their primary role gained in delivering the resurrection message. Along with Peter, both men had been Jesus' closest confidants. Although no clear proof exists that the two had been ranked next to Peter when the expectation of the imminent end faded, one can perhaps still conclude it from Mark 10:35-45, and the man officiating as Judean governor in A.D. 41-44 must have had a reason for killing one of the two brothers, James (probably before the Passover in A.D. 44; Acts 12:2-3). Peter was probably supposed to suffer the same fate but escaped (Acts 12:6-18). The persecutor here was a grandson of Herod the Great, Julius Agrippa I. Agrippa behaved politically in the same manner as his grandfather: as a Hellenistic ruler to outsiders, as an active Jew inside Judea. He demonstrated especially the second role by opposing his emperor Caligula when the latter wanted to have the Syrian commissioner Petronius erect a Jupiter statue in the temple (Josephus *Bello* 2.184-203). It is likely that Agrippa's rage against the Nazaraeans is connected with his need to compensate the temple party for his non-Jewish behavior abroad; the Nazaraeans that had remained in Jerusalem could no longer clearly and totally be considered members of that party after the expectation of an impending Parousia had faded. Yet even that was still not a "Christian persecution." That would even be true if the so-called Apostolic Council had taken place already during the time of Agrippa I and not under one of the three succeeding governors (see 2 below), for it must in any case have taken place after the death of the first James, and even then the defined differences did not make the Nazaraeans appear to outsiders as members of a new religion. The Nazaraeans recognized a second James as successor of the son of Zebedee—if the first one had indeed a leading function in the three-member committee—in this case no longer based on his role as Jesus' apostle but on family charisma. This James was Jesus' actual brother. When Paul came to Jerusalem for the second time, he was met by a leadership committee, consisting of this second James, Peter, and the other son of Zebedee, John (Gal. 2:9).

(2) *From dealing with "Christians" to the caliphate of James.* In Antioch the curious new group of Jews and non-Jews were called "Christians" (Acts 11:26). They had gathered there in an unusual intertwining of everyday circumstances and comprehensive theology; Greeks had simply listened to Stephen's followers, and the call to return to Zion was ultimately directed to all peoples. It is common for participants in unplanned developments to receive their name from outsiders. These might be government authorities forced to tighten their grip, other groups that at some point deem a distinc-

tion necessary, or individual, unorganized contemporaries confused by social tensions. If a program exists at the start of a movement, the instigators usually do the job for their future opponents or partners: they immediately write the name in the program. Paul—who for his part will turn the unplanned mission effort in his designated area into a planned one—has a number of ecclesiological self-definitions at hand that could make sense to those addressed; Christians is, of course, not among them. The application of a name given by outsiders is usually much more than a merely nominalizing act; it is part of the social reality of the group named. Should the group's latent intentions be thereby furthered, it can even appropriate the name. For that reason, only two generations later Bishop Ignatius may have spoken in quite customary fashion in this same Antioch of a christianismos (Magn. 10.1, 3 etc.).

That had its effects on the Nazaraeans in Jerusalem. It is not unlikely that the many names for Jewish-Christian sects, known from later times, are in part an echo of attempts to arrive now at a self-definition and a self-designation. The Nazaraeans must have perceived it as a shock that their pious and legitimate efforts to preserve God's honor wherever God's sacredness dwelled had led to the forming of a new religious community. Here, one had not found a name that they as a group could also have found and given themselves; instead, with the name a new social and religious reality had emerged and was visibly distinct from their own reality and thus called it into question. The most prominent representative of the Christians, Paul, legitimized the justification and self-understanding of this entity called into existence by God, of which the members in Jerusalem were now only a small part. Moreover, he did that in a completely new and shocking way: the "apostles" are not the theocratic leaders of the church but its tools, servants, proclaimers, and messengers of Christ (1 Cor. 3:5; 4:1–3; 2 Cor. 5:20; 6:4). The church in Jerusalem is not the center from which all other churches are offshoots; instead, it has only a claim to respect and material support, which the other, independent congregations are to provide. With its internal hierarchy the Jerusalem congregation does not have a structure required of all other churches; a whole series of open offices were yet to emerge. The person is chosen for office not by an ordination-like ritual, where the most important thing is that those Jesus directly called as apostles administer the laying on of hands; instead, the person is chosen by one part of this ritual, baptism—if not merely through a vision and the inspiration of the Spirit. The congregation is founded not on Peter but on Christ. One did not belong to the church by obeying the Torah, with its focus on circumcision, but through a confession of faith, for which all matters of the law were no longer important for righteousness before God but could be regulated by apostolic authority (Gal. 1:10; 4:16; 5:11).

The Nazaraean congregation now had to anticipate various problems. Among them was a long series of efforts to ascertain either agreement or disagreement. Should Jerusalem with Zion be defined as the center of a circle or as one focal point of an ellipse, with Antioch and later even Rome as the other? Should the relationship between the Nazaraean and other churches be legally formulated, and thus be binding, or only be arranged by mutual consent? In addition, there were discussions about important everyday matters, which at the same time could constitute manifestations of theological and even confessional differences. Today, one is more inclined to view matters from Paul's standpoint not least of all because he has always had people on his side by being the most significant of all, but also because our thought is greatly influenced by his theology. In addition, there is the fact that he had no compunction about considering personal matters to be of public interest. Hence, one never knows whether he is exaggerating or accusing when he says that his opponents charged him with personal gain from the alms collection (2 Cor. 12:16), with secretly committing indecencies (2 Cor. 4:2), or with propagating evil so that good may come from it (Rom. 3:8). Yet even without Paul's having to defend himself against such accusations, he is not hesitant. It seems to him that only false brothers lived in Antioch and entered the church under false pretense in order to spy out Christian freedom and subdue Paul himself (Gal. 2:4); opponents asked to reflect on some matter are "such people" (2 Cor. 10:11); the Judaizers in Corinth are incapable of measuring themselves by themselves (2 Cor. 10:12); they boast beyond limits in other people's work (v. 15); they are super-apostles (2 Cor. 11:5; 12:11); they can be compared with the snake that seduced Eve (11:3) or with Satan, who can assume the likeness of an angel of light (11:13). Some are on the side of the circumcised only so as not to be persecuted by them (Gal. 6:12). Some preach Christ only so they can engage in arguments (Phil. 1:15).

It is uncertain whether such remarks, even if one were to drain them of their emotional content, could provide conclusions concerning the positions and, above all, the methods of the Jerusalem Nazaraeans, since it is disputed whether it was their emissaries with whom Paul argued. Still, the principal points of the argument become apparent here and there. For the Nazaraeans, the law was absolutely binding; lawlessness was sin, and one did not want to allow Jews who had been baptized in the name of Jesus to fall into sin. It was considered irresponsible to permit proselytes not to be circumcised, not to keep the Sabbath, and not to eat kosher food; after all, one could not imagine that God knew two types of Jews, for a proselyte wanted to become a Jew, not a member of some Jewish sect. Meat of which a part was to be sacrificed to idols was not neutral food but was used for worshiping false gods—how could a Jew, whether he believed in Jesus or not, be permitted to eat it? One could not eat in fellowship with someone eating unclean food, even when bringing clean food oneself; after all, it could become mixed up on the table. Mixing was never good, not even in marriage, if one partner kept the law and the other did not.

Among the many attempts to overcome the crisis, the so-called Apostolic Council was the most important (cf. chapters 3, c and 4, b below). The agreement called the apostolic decree (Acts 15:23–29) has probably been made not between the Christians, represented by Paul, and the Nazaraeans, represented by Barnabas, but between two groups among the Nazaraeans: the uncompromising and the moderate, who tolerated Paul's principles concerning a world mission. That was probably possible only because for both Nazaraean groups, the salvific significance of the divine "presence," which had become manifest in Jesus' resurrection (a substantival designation for what has been described in section a, 1 did not exist), began to shift to Jesus' "arrival" (*Parousia*) on earth. Thus, Jesus appeared now as the historic representative of the law's salvific validity; one could live with those not seeing it that way as long as they were given only the status of semiproselytes, which they could become by obeying the precepts set forth in Lev. 17–18 for non-Jews living in Israel. For everyone, both the holy remnant and newcomers, was to return to this Israel Jesus had renewed. It is James whom Luke has speaking this way (15:17), and what James says here matches well whatever else one learns about him. The decree had its proper effect, whether it was delivered by Paul or sent later. That is true not only indirectly, since the unprogrammatic toleration of a law-free mission proclamation, as set forth by the decree, released social forces of ecumenical importance, but also directly: understood as a theologically argued moral law, the decree, likewise ecumenical in nature, made Christianity more concrete in the Jewish sense.

Peter had developed from an eschatological collector to a moderate Nazaraean. He worked in the resulting mission, apparently in systematic fashion (Acts 8:14–11:18), ate in Antioch with non-Jews—the inconsistency in which he did that is to Paul an expression of Peter's wrong understanding of righteousness before God (Gal. 2:11–13) and will have its consequences—and he went to Rome in a year that can no longer be determined. Already before this time, yet after the Apostolic Council, the Nazaraeans must have chosen the second alternative to bring about theocracy (on the first, see b, 1 above): by succession or substitution of a person. James was the born representative. If we disregard the familial character of his charisma, which justified the office in his case, we can describe his office either by the legal church term *curacy* or by the Arabic word *caliphate*. Since centuries later the charismatic milieu of Mecca will resemble that of Jerusalem, it is better to speak in Semitic areas of a caliphate. Even the pope's office in Rome cannot be imagined without this theocratic leadership principle, which Peter no doubt took there. If the substitute character of the office prevails over its succession character, as was possible for both the curacy and the caliphate, the office as God's substitute can coincide with that of one of God's prophets. One no longer knows the particular circumstances in James's case. Yet with him a new world-historical paradigm is created.

(3) *From the murder of James to the departure from Zion.* James's position must have had such a clear profile that now the group he represented was considered to be standing no longer within but beside the Jewish community. The high priest may have regarded James's office as competition. The power of James's person—Hegesipp reports impressively of his righteousness, piety, and holiness (in Euseb. *Hist. Eccl.* 2.23.4–8)—and the traditional distrust of innovations on the part of the Sadducees, who usually provided the high priest, may have also contributed. Therefore, when a vacancy occurred between the premature abdication of the governor Festus (60–62) and the inauguration of his successor Albinus (62–64), the high priest Hannas (Ananos) II was able to add James to the opponents against whom he had death sentences pronounced in the Sanhedrin (Josephus *Ant.* 20.197–200). James was stoned to death. The report Hegesipp provides (in Euseb. *Hist. Eccl.* 2.23.11–18) consists of several versions and already contains legends, but one legend is quite characteristic: the place from which the criminal was pushed from a height of several meters was not the usual wall or cliff outside the city but the pinnacle of the temple.

Thus, intra-Jewish tensions led to a break between two communities of faith, one of which would no longer belong to Judaism. A process no one planned led to an outcome no one could have anticipated. From now on, however, all the religious and social tensions that had gradually separated two wings of a rather complex community could be interpreted as conflicts between Jews and Christians. Now the executions of Jesus, Stephen, and the first James could be interpreted as Jewish opposition. Now Nazaraeans wanting to sing during synagogue worship service had to fear that the "benediction against heretics" in the recitation of the Eighteen Benedictions would refer to them, and as a result, not only they but also members of the community without liturgical function no longer participated in Jewish worship.

Under these circumstances, naturally, Jewish Christians—now we may call them that—did not participate in the Jewish revolt against Rome. In order not to be forced to do so by Zealots, they even gave up Zion. According to a report by Eusebius (*Hist. Eccl.* 3.5.3), when the revolt began, the congregation emigrated to Pella, a secret hideout in a side valley of the east Jordanian high plateau in the vicinity of Greek cities under Roman protection. This must have happened under Simon, the son of Cleopas, upon whom the family charisma devolved after James's death (he was a cousin of Jesus; Euseb. *Hist. Eccl.* 3.11.1).

The historicity of this report has been debated. It had become impossible to leave Jerusalem by A.D. 66; Pella had already been destroyed; Eusebius did not use reliable sources; the report was only a legend by which east Jordanian Jewish Christians wanted to legitimize their presumed origins in the earliest congregation. However, one can also view the outer circumstances differently. Even if the legend hypothesis may correctly assert that certain Jewish Christians came from elsewhere (several places in Samaria and Galilee are possible), joined the congregation, and thus participated in the emigration tradition, everything still indicates that the majority of those living in exile had originally come from Jerusalem. Jewish-Christian history in the East, which now begins, will start developing an inconspicuous though rich *praxis pietatis,* of which the world has learned very little thus far.

Bibliography

Conzelmann, Hans. *Geschichte des Urchristentums.* NTD, supp. series 5. Göttingen, 1971.

Daniélou, Jean. Théologie du Judéo-Christianisme. Paris, 1958. ET: *The Theology of Jewish Christianity.* London and Chicago, 1964.

Dobschütz, Ernst von. *Die urchristlichen Gemeinden.* Leipzig, 1902.

———. *Das nachapostolische Zeitalter.* Leipzig, 1905.

Goodman, Felicitas D. *Speaking in Tongues: A Cross-Cultural Study of Glossolalia.* Chicago, 1972.

Goppelt, Leonhardt. *Christentum und Judentum im ersten und zweiten Jahrhundert.* Gütersloh, 1954.

——. "Die apostolische und nachapostolische Zeit." Part A of *Die Kirche in ihrer Geschichte.* Göttingen, 1962.

Grass, Hans. *Ostergeschehen und Osterberichte.* 3rd ed. Göttingen, 1964.

Grimm, Bernhard. "Untersuchungen zur sozialen Stellung der frühen Christen in der römischen Gesellschaft." Diss., Munich, 1975.

Hasenfratz, Hans Peter. "Die toten Lebenden." ZRGG supp. 24. Leiden, 1982.

Kraft, Heinrich. *Die Entstehung des Christentums.* Darmstadt, 1981.

Kümmel, Werner Georg. *Das Neue Testament: Geschichte der Erforschung seiner Probleme.* 2nd ed. Freiburg and Munich, 1970.

Lohmeyer, Ernst. *Galiläa und Jerusalem.* Göttingen, 1936.

Morgan, Thomas. *The Moral Philosopher in a Dialogue Between Philalethes, a Christian Deist, and Theophanes, a Christian Jew.* 2nd ed. London, 1738. Vol. 2: *Being a Farther Vindication of Moral Truth and Reason. . . .* by Philalethes. London, 1739. Vol. 3: *Superstition and Tyranny Inconsistent with Theocracy,* by Philalethes. London, 1740.

Schoeps, Hans Joachim. *Theologie und Geschichte des Judenchristentums.* Tübingen, 1949.

Semler, Johann Salomo. *Abhandlung von freier Unterschung des Canons.* 4 vols. Halle, 1771–76.

Strecker, Georg. *Das Judenchristentum in den Pseudoklementinen.* Berlin, 1958.

Toland, John. *Nazarenus: Or Jewish, Gentile and Mahometan Christianity.* London, 1718.

Weizsäcker, Carl (Karl Heinrich von). *Das apostolische Zeitalter der christlichen Kirche.* 3rd ed. Tübingen, 1901.

de Wette, Wilhelm Martin Leberecht. *Biblische Dogmatik Alten und Neuen Testaments, Oder: Kritische Darstellung der Religionslehre des Hebraismus, des Judenthums und Urchristenthums.* Berlin, 1813.

Wewers, Gerd A. *Sanhedrin: Gerichtshof.* Talmud Yerushalmi 4:4. Tübingen, 1981.

Important Individual Studies

Adam, Alfred. "Erwägungen zur Herkunft der Didache." ZKG 68 (1957): 1–47.

Baur, Ferdinand Christian. "Die Christuspartei in der korinthischen Gemeinde, der Gegensatz des petrinischen und paulinischen Christentums in der Alten Kirche, der Apostel Petrus in Rom." *Tübinger Zeitschrift für Theologie* 4 (1831): 61–206. See Ferdinand Christian Baur, *Ausgewählte Werke in Einzelausgaben*, 1:1–146. Edited by K. Scholder. Stuttgart, 1963.

Bertram, Georg. "Die Himmelfahrt Jesu vom Kreuz aus." In FS Adolf Deissmann, 187–217. 1928.

Colpe, Carsten. "Das deutsche Wort 'Judenchristen' und ihm entsprechende historische Sachverhalte." *Gilgul* (supp. to *Numen*), FS Z. Werblowski. Leiden, in preparation.

———. "Die *Mhagraye*—Hinweise auf ein arabisches Judenchristentum?" *Internationale Kirchliche Zeitschrift* 4 (1986). FS B. Spuler. In preparation.

Fabry, Heinz Josef. "Der altorientalische Hintergrund des urchristlichen Diakonats." In *Der Diakon*, FS A. Frotz, 15–26. Münster, 1981.

Gager, John G. "Das Ende der Zeit und die Entstehung von Gemeinschaften." In *Zur Soziologie des Urchristentums*, edited by W. A. Meeks, 88–130. Munich, 1979.

Holl, Karl. "Der Kirchenbegriff des Paulus in seinem Verhältnis zu dem der Urgemeinde." *Sitzungsberichte der Berliner Akademie der Wissenschaften*, 920–47. 1921. Also in *Gesammelte Aufsätze zur Kirchengeschichte* (Tübingen, 1928), 2:44–67; *Das Paulusbild in der neueren deutschen Forschung*, edited by K. H. Rengstorf (Darmstadt, 1964), 144–78.

Keck, Leander E. "The Poor Among the Saints in the New Testament." *ZNW* 56 (1965): 100–29; "The Poor Among the Saints in Jewish Christianity and Qumran." *ZNW* 57 (1966): 54–78.

Kretschmar, Georg. "Himmelfahrt und Pfingsten." *ZKG* 66 (1954/55): 209–53.

Kümmel, Werner Georg. Bibliographical reports in *TRu* n.s. 14 (1942): 81–95; 17 (1948–49): 3–50, 103–42; 18 (1950): 1–53; 22 (1954): 138–70.

Lüdemann, Gerd. "Die Nachfolger der Jerusalemer Urgemeinde: Analyse der Pella-Tradition." In *Paulus der Heidenapostel*, 2:265–86. Göttingen, 1982.

Pines, Shlomo. *The Jewish Christians of the Early Centuries of Christianity According to a New Source*. Jerusalem, 1966.

———. *An Arabic Version of the Testimonium Flavianum and Its Implications*. Jerusalem, 1971.

Schiffman, Lawrence H. "At the Crossroads: Tannaitic Perspectives on the Jewish-Christian Schism." In *Aspects of Judaism in the Graeco-Roman*

Period, edited by E. P. Sanders, A. I. Baumgarten, and A. Mendelson, 115–56. Vol. 2 of *Jewish and Christian Self-Definition.* Philadelphia, 1981.

Theissen, Gerd. "Die Tempelweissagung Jesu." In *Studien zur Soziologie des Urchristentums,* 142–59. WUNT 19. Tübingen, 1979.

Waldmann, Helmut. *Vom Ursprung des Diakonenamtes und seiner Geschichte.* In preparation.

3

The Circle of Stephen and Its Mission

Karl Löning

The following chapter of the history of early Christianity could not have been even begun, were Acts not available as a source. Development from the earliest Christian congregation through the earliest diaspora mission to the Pauline mission stands at the center of interest in Lukan historiography.

The post-Easter history of the Galilean Jesus movement, on the other hand, is practically ignored by Luke, and Galilee is mentioned only once as an area where "the church" exists (Acts 9:31; yet not in Acts 1:8). The Jesus tradition is understood by Luke basically not as a document of the history of primitive Christianity but exclusively as a testimony of the pre-Easter time of Jesus. This consistently anachronistic viewpoint of the Jesus tradition can hardly be understood as Luke's sovereign act of creatively interpreting the material; rather, it is first and foremost a misunderstanding, which is useful for questioning the soundness of Lukan historiography. This is more than a matter of the traits that usually spark criticism of Luke the historian: the idiosyncrasies of a dramatic, episodic style, based partially on a reception of legendary tradition. One of the main problems in evaluating Acts as a historical presentation of earliest Christian history is the question, how far Luke's misunderstanding of the Jesus tradition influences his view of history. One aspect of this problem is the question, whether the history of the early diaspora mission should be at all delineated from Luke and Jerusalem, or whether the history of earliest Christianity as a mission history has to be viewed basically from the aspect of the Galilean Jesus movement as its continuation and further development. Here, a far-reaching prior decision is made about the understanding of early Christian mission history. It makes a great difference whether one sees this history as beginning with Luke in the city (Jerusalem) and as spreading first in the urban environment (Sebaste, Gaza, Ashdod, Caesarea, Damascus, Antioch, etc.), whereby the "mission" is transmitted by the existing means of transportation and communication to the cities of the Hellenistic-Roman world; or whether, contrary to Luke, one should look for a common thread with its point of departure in the Galilean Jesus movement. The latter avoids the larger cities (Sepphoris, Magdala, Tiberias, Gischala), seeks its basis—supported by unsettled itinerant charismatics—in villages and small rural towns, and can regard itself as a potential nation of an eschatological kingdom of God in Palestine. The question is not whether there was a development of the Palestinian Jesus movement that reached beyond the original geographic and sociocultural borders to the cities and to an audience in the Hellenistic cultural sphere—one finds indications of that—but whether one can at all sketch the history of the earliest Christian mission in the Diaspora from this angle.

The decision has to be made mainly on the basis of the chronology of the diaspora mission as Luke perceives it. A turning point in the development of the church in Damascus is the conversion of Paul, which must be placed no later than A.D. 33/34. The origins of the Damascus congregation cannot be explained on the basis of the post-Easter development in Galilee or from Galilee. However, Damascus is no exception and can instead be regarded as exemplary for the first phase of an unsystematic, long-distance mission from Jerusalem by means of the existing traffic connections to the more significant cities in the Mediterranean area, facilitated by the connections that the diaspora Judaism residing in these cities had with the temple in Jerusalem. Hence, this chapter about the history of earliest Christianity cannot be written while going against Luke, but only by critically adopting his sketch of history.

a) The Hellenists in the First Christian Church in Jerusalem

The material of Acts 6–8 used to describe the Hellenists in the early Jerusalem church, the conflict of Stephen, and the mission of Philip in Samaria and in the coastal region is quite significant historically and often especially reliable in its details. Yet Luke's material was probably not a coherent "source" but individual pieces. It is possible that Luke received them from an informant with contacts in the church in Caesarea, the final stage of Philip's mission according to Luke (cf. Acts 8:40). That could be indicated by the note in Acts 21:8, the so-called "we" report, on Paul's stay during his last journey to Jerusalem (spring of A.D. 52) in "the house of Philip the evangelist, one of the seven." However, the redactional interpretation of this material clearly bears Luke's signature.

In Acts 6:1, Luke uses for the first time the term *Hellenists* for a certain group within the early Christian church. The term does not mean that the thus designated group follows a Greek life-style (*hellenizein*), meaning not following the law, but that Greek is its native tongue or its vernacular. One can conclude this from the fact that also mainly tradition-conscious diaspora Jews are called "Hellenists" in Acts (9:29). Still, the actual meaning only results when one contrasts "Hellenists" with "Hebrews." This contrast is not found elsewhere. It is apparently a new terminological coinage, which serves to distinguish between Aramaic-speaking Palestinians and Greek-speaking diaspora Jewish Christians within the early Jerusalem church.

The birth of such a usage presupposes a certain development of the Jerusalem church. Luke uses the contrasting terms without further explanation since, according to his report, with the language miracle on the day of Pentecost, baptized diaspora Jews have been a part of the early Christian church from the very beginning (cf. Acts 2:5, 41). If one assumes that the Jerusalem church originated in Galilee in the course of a first collective post-Easter movement, one will be more careful in dating the event. Under the most extensive consideration of Lukan statements, one can imagine the development in such a way that the eschatological gathering, centered on Jerusalem, also reached pilgrims (who had come for the feast of Weeks) from the Diaspora and local diaspora Jews. For a certain group conscience to form based on differing language conditions, still another development is necessary. This development is not described by Luke. He has no interest in describing basic internal distinctions within the earliest Christian congregation. The events leading in Acts 6:1–7 to a differentiation of ecclesiological forms relate to services the church provides and thus describe not the quarrel between Hellenists and Hebrews but its resolution. To Luke the problem is that the earliest Christian congregation, as a result of its rapid growth, can no longer smoothly provide for its members—not because of material poverty but because the distribution of provisions results in disadvantages for the widows of Hellenists. The solution for Luke is for the disadvantaged group to take over the task of justly distributing the provisions among the congregation's members. Luke is less interested in the solution's result—that is, the settling of a conflict of days past—than the solution's method, the differentiation of church tasks. Luke advocates a stronger separation of spiritual and economic leadership positions. The Twelve are no longer willing to be responsible for both areas, but they want to "devote ourselves to prayer and to serving the word," while waiting on tables was to be performed by the circle of the Seven from the Hellenistic group (6:2–4). Luke is not concerned here with a historical but an actual problem, namely, the separation of bishop's and deacon's responsibilities in the post-Pauline church in Asia Minor. Luke advocates a stronger spiritual emphasis in the bishop's office, which as an elected office within the local self-government of congregations is first composed of primarily economic services; in Luke's opinion, however, the office needs to be defined more along spiritual leadership principles, because its original bearers, the "apostles"—that is, the original bearers of charismatic leadership authority, which does not at all derive from the particular demands of a local self-government—no longer represent an element in the present church order. For the reform of church tasks that he advocates Luke wants to derive the principles of order from earliest apostolic times. Hence, the argument between the Hellenists and the Hebrews in the earliest Christian congregation offers him this literary opportunity. When projecting back postapostolic problems of order into the original apostolic era, however, Luke has to narrate the way to a solution in the opposite direction. The office of economic leadership is distinguished from the primarily spiritual office of the "Twelve." The new formulation of the bishop's office in the Lukan church proceeds in the opposite direction.

If that is the tendency of Luke's arrangement in Acts 6:1–7, one can reach two main conclusions for a historical interpretation of the events. The first relates to the ranking of the circle of the Seven; the second to the role of Hellenists as a group within the earliest Christian congregation. The Seven around Stephen were not equivalent to the first deacons of an apostle-led early Christian church. Their service refers neither to the earliest Christian congregation in its totality nor to duties related to economic self-government. Tradition characterizes Stephen—and later Philip; cf. Acts 8:5–7—as a charismatic active in mission. Stephen's appearance in Acts 6:8 as miracle worker and missionary certainly does not correspond to the Lukan distribution of responsibilities between the Twelve and the Seven. Hence, the suggestion made subsequently by Luke that the circle of the Seven became active in mission outside Jerusalem only after Stephen's persecution cannot be maintained. It would also leave unexplained how Stephen, whose martyrdom launched the mission activity of the Hellenists (cf. 8:1, 3), could have prominence as a leading figure in the circle of the

Seven. It is historically likely that the circle of the Seven, headed by Stephen, played an active missionary role in Jerusalem from the very beginning. Hence, the relationship of the Seven to the "Hellenists" in the earliest Christian congregation is that the Seven constituted the charismatic leadership committee of this part of the Jerusalem church. That means at the same time that the Hellenistic part of the earliest Christian congregation, consisting of Greek-speaking diaspora Jews, underwent a relatively independent development. This is also indicated by the argument over provisions, presupposed in Acts 8:1. The argument is certainly not a Lukan invention, since it stands out from Acts' rather harmonious overall picture of the earliest Christian congregation. Also, the argument should not be underestimated as a mere struggle for status ("looking down on the widows"). Luke wants to say that the widows of Hellenists are excluded from the daily provisions doled out by the congregation. He thereby presupposes anachronistically that the earliest Christian congregation has instituted a certain welfare system for the poor. Historically, it is likely that the system catered to the Hellenists as a group. The "Hebrews" refuse to share the means available for their own well-being with those who are not part of the actual Jesus movement and did not surrender their property for the sake of discipleship, but who journeyed as quite ordinary pilgrims to the feast in Jerusalem and thus were not completely unprepared and without means. The latter are expected to solve their own economic problems. Such a demand reinforces the already present tendencies to view the baptized diaspora Jews as a separate group. They come from abroad, speak Greek, and in a sociocultural sense are part of the urban environment of a Hellenistic diaspora Judaism. They were not present in Galilee and know Jesus only from proclamation. They joined the group of actual followers later. Now they even remain to themselves during the congregation's evening meal. That has consequences for the self-understanding of this group as a religious community, since the daily provisions were given out at first in the framework of the eucharistic table fellowship. The place of the early Christian supper celebration is the home (cf. Acts 2:46). Therefore, the necessity of having to take care of their own provisions means that the "Hellenists" have their supper celebrations among themselves and form house churches for that purpose, just as the "Hebrews" do. The home as a decentralized meeting place then encourages the parallel formation of two linguistically different developments of the Lord's Supper. In this area, the language boundary becomes a characteristic, and a corresponding terminology develops to distinguish the Christian house churches by the language they use: Aramaic by the "Hebrews," Greek by the "Hellenists." Thus, the institutional foundations are laid for the "Hellenists"—based on the particular conditions of the cultural tradition of diaspora Judaism—to develop as a group with a distinct profile. The profile's elements, or at least fragments thereof, can be gleaned from reports about the mission of the circle of Stephen.

b) The Circle of Stephen and Its Mission

The members of Stephen's group are mentioned by name in the list of Acts 6:5. All listed names are Greek. That points to non-Palestinian origin. Only two names, Philip and Nicanor, are more frequently found in diaspora Judaism. However, that is no reason to consider the rest of the members non-Jews. That the members could be Gentile Christians is rejected by the particular note according to which Nicolas of Antioch is a proselyte and thus the exception[1] to the rule that all the rest are Jews (Jewish Christians). The reference to Antioch—probably Syrian Antioch—as the place of origin of one of the Seven was also contained in the pre-Lukan list, for as comparison with the list of "prophets and teachers" in the Antiochene church in Acts 13:1 shows, Luke did not construct any overlap in personnel between the circle of the Seven and the pioneers in the Antiochene mission to the Gentiles, even though his point of emphasis was the mission-historical connection between the persecution of Stephen and the mission to the Gentiles (cf. Acts 11:19–20). None of the Seven has a surname. The reason may be that the members of the circle did not trace their authority back to a calling by Jesus. There are no other indications that they belong to the circle of apostles. The Philip in the list of Acts 6:5 must be distinguished from the apostle by the same name (John 1:44; 12:21), who appears in the lists of the Twelve in fifth place (Mark 3:18 par.; Acts 1:13). In the Acts of Philip the two are mistakenly taken for the same. It is unapostolic that the leading members of the circle never appear in the tradition in pairs. Essential for the self-understanding of the Stephen circle as a collegium is the number seven itself. This number may be derived from the number of members in a local synagogal administrative committee and can be seen, at any rate, as a reference to a separate form of organization of the Hellenistic part of the Jerusalem congregation in analogy to the synagogal constitution or to other (perhaps non-Jewish) forms of self-government. Beyond that, the number seven suggests the ideal concept of completion, which is also contained, though in a different way, in the number twelve. At any rate, the coexistence of the circle of Twelve and the circle of Seven in the Jerusalem church is not as easily harmonizable as Luke suggests when subordinating the Seven to the Twelve. One is dealing here on both sides with autonomous ecclesiological models of representation.[2]

Contrary to the Lukan tendency, the tradition used by Luke characterizes at least the two leading men of the collegium of the Seven, Stephen and Philip, as missionaries. The term *evangelist* for Philip in this function (Acts 21:8), however, seems to be secondary. According to deutero-Pauline language usage, the "evangelists" follow in rank the "apostles" and "prophets" but come before the local authorities, "shepherds and teachers" (Eph. 4:11; cf. 2 Tim. 4:5). In Acts 21:8 such a ranking of Philip may be intended. It is not reported that the members of the circle of the Seven were authentically named missionaries. Concerning the earliest missionary activities, the Stephen tradition shows that the Seven were active first in the environment from where they came, namely, the Hellenistic synagogues in Jerusalem. Acts assumes a multitude of such institutions in Jerusalem (Acts 24:12). Concrete references to Stephen's opponents are contained in Acts 6:9. The series of names raises some questions. Concerning the question whether Luke wants to mention one or several synagogues, one has to start with the grammatically clear singular form. At first, people are mentioned that are members of a certain synagogue that is designated the (so-called) "synagogue of the Freedmen, Cyrenians, and Alexandrians." Then come people "from Cilicia and Asia," about whose membership in this or any other synagogue nothing is said. Their mention must be attributed to Lukan redaction. It is important to Luke that here already the opponents are mentioned with whom Paul will have to deal later.[3] From the pre-Lukan naming of Stephen's opponents as members of the "synagogue of the Freedmen, Cyrenians, and Alexandrians," one may conclude that the mission activity of the Stephen circle focused on diaspora Jews of North-African origin, possibly because Stephen himself was African. The New Testament contains some further traces of a rather early relationship of the Jerusalem church with North Africa. The Simon mentioned in the passion tradition or his sons Alexander and Rufus (Mark 15:21) are from Cyrene; so are Lucius, mentioned in Acts 13:1, and possibly other pioneers in the Syrian mission (cf. Acts 11:20); from Alexandria comes Apollos (Acts 18:24). Whether and how far connections exist here with the Stephen circle cannot be determined. Of course, one cannot speak of an African mission at the presupposed point in time. Still, one can assume that the missionary propaganda, presupposed in the Stephen tradition, had consequences among the pilgrims at the feast who had come from the African Diaspora to Jerusalem and, thus, among the respective home synagogues in the Diaspora, especially if we keep in mind that the pilgrims who had come to the temple in Jerusalem traveled in groups and stayed together in compatriot synagogue communities. One will also have to ask whether some Hellenists returned to their homelands as missionaries after their expulsion from Jerusalem. It is hardly a coincidence that two of the members of the Stephen circle, Nicolas and Prochorus, are considered authorities among Egyptian Gnostics. Overall, the point here is not to analyze the incidentally more frequent references to Egypt and Cyrene. It is likely that the indirect distant mission reported here radiated to the remaining Diaspora. The early beginnings of Christian churches in Damascus and Rome, for example, can probably be explained in similar fashion.

One can make only fragmentary observations about the theological profile of the Stephen circle and the concept of its mission because of the scarcity of available material. Our knowledge is based solely on three individual traditions: the martyrdom of Stephen and two episodes on Philip. One should not expand this lack of material in a speculative fashion by freely using Lukan concepts to make Stephen a "predecessor of the apostle Paul" (F. Chr. Baur) and attributing to Luke's theology everything that, as the missing link, could make the development from the early Jerusalem church to Paul understandable.

It is historically certain, first of all, that Stephen's proclamation led to a conflict, which ended in his death and the expulsion of his group from Jerusalem. The essence of this conflict can be gleaned from the accusations made by his opponents: blasphemy against Moses and God (Acts 6:11) or "against this holy place and the law" (6:13). These summarizing formulations, however—at least in this form—go back to Luke. He interprets the Stephen conflict by making the bone of contention the central institutions of Jewish religion, the temple and the law, and making the turning point relations between earliest Christianity and a religioculturally formulated Judaism in general. For Luke the argument over the "law" is a dispute over the obligatory nature of Jewish culture (6:14). Besides all that, essential for Luke is his intention to draw parallels between Stephen and Paul; against the latter, in a similar situation, the same accusations are raised (cf. Acts 21:21, 28 in connection with the ensuing trial chapters).[4] The pre-Lukan essence of the accusation against Stephen is the dispute over the temple as a place of God's presence and of eschatological atonement. One can understand that the dispute is sparked by the concept of the temple and the temple cult, since the Stephen mission seeks its addressees among the members of Hellenistic synagogues who had come from the Diaspora to visit the temple. In the context of this wooing of temple pilgrims, the Christian proclamation has to appear in its essence, at least implicitly, as a denial of the temple cult's soteriological relevancy. Stephen's speech also points in this direction.[5]

The speech's subject is the question about the "place" (cf. Acts 7:7, 33, 49) of God's presence and of the true cult. Based on the foundation of a historical summary oriented toward the Septuagint, the speech develops in Midrash fashion the thesis that this "place" is not the temple in Jerusalem; God's saving wisdom reveals itself in the desert (7:30, 36), and the messengers of this wisdom are denied by Israel (7:25, 35, 39, 52). The building of the temple by Solomon was already a forsaking of the ideal communal cult of the nation of Israel in the desert, where God's presence as an indwelling in the "tabernacle of the covenant" enabled Israel's cultic encounter with God. While the tabernacle was made according to heavenly pattern (v. 44), the "house" Solomon built was made by human hands and was not "the dwelling place" of God (v. 46) David had asked for. The speech deals with Mosaic law only in connection with its cult-critical overall content. The law given by Moses is the basis for Israel's exclusive relationship with Yahweh alone; forsaking the law is viewed in the Deuteronomist sense as an offense primarily against the first commandment of the Decalogue and will be punished by the nation's condemnation to idol worship (7:39–43).

Hence, the text is anything but critical of the law. The criticism of the cult, rather, runs parallel to a radically theocentric interpretation of the law. The cult criticism itself has a fundamental harshness. It cannot be understood as the expression of a—for "Hellenists" typical—liberal, or spiritualizing, concept of religious rites and norms, as if the Stephen conflict was ultimately a dispute between an orthodox and a less orthodox wing in Hellenistic Judaism. Stephen is a charismatic whose spiritual gift expresses itself in wise speech and miracle-working power (Acts 6:8, 10; cf. also on Philip 8:6–7, 29, 39). His death is presented as a visionary event (7:55–56), as an immediate vision of God's glory, not in the temple but in the eschatological opening of the heavens. Hence, the temple critique can hardly be seen as the expression of an enlightened reservation about the cult business in Jerusalem; instead, its true motive has to be related to the soteriological central content of the Christian proclamation, the understanding of Jesus' death as the eschatological atonement event. Although indications for such an understanding are not contained in the Stephen tradition itself, they are contained in the Philip tradition (cf. the use of the quote from Isaiah 53:7-8 in the baptismal catechism of the episode about the court official in Acts 8:32-33). From here, one may also imagine a line of development leading up to the pre-Pauline tradition (cf. Rom. 3:25-26).

The understanding of Jesus' death as an atonement event of universal significance is also the starting point for the development of a mission concept that bursts the boundaries of the cultically defined Israel. This is the programmatic theme of the episode about the court official (Acts 8:26-40), which can be included here[6] in that it explicitly depicts this consequence of the cult critique by the Stephen circle. The minister of finance of the queen of the "Ethiopians"—meant here is the Isle of Meroë south of the fifth Nile cataract, whose queen held the title Candace—is on his way back home from a pilgrimage to the temple in Jerusalem. Since as a high court official he is a eunuch, he is considered ineligible for the cult according to the law (Deut. 23:2-9). On his way back from Jerusalem, he finds in the "wilderness" what the ritual law excludes him from: access to God through Philip's baptism based on Jesus' atoning death. The characterization of the official as eunuch implies a drastic allusion to the demand of circumcision, the requirement for full conversion to Judaism. As a castrated man, the official cannot become a proselyte. When baptism gives him access to the people of God, it appears here as the equivalent of circumcision, namely, at first for a "God-fearer." This, however, shows the way to the fulfillment of the prophetic promise that in the eschatological future even foreigners and eunuchs will gain access to the house of Yahweh (cf. Isa. 56:1-8).

c) The Martyrdom of Stephen and the Beginnings of Diaspora Churches

Luke has turned the martyrdom of Stephen into a central event of mission history. The conflict with the diaspora-Jewish opponents of Stephen (Acts 6:9) escalates to the Sanhedrin trial (6:12-15), while the stoning of Stephen (7:59) escalates to the "severe" persecution of the church of God (8:1). The thereby triggered flight of "all" believers "with exception of the apostles"[7] sets in motion the mission outside Jerusalem. In Stephen's stoning, Saul is merely a participant (7:58); the church's persecution is already to a large degree his work (8:3). For the persecutor Saul, chasing after fleeing disciples becomes a turning point in his life near Damascus and thus a turning point in mission history. The persecutor is called to become the chief witness of the gospel to Jews and Gentiles (cf. 9:15) and returns as such to Jerusalem (9:26–30).

This impressive, dramatic intertwining of the Stephen tradition with the conversion story of Paul is clearly the work of the author of Acts. It is never confirmed by Paul himself. In fact, the idea that the "church of God" persecuted by Paul (Gal. 1:13; 1 Cor. 15:9; cf. Phil. 3:6) can be equated with the Jerusalem church is explicitly excluded by Gal. 1:22–23. Paul declares here that he was not personally known to Christ's churches in Judea; they had only heard of his conversion through the Damascus tradition— whose conclusion Paul alludes to here. Thus, the basis for the assumption of a direct connection between Stephen's martyrdom and Saul's persecution collapses. The two have to be separated.

Concerning Stephen's stoning, one may ask whether it must be understood as the execution of an orderly verdict or as an act of lynch law. The escalation from the dispute to a trial before a high council is probably to be attributed to Luke, who himself creates the trial situation (6:11–12) by a change of scenes (places and persons), but who does not maintain it to the very end (7:57). Still, one cannot simply speak of lynch law, since Stephen is killed by the traditional Jewish form of execution: stoning. The penal nature of this kind of death permits one—in spite of the tumultuous traits of the narrative, which correspond to certain laws of literary form—to envision in the course of a historical classification the execution of an imposed sentence. If that is the case, one would have to search for a corresponding contemporary constellation where a Jewish council had the opportunity to act contrary to the sovereign Roman claim of the *ius gladii*. For that, the short reign of Marcellus in A.D. 36 comes under consideration. After Pilate's dethronement by Vitellius, the legate from Syria, the latter appointed Marcellus, one of his protégés, as his personal representative in Caesarea. One purpose of this measure was, among others, to prepare for the risks which could have resulted from the notoriously anti-Jewish politics of Pilate in Judea during the planned second campaign against the Parthians. The actual holder of power in Judea during Vitellius's absence was not Marcellus, since his position was rather weak and he lacked full imperial authorization, but the high priest Jonathan, one of the sons of Annas, whom Vitellius had replace the weaker Caiaphas. The high priest Jonathan seems to have used the favorable conditions for a form of politics that was directed against Hellenizing tendencies. This constellation offers a possible backdrop to the stoning of Stephen, regardless whether we are dealing here with pogrom-like brutalities of tradition-conscious diaspora Jews or with the execution of a formal trial by a Jewish council. (According to this dating, the death of Stephen would clearly have to be placed after Paul's conversion near Damascus.)

It is likely that in connection with the Stephen conflict the entire Hellenistic part of the Jerusalem church came under pressure, especially if Stephen's death resulted from a court sentence. The Stephen circle was shattered. Afterwards, we find Philip in Samaria and in cities along the coastal plain, namely, Ashdod and Caesarea. Luke seems to have no knowledge of the other members of the Seven. It is appropriate to question Luke's generalizing report concerning the expulsion of "all" (believers) from Jerusalem and the thus prompted mission to Judea and Samaria. Even after the circle of the Seven dissolved, there were probably Christians from the Jewish Diaspora in Jerusalem. (Luke himself presupposes that when counting on Barnabas's presence in Jerusalem in Acts 9:27.) The expulsion of the Seven was not the beginning of a mission outside Jerusalem. (We have already said that Luke does not mean by Acts 8:1 that the first missionaries were all Hellenists expelled from Jerusalem.) More correctly, we might say that the persecuted members of the Stephen circle continued their work in the Diaspora. The mission of Philip is an example of that. This mission has its centers in cities with a Hellenistic population majority.[8] Of course, Luke sees it differently. To him, the mission of Philip is a link between the mission to the Jews and that to the Gentiles, since its proclamation is addressed to both Samaritans and God-fearers, that is, addressees on the fringe of actual Judaism. This view cannot be historically supported. It leads in Acts 8:4–25 to the misleading connection of the Philip-Samaria tradition with the Simon Magus tradition.[9] Luke synchronizes both and thus follows his idea of proclamation history as a linear process in which the unity of time, place, and action is always presupposed. Historically the two accounts have to be separated. The mission of Philip was in all likelihood first directed toward Jewish minorities in the cities, while the mission among the heterodox Samaritans, the rural population, was not only at the center of the Peter-John tradition (Acts 8:14ff.) but also of the Gospel of John (ch. 4) and possibly of Luke's special material (cf. Luke 9:52–56; 10:30–35). In a chronological sense, the Simon Magus episode probably belongs in the time of Peter's missionary activity after the martyrdom of James in A.D. 42. In terms of a sociology of religion, it belongs close to the Judean mission.

As an urban mission, Philip's mission probably stands basically in the tradition of Jewish propaganda to prospective proselytes. However, our sources concerning the Philip mission are too meager to provide further detail. More concrete is the tradition about Damascus. As already indicated, it is impossible for reasons of content[10] and chronology to connect the beginnings of the congregation in Damascus with the persecution of Stephen. The Damascus congregation already exists before Paul encounters it in the year of his calling (A.D. 34 at the latest). The terminology Paul uses to describe his persecuting activity may not show whether we have to imagine Paul as a Jew residing in Damascus, who possibly as a young teacher of the Torah had a synagogal office and was confronted ex officio with the new teaching, or whether, as legend has it (Acts 9:1–19), he proceeded from the outside as an enraged enemy of God against the disciples in Damascus. Yet it is clear that the group he persecuted had developed a theologically articulated self-understanding as the "*ekklesia* of God"—or was seen that way by Paul in retrospect (Gal. 1:13; 1 Cor. 15:9; cf. Phil. 3:6). In line with his view of history, Luke relates this incorrectly to the Jerusalem church (Acts 8:3) by transferring the term *ekklesia* from the Damascus tradition to the report of the persecution of Stephen.

The Damascus tradition reports in quite detailed fashion on the self-understanding of the congregation in Damascus and is of particular value to us for that reason and as a document of the early diaspora mission. The tradition contains *in nuce* a soteriology and an ecclesiology. In the programmatic word of the Lord to Ananias (Acts 9:15), Saul is called a "chosen vessel" (NRSV: "instrument"). Hereby, the word *chosen* has to refer to the eschatological choosing activity of God. By God's free choice, the "vessels" receive their calling either to destruction as "vessels [NRSV: "objects"] of wrath" or to glorification as "vessels of mercy" (cf. Rom. 9:11, 22–24). As Luke (cf. his paraphrase in Acts 22:14; 26:16) and with him most interpreters see it, the phrase does not formulate the future calling of Paul as a "special instrument" in the mission to the Gentiles, but rather Paul's salvation by God's graceful election. This is connected with his fate as a suffering witness of Jesus: "to bring my name before Gentiles and kings," which does not allude to Paul's apostolic role (as Luke says by his addition "and before the people of Israel") but corresponds to the situation of any of Jesus' disciples. The ecclesiology indicated here is based on the self-understanding of the diaspora synagogue and its claim to be God's witness among the nations.

One finds here decisive alterations in the Christian self-understanding, in the concept of mission, and thus in the theological evaluation of its results. Christian self-understanding now develops forms of expression under the conditions of the cultural life of Jewish minorities in the Hellenistic Diaspora.

Subsequently, Christian mission relies in essence increasingly on the traditional mediating role of the diaspora synagogue in the cities of antiquity, where "for generations past Moses has had those who proclaim him" (Acts 15:21). In the first century A.D., the Jewish mission flourished under the favorable external conditions of the Roman rule in the Mediterranean region. The readiness of the "Gentile" population to become interested in the Jewish religion is connected with the collapse of the political and economic foundations of traditional religions because of the Hellenization of the Near East and with the inability of the Hellenistic imperial cult and its peace concept to lend meaning in the subjugated areas. The Jewish religion offers certainly many things that the Hellenistic city dwellers lack, especially a true monotheism that is not suspect as a political ideology yet withstands the criteria of a philosophical critique of religion, as well as a morality that connects the individual personally with the deity and at the same time influences one's daily life. The institutional basis for Jewish culture to spread to the Hellenistic city is the synagogal worship service, which is an intellectual ritual of particular magnetism. In distinction to the Palestinian homeland, the diaspora synagogue offers its Gentile sympathizers more varied forms of participation. Both synagogal forms direct their missionary activity toward winning Gentiles for a full conversion to Judaism as soon as the latter have become proselytes. Still, in contrast to Palestine, in the Diaspora not only are proselytes (after proselyte baptism and circumcision) considered members of the synagogue but also the "God-fearers."

God-fearers, whose number must have even exceeded the already considerable number of proselytes—Josephus emphasizes the latter especially in Antioch—were admitted to the worship services; they were not obliged to keep the entire Mosaic law but only some precepts indispensable for living in community with Jews, namely, the Sabbath and the food commandments. Full conversion to Judaism was made more difficult for men than women because of the demand of circumcision, a procedure not only painful and dangerous to one's health, but also disfiguring. It constituted a stumbling block even apart from the subsequent obligation to keep all parts of the Mosaic law.

The early Christian diaspora mission can begin here. At first, it is a form of mission to the Jews and stays within the diaspora tradition even when wooing proselytes and God-fearers, whether in the synagogue or outside. The further development toward a circumcision-free mission to the Gentiles, however, cannot be explained without the bridgehead of the synagogue and its mission concept.

d) Antioch as a Mission Church

Acts connects this step with the initial history of the church in Antioch (Acts 11:19–20). Luke ties this history directly to Stephen's persecution. The missionaries in Antioch are part of those "scattered" by Saul's "severe" persecution, and they are still, so to speak, on the run from the one who will join their work a little later (11:26), as soon as Barnabas, Paul's mentor already in Jerusalem (9:27), has fetched him from his hometown, Tarsus. This personal drama is certainly a Lukan fiction. Also Lukan is the report that the mission in Antioch was at first directed "to no one except Jews," but that then a few of the scattered, originally from Cyprus and Cyrene—they too had come from Jerusalem—began to proclaim the gospel "to the Hellenists also." These ideas must be interpreted in analogy with the model pericope in Acts 13:14–52 (Paul and Barnabas at Antioch of Pisidia): Luke already imagines a separate mission to the Gentiles as a second phase after the mission to the Jews that was directed from the synagogue outward (cf. 13:44–48). Hence, in 11:19–20 he summarizes what is to be seen historically as a much longer development. Luke can do so because in terms of salvation history and theology this sequence of two phases is already fully legitimized (cf. the doctrine in 11:18) to the reader of Acts by the Cornelius tradition (Acts 10), which is interpolated prior to that.

According to Luke, nothing new happens in Antioch, as compared with Peter's mission to Caesarea. Luke does not permit the thought of a breakthrough in the actual mission to the Gentiles in Antioch because of his understanding of Paul's role. In Acts 11:19–20 Luke already anticipates the later practice of Paul, thus exonerating him from responsibility for developments dealing with the dissociation of the Christian proclamation and the church from Judaism. From the Lukan perspective, Paul is the chief witness of the gospel who changes from persecutor to proclaimer. The momentum of his testimony to Judaism is based on the fact that his conversion to the other side does not alter in the least his Pharisaic loyalty toward the traditions of the fathers (cf. Acts 23:6; 26:4–6). The accusation that he teaches forsaking Moses (cf. 21:21) cannot touch him. For that reason Paul must in no way be considered a pioneer or innovator. For the same reason the Gentile mission has to be in full swing both theologically and practically—in that order—before Paul joins it.

When one knows how to read Luke, the note about the mission to the Gentiles in Antioch gains relevance. The information about the origin of the missionaries, coming from Cyprus and Cyrene, is significant because it cannot be deduced from the idealized geography of Luke's salvation history, for the straight line of Peter's mission over Lydda–Joppa–Caesarea (Acts 9:23–11:18) is not continued here. The importance of Phoenicia for the course of the mission to the Gentiles is confirmed by pre-Markan tradition (cf. Mark 7:27–30; cf. 3:8). However, Luke appears to consider here anachronistically later conditions.[11] The breakthrough occurs in Antioch, where the disciples are first called *Christianoi*. That means that here for the first time the church emerges as a group distinct from the synagogue. Originally, this was hardly a name the group gave itself. The term is formed like a party name (like the *Herodians*) and, at any rate, intended for use outside the group. The distinguishing criterion of this group's identity is thus its association with *Christos*.[12] That this criterion serves as the group's distinction from the synagogue is something new, and it presupposes a corresponding decisive development. The beginnings of the church in Antioch lie in the dark. In A.D. 37 at the latest, Paul enters the Antiochene mission work after his conversion, his three-year stay "in Arabia," and his first stay in Jerusalem (cf. Gal. 1:17ff.). About the development up to this point, however, one can only speculate. That Antioch *originated* as a mixed congregation is an unlikely assumption, which is also rejected by Acts 11:19–20 rather than being confirmed. It is possible that the beginnings are connected with the indirect long-distance mission from Jerusalem: Jewish pilgrims come to the feast from Antioch, make contact with the Jerusalem church, and return as baptized followers to Antioch; there they continue to express their new life in the common meal of a small community that does not abandon its earlier relationship to the synagogue but, on the contrary, intensifies it in a missionary sense. Since the places of origin of the Antiochene missionaries are concretely named as Cyprus and Cyrene (Acts 11:20), one can also assume that Antioch was already formally missionized by out-of-town itinerant charismatics; whether by way of Jerusalem is another question. On the basis of these observations the Lukan concepts can be clarified. That the note about the missionaries' places of origin is not merely adapted from the list of coworkers in Acts 13:1 (Barnabas is from Cyprus, Lucius from Cyrene) can be clearly seen by the fact that

Barnabas comes from Jerusalem to Antioch only later (11:22–23) and thus is not counted by Luke as being among the first missionaries.

Regardless of how one imagines the "founding" of the church, the development of the Antiochene group of disciples into a mixed congregation is based on a purely Jewish-Christian core community, for which the self-understanding based on baptism in Jesus' name is definitive. Accordingly, the process of relativizing identity concepts in the diaspora synagogue begins when circumcised, full-fledged members of the synagogue no longer see their membership in the synagogue community as the soteriologically relevant criterion of their existence. That is the starting point for an escalation whose phases can be basically imagined. The relativizing of circumcision as a criterion for belonging to Israel, which started among the Jewish Christians themselves with the Christian understanding of baptism, has its effects on their relationship with God-fearers. Christian baptism appears to supersede both proselyte baptism and circumcision. If in the eyes of the diaspora synagogue the uncircumcised God-fearer was already more than only a guest in the synagogue, now, with the Christian understanding of baptism, the still existing reservations can be radically overcome. These reservations concern mainly the circumcision-related obligation on the part of both Jews and proselytes fully to observe the Mosaic law. It is likely that the Christian core community assumed quite early a firm attitude on questions of ritual discipline, since the basic form of expressing its new identity, the eucharistic communion, did not allow for half-measures. The common meal of the circumcised and uncircumcised is not just a discipleship problem of the Christian mission to God-fearers but was already a cardinal point in the self-understanding of Jewish Christians in the Diaspora because the synagogal membership conditions for God-fearers, on the one hand, and the common meal of the baptized Jesus followers, on the other, represented institutional conditions that could not be reconciled with each other on the basis of a ritual understanding of Judaism's identity. Thus soteriological relativism of circumcision by means of baptism and the disciplinary one by means of the eucharistic meal practice belong together both in fact and (therefore also) in time.

One looks in vain in Acts for a description of the life of these mixed congregations. Luke considers this phase merely a transition to the actual mission to the Gentiles and to a Gentile-Christian church, which represents, in contrast to a law-abiding(!) Jewish Christianity (cf. Acts 21:20), a culturally independent type of Christianity. An idea of the enthusiastic élan of the early diaspora mission is mainly conveyed by the much later

Letter to the Ephesians, which understands this very unity of the circumcised and the uncircumcised as the fruit of a cosmic peace brought by
Christ (cf. Eph. 2:11-22). These new experiences find theological expression in the views that we encounter mainly in the Pauline letters as tradition received from Paul. The kerygma of the Hellenistic church before and
beside Paul connects the traditional synagogal demand to be converted to
the one God with the expectation of the Parousia of the "Son of God" as
eschatological judge (cf. 1 Thess. 1:9-10). At the center of the salvation
event is the universal atonement event of Jesus' death, presented in cosmic
dimensions as the divine Redeemer's descent into the mortal destiny of
people and as their liberation from it through their absorption by baptism
into his ascension to the sphere of God (cf. Phil. 2:5-11). One should not
simply see the soteriology of the completed cosmic reconciliation through
Jesus' death, the corresponding Christology (preexistence Christology),
and the corresponding understanding of the Christian existence as the further development of Jesus' proclamation of the kingdom of God and of the
kerygma of the early Jerusalem church; instead, these concepts represent
theologically an original point of departure that expresses not the thought
of an eschatological "movement" but that of an urban "subculture."

Of course, one cannot directly relate these necessarily sketchy and generalizing references to the concrete history of the church in Antioch. This
congregation's particular importance as a center of the diaspora mission
becomes concrete only in connection with the events in which Barnabas
and, later, Paul participate. The universality of the salvation event is
viewed, in correlation with the syncretistic milieu of the Hellenistic city, as
a cosmic reconciliation of the human world with God.

Barnabas is one of the first "missionaries" in Antioch. According to
Acts 11:22, he goes there when commissioned by the Jerusalem church
after the Gentile mission has already begun. This recalls the role both Peter
and John played in Samaria according to Luke (cf. 8:14): the aim is to
preserve continuity with the origin of the church. For Luke, Barnabas is
above all a mediating figure in the sense of Luke's idea of continuity. Barnabas is both a Levite and a Cypriot—hence a "Hellenist" of priestly descent. He owns property in Jerusalem and thus belongs to the pious
diaspora Jews who want to have their residence in the kingdom of God in
expectation of God's rule. As a Christian, he sells his field because his
hope for salvation is now newly articulated in the early Christian community in the ideal of poverty and brotherhood (cf. Acts 4:36-37). Now he

comes to Antioch with the order to confirm the results of its mission (11:23). In a historical sense, also, one must view him as a figure between Jerusalem and the development originating in Antioch, yet in a different sense. Up to his entering the work of the Antiochene church, we have to imagine this congregation's missionary practice like the growing of a cell by osmosis: the salt content within the cell absorbs substances from the environment and by diffusion brings them through its outer layer, which acts like a semipermeable membrane, permeable only toward the inside. Barnabas represents another type of missionary activity that is literally directed outward into the mission field in accordance with the commissioning principle, as was always characteristic of the Palestinian Jesus movement. According to Acts 14:14, Barnabas is an "apostle." This title cannot have originated with Luke, since he reserves it for the Twelve. The historicity of this detail is also shown by the fact that *Barnabas* is a prophetic surname given by the apostles (cf. 4:36); it has replaced the original proper name *Joseph* in the tradition. Barnabas works according to apostolic pattern as an itinerant missionary and in pairs, as was customary. We find in Acts 14:14 (cf. 13:2, 7) that his partner is Saul, after Barnabas had persuaded him to join the work of the Antiochene mission. Still, the external mission according to apostolic pattern probably had already started earlier, namely, through what Acts 13:1 calls "prophets and teachers," who could form two apostolic pairs without Saul, who is mentioned here last. The description of the mission of Barnabas with Saul on the so-called first missionary journey still shows traces of the transition from the older growth model to the commissioning principle of external mission, in that the latter grows out of the worship of the congregation (13:2–3).

Through this development, Antioch becomes a center of apostolic mission beside Jerusalem but at first, of course, of much less importance. Since in the practice of the diaspora congregations, however, the foundations were already laid for a circumcision-free acceptance of "God-fearers" into the community of the baptized, the "Gentile" mission develops at the latest in the wake of the external mission and addresses its proclamation to an interested Hellenistic public outside the synagogue (e.g., in Lystra; Acts 14:8ff.). But here too, the transitions are smooth. Acts shows that tying into the synagogal audience first remains a common method long afterwards (cf., e.g., the certainly pre-Lukan report about Philippi in Acts 16:13–15); for the Lukan redaction this is a matter of course (cf. Acts 13:14ff.; 14:1; etc.).

e) The Argument over the Legitimacy of the Mission to the Gentiles: The Antiochene Incident and the Apostolic Council

The significance of Antioch for the history of early Christian missions would not be complete, however, if we did not consider the conflicts between Antioch and Jerusalem sparked by the first mission to the Gentiles. These conflicts lead eventually to the point where the mission to the Gentiles and its results are legitimized by the earliest Christian church. Barnabas and Paul are representatives of the Antiochene mission and are instrumental in this decision, though in very different ways.

Since Paul describes these events in the Letter to the Galatians, the available sources are now much more favorable than in the presentation of the beginnings of the mission in the Syrian area. It is well known, however, that definite tensions exist between the report in Acts (11:19–15:41) and the report in Galatians (Gal. 1–2). In light of this situation, scholars agree that in case of doubt, Paul's report should take precedence over Luke's. Still, the question remains as to how great these tensions really are. It is central whether the argument described in Acts 15:1–2 between the people from Judea and Paul and Barnabas concerning the need of circumcision, which in Luke's view sparks the Apostolic Council, can be identified with the Antiochene incident (Gal. 2:11, 14) on the basis of the information in Gal. 2. This possibility, in contrast to the common perception that the two have to be distinguished and that the Antiochene incident has to be placed after the Apostolic Council, offers the substantial advantage that one no longer has to ask how a dispute could possibly arise over the results of a mission practice after the council had approved that practice. The conflict would then already have been solved on a basic level (Gentile mission) and would have then focused on the practical consequences (table fellowship). The earliest Christian church would then have agreed to a mission practice without acknowledging its results. That is hardly possible, especially in light of the actual Antiochene development from a mixed congregation to an apostolic mission congregation, which is preceded by and based on the table fellowship of both the circumcised and uncircumcised within the mission to the Gentiles. The opposite view—that the Antiochene incident can be identified with the situation indicated in Acts 15:1–2—is supported[13] with the argument that Gal. 2:11–14 (the Antiochene incident) does not continue in the chronological sequence of events of Gal. 1:13–2:10 (Paul's contacts with the earliest Christian church), but that in Gal. 2:11–14 Paul extracts one point from a series of events to help sharpen the argument that his apostolate cannot be derivative by means of a crucial fact: namely, that his apostolic authority prevailed in a confrontation with Peter. The following reconstruction assumes this hypothesis.

According to Gal. 2:1, between Paul's first visit to Jerusalem (A.D. 36) and the so-called Apostolic Council lie fourteen years (if one does not subtract the three years between conversion and the first Jerusalem visit). During this relatively long period, not only has the order of the mixed Antiochene congregation stabilized, but also the practice of the circumcision-free special mission to the Gentiles. The fact that resistance against it in Jerusalem only now begins to form is not explained by emerging grievances in Antioch but by Jerusalem's stricter understanding of the law, which is accompanied by a central claim to leadership on the part of Jerusalem authorities. In the forties, probably shortly before the so-called Apostolic Council (A.D. 47 or 50), conflict arises (cf. Acts 15:1).

If Gal. 2:11–14 precedes the Apostolic Council, one will have to presuppose Peter's presence in Antioch at the time in question. Acts has Peter depart from Jerusalem (12:17) yet remains consistently silent about his ensuing journey. Peter's departure from Jerusalem must be understood as resulting from a shift of competence in the relationship between James and Peter, in consequence of which Peter apparently at an early point moves the focus of his activity (again) to mission. Indications of that include, for example, the Peter traditions about Lydda and Joppa (Acts 9:32–43). Also the Cornelius tradition can be placed in this connection, not, of course, as proof of Peter's mission in Caesarea—which is the center of Philip's mission—but as an indication of a transregional claim of authority on Peter's part for the mission congregations even outside Judea and Palestine.[14] The presence of Peter in Antioch at the time of the Antiochene incident (prior to the Apostolic Council) has to be seen against this background.

From Gal. 2:12a it follows that Peter not only approved the situation he found there (cf. the Cornelius tradition!) but also himself joined in the practice of a law-free common meal. Only after the appearance of members from the Jerusalem congregation does he change his behavior. While Luke calls these "persons" incompetent disturbers of the peace (cf. Acts 15:24) with theological views (cf. Acts 15:1b) that are outdated in salvation-historical terms (cf. Peter's speech in 15:7–11 with explicit reference to the Lukan precedence of the Cornelius story), Paul sees them as coming from James's group (Gal. 2:12). Of course, he does not say anything about their competence. However, Peter's behavior after their appearance (his separation from the congregation's common table) is in Paul's interpretation not an act of (wrongly) considering the sensitive conscience of the brothers from Jerusalem but a giving in out of fear of them. They seem to be in the stronger position. James controls Peter.

At this point, the demand of the Jerusalemites can be seen in Peter's behavior. Jewish Christians are obliged to observe the law and need, for that reason, to discontinue their common meals with uncircumcised Gentile Christians. It is not the practice of the mission to the Gentiles as such—baptism or circumcision—that sparks conflict, but the breach of traditional purity concepts. Since already both circumcision-free baptism and the unrestrained table fellowship of mixed congregations have become customary, one has to view this incident from the Antiochene perspective as a meddling of people from James's group with the internal affairs of the diaspora mission (cf. Gal. 2:4). Antioch's defense against it is due mainly to Paul and even to him alone if we want to believe Gal. 2:13, according to which all Jewish Christians, Barnabas included, submit to the Jerusalemites' concepts of order. That is certainly exaggerated, since Paul alone could not have forced the Apostolic Council.

The descriptions of the council itself (Acts 15:6–29; Gal. 2:1–10) can only be compared on the basis of the pre-Lukan tradition in Acts 15.[15] The two descriptions of the council, that of Paul and that of the pre-Lukan tradition, distinguish two aspects in the matter under discussion: on the one hand, the question about the freedom from circumcision as a basic problem of soteriology; on the other, the question about the validity of the law for Jewish Christians and the resulting disciplinary consequences for the ordering of mixed congregations. The traditions establish different priorities and thus reflect the contrasting interests of the parties. For Paul it is basically a matter of defending the legitimacy of his proclamation and of his Gentile mission without circumcision (Gal. 2:2). In a demonstrative way, he takes the Gentile Christian Titus along to the meeting (2:1) and concludes in retrospect that the latter was not forced to circumcision (2:3). Besides that, Paul has successfully opposed the pressure of the "false brothers," who wanted to abolish disciplinary freedoms in the practice of the circumcision-free mission to the Gentiles (2:4–5). The authorities in Jerusalem had added nothing to him (2:6); on the contrary, they recognized the differing concepts of the Petrine and the Pauline missions and shook hands on their legitimacy and coexistence (2:7–9). The Pauline mission concept is here *again* acknowledged in its autonomy, after it was defined earlier, during Paul's Jerusalem visit, between Peter and him in the sense of Galatians 2:8. In Paul's view the Apostolic Council has now also placed the rest of Jerusalem's authorities ("pillars") behind the agreement in Galatians 2:8 and has managed thereby to oppose the attempt of the "false brothers" to dilute the concept according to their particular understanding of the law. If their demands had been granted, it would have meant for Paul that the "truth" of his gospel was revoked (2:5).

The pointed formulation in Gal. 2:6 that to Paul nothing was added already indicates that such additions were not only discussed at the council, but that they were also made obligatory for others. (According to the context, only Barnabas can be meant here.) This side of the coin becomes clearer when we evaluate the pre-Lukan tradition in Acts 15. It is marked by the interest of Jerusalem's authorities in incorporating the restrictive tendencies in Jerusalem concerning the law's observance into a compromise, which basically obligates even the mixed congregations to the Mosaic law, without bursting their unity and in spite of freedom from circumcision for Gentile Christians. The compromise as such is contained in the so-called apostolic decree (Acts 15:23–29); its argumentation is in the speech of James (15:14–21).

James's formulas in the version of Acts 15:29 (cf. 21:25) are the core of the apostolic decree. They prescribe that for uncircumcised members of Christian congregations, those purity precepts are binding whose area of validity extends the law of holiness (Lev. 17:1–26:46) even to foreigners in Israel. Hence, Gentile Christians in mixed congregations are basically obligated to the Mosaic law. They are not held to the complete observance of the law as are the circumcised members of the congregation—that is implied, of course—but this is not due to the soteriological understanding of Jesus' death, which makes the law obsolete as a way of salvation, but in reference to the law itself with its differentiated claim of validity for the circumcised and the uncircumcised. James's speech develops the corresponding ecclesiology (and soteriology). Only the eschatological restitution of the fallen house of David makes possible a mission to Gentiles; hence, this mission is based on the restitution of Israel and takes place as foreigners migrate to a restored Israel (cf. the scriptural arguments in 15:16–17). In view of the situation in the Diaspora, the basic obligation of foreigners to the law is not unexpected; since ancient times the Mosaic law has been propagated in the cities by the synagogue (cf. 15:21), and the Gentile world has been confronted with the revealed will of God. That is not to be revoked in the Christian church.

The decree is delivered by a Jerusalem delegation (Judas and Silas) to

Antioch and is to be observed in both Syria and Cilicia. Antioch has to live with it. Hence, Antioch is no longer a base of operation for Paul. Barnabas, on the other hand, seems to have accepted the compromise for Antioch and the Antiochene mission. Thus, his work with Paul loses its footing. A dispute ensues when Barnabas prepares to take the decree to the urban congregations of their common mission (cf. 15:36ff.). The argument over John Mark is only the occasion. This begins a new period in the history of the early Christian missions.

The apostolic decree has its own history of influence. The "western" text transmits an ethicized version. It probably stems from a Gentile-Christian congregation that was no longer familiar with the original meaning of the formulas. This development is indicated in Luke. He transposes the order of the formulas in Acts 15:20 as compared to Lev. 17–18 and thus betrays that he no longer knows their origin and argumentation. Yet he still knows that the problem dealt with respecting Jewish ideas of order. But Luke is not thinking here of Jewish Christians but of diaspora Jews in the cities of the Christian mission. The latter should not be given an excuse when staging disturbing actions of protest. (Cf. 16:3–4: the circumcision of Timothy "because of the Jews" and the delivery of the apostolic decree to the congregations belong together.) For Luke, the James formulas have only a culture-affirming meaning. (Each culture deserves respect, not only the foreign Jewish but also the Greek.) Overall, Luke understands the decree of the council primarily in the Pauline sense, where Gentile Christians are entitled to unrestricted freedom from the law. As a Gentile Christian, he is not interested in the problem of mixed congregations. For Luke, Jewish Christianity in Palestine (cf. Acts 21:10) and Gentile Christianity beyond Acts 28:28–31 form two culturally distinct church regions. The results of the continued history of Paul's mission, as Luke sees it, are thereby presupposed.

Bibliography

Bihler, Johannes. *Die Stephanusgeschichte im Zusammenhang mit der Apostelgeschichte.* 1963.
Cadbury, Henry J. "The Hellenists." In *The Beginnings of Christianity,* edited by Frederick J. Foakes-Jackson and Kirsopp Lake, 1/5:59–74. 1933.
Conzelmann, Hans. *Geschichte des Urchristentums.* 1969.
Cullmann, Oscar. "Von Jesus zum Stephanuskreis und zum Johannesevangelium." In *Jesus und Paulus,* FS Kümmel, 44–56. 1975.

Derwacter, F. M. *Preparing the Way for Paul: The Proselyte Movement in Late Judaism.* 1930.

Gaechter, Paul. "Die Sieben (Act 6,1–6)." In *Petrus und seine Zeit,* 105–54. 1958.

Georgi, Dieter. *Die Gegner des Paulus im 2. Korintherbrief: Studien zur religiösen Propaganda in der Spätantike.* 1964.

Gressmann, Hugo. "Jüdische Mission in der Werdezeit des Christentums." *ZMR* 38 (1924): 169–83.

Grundmann, Walter. "Das Problem des hellenistischen Christentums innerhalb der Jerusalemer Urgemeinde." *Zeitschrift für die neutestamentliche Wissenschaft und die Kunde der älteren Kirche* 38 (1939): 45–73.

Hahn, Ferdinand. *Das Verständnis der Mission im Neuen Testament.* 1963.

Harnack, Adolf von. *Die Mission und Ausbreitung des Christentums in den ersten drei Jahrhunderten.* Vol. 1. 1915.

Hegermann, Harald. "Das griechischsprechende Judentum." In *Literatur und Religion des Frühjudentums,* edited by Johann Maier and Josef Schreiner, 328–52. 1973.

Hengel, Martin. "Die Ursprünge der christlichen Mission." *NTS* 18 (1971/72): 15–38.

———. "Zwischen Jesus und Paulus: Die 'Hellenisten,' die 'Sieben' und Stephanus (Apg 6,1–15; 7,54–8,3)." *ZTK* 72 (1975): 151–206.

———. *Zur urchristlichen Geschichtsschreibung.* 1979.

Kasting, Heinrich. *Die Anfänge der christlichen Mission.* 1969.

Köster, Helmut. *Einführung in das Neue Testament im Rahmen der Religionsgeschichte und Kulturgeschichte der hellenistischen und römischen Zeit.* 1980.

Kraft, Heinrich. *Die Entstehung des Christentums.* 1981.

Lüdemann, Gerd. *Studien zur Chronologie.* Vol. 1 of *Paulus, der Heidenapostel.* 1980.

Neudorfer, Heinz-Werner. *Der Stephanuskreis in der Forschungsgeschichte seit F. C. Baur.* 1983.

Pesch, Rudolf. *Die Vision des Stephanus: Apg 7,55–56 im Rahmen der Apostelgeschichte.* 1966.

———. "Voraussetzungen und Anfänge der urchristlichen Mission." In *Mission im Neuen Testament,* edited by Karl Kertelge, 11–70. 1982.

———. "Das Jerusalemer Abkommen und die Lösung des Antiochenischen Konflikts: Ein Versuch über Gal 2, Apg 10,1–11,18; Apg 11,27–30; 12,25 und Apg 15,1–44." *Kontinuität und Einheit,* FS F. Mussner, 105–22. 1981.

Plümacher, Eckhard. "Die Apostelgeschichte als historische Monographie." In *Les Actes des Apôtres*, edited by Jacob Kremer, 457–66. 1979.

Reicke, Bo. *Glaube und Leben der Urgemeinde: Bemerkungen zu Apg 1–7.* 1957.

Safrai, S. and M. Stern. *The Jewish People in the First Century: Historical Geography, Political History, Social, Cultural and Religious Life and Institutions.* Vol. 1, 1974. Vol. 2, 1976.

Scharlemann, Martin H. *Stephen: A Singular Saint.* 1968.

Schneider, Gerhard. "Stephanus, die Hellenisten und Samaria." In *Les Actes des Apôtres*, edited by Jacob Kremer, 215–40. 1979.

Schüssler-Fiorenza, Elisabeth. *Aspects of Religious Propaganda in Judaism and Early Christianity.* 1976.

Simon, Marcel. *St. Stephen and the Hellenists in the Primitive Church.* 1958.

Strobel, August. "Das Aposteldekret als Folge des antiochenischen Streits." In *Kontinuität und Einheit*, FS F. Mussner, 81–104. 1981.

Weiser, Alfons. "Das 'Apostelkonzil' (Apg 1,1–35): Ereignis, Überlieferung, lukanische Deutung." *BZ* n.s. 28 (1984): 145–67.

Notes

1. That the proselyte Nicolas might be the authority in the sect of Nicolaitans (cf. Rev. 2:6; 14–15, 18ff.; cf. Irenaeus *Adv. Haer.* 1.26.3, where the Nicolas of Acts 6:5 is explicitly called the "master" of the sect; and Clement of Alexandria *Strom.* 2.118, who has in mind only a usurpation of the authority of a member of the circle of the Seven) does not seem to play a role either in the transmitting of the list of the Seven or in its Lukan reception. Although the fact that Nicolas is named last implies a subordination in rank, it does not convey either a negative picture or an exception to the positive picture in Acts 6:3.

2. A particular problem is the question of a possible relationship to the Markan feeding-miracle traditions, where the numbers twelve and seven are likewise used as symbols of completeness (Mark 6:43; 8:8; with the explicit reflection of the evangelist in 8:19–21). It is hardly possible to see here the founding legends of the "Hebrew" and "Hellenistic" earliest congregation. The Hellenists would have hardly appealed to a Galilean Jesus tradition.

3. Luke is working here for the first time toward the special relationship between the "witness" Stephen and the "witness" Paul (cf. especially

Acts 22:20 in connection with 22:15) by providing both with opponents who are Jews from Asia. Thus, a dramatic connection develops between the Stephen trial and the trial against Paul (cf. on the latter Acts 21:27; 24:19), as well as a corresponding thematic one (cf. Acts 8:13 with 21:28). Hence, the expanded list of opponents in Acts 6:9 proves to be an element of the Lukan picture of Paul. The same is true for the mentioning of Cilicia, Paul's homeland, as the opponents' area of origin in addition to Asia.

4. This parallelism is an essential component of Luke's image of Paul. During the stoning the Lukan Paul is introduced as an indirectly involved sympathizer of Stephen's opponents (Acts 7:58b; 8:1a). Hence, his opposition is directed at the gospel, which he himself will proclaim as a persecuted witness of Jesus. In this way he becomes the chief witness of the gospel to official Judaism, which he himself represents as a persecutor (cf. Acts 9:1–2). Stephen's indirect characterization by the summarized "indictment" of his opponents serves this Lukan Paul concept in two ways: temple criticism and law criticism. In this way the impression is given that the "Hellenists," represented by Stephen, formed a bridge from the earliest congregation to Paul, which proves to be a typical Lukanism.

5. It should be clear that Acts 7:2–53 is not Stephen's authentic defense speech or its paraphrased rendering; it is also clear that the essence of the speech cannot be considered Lukan. One cannot compare it to the other speeches in Acts. It is enough to assume here that the speech is in general part of the traditional material about the Stephen circle.

6. Contrary to the Lukan view, Acts 8:26 speaks for a location near Jerusalem. The indications of place, of course, are part of an ideal scene. One searches the map in vain for the road leading from Jerusalem south to Gaza. It is the road leading from the temple into the "wilderness." (On the attributive *erēmos* in Acts 8:26, cf. the wilderness theme in Stephen's speech in Acts 7:30, 36, 38, 44.)

7. Since F. Chr. Baur, Acts 8:1 has been mostly understood to mean that only the "Hellenists" were expelled, not the "Hebrews." Yet that is not what it says and would also be against the thrust of Luke's (redactional!) note. The "apostles" not expelled would then become the representatives of only a part of the earliest Christian congregation, which would be completely un-Lukan. Luke emphasizes with Acts 8:1 that in spite of the expulsion of the entire congregation from Jerusalem, the time of proclamation to the "people" still continues. Hence, Luke does not say that the mission outside Jerusalem was only carried out by "Hellenists."

8. That is especially true for "the city of Samaria," Sebaste, which with

its Hellenistic history since Alexander the Great had been newly founded by Herod the Great and named after Emperor Augustus (Sebastos). Whether Gaza needs to be counted as part of the Philip mission in Acts 8:26 cannot be determined. The composition of the population of Ashdod, which definitely was a part of Philip's mission (8:40) is not known. Caesarea, the Roman administrative center by the coast, is according to Acts 21:8 the center of Philip's mission during the fifties.

9. The Simon Magus episode is a Peter tradition. Luke incorporates the news about the Philip mission in Sebaste into a preliminary story of the former. Yet it is impossible to extract from Acts 8:4–8 a nucleus of pre-Lukan tradition that can be supported from a literary perspective.

10. In terms of content, the main question is what possibilities the high priest could have had for taking action in Damascus (cf. Acts 9:2). Yet the entire course of events is unlikely. Anyone who starts the search in connection with the persecution of Jesus' followers in Jerusalem should be successful at the latest in Galilee. Why do the letters of authorization refer to measures in Damascus?

11. According to Acts 21:2–7, Paul stays with some disciples in Tyre and Ptolemais on his way to Jerusalem. The question whether one finds traces of the development of a mission to the Gentiles based in Galilee is controversial. The fact that Syrophoenicia (Mark 7:24, 31), the Decapolis (Mark 5:1–20: Gerasa or Gergesa?), and Caesarea Philippi (Mark 8:27) appear in the Jesus tradition as places of Jesus' ministry speaks for a relationship of the Galilean Jesus movement with these areas and a corresponding missionary interest. However, one needs to ask whether these events can be dated early enough to say something about the beginnings of the mission to the Gentiles. In terms of the sociology of religion one has to distinguish the long-distance mission of Jerusalem to the urban synagogues of the Diaspora from a branching-out of the Jesus movement in Galilee beyond its original geographic and cultural borders. At any rate, Damascus was not reached from Galilee any more than Alexandria, Antioch, and Rome were.

12. Cf., on the other hand, Suetonius's report that Claudius had expelled the Jews from Rome because they, incited by *Chrestus*, continued to disturb the peace (*Claudius* 25.4). Here *Chrestus* is so much perceived as a Jewish figure that one cannot see whether a title (*Messiah*) or a name (*Jesus Christ*) is meant, that is, whether this passage can be at all a valid testimony for the existence of a Christian community in Rome.

13. Gerd Lüdemann, *Studien zur Chronologie,* vol. 1 of *Paulus, der Heidenapostel* (Göttingen, 1980), 58ff.

14. The Cornelius legend legitimizes not—as Luke thinks—the mission to the Gentiles but the communion of the circumcised and the uncircumcised and thus a situation like that in Antioch (cf. Acts 10:15 in connection with vs. 23a, 28, 34–36 and 11:3).

15. That Luke used tradition in Acts 15—but not various sources—can be concluded from the following. (1) The exposition contains a doublet in the indication of the matter under discussion (15:1, 5); the pre-Lukan element is in v. 5b. (2) The messengers of the apostolic decree coming to Antioch are not Paul and Barnabas, as could be expected from the Lukan context, but Judas and Silas (v. 22); Luke wants to merge all four into a delegation. (3) Tradition calls the apostles and the elders an authoritative body (vs. 6, 23); for Luke it is a plenary session (vs. 4, 12, 22). (4) The apostolic decree, in its address (Syria and Cilicia), is not consistent with Acts 14 (first missionary journey). (5) Of the two variations of the apostolic decree, only the second (15:29; cf. 21:25) has preserved the traditional sequence of clauses in accordance with Lev. 17–18, while the first (15:20) regroups them and hence is apparently a redaction. (6) The scriptural quotation in James's speech (15:16–18) departs partially from the text of the Septuagint and thus cannot be (completely) attributed to Lukan redaction. The pre-Lukan tradition cannot be proved in Peter's speech; the connection with Acts 10:11 is redactional.

4

Paul and His Churches

Jürgen Becker

a) Paul as Pharisee and as Apostle to the Gentiles

With numerous figures of antiquity Paul shares the fate that we have sufficient knowledge about only that period of his life that had a significant impact on later history. Paul is no doubt also one of the few persons whose lives are divided into two parts because they experienced a profound identity crisis at some point in their lives. For Paul this event created such a break that he dissociated himself from the first phase of his life; for him his real life began with the second phase.

Paul's correspondence with the churches dates from the middle of this second period. Based on the available evidence, only Romans, 1 and 2 Corinthians, Galatians, Philippians, 1 Thessalonians, and Philemon should be attributed to Paul himself. A few of the letters (2 Corinthians, Philemon) should also be considered collections of letters. Through these sources we have more extensive and more direct knowledge of Paul than of many figures of antiquity—including Jesus. Yet Paul is not interested in his own biography. In retrospect he hardly provides any information at all on the first phase of his life. And again at the end of his life we are left largely in the dark. The period of Paul's independent missionary activity (say, A.D. 48/49 to 56/57) offers the historian a clearer picture, even though here too, many questions remain unanswered.

Apart from the apostle's own accounts, we can draw on statements from Luke's Acts. Yet the problems in drawing conclusions about Paul's life are formidable and often insurmountable. Paul's own accounts (which are certainly not always unbiased) frequently contradict Luke's statements, which were written a generation later. In other instances—for example, in the case of the church in Corinth—Acts reports very little in contrast to Paul's letters to the Corinthians. Finally, we must ask, Is Acts really reliable in cases where it cannot be verified by comparison with Paul, when in verifiable cases it often does not hold up to criticism? To be placed in the same category as Acts, although clearly distinguished from it, is *1 Clement,* since it obviously is a witness for a date in Paul's biography, namely, his martyrdom under Nero (*1 Clem.* 5). The deutero-Pauline writings (Ephesians, Colossians, 2 Thessalonians, 2 Timothy, Titus) do not really tell us any more than what we already know from Paul himself. And there are no non-Christian texts that contain information on Paul—a fact that should not be surprising at all.

Paul was born about two decades after Augustus made peace with the Parthians, which brought the beginning of a period of political tranquility and economic prosperity to the eastern Mediterranean. In the past lay both the wars of Julius Caesar and those of his heirs and murderers, with their terrible consequences for the population. In the flourishing period of the *pax Romana,* life was characterized by stable political conditions and a considerable economic upswing. The Teutonic wars on the northern border of the empire had practically no effect on the people of the Mediterranean. Paul experienced the entire reign of the Julian-Claudian dynasty (Augustus, Tiberius, Caligula, Claudius, Nero). Under Nero, its last representative, Paul was executed. Thus he lived in one of the most flourishing and most peaceful periods of the Roman Empire.

Acts reports that Paul was born in Tarsus in Cilicia (21:39; 22:3). There his parents were members of the diaspora synagogue (Phil. 3:5) and possessed municipal (Acts 21:39) as well as Roman citizenship (Acts 16:37–38; 22:25, 28). Thus they were among the respected and financially well-to-do families. This information, which is provided only by Acts, would seem to be reliable. It is indirectly verified by Paul, who speaks the Hellenistic vernacular, the Koine, without strong Semitisms. He quotes Jewish scripture in the Greek version, that is, according to the Septuagint. He is familiar with Stoic ideas, uses illustrations from popular philosophy, and knows how to write in the style of the Cynic-Stoic diatribe. At times he employs the means of Greco-Roman rhetoric, and he knows how to use material borrowed from the mystery religions. The rural world that dominates the proclamation of Jesus is replaced by the urban world of Hellenism (see, e.g., the vices in Rom. 1:26–31 and the motifs from the gymnasium in 1 Cor. 9:24–27). Though the same can also be assumed to a limited extent for some members of the Jerusalem church (including, for example, members of the group around Stephen), it is Paul who later employs a mission strategy that is in line with this background. He conducts his mission in the cities of the Roman Empire and is as familiar with these cities as a fish is with water. Even if others may have used similar methods, Paul must still be regarded as the missionary who especially promoted the spread of Christianity in the empire outside of Palestine as urban Christianity.

What characterized Tarsus at that time was generally also true for all of Paul's mission sites. Tarsus was the capital and official seat of the Roman governor of Cilicia. The city was very accessible via the navigable lower reaches of the Kydnos river and via the important trade route running from Antioch on the Orontes to the Aegean coast of Asia Minor. Because of the city's loyalty to the party of Caesar, Antonius and Augustus had been kindly disposed towards it. As already indicated, this urban milieu is the environment in which Paul felt at home. One only has to recall briefly the main stops of his mission. Antioch in Syria, the third largest city of the Roman Empire after Rome and Alexandria, was a center of commerce at the crossroads of the trade routes from east to west and from north to south. It had access to the sea via the Orontes and was the capital of the province of Syria. Philippi was an important city on the *via Egnatiana,* which connected Rome and Byzantium; its prosperity came from mines (silver and gold) and a fertile surrounding countryside. Also located on the *via Egnatiana* was Thessalonica, the main port and trading capital of Macedonia and seat of a proconsul. Corinth, the Carthage of the eastern Mediterranean and center of trade between the East and the West, was a port and a city of international commerce. It was the seat of the proconsul of Achaia. In addition, it had been founded, like Philippi, as a Roman military colony a little more than a generation before Christ. This picture is completed by the Pauline sites in Asia Minor, most notably Ephesus, as well as by Rome, which needs no special introduction.

Paul was thus selective in choosing the targets for his mission. It is his social background that plays a dominant role here and elsewhere. Did his origins not perhaps force him to go into the cities because he did not speak the respective provincial dialects? Did he have to trust that the urban Christianity of a particular city would spread into the provinces through some degree of multilingualism? If this was the design of his mission, it was evidently successful, as Pliny the Younger (*Letters* 10.96), an impartial witness, confirms a little more than two generations after Paul: "The plague of the superstition [i.e., Christianity] has not only spread over the cities, but also over the villages and rural areas." Later still, Tertullian (*Apologeticum*

1.7) will confront the emperor with the statement: "There are loud complaints that we have taken over the entire city, and [that there are already] Christians in the countryside, the villages, and the islands."

The cities at that time were places where economy and culture especially flourished. This required not least of all a cosmopolitan, enterprising people with a pioneering spirit, who were enthusiastic and willing to take risks, who possessed vocational flexibility, who were open to new things, and who, in good Greek and Roman tradition, also had a sense of the public welfare of the polis, even to the point of being willing to make generous sacrifices and help others. One might, for example, wonder whether the couple Aquila and Prisc(ill)a (Acts 18; Rom. 16:3; 1 Cor. 16:19) did not perhaps represent this type of person. Paul's parents might also come to mind. It can at least hardly be denied that Paul himself was a cosmopolitan and enterprising person. His incomparable missionary work testifies to this. His enthusiasm and willingness to take risks can also hardly be overestimated. One only has to think of the dangers and difficulties he repeatedly accepted as a matter of course (see 2 Cor. 11:23–30). A pioneering spirit is evident not least of all in the plan to carry the message of Christ to the end of the world (Rom. 15:23–24). Even if we conjecture more than we know about the mission parallel to Paul's, this much seems certain: presumably none of his Christian contemporaries was equally skilled in planning and organizing missionary work, in looking after the extensive network of new congregations, in his commitment of himself and his coworkers, and, in addition to all this, in reflecting on his work in writing. Paul's view that he has worked more than the other apostles (1 Cor. 15:10) has also this aspect.

Yet Paul is not merely a Hellenistic urbanite. He is also a Jew of the Hellenistic Diaspora. It is true that (in a Roman-Hellenistic environment) he only calls himself Paul. Acts 13:9, however, provides evidence of a double name, which he presumably bore from birth. The name Saul, which he was given in memory of the tribe of Benjamin and the first king of Israel, points to the fact that Paul belonged to that tribe too (Phil. 3:5). In his youth he was trained as a tentmaker, his father's vocation (Acts 18:3). This craft, which cannot be precisely defined but included all kinds of work with leather, allowed him later as missionary to support himself largely through his own occasional work (1 Cor. 9:14–18). But in still another respect Paul was ahead of all the apostles and missionaries of his time about whom we have detailed knowledge. He was highly educated, as was customary at that time for a (Jewish) urbanite from a respected family. He went to school because his pious Jewish parents evidently intended for him to become a Jew trained in Pharisaism (Acts 23:6; Phil. 3:5). A prospective rabbi, incidentally, also supported himself with his craft. It is doubtful, however, that Acts is correct in seeing Paul in Jerusalem at the feet of the great Gamaliel I (Acts 22:3). This was impressive news indeed: the great apostle as a student of the great rabbi of the school of Hillel! Before and after his calling we find Paul in Damascus (Gal. 1:17), then in Syria and Cilicia (Gal. 1:21), but not in Jerusalem (contra Acts 8:3; 9:1–2). Nevertheless, a temporary period of study in Jerusalem, although without the conclusion of being ordained rabbi, is historically conceivable. Was it at that time even possible to be adequately trained in Pharisaism without visiting Jerusalem? Did Paul perhaps go to Jerusalem before Christian churches existed there? In this case, his stay in the city would at least not contradict Gal. 1:22. In any case, it is hardly accidental that the early, nonliterary phase of Christianity had but one exception, namely, Paul, who had mastered the medium of written proclamation and consciously used it to look after his churches. As far as his education is concerned, he undoubtedly held a special position among the first generation of Christians, even though a number of them certainly might have mastered in principle cultural skills such as reading and writing.

We really would like to know more about the Pharisaic views of the pre-Christian Paul. But in this respect we can only speculate. For it is very difficult to draw a sufficiently reliable and at the same time concrete picture of Pharisaism in those days. The next question would then be to what extent such a general and typical picture would specifically describe Paul. Here the following consideration can help us. Paul's writings contain statements about Judaism from the Christian perspective of the apostle. When Paul characterized Judaism, he certainly did not have to acquire his views after his conversion to Christianity through anonymous material. Rather, his former Judaism played a crucial role here. This insight has not had its full impact up to now, because work on the anonymous tradition of the Gospels almost inevitably influenced the treatment of the Pauline materials. Now, by nature the two sources are equally anonymous, but in the case of the apostle and former Pharisee we can identify the medium of the tradition behind such statements. For Paul still carries Judaism within him as a latent personal conviction that has been replaced but is still present.

For Paul the Jew, faith in Israel's one and only Creator-God was essential. Through an uncompromising monotheism the Jews of the Diaspora set themselves thoroughly and distinctly apart from their environment. This was part of the strangeness of the Jewish religion for Hellenism, even though it too contained henotheistic tendencies. For a Jew gods are demons or nothing at all (1 Cor. 8:4–5). Not to know the one God is a culpable transgression that leads to grave sins in the created order (Rom. 1:18–32). Christians take up this thought in their early missionary proclamation to the Gentiles (1 Thess. 1:9). At this point we find an unbroken continuity between Jews and Christians. Jews had to avoid everything that was even remotely related to the cultus of foreign gods. In most cases this intransigence led to the isolation of Jewish minorities from the rest of the population. As a Christian, Paul became decidedly more open in his thinking and in the name of the one Creator-God assimilated part of the "heathen" world. Hellenistic (Jewish) Christians generally rejected the Levitical purity laws entirely, thereby breaking down a major barrier separating them from non-Christians.

This universal starting point of the Creator-God is then differentiated with an emphasis on the particularity of salvation history. Israel alone is elected among the nations, who are all sinful (Rom. 1:18–32; 9–11; Gal. 4:8). Only proselytes—non-Jews who through circumcision have converted to Judaism—can still be included in the election (see Matt. 23:15). Thus the apostle to the Gentiles, who by now holds that all nations are elected in Christ, can still speak in "Jewish" fashion when he talks about the nations as a "crooked and perverse generation" (Phil. 2:15), or about the "unrighteous" (1 Cor. 6:1). On the other hand, from the Jewish conviction of being chosen, Israel's privileges are apparent: it possesses sonship because of the covenant made with the fathers. It has been given the law as a way to know God's will and as a promise to give life to the person completely dedicated to the law. And, finally, Israel possesses the cult as an expiation for transgressions (Rom. 3:1–2; 9:4–5; 11:2, 28–29). A Jew can therefore rely on the law, boast in God, judge right and wrong, and be a guide of the blind and a teacher of the ignorant (Rom. 2:17ff.). Pharisees in particular seek to apply the law, this embodiment of being chosen, in all situations of life, even if this goes against their own personal advantage.

The Creator of the world, who chose Israel, is at the same time the Judge of all, the living and the dead. As a creature owing obedience to its Creator, every human being lives in the face of the coming judgment (Rom. 1:19–21; 9:18–24). The distinctive mark of this judgment is not temporal proximity (as in the earliest stage of Christianity). It is rather a theme that serves to stress the fundamental responsibility of every human being at all times. The time for human obedience and divine patience will last until the day of judgment. On the day of wrath God will hold a fair trial and deal with each human being according to his or her deeds, without respect to person. The sinner will face wrath; the righteous will receive life (Rom. 2:1–11). In this judgment, elected Israel cannot be lost in its entirety (Rom. 11:2, 28–29).

In the context of these views, whose elaboration and extension in Jewish literature we must forgo here, Paul takes a decidedly legalistic and uncompromising stance (Gal. 1:14; Phil. 3:6). Zeal for the law of the fathers leads him to persecute the young Jewish-Christian church at the synagogue in Damascus (Acts 9:2, 19–20). For the apostle this remained a dark spot throughout his life and weighed heavily on his mind (1 Cor. 15:9; Gal. 1:13; Phil. 3:5–6). Persecution by Paul was confined to Damascus (Gal. 1:13; Phil. 3:5–6). Therefore Paul had nothing to do with the persecution of Stephen. This is indeed claimed only by the Lukan redaction (Acts 7–8; 9:1–2), in order to establish a historical and biographical connection between two formerly independent strands of tradition. Yet this secondary linkage is justified in substance, for if he had known about it, Paul the Pharisee would have approved of the Jewish actions against Stephen.

Exactly what happened in Damascus remains obscure because Paul speaks of this incident only to disparage himself in retrospect but remains silent about the specific details. At any rate, he was seriously determined to destroy the Christian group within the synagogue (Gal. 1:13). It also remains unclear whether Paul acted alone or in concert with others. The latter is probably more likely. The use of the term *zeal* (for the law) may be a reference to Phinehas (Num. 25). His example inspired the Maccabean revolt (1 Macc. 2), which set the tone for more than two centuries. This kind of zeal led the Essenes in Qumran to hate other nations and those within their own nation who were unfaithful to the covenant (1QS 4.5–6, 17–18). It incited the revolutionary groups and Zealots in the post-Herodian period up until A.D. 70/71 (conquest and destruction of Jerusalem by Titus) to engage in a bloody fight against everything foreign. This zeal runs through Jewish history like a common thread from the Maccabees to the second revolt (132–35), which Hadrian bloodily suppressed.

In the very context of his persecuting activity, Paul had a sudden experience that redefined his whole existence and led him to become the Christian apostle sent especially to the Gentiles. This conversion or calling must not be conceived according to the biographical legend in Acts 9:1–9 with its traditional traits (cf. Acts 22:3–21; 26:9–20). Rather, it must be based on the statements in 1 Cor. 9:1–2; 15:8–10; Gal. 1:10–17; Phil. 3:2–14, according to which Paul interprets the event as the moment in which God, whom the Christians worshiped together with the synagogue, allowed him to see the exalted Lord of the Christians—the very same Lord whom he had persecuted in the form of the Christian church. Thus before his calling Paul already knew about this Jesus whom the Christians confessed as their Lord. For since Paul did not persecute the Christians without a reason, he was presumably acquainted with their faith and its practical consequences. Unlike Acts, Paul himself does also not describe the event as an audition, but as a vision through which the apostle found himself redefined in a direct and immediate way.

The vision releases insights that provide a new basis for Paul's existence. In the process he does not simply change from a Jew into a Jewish Christian, who now acknowledges as true the teachings he once persecuted. Rather, the Pharisaic persecutor, who had fought with particular dedication for the laws of the fathers and who for this reason had persecuted the Christian group at the synagogue, now becomes the Christian apostle— specifically, the apostle to the Gentiles—who questions the law itself (Gal. 1:14, 16; Phil. 3:5–6; Rom. 1:5, 14). Paul thus becomes the messenger of Jesus Christ, a messenger who through the gospel knows that those who before the Jewish law were sinners by definition are now the called (Gal. 2:15). They are now considered directly and newly chosen through the gospel (1 Thess. 1:4–5). God's eschatological election through the gospel replaces the age of the law.

The apostle was probably not immediately aware of all the profound consequences of this new starting point; right after his calling Paul could not have written the Letter to the Romans. But nothing in his correspondence gives rise to even the slightest doubt that from the very beginning Paul considered the central issue in his calling to be the opposition between the exalted Lord as the embodiment of the God who elects in the gospel, and the law as the embodiment of the Jewish conviction of being chosen. As a Jew Paul had upheld the claims of the law in an uncompromising way against the Jewish Christians (including the attempt to liquidate them—see Gal. 1:13). This is the reason why now, in his calling, the opposition between Christ and the law became so sharply defined and may have been more pronounced than in the contemporary views of the Christians in Damascus.

This interpretation of Paul's conversion presupposes, however, that the Jewish Christians in Damascus already acted less in accordance with the law than a strict, law-abiding Pharisee could have allowed. This is why their incipient critical attitude toward the law led to a life-and-death conflict with Paul and not just to the problems of ongoing debates over interpretations of the law. The attempt to wipe out the Christian church indicates the end of such disputes, for from now on it was merely a question of submission or death. What views so offensive to the law might the Christians in Damascus have held? In chapter 3, *b* above it was suggested that the issue was merely a dispute within the framework of the law over the proper place of worship; according to this view the Jewish temple as the salvific place of atonement was replaced by Christ as the eschatological sacrifice of atonement. But if this were the case, would it then not have been possible to deal with these Jewish Christians in the same way as with the Essenes of Qumran? The Essenes understood themselves as the "place" of atonement for Israel and criticized the current temple cultus so severely that they stayed away from it and declared it illegal. But is it possible to solve the difficulties of the tradition history of Stephen's speech (Acts 7) by regarding the oldest stratum as a direct reflection of the views of the group around Stephen? Furthermore, the interpretation of Jesus' death as a sacrifice of atonement cannot be found in this text at all. It has to be borrowed from Acts 8:32–33, that is, from a text that was extensively shaped by Luke himself, as Luke 4:16–21 and 24:17–27 prove. It is therefore more natural, on the one hand, to reconstruct the conditions in Damascus from Paul's own texts and, on the other hand, to remember that the Hellenists were able to utilize Jesus' critical attitude toward the law in their situation.

This may have happened in about the following way: the Christians believed that through his resurrection Jesus had been installed by God as the eschatological Son of man and the imminent Savior of the church (1 Cor. 16:22; 1 Thess. 1:10). Baptism in the name of this Lord incorporated a person into this church. Circumcision, therefore, was obviously no longer the sole and sufficient basis for salvation at the end of time. Furthermore, in the Diaspora (uncircumcised) God-fearing Gentiles were very often among those visiting the synagogue. What if one of them, bypassing the troublesome circumcision, desired to be baptized? Was it permissible to baptize him as an exception, since the Jesus tradition obviously included reports that in exceptional cases the Lord had also crossed Jewish boundaries and ministered to non-Jews? Had this Lord not also spoken rather critically about the purity laws separating Jews and non-Jews (Mark 7:15)? For a strict Pharisee this position certainly constituted a casus belli. It is equally plain that the Christian Paul quickly came to regard such a view as provisional and not very consistent. If this was to become a clear Christian position, the question of the law had to be tackled in a more fundamental way from the perspective of the new message of salvation.

Paul considered himself to be directly called by the same power as the other Easter witnesses. Damascus was his "Easter" (1 Cor. 15:8–9). He therefore immediately starts an independent mission in the area of the Nabataeans and in Damascus (Gal. 1:16–17), in northern Syria and in his native Cilicia (Gal. 1:21). However, neither he nor Acts notes any particular successes. This changes only when he belongs to the church in Antioch for about ten or twelve years. There he matures into one of the leading figures of primitive Christianity. His eventual departure from this church in 48/49 marks the commencement of his worldwide mission (see Rom. 15:14–29) as the apostle to the Gentiles, which lasts for about ten years and has Corinth and Ephesus as focal points in terms of both time and effort. In retrospect, it is safe to say that through this missionary enterprise Paul became the most significant person of the first generation of early Christianity. He is then arrested while bringing the collection from the other churches to Jerusalem, is transported to Rome, where he had intended to go for a long time, and is executed there in the early sixties (see *1 Clem.* 5). The last sign of life from Paul is his letter to the Romans, which he wrote on the way to Jerusalem for his last visit (Rom. 15:25). Thus it unintentionally became his final testimony.

Everywhere his missionary activity faced competition. Itinerant preachers did not exist only in the form of those itinerant Jewish-Christian radicals who usually appeared on Paul's mission field after he had left. The group around Stephen was also partially composed of itinerant missionaries. The Jews too promoted their religion in the Diaspora (Matt. 23:15). In addition, there was extensive communication between the synagogues. As members of baptizing communities the disciples of John the Baptist were also actively involved in missionary work (see John 1; Acts 19:1–7). Hellenism presented an even more colorful picture. Market places, schools for rhetoric and philosophy, and inns at the crossroads of the trade routes were popular meeting places for wandering Sophists, rhetoricians, philosophers, magicians, and holy men like Apollonius of Tyana, who was the most famous and a contemporary of Paul. Such figures were a familiar sight not only to Athenians; they were not alone in their desire to listen to anything that was new or concerned religion (Acts 17:18–21). Especially plentiful were itinerant preachers who promoted a particular way of salvation. The main route of these missionaries ran from east to west. They can be roughly

characterized as follows: First, their personal appearance attracted attention. They tried to outdo others in beauty or in unkempt appearance. In
demand were detachment from the common people, a pompous style designed to impress, and an air of sovereignty. They also cultivated a particular life-style: living in isolation without a family, displaying poverty and
frugality, and begging. Also not uncommon were ascetic attitudes, such as
abstinence from wine or meat. They slept in temples, in holy places, or out
in the open, and moved around from city to city. Rhetoric was especially
popular; speeches were used to captivate the crowd (for typical features, see
Acts 12:21-22). Proficiency in eloquence and disputation were the most
effective means of advertising. These were complemented by the display of
charismatic power and sensational demonstrations. The superhuman quality and divinity of an individual were demonstrated through miracles performed on nature or on human beings, through prescience, prophesy,
interpretation of dreams, and ecstasy. It was an age craving for miracles.
And, finally, these itinerant preachers sought followers: travel companions,
disciples, and apprentices.

How does Paul fit into this picture? In his personal appearance, he was
just the opposite of the competition. He gave the impression of weakness,
not strength (1 Cor. 2:3; Gal. 4:13-14). Carrying himself in a bombastic
manner was not his style (1 Thess. 2:7-8). He exerted more influence
through his letters than through his presence (2 Cor. 10:1-2). In life-style
similarities are more in evidence. Paul also lived without a family (1 Cor.
9). He lived frugally (Phil. 4:11-12) but not ascetically (1 Cor. 8; 10:26).
Abstinence for the sake of a brother, however, is one of the main topics of
his social ethics. He definitely did not gain his livelihood through begging—in stark contrast to the itinerant Jewish-Christian radicals (1 Cor. 9;
Phil. 4:10ff.). He lived in Christian homes within his churches. His rhetorical skills were quite poor, in the opinion of the Corinthians (1 Cor. 2:1-5),
but with charismata the apostle was richly endowed. He was a charismatic,
for the churches generally had a charismatic orientation (1 Thess. 4:8-9;
5:19-20; 1 Cor. 1:6). His preaching was accompanied by signs and miracles (Rom. 15:19; 2 Cor. 12:12). He experienced the ecstasies of glossolalia more frequently than the Corinthians, who were especially gifted in this
respect (1 Cor. 14:18). He had special revelations (2 Cor. 12:1-9), and
with respect to spiritual insight he compared quite well with the Corinthians (2 Cor. 2:10-16). However, he deliberately brings all this into play
only in passing. In part, he exercises these gifts only in private and never
uses them to show off. Most of this he mentions only as a fool in Christ (2

Cor. 11:16, 30; 12:1, 11). He thus wants to set himself apart especially from the "super-apostles" mentioned in 2 Corinthians, who so closely resemble the Hellenistic charismatics. It is his desire that only the content of his message should make an impact, and he wants to be found in conformity with the Christ who is the topic of this message. The brother and the person to be won dictate his conduct (2 Cor. 10–12; 1 Cor. 2; 8; 9).

If Paul set himself so consciously and clearly apart from his environment, what then did he consider to be his apostolate to the Gentiles? How did he conduct his mission, and how did he look after his churches? It is his ambition to go only to places where no missionaries had been and to seek these places throughout the world (Rom. 15:20–24). To do that he usually went to the local synagogues and spoke there in the customary synagogal style (Acts 13:5, 14–16; 14:1; etc.; note that Acts standardizes). In the inns attached to the synagogues he presumably also found lodging initially, when he was still new to a particular location. But he also speaks in lecture halls and market places (for typical details, see Acts 14:18ff.; 17:17; 19:9). On the long journeys and in the unfamiliar locations this kind of groundbreaking missionary work had to be self-sufficient in terms of travel expenses, accommodation, and food. This required Paul to earn as much of his own living as possible. Only as an exception did he accept gifts from the churches (2 Cor. 11:7–12; Phil. 4:10–20; 1 Thess. 2:9). This involved forgoing a middle-class life-style and personal self-development. He was totally committed to being a servant of Jesus Christ—at the permanent risk of his life (2 Cor. 11:23–29). As one who is free he used his freedom to become a Jew to the Jews, to be as one outside the law to those outside the law, and to be weak to the weak, so that he might save some (1 Cor. 9:19–23). The maxim of his work was not self-promotion but empathy with others. One day he wants to stand before his Lord with his churches (1 Cor. 3:5–15; 9:1–2; 2 Cor. 11:2). Apostolate and parental concern for the churches belong together (1 Cor. 9; Gal. 4:12–30; 1 Thess. 2:1, 7–12). These churches are urban, middle-class house churches that win others for Christ through their good reputation (1 Thess. 1:7ff.), through their worship services that are open to strangers (1 Cor. 14:23), and through the testimony of individual members in everyday life (1 Cor. 7:16). What makes them grow is the exemplary conduct they display to the outside world (1 Thess. 4:11–12; Rom. 12:14–21; Gal. 6:10) and the amazing internal ability to integrate new members.

In addition to this, Paul trained a circle of coworkers, which is a unique feature of his mission (Ollrog). Paul's model was Antioch where he himself had served as a coworker in the church (Acts 13:1). Several of the later coworkers, such as Titus, Silvanus, and John Mark, came from Antioch too. But Paul chose his coworkers mainly from churches that he had founded himself. Among these were Timothy, Syzygus, Apollos, and Epaphroditus. With few exceptions, they worked with him only on a temporary basis. They were emissaries of the churches and carried out the missionary task of the churches together with and alongside Paul (1 Cor. 16:15–18; Phil. 2:29–30). Only a few fellow missionaries, such as Timothy and Silvanus, worked closely with Paul on a permanent basis. Still others, such as Apollos and Titus, worked independently. This entire circle significantly strengthened Paul's mission and his contacts with the churches.

Finally, a decisive factor in this context is the apostle's correspondence, which has been preserved only in part. The consistent use of this medium is another typical feature of Paul's mission. To look after churches with so many branches, to share personally in their development, and to help them theologically required more than visiting them occasionally and employing coworkers. These letters of Paul are the only written testimonies of earliest Christianity that we have. They have survived churches and coworkers and, because of their depth, have had a history whose influence can hardly be overestimated. These letters became the core of what was to be the New Testament canon.

b) Paul and Antioch

It can hardly be overestimated how significant the period between Paul's calling (c. A.D. 33) and his departure from Antioch (c. 48/49) was for the history of Christian theology and missions. The apostle's early writings (1 Thessalonians; 1 and 2 Corinthians) already contain traditional and typical statements on Christology, eschatology, and ecclesiology, as well as on the life and self-understanding of the church. When these are compared with the Jesus stratum in the Synoptic tradition, the earliest interpretation of Easter that can be reconstructed, and the views of the group around Stephen that are still to some degree discernible, it becomes clear that major changes must have taken place.

The foundation for these statements of Paul, as well as their main elements, were undoubtedly developed during his stay in Antioch. Without intending to downplay the contacts between the Palestinian churches and those in Syria and Asia Minor, it is safe to assume that a leading role in this development was played by cities that traditionally contained a large Jewish

Diaspora, and also by the first Christian mission churches, such as Antioch, Damascus, and Caesarea. Even if one does not want to construct a false dichotomy between Jerusalem and Galilee, on the one hand, and these new churches outside of Palestine, on the other, it is evident that their respective situations and interests were at variance on important points. The development of Christian faith and life during this period was therefore presumably not always synchronous and uniform in every place, notwithstanding the fact that we only have a very vague picture regarding specific details.

Yet one thing ought to be clear: Antioch and not least of all Paul himself as prophet and missionary teacher of this church (Acts 13:1) played a conspicuously prominent role in this development (Acts 11:19-30; 15; Gal. 2). In characterizing this development in Syria and Asia Minor, it therefore makes sense to concentrate, in a somewhat simplified way, primarily on Antioch and its pioneering role. This approach is based on four historical facts, which apply only to Antioch and which specifically characterize the exceptional and pioneering role of the metropolis on the Orontes. First, it is Antioch that programmatically initiates the mission to the Gentiles (see chapter 3, *d*). Also, the designation *Christianoi* (Acts 11:26; see chapter 3, *d*), which emerges in Antioch, signals that here a Christian group within the confines of the synagogue for the first time became an independent and autonomous church outside the synagogue. And, finally, the two events of the Apostolic Council (Acts 15; Gal. 2) and the clash between Peter and Paul in Antioch (Gal. 2:11ff.) testify to the fact that the Christian churches in Judea, Galilee, Syria, and Asia Minor all considered this very church to be the leader of the development of earliest Christianity in terms of theology, missions, and church organization. It cannot be merely accidental that a critical reading of Acts and of the Pauline accounts in Gal. 1-2 leads to the same basic assessment of this situation. It is presumably also not a historical distortion when Paul sees himself as the spokesman and protagonist both at the Apostolic Council and in the clash with Peter in Antioch, even if one would wish to grant Barnabas a somewhat greater overall role than Paul now gives him.

The life of the church in Antioch and the life of Paul were very closely interwoven in the period of Paul's stay there, if we can assume two things: that the church in Antioch indeed played a leading role in the subsequent development of earliest Christianity outside of Palestine in the way indicated, and that beside Barnabas, who apparently acted more cautiously and more in line with Palestinian Jewish Christianity (see Gal. 2:13), Paul himself became the crucial figure within the church who helped to promote this course of history. Is it mere accident that after Paul's departure from Antioch this city was, for the time being, again lost in the mists of history? Can this be taken as an indicator of the great significance Paul had for Antioch? Unfortunately, there is very little direct material that would enable the historian to draw a comprehensive and reliable picture of these years. This material consists of two sources: the news from Antioch in Acts (see chapter 3, d), which must, however, be stripped of its Lukan redaction, and Gal. 2, where Paul, with a focus on the Galatian problem, describes the events from his own perspective. But we can and must go even further by listening to indirect witnesses. If Paul wrote 1 Thessalonians about one year after his departure from Antioch (c. A.D. 50), then it is safe to assume that at least the typical statements of this letter are characteristic of Paul's period in Antioch. For it is hardly likely that Paul changed this quickly, and, precisely because of his new missionary activity, he presumably also strove for continuity in his basic views. It is further best to assume that the traditional material, which Paul treats in his letters as commonly known, was in essence also created in this early period. In any case, whoever concedes that Paul used traditional material and held standard views that are older than 1 Thessalonians necessarily has to think primarily of Antioch.

The church in Antioch carried out its missionary work not merely among proselytes of the local synagogue; even in Jerusalem this kind of mission was theologically possible and was practiced with limited success (see Acts 6:5). It also did not merely on occasion make an exception and baptize a God-fearer who requested this himself (see a above), as was perhaps done in Damascus. For the history of the church the decisive step of the church in Antioch was the fact that this group, which originally still consisted of Jewish Christians, was able to theologically relativize its affiliation with the synagogue to such an extent that it gradually shifted to a mission that was specifically addressed to Gentiles (Acts 11:19–20), without requiring them to be circumcised. This process was presumably to a very large extent due to the rapidly growing group of Gentile God-fearers who had become Christians. Thus, unconnected with circumcision, baptism became the sole uniting bond that visibly marked conversion to Christianity. At the beginning of this development Barnabas comes to Antioch (chapter 3, d). He actively promotes this new line of thinking and recruits Paul as his coworker (Acts 11:25–26). From then on both of them are part of the church's governing committee of five (Acts 13:1), with Paul still holding the lowest rank, apparently because he was the last to join the church. Simultaneously, both of them work as missionaries for the church (initially with Barnabas in the preeminent role) by carrying out missionary work in the surrounding region (Acts 13–14). A majority of scholars currently hold that, contrary to the Lukan order, this missionary journey in the North, above Syria and Cilicia, took place after the Apostolic Council (Acts 15). However, much can be said in favor of the Lukan sequence of events (Hengel, *Geschichtsschreibung*, 91–92). This would mean that what Acts portrays in stylized fashion as a mission originating from Antioch as its center would actually point to the fact that the Antiochenes carried out their new missionary concept in an expansive way. Through his active role in the Antiochene church, and based on the experience of his calling, Paul then apparently emerges more and more as the leading figure in this development. At least this is what is portrayed in the accounts of the Apostolic Council and the incident during Peter's visit in Antioch (Acts 15; Gal. 2).

The question might arise, Why did Barnabas bring in Paul rather than someone else? The answer should be clear: Paul was by then known as a theologian who, through his critical attitude towards the law, was very much in line with the development in Antioch. Since Paul accepted this task and decisively helped to shape Antioch's path, the history of the church in Antioch also became a reflex of his own calling. It is safe to assume that Paul himself was responsible for the strong promotion of the mission to the Gentiles. And it was also Paul who went to the Apostolic Council and, as a crucial test case—one might almost say provocatively— took along as his partner Titus, the uncircumcised Gentile Christian (Gal. 2:3). This shows how he understood himself as he appeared there, namely, as apostle to the Gentiles.

Antioch apparently had considerable success with this new direction of its mission. To the extent that it was successful, the church had to clarify its relationship to the law and the synagogue in a definitive way. To remain attached to the synagogue, as was the case in Damascus, meant to force Gentile Christians to observe a minimum of the purity regulations contained in the law (e.g., Lev. 17–18). But even then the relationship with the synagogue would turn into a permanent state of conflict. From Damascus Paul was somewhat familiar with these problems. There can be no doubt about the new solution Antioch adopted: the name *Christianoi* (Acts 11:26; see chapter 3, *d*) is an unmistakable indication that the church detached itself from the synagogue. With this step it had freed itself from the obligation to observe Jewish purity laws and the circumcision commandment but had also placed itself outside Judaism and the affiliation with the people of salvation. Until then this connection had not been severed by any Christian group within the synagogue. This solution, however, provided the freedom to proclaim the gospel directly to the Gentiles and to shape the life of the church on the basis of the gospel alone. But the new problems were still serious enough: How should one work out the relationship to those Jewish-Christian communities that remained within the synagogue? How could one cope without the significant political protection that Judaism enjoyed? How, without circumcision, could one describe one's spiritual descent from Judaism, especially since Jesus and the apostles were Jews? Antioch's step was a very risky venture into rough, uncharted territory! Only much later did this step prove to have set the course to which the future belonged. Success does not usually have to justify the truth of its actions. This is why in retrospect Antioch's path is considered obvious and correct. At the time of Antioch's decision, however, the picture looked rather different. Antioch faced a host of problems and was the outsider that had to justify its truth. Paul himself will consistently defend this freedom from the law throughout his life. Later, as an independent missionary, he will be stoned once and receive five times the synagogal punishment of 39 lashes (2 Cor. 11:24–25)—apparently because of his position on the law. Can it be denied that such a man was a protagonist in Antioch, who helped to bring about the events there?

So Antioch no longer accepts circumcision, the ritual law, and the Jewish cult as a bond of unity. This function is taken up by election through the gospel, baptism in the name of Jesus, the gift of the Spirit, unity with Christ, brotherly love, and the common hope for the imminent return of the Lord. How does the new name *Christianoi* fit into this picture? It is hardly likely that it originated as a self-designation; rather, it was attributed to the young church from the outside (by non-Jews?) when the church became known as an independent, private religious community. Christians called themselves "brothers" (1 Thess. 2:1, 17; 4:1, 13; etc.), "beloved by God" (1 Thess. 1:4), "saints" (1 Cor. 1:2; 6:2; etc.). Jews probably called them the "sect of the Nazarenes" (Acts 24:5). The designation *Christianoi* seeks to denote the affiliation with Christ. Thus the honorific title *Christos* must have been the norm in this church at that time. As a designation of the new unity "in Christ" it indeed appears in ancient baptismal traditions, which also speak of the removal of the opposition between Jews and Gentiles (Gal. 3:26–28 et al.). Yet another ancient source is the old christological creed in 1 Cor. 15:3b–5 that interprets what happened to Christ as the basis of salvation for Christians and Jesus' death as a salvific death "for us." Did this creed perhaps originate in Antioch as a baptismal creed? If Christ is the sole basis of salvation, is the Jewish cult then not tacitly invalidated? At least Paul himself can later still speak of how at this very point in time Antioch had embraced a new approach that was based on the gospel and invalidated the law: the Galatians' relapse into submission under the law forces him to revive and employ once again old Antiochene "slogans" such as "the freedom we have in Christ" (Gal. 2:4), which is "the truth of the gospel" (2:5, 14). Paul will defend this freedom (from the law) throughout his life. His mission is a part of the history of freedom. In the post-Pauline period the concept of freedom will soon be forgotten—for the time being.

It is important to understand these theological connections even more clearly. To do this one can start with the established sermon outline that Paul uses in 1 Thess. 1:9–10. Paul reminds the Thessalonians:

" . . . how you turned to [the one] God from idols,
   to serve a living and true God,
and to wait for his Son from heaven,
   whom he raised from the dead—
Jesus, who rescues us from the wrath that is coming."

The division into doctrine of God and Christology is a necessary consequence of the turn to the Gentiles. Christians had monotheism in common with the Jews. From the Hellenistic synagogue they adopted the preaching format that called on hearers to abandon idols in favor of the one true God. Turning to this God means turning away from the temples and holy places, the municipal and national cults, the mysteries, the house gods and the gods of associations, etc.; it means a religious and social uprooting, as well as a reorientation in the moral sphere. For both Jews and Christians considered the nations morally depraved (Rom. 1:18–32; 1 Cor. 6:9–11). Worship of the gods and an immoral life-style were two sides of the same coin. But Christians were also able to speak of this one God in a new way. Palestinian Jewish Christians had already called him "Abba" (Rom. 8:15), and this practice was continued. But now he was above all the "Father of the Lord Jesus Christ" (2 Cor. 11:31 etc.), "our God and Father" (1 Thess. 1:3; 3:11, 13), but also "Father" in the sense of Creator of the world (1 Cor. 8:6; Phil. 2:11). This means the church was able to speak of a new, intimate relationship with God and to interpret this God at the same time as the Father of the world. This latter point was not without significance for the church's mission.

This God was "the one who calls" (1 Thess. 1:4; 5:24; Gal. 1:6, 15) in Christ and through the "gospel" (1 Thess. 1:5; 2:2, 4, 8, 9; Gal. 2:5, 14). It is in this Antiochene context that the language of Christianity came to include both the concept of God as the one who calls and the concept of the gospel as a standing expression in the missionary proclamation that focused on the act of salvation in Christ as recorded in the creed (see Rom. 1:1, 9; 1 Cor. 15:1). This implied a complex process of adoption and transformation of Jewish theology. The election of Israel at the time of the patriarchs is now replaced by the eschatological election of the nations by the Father of Jesus Christ. The law is replaced by the gospel, or the church's being "in Christ" (see 1 Thess. 1:1; 2:14; but esp. 2 Cor. 5:17; Gal. 3:26; 2:4). The way of the law as the sum and substance of moral conduct is replaced by "sanctification" (1 Thess. 4:3, 4, 7). Conversion and acceptance into this new context of salvation are sealed in baptism. It provides admission into the church, just as circumcision provided admission into Judaism. It is interpreted as an event of radical change through which the old being becomes a thing of the past and human beings are so thoroughly renewed in their whole constitution that they are regarded as purified, sanctified, and justified (1 Cor. 6:11; 1:30), as a "new creation" (2 Cor. 5:17), and, being guided henceforth by the Spirit, are able to accomplish their sanctification (1 Thess. 4:1–12). This is how the new Christian freedom is interpreted. This guidance of the church by the Spirit should not be seen in a way that is too abstract. According to Paul's account, his transport into the third heaven falls into this period (2 Cor. 12:1–5). He travels to Jerusalem because he is prompted by a "revelation" (Gal. 2:2). Immediately following his departure from Antioch he writes to the Thessalonians not to quench the Spirit (1 Thess. 5:19). Thus the Spirit manifests itself very concretely in such phenomena.

In our exposition of the first theme of the sermon outline from 1 Thess. 1:9–10 we already had to refer repeatedly to the underlying Christology. This Christology is then laid out extensively and prominently in the second part as the goal of the sermon: Jesus, as the one whom God has raised and exalted, is the one who delivers from the coming wrath. This implies the imminent expectation of the Lord (see 1 Thess. 2:19; 3:13; 4:15). What is awaited is not so much the kingdom of God that Jesus announced (this view is still present in 1 Thess. 2:12; 1 Cor. 6:9–11) but rather the *Parousia* of the Lord (1 Thess. 2:19; 3:13; 4:15; 5:23), which alone will deliver those who are baptized from the eschatological wrath (1 Thess. 4:17c; 5:10). The emphasis on Christ as Savior also tacitly eliminates the law as the criterion for the coming judgment. Once again, we gain a glimpse of the church in Antioch as freeing itself from Judaism, and thus of an aspect of its new freedom.

The Antiochenes, however, continued to develop Christology in other respects also. We will mention only three issues, which were of fundamental importance for Paul and for the subsequent history of doctrine in general. It was apparently the Greek-speaking Jewish Christians in Syria who for the first time interpreted Jesus' death as an expiatory suffering on our behalf (1 Cor. 15:3b–4; 1 Thess. 5:10). This is also the time when a statement about Christ's preexistence takes shape (1 Cor. 8:6; Gal. 4:4). Still implicit and not yet independent, it addresses the issues of Jesus Christ as mediator of creation and of his sonship. Finally, it is here that the designation Lord as an exclusive title for Jesus is introduced into Christology. It answers the question, who is Lord of the world (Phil. 2:10–11) and of the church (1 Cor. 12:3; Rom. 10:9). It is true, the Palestinian church was already familiar with the address Lord for the Son of man (1 Cor. 16:22), but it does not yet use the honorific title Kyrios (= Lord). This honorific title quickly gained acceptance and probably contributed to the fact that the title Christos soon became Jesus' proper name in the form "Jesus Christ." All three statements are deeply rooted in the specific problems Antioch had to face. With the latter two propositions the church explains the increased involvement of its mission with the world; with the first, it defines the basis of salvation on which its new understanding of baptism rests. The freedom of the gospel, which at its core is a proclamation open to the world, is based on Christology.

How, one might ask, did this young and now independent church live? With respect to its sociological form one would have to describe it as a private religious association in the form of a house church (see d). While Christians still belonged to the synagogue, as one of the groups within Judaism they had—in addition to attending the synagogue on the sabbath—presumably already held other private meetings in houses. Leaving the synagogue, however, not only meant being no longer politically recognized as a particular religion in the Roman Empire and losing the special privileges of Jews, which varied from city to city; from now on the life of the church also had to be organized alone and without support. The supplementary gathering in private homes thus became the official and sole meeting place of the church. In this respect it differed decidedly from its environment. It did not have a special place of worship, let alone a temple or a sacred grove. It also had no cultic apparatus, no sacrifices or cultic vestments, and no processions like those enjoyed by the Greeks. In short, the things typically associated with the practice of religion at that time were not (yet) to be found in these young mission churches. However, this situation certainly also had a missionary advantage, namely, that it was possible to gather anywhere without problems. This too is part of the freedom that was gained through separation from Judaism.

The system of private associations (*collegia*) in general had a heyday during the imperial period. Associations were often formed by people who for the most part belonged to the lower class, for example, or by foreigners, who were present in every city because of the considerable mobility of that age. Associations were organized on a private level, based on common interests. Common professions, geographical origin, and education were factors that played a role here. Of course, such associations chose a tutelary deity for themselves, so that, as was typical in antiquity, there was always some religion involved. Almost all associations also arranged funerals and took care of grave sites. Associations usually had a democratic structure. A general meeting determined the policies. Officers and small committees were elected to conduct current transactions. These associations were politically desirable and thus generally had the right to assemble and conduct their own financial affairs. This legal form was also adopted in principle by the Jews in the Diaspora, who then also acquired special privileges. For its organizational structure, therefore, Christianity adopted a quite typical model.

During the apostles' stay in Antioch there were two events that cast a bright light on the problems associated with the course Antioch was then taking, and their significance for the subsequent history of Christianity can hardly be overestimated. Both events, the Apostolic Council (Acts 15; Gal. 2:1–10) and Peter's visit in Antioch (Gal. 2:11–21), were to a significant degree shaped by Paul.

Most recently, however, a sequence of events has been suggested which is at variance with this traditional order (Lüdemann, *Paulus*, p. 58ff.; in its essential features it is adopted above in chapter 3, *e*): (1) Paul's description of the Apostolic Council contains an old personal tradition whose content has, up to now, always been considered part of the core of the agreement that was reached at the Apostolic Council (vs. 7–8). It goes back to a short, private visit Paul paid to Peter (cf. Gal. 1:18). (2) This private agreement is followed by Peter's visit in Antioch (Gal. 2:11ff.). (3) This incident demonstrates that the relationship between the Gentile-Christian and the Jewish-Christian parts of the church required a general solution. This solution is found at the Apostolic Council in the form of the apostolic decree (Acts 15:19–21, 28–29). In Gal. 2 Paul would thus allegedly reverse the historical sequence. Acts 15 and Gal. 2 certainly leave a number of problems unresolved. But this new suggestion contains so many hypotheses and unnecessary constructs that clear preference must be given to the traditional assumption, based on Gal. 2, that the incident in Antioch occurred after the Apostolic Council. What would have forced Paul to declare the agreement, which was actually reached in the context of Gal. 1:18, to be a result of the Apostolic Council, thereby contradicting the historical facts that the Galatians knew or were able to check? It also remains unclear how it would be possible to break up the single complex sentence in Gal. 2:6–9, declaring just vs. 7–8 to be an already existing tradition. If Paul followed the rules of Greek rhetoric in his composition of Gal. 2, then he was free to rearrange the historical sequence of events should this be required for the portrayal of his position; the historical sequence was the standard, however (see the references in Lüdemann, pp. 77–78). On the crucial points Acts 15:1–12 and Gal. 2:1–10 are in agreement. At issue is the question of circumcision, that is, whether Gentiles who want to become Christians have to become Jews first, or whether it is possible to have a Gentile Christianity independent from Jewish Christianity and with equal rights. In Luke's account Peter takes the Gentile-Christian position, since it was he, according to Luke, who began the mission to the Gentiles (Acts 10:1–11:18), and because Luke wants Paul to appear faithful to the law (Acts 21:18–26; 23:1–10). In Gal. 2:6–9 Paul takes the Gentile-Christian position himself, which is historically certainly correct. It should be noted, though, that Peter's role and the portrait of Paul are, notwithstanding Luke's bias, identical or very similar in a remarkable number of details. Paul and Barnabas appear in Jerusalem as Antioch's authorized representatives (Acts 15:2–3; also to be inferred from Gal. 2:9). Therefore, Paul's remark that nothing, not even a minimal requirement of observing the law (Gal. 2:6–7), had been imposed on him also applies to Barnabas (v. 9), as well as to the church in Antioch. What is portrayed in Acts 15:13ff. as the position of James, consisting essentially of the so-called apostolic decree, can therefore not have been the issue under debate at the Apostolic Council. Thus, much speaks for the assumption that, sparked by the incident in Antioch, an agreement was soon reached between Jerusalem with James and Antioch with Barnabas and Peter. They all acknowledged that the Antiochene church, comprised of Jewish and Gentile Christians, could only live together if the Gentile-Christian segment recognized the main demands of Lev. 17–18. Luke has merged this second agreement with the Apostolic Council, since, apart from Paul, it had the same participants and was a problem that arose as a consequence of the council. In his own churches Paul most certainly did not, on a Jewish-Christian basis, abide by this additional agreement, which was apparently reached after his departure from Antioch (see, e.g., 1 Cor. 8). In his view, Jewish Christians did not need any Levitic regulations to protect them; this would be legalistic and would run counter to the gospel. For him Jewish Christians had also "died to the law" (Gal. 2:15–21).

At the council the delegates from Jerusalem and Antioch—with Titus, an uncircumcised Gentile Christian, demonstratively present (Gal. 2:3)—were in agreement that the Spirit that was working through Peter in the formation and life of the Jewish-Christian churches was the same Spirit that was effecting Paul's Gentile-Christian missionary successes (cf. Rom. 15:18–19; 2 Cor. 12:12; Gal. 3:2, 5). Therefore, they all acknowledged the "grace" given to Paul by God, namely, his apostolate (Gal. 2:9; cf. Rom. 15:15). That meant that the Jerusalem delegates gave their basic consent to the mission to the Gentiles. With this consent the Jewish Christians declared that from now on they accepted, although presumably as an exception, a Christianity independent of the synagogue. Jewish Christians also considered the community of all Christians under the gospel to be of greater importance than the acceptance of the law. It is possible to become a Christian without having to become a Jew first. Baptism was more important than circumcision, even though for Jewish Christians it certainly was the norm that a Christian would be circumcised and baptized.

At that time presumably no one, except perhaps Paul, foresaw that within a few years Gentile Christians would increase in number to such an extent that Jewish Christians would have become a mere minority. This outcome was not least of all the result of Paul's mission. The fact, however, that Paul's mission moved away from Antioch and the territory of its mission and that, based on the borders of the greater Roman Empire, Paul spread Christianity throughout the whole world—that is, from Syria and Asia Minor to Europe—is in all probability related to Peter's visit in Antioch. After initially participating with the whole congregation in the Lord's Supper on a Gentile-Christian basis—as was considered legitimate after the Apostolic Council—Peter and the Jewish Christians withdrew after the arrival of supporters of James. For Jewish Christians, but not for the church as a whole, the law should remain binding. Apparently Barnabas and at least significant groups within the church shifted to Peter's side. Would the outcome of all this be a re-Judaization, resulting in two local Christian churches? Paul refused to take this path. But the church preserved its unity in celebrating the Lord's Supper by adhering to the apostolic decree already mentioned. Soon afterwards Paul left the city to which he owed much and which was also much indebted to him. No longer did he consider himself attached to Antioch. And since that time his relationship with Peter was also no longer without a note of discord. Paul became an independent missionary who made it a point of honor to preach the gospel wherever Christ was not yet known (Rom. 15:20). This means the strategy of his mission had changed; he no longer conducted his mission from a single base (Antioch) but instead established new centers for mission himself.

c) The Apostle to the Gentiles and the New Churches He Founded

After breaking away from Antioch Paul must have thought almost immediately of a worldwide mission. With good reason he is therefore up to this day considered the apostle to the Gentiles. His plan to visit Rome, the capital of the empire, was thus presumably conceived quite soon after his Antiochene period. As with a good many of the apostle's missionary schemes, this plan could not be realized immediately, in spite of repeated attempts (Rom. 1:13; 15:23). Later, Paul modifies his plan; Rome is to become an intermediate stop on a mission to Spain (Rom. 15:23–24).

With this strategy the western border of the then known civilized world comes into view. The global dimension of Paul's mission is emphasized in similar fashion in Rom. 15:19 when, just before turning to the western part of the Mediterranean, he sweepingly includes the empire's entire eastern hemisphere in the range of his past mission: "From Jerusalem [the world's salvific center according to the Jewish view] and as far around as Illyricum [the northwestern border of Macedonia] I have proclaimed the good news of Christ." Paul sees himself called as a "debtor" primarily to the non-Jewish world and takes this call seriously in a geographical sense (Rom. 1:14). This is confirmed, for example, by the fact that Paul quotes Ps. 19:4 in Rom. 10:18, thereby describing the Christian proclamation as having gone out "to all the earth" and "to the ends of the [inhabited] world." Certain analogies to having this global horizon can undoubtedly be found in the Stoics and in men such as Appolonius of Tyana. The unity and inner stability of the Roman Empire provided the political foundation for such an outlook. But Paul is not simply a "cosmopolitan"; rather, he relates himself and his work over and over again to his calling to be the apostle to the nations. It is surely no accident that we know of no other missionary of the first generation of earliest Christianity whose horizon was equally global and comprehensive. There was certainly a lot of Christian missionary work that was not connected with Paul; these efforts, for example, reached Rome before Paul and the North African coast entirely without his assistance. But all this was the work of many missionaries with narrower goals.

Yet we must also ask to what extent a statement such as Rom. 15:19 is based on reality. Are there really no missionary tasks left for Paul in the eastern part of the empire, even assuming that he intends to carry out missionary work only in places where Christ has not yet been proclaimed (Rom. 15:20)? Certainly, Paul founded churches in Syria, Asia Minor, Macedonia, and Greece, but in so doing he confined himself to large cities and only to a certain number of them, with the two centers Corinth and Ephesus being especially noticeable. It would appear that in his view provinces had heard the message of salvation even if only small churches existed in the cities. Once he had given his basic testimony of Jesus Christ in the cities (1 Cor. 3:6–13), his task was completed. Even baptisms are largely left to others (1 Cor. 1:14–17). Paul apparently sought to have Christ's name mentioned in a representative way throughout the entire *oikoumene* before the coming of his Lord for the final judgment (1 Cor. 15:24; Rom. 15:16). He wants to be able to stand before the one who commissioned him as the apostle to the Gentiles (Rom. 1:5), joined by his churches throughout the world as his work and his honor (1 Cor. 3:6, 13; 9:1, 15–18; etc.).

In order to get a preliminary picture of the characteristic features of Paul's churches, one might attempt to gain certain clues from statements in Paul's earliest letter. Especially suited for this purpose are the passages 1 Thess. 4:1–12 and 5:12–24. These texts read:

4:1 Finally, brothers and sisters, we ask and urge you in the Lord Jesus that, as you learned from us [as an admonition] how you ought to live and to please God (as, in fact, you are doing), you do so more and more.
²For you know what instructions we gave you through the Lord Jesus.
³For this is the will of God, your sanctification:
[namely,] that you abstain from fornication;

⁴that each one of you know how to control your own body in
  holiness and honor,
⁵not with lustful passion, like the Gentiles who do not know
  God;
⁶that no one wrong or exploit a brother or sister in this matter
  [= in trade],
  because the Lord is an avenger in all these things,
  just as we have already told you beforehand and solemnly
  warned you.
⁷For God did not call us to impurity but [to live] in holiness.
⁸Therefore whoever rejects this rejects not a human authority but
God, who also gives his Holy Spirit to you.
  ⁹Now concerning love of the brothers and sisters, you do not need
to have anyone write to you, for you yourselves have been taught by
God to love one another;
  ¹⁰and indeed you do love all the brothers and sisters throughout
Macedonia.
But we exhort you, beloved,
  to do so more and more,
  ¹¹to aspire to live quietly,
  to mind your own affairs,
  and to work with your hands,
  as we directed you,
    ¹²so that you may behave properly toward outsiders and be
    dependent on no one.

5:12 But we appeal to you, brothers and sisters, to respect those
      who labor among you, and have charge of you in the Lord
      and admonish you;
  ¹³esteem them very highly in love because of their work.
Be at peace among yourselves.
¹⁴And we urge you, beloved,
  to admonish the idlers,
  encourage the faint hearted,
  help the weak,
  be patient with all of them.
¹⁵See that none of you repays evil for evil,
  but always seek to do good to one another and to all.

[16]Rejoice always,

[17]pray without ceasing,

[18]give thanks in all circumstances;

   for this is the will of God in Christ Jesus for you.

[19]Do not quench the Spirit,

[20]do not despise the words of prophets,

[21]but test everything; hold fast to what is good,

[22]abstain from every form of evil.

[23]May the God of peace himself sanctify you entirely; and may your spirit and soul and body be kept sound and blameless at the [Parousia] of our Lord Jesus Christ.

[24]The one who calls you is faithful, and he will do this.

Both these texts represent typical forms of paraenesis. They deal with the usual, the standard case, not with what is extraordinary or under dispute. This makes them especially suitable for answering the question, What form of Christianity was typical in Paul's churches? Clearly, they are addressed specifically to the church in Thessalonica, but it is also clear that Paul could generally speak in this way to any of his churches. Both texts have an intentional structure. The first sets out with a general introduction (4:1-2) and then in verses 3-8 provides directions for the daily life of Christians under the catchword *sanctification* (v. 3a = v. 7). A second main section (vs. 9-12) then issues further exhortations under the predominant theme of brotherly love (vs. 9-10). The first part of the second text (vs. 12-13) begins by instructing the members of the church about their relationship to the leaders of the church and then speaks to the latter about their responsibility to the former (5:14-15). A second part first addresses the issue of how the church as a whole ought to express itself in worship (vs. 5:16-18) and then deals with special manifestations of the Spirit in individual prophets (5:19-22). Verses 23-24 form a typical closing.

Both texts portray a fraternally structured church life. It is marked by the imminent expectation of the Parousia (5:23-24) and by contrast with the nations who do not know the one God (4:5). Thus it has a Gentile-Christian orientation and is, therefore, a reflection of the missionary preaching to Gentiles in 1 Thess. 1:9-10, which we have summarized briefly. The strongly emphasized keyword *sanctification* (4:3, 4, 7) provides the link with baptism (see *b* above). Therefore, what we have here is a volunteer church, a small, holy group in the midst of the non-Christian majority. This church, devoted to the pursuit of holiness, is mainly occupied with regulating its own internal affairs. An outward perspective is quite limited and plays merely a marginal role; to those on the outside (an expression inherited from the synagogue) Christians were to set an example of a respectable, normal life-style (4:12). As a church they did not feel responsible for matters of politics, the economy, or social issues in the civil community. Instead they developed a holy brotherhood in which worship and everyday life were intrinsically linked. They do not aim at improving the world through theological schemes; they do not give recommendations on how to govern a state, how to solve social questions in the political sphere, etc. Rather, they focus on the new kind of community they have with one another as Christians. It was the entire first generation that basically chose this option. This whole generation espoused the internal consolidation of the small group and defined its relationship to the outside world merely in terms of individual respectability and decency of its members, so that the church could prosper. Yet over time it was not possible to maintain this basic attitude in the same way.

The norms of this community do not consist of sayings of Jesus, even though connections in substance, both implicit and intentional (e.g., in the case of monogamy), are clearly discernible. Jesus is not a legal authority but first and foremost a salvific figure (1:10; 5:10). Besides, behind Paul's authority stands the exalted Lord (4:1–2; 5:18), whose reality is present in the current experience of the Spirit. This experience of the Spirit is subject to examination by the congregation (5:19–22). The entire congregation is instructed about the Spirit directly by God (4:8–9). In this sense we have an enthusiastic understanding of the church, which assumes everyone to be equal before Christ. Paul too does not impose new norms on the church (4:1, 6). Rather, he reminds them of his initial proclamation and of the knowledge given in the Spirit to each member (4:1–2, 9), which is identical with this initial proclamation. His exhortation means to ensure a continuous formation of life according to this undisputed basic conviction (4:1). It therefore also does not come as a surprise that Holy Scripture, which is being taken over from Judaism in the form of the Septuagint, is used to describe the Christian situation (4:6 = Ps. 94:1; 4:8 = Ezek. 36:26–27; 37:14; Jer. 31:33–34) or to characterize the nations (4:5 = Ps. 79:6), but is not the obvious ethical norm in and of itself. Instead, it plays more of a marginal role (5:22 = Job 1:1, 8) as a resource of expressions with which to describe established norms for the church. Of course the ritual and cultic law is tacitly put aside. The basic decision has long been made. It no longer requires discussion or justification, nor do these laws first have to be laboriously reinterpreted allegorically, as, for example, in Philo. Rather, they are disregarded as a matter of course. Thus a compromise, like the one recorded in Acts 15:19–20, 28–29 as a minimum ritual requirement, could not find a place in the actual life of these churches.

All norms regulate the life of the community. Cultivation of one's individuality and development of one's personality are banished from sight. By invoking the rule of strict monogamy, the Hellenist, who was used to visiting a hetaera, has this individual right revoked, though up to then it was granted to him by the society of his time as a matter of course (4:4). Even the prophet has to let his expression of the Spirit be judged by the congregation (5:21–22). Particular emphasis is placed on the communal by exhortations to love the brethren (4:9–10), to keep the peace (5:13), and to care for all those that are weak (5:14). Protection of the community is advocated in 4:6, 11–12, 15. In all this, however, the community is not on its own, since it is focused on the coming Lord (5:23), grounded in God's faithfulness (5:24), and guided by the Spirit; this means that it sees itself as being related to another, through whom it is sanctified and who is not subject to its own control.

What are the specific matters being regulated? In typical fashion 4:3–8 deals with two themes, which concern the urban life of such citizens who are neither seriously involved in politics (see Pol. *Phil.* 12.3) nor exempt from earning a livelihood because of considerable wealth; these citizens are instead settled and have a family; they are married to one spouse and earn a living for their families through a combination of trading and working as craftsmen (4:6, 11; cf. 2 Thess. 3:12; *Did.* 12.3; *Barn.* 10.4). This also clearly implies that, in conformity with the then current system, the man is consistently regarded as the paterfamilias. Early Christianity did not disturb the general social structure of antiquity, even though it can be assumed that certain functions in the life of the church that did not touch on the prevailing social structures of antiquity—for example, new internal functions of the church such as church leadership and prophesy (5:12, 20)—could also be carried out by women (Rom. 16:1ff.; 1 Cor. 11:5). The texts provide certain clues that can quickly substantiate this in detail: the address throughout (in Greek) is "brothers" and not, for example, "sisters and brothers." The marital relationship is described from the perspective of the man; the woman is seen as his "vessel" (4:4, literal). According to 4:6, it is the "brothers" who conduct trade with one another. In a different way this social structure is also at issue in 4:11–12: the experience of the Spirit and the near expectation of the Parousia led to the temptation to sever the usual social relationships even before that time, and indeed the itinerant radicals, for example, provided the churches with a practical demonstration of this course of action. But in our texts the members of the church are instructed to prove themselves through a normal life-style in their community, thus not becoming a burden to the church or giving non-Christians any grounds for gossip.

This church may be a brotherhood, but it nevertheless has "leaders" right from its inception (see Rom. 16:1ff.). The church is instructed to look to them, not in submission but in understanding acknowledgment. And these leaders in turn are reminded of their duties toward the church (1 Thess. 5:12–15). There are no established offices yet or any organizational structures beyond the local churches, let alone any kind of hierarchy; this is why all are addressed as "brothers." The universal brotherly kiss expresses this sense of being equal and of belonging together (1 Thess. 5:26; Rom. 16:16; 1 Cor. 16:20; etc.).

What definitely needed to be reorganized was worship. Three elements are discernible in our text: exhortations to the church by the leaders (5:14b), expressions of the church as a whole such as hymns of praise (articulating the "joyful anticipation" of the coming Lord; see Phil. 4:4–6), prayers of supplication and thanksgiving (5:16–18), as well as unplanned, spontaneous expressions of the Spirit (see 1 Cor. 14). In addition, one of the apostle's letters was of course also read to the congregation (cf. 1 Thess. 5:27). Since Paul expects even Gentile Christians to have a sound knowledge of the Septuagint (see, e.g., 1 Cor. 9:9; 10:1–13; 14:21; 15:21–22, 44–49), one can presume that it was used with a Christian exposition during congregational meetings. It is therefore likely that the reading of scripture was adopted from the synagogue. Baptism and the Lord's Supper naturally played an important role in the services (see, e.g., 1 Cor. 11:17–34; Gal. 2:12). In 1 Thess. 5 this is taken for granted. However, the very fact that the statements in 1 Thess. 5 are fragmentary and of a general nature indicates how fluid the structure of the service still was.

The overall impression of these texts is that they are controlled by a determination to have a strong integrating power within the brotherhood. The life of this church is based in practice on the equality of all its members, with few functions above that general level. Life is governed not by individual laws or even casuistry, but by the general rule of brotherly love. Its fulfillment places high demands on the responsibility of each church member. Above all, each member has to make substantial sacrifices and show serious consideration for the community. In such cases everyone is called to give without reservation. If, on the other hand, a member happens to be the weak one at some time, he or she can count on support and assistance, even though as a general rule no one was to become a financial burden on the church. This fusion of worship and everyday life, of religion and morality, which was practiced in the church, was to a certain degree surely not an entirely foreign notion in antiquity. Yet this consistent correlation of theological explication and demanding life-style can hardly have failed to make its impression on the ancient world (see Phil. 2:14–16).

In this context attention must once again be called to the fact that this life-style of the Christians was embedded, on the one hand, in a specific understanding of baptism and, on the other, in the expectation that the end of all things was very near. The former meant the eschatological recreation of the human constitution by the Spirit (1 Thess. 5:5, 8; 1 Cor. 6:11; 2 Cor. 5:17; Gal. 6:15) and thus deliverance from the old being, which now lay in the past (1 Cor. 6:9–11). This was, no doubt, a tremendously ambitious claim, which now had to be fulfilled in practical, everyday living. For this very reason the expectation of the end (see, e.g., 1 Thess. 4:15; Rom. 13:11–12) does not generally lead to an escape from the world, but rather to living life even more conscientiously as a new creation (Rom. 13:11–14; 1 Thess. 5:7–8). This includes, for example, honesty on taxes (Rom. 13:6–7) and forgoing personal legal claims (1 Cor. 6:7). Christians thus understand themselves as "children of God without blemish in the midst of a crooked and perverse generation, in which" they "shine like stars in the world" (Phil. 2:15). This claim was also backed up by radical church discipline (1 Cor. 5:1–8), to be used as a last resort. Thus there seems to be little reason to assume that in the early period of Christianity claim and reality would have widely differed in regard to this life-style. It is equally clear that a community that was becoming increasingly larger, as was the case by the time of the third generation, would have to face new problems and cope with different conditions.

The picture of the church implied in this typical paraenesis is consistent with the way in which Paul touches on aspects of a doctrine of the church (ecclesiology). He neither speaks about the subject of church and state, or church and society, nor is already conscious of a history of the church. He does, however, deal with the relationship of the church to Israel and its history. Because the God of Abraham is the one who calls the nations, the church can be regarded as the children of Abraham (Gal. 3:29) and as the true Israel (Gal. 6:16). But this does not imply an unbroken continuity with the existing Israel, for membership in the church is solely dependent on the gospel, and the gospel itself is not tied to the law. Here it is typical for Paul to describe the reality of the church as the "body of Christ" (1 Cor. 12:12ff.; Rom. 12:5) even, and particularly, in contexts that do not refer to salvation history. His remarks on this issue not only make it clear that for him Christology takes precedence over ecclesiology but also show how Paul considers the variety of gifts of the Spirit within the church as a unity and how he relates the different individual members of the church to one another. It is possible that the notion of the "body of Christ" was a typically Pauline concept and initially was at home only in the Pauline churches (even as late as *1 Clem.* 37.5–38.4). This is most certainly not true for *ekklesia*, the word most frequently used for the church. This is the term Paul uses for the individual congregation (e.g., in the headings of his letters), as well as for all Christians as a whole (1 Cor. 15:9; Gal. 1:13). The individual congregation, in his usage, represents the church as a whole, and no church is more important than any other. The churches are equal to one another in principle, just as the individual brothers are in the local congregation. *Ekklesia* always means "body of Christ," wherever it may exist. It is not the sum of all local congregations that constitutes the total church as "body of Christ"; rather the "body of Christ" exists wherever the gospel of Christ is accepted. The concept of the church contains yet another element that is very crucial: the *ekklesia* is fundamentally separated from the world. The believer experiences this radical break and its exclusive quality in baptism (1 Cor. 6:9–11). Having been baptized, he or she has escaped death (1 Thess. 4:13)—unlike those outside—and no longer does the "works of the flesh" (Gal. 5:13, 19–21). The notion of a church consisting of saints and sinners, as it was advanced in the third generation, for example, by Matthew (Matt. 13:47–52), would not have been an acceptable ecclesiological concept for Paul (see 1 Cor. 5).

d) The General Situation of the Churches from the Perspective of Social History

The missionary success of earliest Christianity, the life of the young volunteer church as a still exceedingly small minority in the Roman Empire, and the possibility of living as a brotherhood guided by the Spirit were all based on the private house church. After his departure from Antioch, Paul continued to use this model for the new mission churches he founded. Paul, the former diaspora Jew, naturally opted for the ancient *oikos*, even though the other religious communities, which progressively advanced from east to west, organized themselves in ways that were essentially independent of family structures. For over the centuries in the Diaspora, Judaism had had positive experience with the family as an important environment in which religion could develop. Since the time of the first independent churches in the area around Antioch, this design was apparently also considered by Paul a proven form of organization for Christianity. Thus the ancient *oikos,* in the sense of the house as living space and family household in general, became missionary base, organizing center for a local congregation, gathering place for worship, lodging for missionaries and delegations, and at the same time, of course, the immediate and crucial place for living a Christian life. Recently this has been explored in several studies (see Klauck, incl. bibliography). Especially Paul's letters and the corresponding material in Acts contain fundamental statements on this subject.

The ancient household, headed by the paterfamilias, was the crucial constituent of the polis and of the state in the Roman Empire. Not only did the prominent families control the political affairs of a community, but the family usually also served as the principal social insurance for its individual members. Life's risks and fortunes (social and political ascent or descent, education, choice of profession, illness, old age, effects of war, natural disasters, etc.) were to a very large extent tied to the family. They were also borne by the family and not mitigated by a welfare system of the state or by institutions outside the family, such as insurance companies. The Roman state was not a welfare state, even if it took care of veterans and provided food for the poor. The ancient household, especially in the form of the father of the family, consequently enjoyed considerable independence— approved by the government—in legal, social, and religious affairs. It is one of the most impressive cases of a linkage of rights and duties. In this context we have to draw particular attention to the fact that the house—apart from very few larger structures used for manufacturing—was not only the basic economic entity in antiquity; it also had a very high significance as a religious site. Well known is Cicero's statement in *De domo sua:* "What is more holy, more protected by every religion, than the house of every individual citizen? Here are altars, hearths, the divine penates. Here holy shrine, worship, and cult are united. This sanctuary is so holy to all that it is a sacrilege to tear anyone away from here" (41.109). It might be added that the legal form of private associations (*collegia*—see *b* above) provides solid documentation for the transition from house-based religion to private cults, which, though not confined to the family, were centered around the family and practiced in private homes.

The fact that Christianity chose an organizational structure centered in the home must be considered a particularly fortunate decision when one looks back as a historian. Christianity was at that time a movement that could not yet even dream of ever being able to participate in state and society as a shaping force. For Christians were, after all, an officially despised minority, who hoped to see the imminent end of the world. Christianity's decision to choose an organizational structure centered in the home provided that movement with a space that was exempt from external authority and especially suitable for pursuing its own development; it also made it possible for Christianity to design worship and everyday life as an integral whole and according to its own ideas, with the additional advantage of being able to utilize an established network of close personal, economic, social, and religious relationships as an already existing infrastructure. In normal, everyday situations Paul and his churches consequently show loyalty toward state authorities (Rom. 13:1–7). This is the general spirit in which Paul addresses the church. He does not speak to the magistrates, the *gerusia*, the imperial officials of the provinces, or the officer corps of the Roman army; he does not write a *speculum majestatis*. The power of the state is a foreign, non-Christian entity facing the church. Consequently, Paul does not propose programs to change society, addressing, for example, the question of slavery, social justice, the distribution of political power, or the emancipation of oppressed groups in society. We can leave aside such questions as whether the imminent expectation of the Parousia would have permitted such global, long-term perspectives at all, and whether Paul and his churches were generally in line with most of ancient society in regarding an unequal participation in rights and duties, property, liberty, and power as the natural state of affairs or as ordained by God. Paul implements the choice of the *oikos* by consistently relating Christian conduct to the space of the family, as it existed below the level of state and society. He also makes sure that the network of Christian relationships within the household gives no offense to the outside world.

The references to house churches within the area of Paul's mission allow us to draw the following overall picture. First, we have the couple Aquila and Prisc(ill)a, who were apparently expelled from Rome by the Claudian edict concerning the Jews. In Corinth Paul stayed and worked with them in their home (Acts 18:1–3), and it was presumably also in this couple's home that the first house church in Corinth was formed. Almost two years later Paul and this couple once again worked together in Ephesus, gathering a house church around them (Acts 18:18–19; 1 Cor. 16:19). It can be assumed that Apollos, coming after Paul, employed the same approach in Corinth: he concentrated on one *oikos,* which later remained particularly loyal to him (Acts 19:1; 1 Cor. 1:12; 3:4–6). The rivalries, to which Paul alludes in 1 Cor. 1–4, are, generally speaking, most likely related to missionary bases being located in private homes and to the different baptismal practices to be found in each of them. On the basis of 1 Corinthians, for example, it therefore seems necessary to assume the existence of several house churches in the city, as well as a "branch" in Cenchreae (Rom. 16:1). Apart from 1 Cor. 1–4, there is also evidence of a Corinthian house church of the *archisynagogos* Crispus (Acts 18:8 together with 1 Cor. 1:14), a house church of Stephanas (1 Cor. 1:16 and 16:15–16), and a church at the house of Gaius (Rom. 16:23 and 1 Cor. 1:14). Is it safe to assume further house churches at the home of Titius Justus (Acts 18:7) and that of Erastus (Rom. 16:23)? The list of greetings in Rom. 16 also makes mention of several house churches (vs. 5, 14, 15), which are to be located in Rome or Ephesus, depending on whether Rom. 16 is seen as part of the original letter to the Romans or as a different letter addressed to the church in Ephesus. And then, of course, we must mention the house church of Philemon in Colossae, to whom Paul writes a separate letter (Philemon).

Assuming that several house churches coexisted in larger cities like Rome, Corinth, and Ephesus, the question arises as to how these were related to one another. In the case of Corinth it is possible to discern alternate meetings in houses and gatherings of the city's church as a whole (1 Cor. 14:23). Regardless of the particular kind of architectural design of the ancient house, there usually was enough room to accommodate at least ten to twenty people. When the church grew, it was natural to split up into smaller groups, provided there were house owners. Then, when the church wanted to celebrate worship as a whole, there was perhaps an even larger room or an inner courtyard in one of the houses, as perhaps in the house of Gaius in Corinth (Rom. 16:23). From his time in Antioch, Paul was presumably already familiar with the alternation between meetings in houses and gatherings of the local church as a whole. One can imagine the following scenario: at the time of Gal. 2:11–12 Paul, Peter, and the group associated with James lived in different house churches, which had either a Jewish-Christian or Gentile-Christian orientation. After the group associated with James arrived, there was a demand for these two wings to be totally separated, so that the Jewish-Christian house churches could observe the Old Testament ritual laws. This issue is debated and decided at a general meeting (Gal. 2:14: "before them all"). Does the example of Antioch thus uncover yet another reason why several house churches could form in the same city? Was this reason perhaps Jewish-Christian versus Gentile-Christian orientation? In any case, according to 1 Cor. 1–4 it is also clear that the house churches in Corinth at least developed certain theological emphases. This opens up the general possibility that different trends could exist within the same church in a city, assuming, of course, that there was interaction between different house churches and gatherings of the church as a whole.

Being centered on the household also provided an inner structure for the churches. The house owners and hosts most likely assumed certain leading functions by default (perhaps 1 Thess. 5:12?). The family table became the place for the Lord's Supper. Since women enjoyed more independence inside the house than was granted to them in the general public sphere of the polis, they enjoyed more freedom within the Christian house churches to develop their abilities. The slaves, being property of their masters, could be respected by them in quite a different way if they were Christians. The admission of individual Christians from all classes who were not members of the family was governed by the hospitality code of the hosting house owner. Yet baptisms of entire households must not be imagined as being forced conversions or baptisms; Philemon, a Christian head of a household, still has an unconverted slave (Philemon).

These observations also provide us with the first clues about the social conditions within the churches. What, for example, was the social stratification of the churches? It is again Corinth about which we have the most concrete information, but the situation in the other Pauline city churches was presumably very similar. An evaluation of the social conditions depends fundamentally on one's judgment of social stratification in the Roman Empire in general. It is most helpful to work with a system that is roughly divided into the following three parts (Grimm, 5–17). The position at the top was occupied by the Roman class of senators and, just a little below them, the Roman class of knights. Here we find the highest level of public prestige, wealth and income, influence and power in politics, a preeminent legal status, and freedom to determine one's own life-style and education. While the class of senators was numerically extremely small, the class of knights had increased very considerably since the reign of Augustus. The knights also provided the representatives of Roman power heading the provincial governments, but in relation to the population as a whole they too were of course only a very small group. The numerically largest group was the huge mass of those without possessions who, free or slaves, earned their living by working with their hands. They were the urban and rural proletariat, the unemployed, day laborers, slaves, laborers, small-scale manual workers, and farmers. The rural population made up the majority of this class; in the post-Augustan period in general the large majority of people initially still lived in the country, did not participate in urbanization and cultural life, and existed under particularly primitive living conditions. Through support by the emperors (granting of citizens' rights and other privileges), the economic boom, and the process of urbanization a middle class developed in between the two other classes just mentioned; the rate of this development was characterized by strong fluctuations. This middle class consisted of a self-confident, urban bourgeoisie with an entrepreneurial spirit and sizable wealth. It comprised trade and land owners, small industries and finance, independent manual trades, and special professions such as teachers and physicians.

It is not surprising that initially Christianity did not gain any ground at all among Roman senators and knights. This upper class led such an exclusive, traditional Roman life-style that such early identifiable missionary successes could really not be expected. Apart from rural Palestine, missionary churches developed primarily in the cities, not least because of Paul's journeys. Urban character is a hallmark of the dispersed churches of the first generation in the Roman Empire (cf. *a* above). One can therefore assume that the members of the middle and lower classes in the cities were open to the Christian message. In the provinces the Roman class of knights was represented only to a very limited degree and in part only on a temporary basis. In addition, Rome allowed the cities to be relatively self-governing. In the cities the middle class of the empire could therefore practically consider itself the dominant upper class for that particular city and was presumably also regarded as such by the lower class.

It is clear that house churches could come into being only if families of a city's upper class converted to Christianity. If one applies the evidence just outlined to house churches in cities such as Corinth, Rome, and Antioch, it becomes clear that the Christian churches in Paul's mission field included a significant and influential number of affluent citizens (and their families) from the very beginning.

This impression is supported by another consideration: from its beginning the Pauline mission benefited from the synagogue (see Acts 13:48; 14:1; 17:4, 12; 18:4), for Paul's gospel aimed first at the Jews and then at Gentiles (Rom. 1:16; 2:9–10; 3:9, 29; 9:24). However, among diaspora

Jews, who had old Jewish family traditions, the Christian mission could presumably register only meager success. (Is Acts 18:8; 1 Cor. 1:14 perhaps an example?) It is also unlikely that former non-Jews, who through circumcision had converted to Judaism and were called proselytes, made up a large portion of the Christian missionary success, especially since they constituted presumably only a very small segment of the synagogue's total membership. This group was also much too firmly integrated into Judaism, especially since it most likely comprised a significant number of slaves and formerly non-Jewish women who were now married to Jewish husbands. The situation was different, however, in the case of the "God-fearers," that is, non-Jews who associated themselves with the synagogue but shied away from circumcision and the adoption of the entire ritual law. This group was certainly not small in number. They were impressed by Jewish monotheism, the worship of the invisible and only true God and Creator, by the ethical sincerity of the Jewish congregations, and presumably also by the age of this religion. But they did not want to give up their relationships within their non-Jewish families or their professional and social integration in the ancient polis, nor were they willing to expose themselves fully to the latent anti-Semitism of the time. Therefore, they merely associated with the synagogue. It is likely that in many cases they came from good families. The socially underprivileged and powerless (laborers, slaves, women, adopted children) were more likely to gain through a conversion that required circumcision or were forced to convert for practical reasons. A non-Jew of higher standing had to take his family and professional circumstances into consideration (Kuhn and Stegemann, pp. 1266–67). The Jews often cultivated this affiliation of non-Jews to their own advantage. Religiously, they held the view that one could participate in the worship of the Jewish God even without being circumcised (Josephus *Antiquitates* 20.41–42). At the same time the God-fearers could often be expected to make considerable donations to the synagogue. They, on the other hand, could serve as intermediaries between the Jews and the polis. In the Christian church these God-fearers now found the same monotheism, an even more radical sincerity with regard to life-style, and full acceptance without circumcision and ritual law. In this respect they could see Christianity as Judaism "freed from restrictions" (Harnack, p. 2). For them the Christian antithesis to Judaism (Christology, election of the Gentiles, imminent expectation of the Parousia) was a kind of discontinuity that fittingly built upon this continuity. For them the transition to Christianity was therefore accompanied by a relatively balanced ratio of continuity and contrast, of familiarity and strangeness. For this very reason, however, one also has to assume that there was a fierce competition over these God-fearers between the local Jews and the newly developing Christian mission church in that particular city (see Acts 18:13). The Christian churches frequently won in this competition, which led to a decrease in the membership of the synagogues. It is likely that part of the persecutions Paul suffered from the Jews arose out of this situation (see 2 Cor. 11:23–27), and it explains why he could write in an anti-Jewish tone, for example, in 1 Thess. 2:14–16. But this situation also brought a class of people into the church who for the most part could presumably be described as affluent (see Acts 18:2, 7; etc.).

Finally, in 1 Cor. 1:26–29 Paul himself provides evidence that the affluent class of the provincial cities had found their way into the churches. Given the underlying theological train of thought, Paul would really have to say here: the church consists of those who have no status at all in the world. The wise, the powerful, and people of noble birth are missing, because God has chosen the foolish, the weak, and those of low birth. This is how the text was frequently understood even up until modern times. Origen already used 1 Cor. 1 in his defense against Celsus (Contra Celsum 3.48), contradicting Celsus' thesis that early Christianity had been proletarian in character. For in this passage it is striking that the apostle concedes the presence of "not many" of those who are socially more privileged, although this admission runs counter to his theological aim. For Paul the reality of the church can therefore not be squared with his concept of election in a simple and direct fashion, because from their inception the Pauline churches comprised a representative segment of affluent people. The information about the houses and the number of former God-fearers, who at the beginning were proportionally overrepresented and, for the most part, socially privileged, permit the conclusion that in the churches the number of people from the urban, upper middle class was proportionally higher than in the general population of a city such as Corinth.

This observation serves as an argument against the simple association of Pauline Christianity in the Hellenistic cities with the urban proletariat. But we must now also state just as clearly that in absolute numbers the largest segment in a church such as Corinth was of course made up of people from the lower class. This can already be inferred from the demographic ratio of the city population. But the situation in Corinth itself also provides evidence for this fact. Recent studies (esp. Theissen, Studien, pp. 231–317) have shown how Paul dealt with tensions within the church by taking a theological position that also had an equalizing effect on a social level.

Such tensions were in part related to questions of social class. *First Clement* is in all probability another welcome confirmation of this assumption, for it provides evidence that by the end of the first century the social structure in the church in Corinth was apparently still rather analogous (*1 Clem.* 37–38). For the period of the apostle, we can find specific clues in 1 Corinthians: Paul apparently speaks of the "rich" when he condemns the lack of love during the Lord's Supper in the church; for these people begin with the general meal before the "poor," who have only limited control over their own time, are able to join. The "poor" can still participate in the Lord's Supper as a cultic meal of the church, which in Corinth was theologically highly esteemed. In the general meal, however, they receive (next to) nothing (1 Cor. 11:17–34). The dispute over eating meat that had been offered to idols (1 Cor. 8; 10:4–11:1) most likely had a social dimension too. The privileged social position of the "rich" implied naturally and as a matter of course that at their own meals they would serve meat more frequently. They also repeatedly participated in events such as social receptions where, as everywhere in antiquity, at least certain elements of Hellenistic religion played a role, especially in the case of meat and wine. The "poor" were probably never—or only as an exception—invited to such functions. Only at the few public festivals could they generally participate in a distribution of meat. Apart from such occasions their daily diet usually did not include meat. This is why they can more easily comprehend the taboo imposed on meat that had in any way come into contact with the pagan cult, even if only during slaughtering. For them it was of course also much easier to break off social contact with the non-Christian world or to act in such radical ways as to advocate separation from all "idol worshipers." This was a position that Paul in 1 Cor. 5:9–11 assumes and corrects as the view held in (part of) Corinth. If the "rich" wanted to act in this fashion, they usually had to give up their profession, for example; in any case, they had to readjust completely as far as their relation to society was concerned. It thus seems reasonable to assume that the position of the strong was mainly endorsed by the "rich." On the basis of the idea of monotheism the strong considered the gods to be nothing at all and therefore took no offense at eating meat in spite of its contact with pagan cults. On the other hand, it seems likely that the more timid view of the weak, who had scruples about participating in such festivities and meals, was to be found among the "poor."

It would of course be wrong to assume social problems as the cause of all conflicts that can be detected within the Corinthian church. It should be obvious, however, that the integration of people from all classes and ranks in society into the Christian house church, which was something quite uncommon in antiquity, could lead to problems. We must therefore ask exactly how this integration was carried out.

e) The Integrative Power of the Churches

In sections c and d we have already noted repeatedly that the missionary churches established themselves in sharp contrast to their environment and that they spent much energy regulating their internal affairs according to a brotherly love that was guided by the Spirit. The mission addressed not only selected groups that were already connected, for example, by ethnic, professional, or social ties; it addressed everyone without exception. This, together with the fact that each individual was nevertheless expected to lead a radically different life after baptism, made the task of integrating everyone in the house church especially formidable. This task was all the more crucial as it challenged every aspect of life of every Christian, for at issue was not merely a ritual and limited participation in, for example, one of several Hellenistic mystery cults. What then did new converts gain? Could the Christian church give them so much that they had the strength to make a definite break and then subsequently endure permanent conflict with their environment?

If asked this question, Paul would undoubtedly have cited participation in the gospel as the chief gain. In other words, the chief gain was a common conviction about an established set of beliefs within the young Christian community. Paul gives the churches no new temple, no statue of a god, no cultic drama. He supplies them with a message that renews the individual in his or her existence, that is, from within (2 Cor. 4:3–6). This message he calls the "gospel." It is the interpretation of what happened to Jesus Christ for the benefit of all human beings (1 Cor. 15:1–11). It is a manifestation of God's love itself (Rom. 5:8–9). This turning to all people, which has its foundation exclusively in God himself, creates the new, intimate relationship the Christian has with the Father of Jesus Christ. The gospel, which announces this fact, proves its power by turning sinners into righteous human beings, and people who are subject to judgment into those who can hope for the life to come (Rom. 5:12–21; 2 Cor. 2:15–16; etc.).

It was probably especially this hope concerning life beyond the grave that met with a positive response from those addressed. At any rate, the Pauline churches understood when the apostle wrote to them (Phil. 3:20–

21): "But our citizenship is in heaven, and it is from there that we are expecting a Savior, the Lord Jesus Christ. He will transform the body of our humiliation that it may be conformed to the body of his glory, by the power that also enables him to make all things subject to himself." Even after Paul, this conviction remains. Christianity consists, according to 1 Peter, in the fact that the believers have been given "a new birth into a living hope through the resurrection of Jesus Christ from the dead" (1 Peter 1:3). Tertullian also writes (*De resurrectione* 1): "The confident faith of Christians is the resurrection from the dead; through it we are believers." For a proper evaluation of this hope it is also important to note that this hope was represented by the imminent expectation of the Parousia, that is, the announcement that the end of the world was to come soon. All of first generation Christianity was enthusiastically oriented toward the imminent end of all things (Rom. 13:11; 16:20; 1 Cor. 7:29–31; 16:22; Phil. 4:5). For those who are convinced that the world will pass away in a short while and that even now they themselves belong to the eternal kingdom of life, it is comparatively easy to distance themselves already from the present world by breaking with the way they live their lives; they can succeed in enduring conflicts with the status quo more easily if it is for only a short time.

Also part of the gain was participation in the life of the community. Acceptance of the gospel and admission into the church cannot be separated. How closely Paul relates these two can be seen in the fact that he consistently holds that Christ in his Parousia will assume the church as a whole into the final community with him, and the individual only as a member of this church (see 1 Thess. 4:17; 5:10; 1 Cor. 15:51–52, 57). How pronounced this communal life was is attested, for example, by the expressions with which the community labeled itself and non-Christians. Both sets of expressions always consist of absolute terms; they are used without any internal differentiation. Christians are collectively called the "saints" (cf. the openings of the Pauline letters) and the "chosen" (1 Thess. 1:4; 1 Cor. 1:27). They are "loved" and "known" by God (1 Cor. 8:3; Gal. 4:9; 5:8) and therefore "called" (1 Cor. 1:9; Gal. 1:6). Among themselves Christians understand each other as "brothers" (the regular form of address in the letters) and as "children of God" (Rom. 8:16, 21; Gal. 3:26). What characterizes the self-understanding of the churches is therefore a combination of religious statements about being elected and a terminology taken from the context of the family. In contrast, "those outside" (1 Cor. 5:12–13; 1 Thess. 4:12) are characterized by terms that emphasize separation and distance. They are not only "the nations" or "the cosmos" (used frequently) but those "who do not know God" (1 Thess. 4:5; Gal. 4:8), "who have no hope" (1 Thess. 4:13), the "unbelievers" (1 Cor. 6:6 etc.), or the "unrighteous" (1 Cor. 6:1, 9). For Paul, however, these expressions with their clearly negative bias do not lead to the separation from humanity that some Corinthians sought (1 Cor. 6:9–13); rather, they apply precisely in connection with the demand to live together with non-Christians. The rule of the church not to leave the world but to prove oneself in it, is used as a chance to proclaim Christianity everywhere and to win outsiders for Christ (1 Cor. 10:32–33).

Another significant factor for the cohesion of the churches is the fact that the community chose a physical-concrete and not a spiritualistic-Gnostic orientation. Participation in the community means baptism of the whole person and the total renewal of that person; the entire old self dies and becomes a new creature (1 Cor. 6:11; 1:30; 2 Cor. 5:21). The Spirit manifests itself in different charismata; among these are some that are socially especially relevant, such as *diakonia* (Rom. 12:7), *agape* (Gal. 5:22), and the ability to cure diseases (Rom. 15:19; 1 Cor. 12:28; cf. Rom. 15:18; 2 Cor. 12:12). The church is the "body of Christ" (Rom. 12:3ff.; 1 Cor. 12:4ff.), in which the members are related to each other through their various gifts. The Lord's Supper still combines a meal for nourishment with a cultic meal. The uncaring behavior shown at this ceremony led, according to Paul, to specific illnesses within the church (1 Cor. 11:20–34). The baptismal paraenesis in Rom. 6:12–13 states: "Do not let sin exercise dominion in your mortal bodies. . . . No longer present your members to sin as instruments of wickedness, but present yourselves to God as those who have been brought from death to life, and present your members to God as instruments of righteousness." And at the beginning of the paraenesis in Rom. 12:1–2 Paul writes: "Present your bodies as a living sacrifice, holy and acceptable to God."

It was then also especially important for the community that it was characterized by equality. This was particularly significant because those addressed by the gospel came from the most diverse circles and social levels. Equality is an especially prominent element in the pre-Pauline baptismal tradition, which Paul uses in Gal. 3:26–28. The context of this tradition is a group of statements that understand redemption as a spiritual and eschatological new creation, which is presently already in effect "in Christ," and that means in the church (see 1 Cor. 7:19; 12:13–14; 2 Cor. 5:17; Gal. 5:5–6; 6:15; see also Col. 3:9–14). The text reads: "For in Christ Jesus you are all children of God. . . . As many of you as were baptized into Christ have clothed yourselves with Christ. There is no longer Jew or Greek, there is no longer slave or free, there is no longer male or female; for all of you are one in Christ Jesus."

In the context of this passage one thing becomes clear: if one understands baptism, through either the metaphor of a new creation (2 Cor. 5:17; Gal. 6:15) or the image of a new garment, as becoming a new person in Christ (Gal. 3:27)—which is seen as a result of the renewing Spirit, as it is given in baptism (1 Cor. 12:13; Gal. 5:5)—then one takes up that prophetic tradition which promises a constitutional, creative change of the human inner being in the last days (Jer. 24:7; 31:33–34; Ezek. 36:26–27; Joel 2:26–27; 3:1–2). The "old" in the form of the differentiations into Jew and Greek, slave and free, male and female is no longer a basis for salvific status or special rank or depreciation within the church. Whoever has undergone baptism and is endowed with the same Spirit is equal "in Christ." This is true not only spiritually before God but also in the concrete life of the church. All have a share in the charismata (1 Cor. 12–14), can thus speak during worship, and have a place of equal rank with everybody else at the Lord's Supper. Nobody can claim privilege on the basis of position (e.g., a Jewish Christian wanting to observe the Mosaic law, see Gal. 2:11–21), nor can anyone be discriminated against (e.g., in worship a woman may take the role of prophet; see 1 Cor. 11:4–5). But even beyond the worship service, much within the Christian household has now become new. Within a Christian marriage both partners, through a mutual focus on the other partner's welfare, are now placed under the obligation to love one another (1 Cor. 7:3–4 etc.). The relationship between master and slave is changing too, provided both of them are Christians (Philemon). Within the existing structures of the time, baptism and Spirit thus create a new fundamental equality for all, both in worship and in daily family life.

Closely related to the aspect of equality is Paul's central concern for the unity of the church. Groups that rival one another are a danger for the church. They are not a sign of vitality but an indication that the unity is threatened (1 Cor. 1–4). Christians must "together . . . with one voice glorify the God and Father of our Lord Jesus Christ" (Rom. 15:6). This requires making concessions in dietary customs, which are not relevant for salvation, for the sake of the weak brother (Rom. 14:1ff., esp. v. 17). In worship members cannot exercise their charisma whenever they want. They must focus on the "upbuilding" of the church (on this point, see Rom. 14:19; 15:2; 1 Cor. 8:1); their utterance must be comprehensible to all and must fit into the order of service (1 Cor. 14). Of primary importance are peace (Rom. 15:33) and unity of mind (1 Cor. 1:10).

It was also crucial in the Pauline churches that the Spirit, which some-times overflowed as in Corinth, not be permitted to claim the heaven of ecstasy as its natural habitat but instead demonstrate its power within the social structure as its assigned place. The Spirit induces brotherly love (1 Thess. 4:8–10). Christian liberty is taken as an opportunity to learn to serve one another in love (Gal. 5:13–15). Such love is the fulfillment of the commandments contained in the so-called second table of the Decalogue (Rom. 13:8–10). Love means accepting the "weak"; its standard in this respect is Christ as the archetype and example (Rom. 15:7ff.; Phil. 2:1–11). When compared to all other charismata, love is the "more excellent way" (1 Cor. 13). Being oriented toward love, the life of the churches thus seeks to promote integration. This understanding of love was not accompa-nied by a lax attitude toward norms; rather, the church had clear duties, which all were required to obey and which presented a radical challenge to those who had been baptized. Holiness and sanctification belonged to-gether (see Rom. 6:19; 15:16; 1 Cor. 3:16–17; 6:11; 1 Thess. 4:3–4, 7). Especially visible was the negative morality of dissociation from non-Christians: Christians no longer had anything to do with idolatry and pagan depravity (Rom. 13:11–14; 1 Cor. 6:9–11; Gal. 5:16–24; 1 Thess. 5:4–10). But there was no legal or catechetical norm; rather, it was ex-pected that all would, without external control, honestly put the new life into practice and would also examine on their own what was the will of God (Rom. 12:1–2; Phil. 4:8). Yet this did not lead into an arbitrary sub-jectivism, for the new creation had its origin in the Spirit, who could not speak with two voices. That is why virtues and vices could be clearly identi-fied, and why, in extreme cases, members could, as an *ultima ratio,* be ban-ished from the church (1 Cor. 5:1–5). The integration of the church was thus also promoted by a morality that challenged each Christian in the same way.

Integration takes place and is accepted if personal responsibility and the ability to compromise are allowed to come into play. Presumably in no other literature or church (group) of early Christianity was the personal responsi-bility of the individual members so clearly and consistently emphasized as in Paul's letters and in his churches. Paul would rather accept the turmoil in Corinth than to restrict freedom in a legalistic way. Even in the case of such a young church as Thessalonica, he does not make allowances for the lack of experience with the Christian life-style. For after his sudden departure he writes to them that they need no exhortation concerning brotherly love (1 Thess. 4:9–10). He continues to advocate freedom, even though the Corinthians made this task rather difficult for him (1 Cor. 3:21–22; 6:12; 10:23–24). In spite of his experience in Corinth he holds fast to this line, for example, in his letter to the Philippians (4:8). Paul can also suggest compromises wherever he finds them acceptable in some way. In his view, disputes over property are un-Christian, because Christians will suffer injustice themselves rather than inflict it on others. As a last resort, a wise person in the church, rather than a pagan court, should settle disputes (1 Cor. 6:1ff.). In view of the turmoil of the end time all Christians should actually remain celibate like Paul, but most of them are not endowed with this particular charisma; therefore the apostle can suggest a whole list of flexible solutions for entering into marriage, marriage itself, as well as for divorce (1 Cor. 7). With regard to eating meat offered to idols, Paul also rejects a radical solution and, after looking at different situations, outlines various modes of behavior (1 Cor. 8; 10:14ff.). For problems related to worship he attempts to find a solution by distinguishing between the private sphere and gatherings of the congregation (1 Cor. 11:21–22; 14:18–19).

Finally, the pressure of suffering from the outside, to which the churches were exposed against their will and which they withstood together, presumably also promoted the internal unifying process (on this aspect, see also g below). What the young church in Thessalonica experienced in this regard right at the beginning of its existence, for example, was presumably not altogether atypical (1 Thess. 1:6; 2:2, 14). This is why one probably cannot deny that a general exhortation such as that in Rom. 12:12–19 had this kind of concrete background, which was all too familiar to the church, when it says there: "Be patient in suffering. . . . Bless those who persecute you; bless and do not curse them. . . . Do not repay anyone evil for evil. . . . If it is possible . . . live peaceably with all. . . . Never avenge yourselves." The principle that served as a rule for the church was the memorable phrase from 1 Cor. 12:26: "If one member [of Christ's body] suffers, all suffer together with it."

f) Ways of Easing Specific Tensions Within the Churches

These general observations on integration in the previous section would remain incomplete if they were not complemented by a description of the concrete ways in which tensions within the churches were reduced and existing differences mitigated. According to the baptismal tradition in Gal.

3:26–28 already cited above, the churches included primarily the opposites of Jew and Greek, slave and free, male and female. An additional opposition is that between rich and poor, which has already been discussed in section *d* above.

The fact of Christians coming from either Judaism or the non-Jewish world led to a variety of problems in early Christianity. Paul's first contact with Christianity was his encounter with Jewish Christians in the synagogue in Damascus. As a missionary in Antioch he lived in a church that before long comprised a Gentile-Christian group as its dominant segment, which succeeded in having the entire church live in a Gentile-Christian way until Peter and the supporters of James insisted on a separation. Once Paul had left Antioch, he established new churches only on a Gentile-Christian basis. His Jewish-Christian coworkers also agreed with him on this point. Yet his missionary work often started at the synagogue. The extent to which this approach helped to convert not only God-fearers but also Jews to Christianity certainly differed from city to city. In this regard the situation in Rome was probably comparable to that in Antioch. As Jewish Christians, Aquila and Prisc(ill)a, together with other Jewish-Christian believers, were evicted from Rome by the edict of Claudius (Acts 18:1–2). The Gentile-Christian segment of the church was apparently not affected. This means that a church that had grown out of the synagogue now became a Gentile-Christian church. The Jewish Christians who returned under Nero found the situation changed. It is clear that Paul addresses the church as a Gentile-Christian church when in Rom. 9–11, for example, he speaks to Gentile Christians (11:17) about Israel. The reading of Rom. 14–15 that interprets the conflict between the strong and the weak as a conflict between Gentile and Jewish Christians would then indeed show how Paul pushed for a solution to the conflict. However, such an easy solution is not convincing for the simple reason that Aquila and Prisc(ill)a, who by that time were presumably back in Rome again (Rom. 16:3), were certainly of Pauline persuasion. In addition, the text itself does not provide any direct clue to support such an interpretation. At the time when Paul wrote his letter to the Romans, apparently no specific problem existed between Jewish and Gentile Christians in that church.

The situation in the churches of Thessalonica and Corinth was similar. Since the missionary preaching in 1 Thess. 1:9–10 is addressed to Gentiles, and since Paul reminds the Thessalonians of this message, it can be assumed that the church consisted (primarily) of Gentile Christians. This church had no Jewish-Christian problem. In Corinth Paul began his mission at the synagogue, according to Acts 18. When it came to a clash, Paul stayed with the God-fearing Titius Justus. And Crispus, the overseer of the synagogue, also became a Christian. The Jewish Christians Aquila and Prisc(ill)a, whom Paul met in Corinth for the first time, had no disagreement with him about the Gentile-Christian orientation of his mission. The Alexandrian Jew Apollos, who worked in Corinth after Paul (1 Cor. 3:6), also had no Jewish-Christian reservations vis-à-vis Paul. At least the overwhelming majority of the church was Gentile Christian. It can be assumed that in this respect Paul regarded Thessalonica and Corinth as model cases for the kind of solution he had already endorsed and practiced in Antioch, namely, that the churches were to live in a Gentile-Christian way. Since the priority of Judaism is abolished in Christ (Gal. 2:14–16), Jewish Christians were to follow Paul's example and live out a Gentile-Christian understanding of election and the law.

In Philippi and Galatia the problems were different. The churches in Galatia consisted of Gentile Christians (Gal. 4:8–9) or more precisely of Hellenized Celts (3:1). Judaists who traveled in Paul's wake and insisted on circumcision (6:12–13) sought to turn the church around. In Philippi we also find a Gentile-Christian church (cf. the names in Phil. 2:25ff.; 4:2–3, 18) that was infiltrated by Judaists, who then tried to force it to accept circumcision (Phil. 3:3). In both cases Paul's reaction is firm and without compromise. He considers the Judaists to have betrayed the gospel and the freedom it entails (Gal. 2:4–5), and they have broken the agreement reached at the Apostolic Council (Gal. 2). He can therefore only urgently recommend to his churches that they dissociate themselves from these missionaries. Thus we can conclude that, apart from external influences through rival missionary activities, the Pauline churches solved the problem of the relationship between Jewish and Gentile Christians on a Gentile-Christian basis. The prime example of this solution is Paul himself. When faced with rival influences, he insists without compromise on this very solution and on a separation from the opponents.

Paul's fight against the Judaists must be kept separate from the cultivation of his relationship with the Jewish-Christian mother church in Jerusalem. Paul consciously cultivated this relationship through the collection that he had his churches gather over several years (Gal. 2:10; 1 Cor. 16:1–3; 2 Cor. 8; 9; Rom. 15:26–28; also Acts 11:29–30; 12:25; 24:17). Gal. 2:10a reports that upon request of the authorities in Jerusalem, Barnabas and Paul made an additional, voluntary pledge on behalf of the church in Antioch to support financially the needy members of the church in Jerusa-

lem, the earliest Christian congregation, over and beyond the actual agreement reached at the Apostolic Council (cf. Rom. 15:26). After leaving
Antioch, Paul voluntarily and on his own initiative continued in his newly
established churches with this assistance to the church in Jerusalem (Gal.
2:10b). As a reason for this collection Paul only mentions the poverty in
parts of that earliest Christian church (Rom. 15:26). Luke stylizes and
idealizes the situation in Jerusalem to fit a Hellenistic ideal of community
property (Acts 2:42–47; 4:32–37; etc.). We must therefore rely on assumptions (famine under Claudius: see Acts 11:27–30; imminent expectation of
the Parousia with the result of giving up regular work: see 1 Thess. 4:11; 2
Thess. 3:7–12). Paul does not inquire about causes but instead seizes the
chance to use this situation as a means of joining his Gentile-Christian
churches (as a unified block) with the earliest Christian church by promoting a sense of being one single church. It must be noted that although Paul
advocates the collection on his own initiative after leaving Antioch, he
does not make it mandatory for the churches to participate; rather, he accepts it only as a voluntary gift (2 Cor. 8:3, 8), which the churches themselves decide to give upon his recommendation (2 Cor. 8:4; Rom. 15:2–3).
The gift is based neither on a right Jerusalem might have (a possible analogy: the Jewish temple tax) nor on an obligation imposed on Paul at the
Apostolic Council, which would be binding for his post-Antiochene period. Rather, even the members of the church in Jerusalem consider it an
act of love to which they have no claim. It is a one-time undertaking (does
Gal. 2:10a suggest that it was more permanent for the church in Antioch?),
which seeks to remedy the "needs of the saints" (2 Cor. 9:12) to the glory
of God (2 Cor. 8:19; 9:12–13). These observations indicate that the
deeper meaning of this collection is characterized by the concepts of
diakonia and *koinonia* (Rom. 15:25, 31; 2 Cor. 8:4; 9:1, 12–13). This
means that the Gentile-Christian churches have become participants in
the gospel through Jewish Christianity, represented by Jerusalem. Through
this financial assistance they now repay their common debt of gratitude
(Rom. 15:27). The unity among themselves is proof of their solidarity with
Jewish Christianity. Paul thus promotes the sense of unity of the church in
an age in which missionary expansion posed the danger of fragmentation.
This was especially important since operational structures beyond the local
level were still confined to delegations of envoys (on the circle of coworkers, see *a* above) and the hospitality they enjoyed with a local congregation
(Rom. 12:13).

The collection was of such importance to Paul that even in the face of the dangers in Jerusalem that delivery by the apostle entailed, he vigorously pressed on with it and wanted to be personally present when it was handed over to the church there (Rom. 15:31). These dangers consisted in part of the Jewish hostility towards him and to that extent proved to be real (Acts 21:10ff.). But they originated in part also in the Jerusalem church itself: Paul fears it might reject the Gentile-Christian gift, the symbol of community. We can only speculate about the cause of this sentiment. Two interpretations are possible. First, the Jerusalem church might accept fellowship with the Gentile Christians but no longer be able to accept the gift because of the political and religious situation in Judea. For the prevalent mood, which was characterized by nationalism and zealotism, called for separation from everything Gentile (cf. Josephus *Bellum* 2.408–9). A second possibility is that since the Apostolic Council the Judaist potential had significantly increased within the Jerusalem church itself (Gal. 2:4; cf. Acts 15:1, 5). The Judaist opponents, who visited the Pauline churches in Galatia and Philippi, had since gained a much stronger position in Jerusalem. Paul still hoped that upon his arrival the moderate faction of the mother church would prevail and once again push back the radical forces, as it had at the time of the Apostolic Council. Both of these interpretations might also be combined. However one decides in this regard, one thing is certain: the idea of community was of such importance for Paul that he did not shy away from the danger.

The second contrast mentioned in Gal. 3:26–28, namely, that between being a slave and being free, did not lead to any serious problems in the Pauline churches. Slavery was generally an unquestioned institution. A Christian head of a household, such as Philemon, could own slaves without drawing any criticism from the church or from Paul (Philemon). He was presumably not an exception, for the apostle neither requires of him, as a head of a household who is also a Christian, to set his slaves free, nor suggests anything to him that would infringe on his rights as a slave owner. On the contrary, Paul's wishes remain strictly confined to the individual case of Onesimus, a runaway slave. They are personal requests, which the slave owner is asked to fulfill voluntarily and within the framework of his lawful position, but which he may also turn down. In the latter, unexpected case this would likely cause a personal disappointment on Paul's part, but it would in no way discredit Philemon as a Christian slave owner (see Pliny *Epistulae* 9.21, 24). The slave who ran away as a non-Christian is returned to his owner, in spite of the fact that in the meantime he has become a Christian; in addition, Paul vouches for any losses that may have resulted.

Paul also does not ask for him to be set free (manumission) from being a slave (*status servitutis*) but merely that his master grant him a temporary leave in order to serve Paul. He leaves it up to Philemon whether to grant Onesimus a leave at all for this purpose and also to choose the legal form (release or temporary loan), should he indeed decide to do so. The Letter to Philemon is a classic case, which shows how, within the existing legal framework and without seeking to change or even abolish it, one could to some extent on a private level alleviate the harsh conditions between slave owner and slave (as an analogy, see Pliny *Epistulae* 8.16): the Christian slave would from then on carry out his or her tasks in a particularly conscientious manner (Philemon 11); the Christian slave owner would, in turn, regard him or her as a "beloved brother" (v. 16) or sister.

The Letter to Philemon was written because of a special case: a non-Christian slave runs away—be it to escape slavery or to seek protection from punishment—from a Christian head of household with whom the apostle is well acquainted; this slave then meets the imprisoned apostle, who converts him to Christianity. Something like this does not happen every day. It is much more difficult to gain a picture of the average situation of slaves in the Pauline churches. There are only three texts that speak of slavery (1 Cor. 7:21–22; 12:13–14; Gal. 3:26–28). They all mention it only in passing in the context of other topics. This shows that on this issue the churches had an established solution that was generally followed. Apart from that, it is difficult to assess how large a segment of the churches consisted of slaves. They were certainly not proportionally overrepresented. It is possible that the non-Christian houses in Rom. 16:10–11 and Phil. 4:22 comprised slaves. Chloe (1 Cor. 1:11) might also have been a non-Christian woman whose household included Christian slaves. In Philemon we have at least one definite case of a Christian slave owner. To complete this list, we could add the household of Lydia mentioned in Acts 16:14 and that of the prison warden referred to in Acts 16:31ff. This is a small and unreliable yield. Reviewing typical names of slaves does not help us much either. In this respect, one might point to the names of Ampliatus (Rom. 16:8), Eutychus (Acts 20:9), Fortunatus (1 Cor. 16:17), Hermas (Rom. 16:14), Persis (Rom. 16:12), Stachys (Rom. 16:9), Syntyche (Phil. 4:2), Tertius (Rom. 16:22), Tychicus (Acts 20:4), and Urbanus (Rom. 16:9); it is likely that several of these were slaves. But these names were also used during the imperial period for people who were free. And slaves who had been set free usually kept the names they had as slaves. Thus the result remains vague, especially since it was not really unusual for slaves to be set free. Texts such as Gal. 3:26–28 testify to the fact that slaves were integrated into the churches as a matter of course, but it seems that slaves were rather weakly represented. The difference between rich and poor apparently posed a comparatively more serious problem for the social life of the churches, especially since many slaves were better off than, for example, day laborers, small-scale manual workers, and impoverished peasants.

Decisive for the integration of the slaves into the church were such general theological premises as that Christ himself had taken on "the form of a slave" to secure our redemption (Phil. 2:7), that the form of his death, crucifixion, was the chosen punishment for slaves and those without rights, and that as one who willingly had become poor he made the believers rich (2 Cor. 8:9). To be a "slave of Jesus Christ" became a title of honor for the apostle, for example (Rom. 1:1; Gal. 1:10; Phil. 1:1). Given this background, Paul can say in his dialectical style that a slave is one set free in Christ, and a free person is a slave of Christ (1 Cor. 7:22).

Because of statements such as these, the Christian church, within its domestic boundaries, did not deny slaves access to worship. Nor were baptized slaves denied equal rank within the church; they were also members of the body of Christ, gifted with charismata, and they participated in the Lord's Supper just as their master did. He could no longer regard them as objects but had to respect them in principle as persons, as brothers and sisters. This also had great significance for everyday life, for it meant being treated accordingly by their master. Slaves, in turn, were bound not to use the Christian faith as a basis for promoting the release of slaves as a sociopolitical agenda. Like all others, they were basically to remain in the state in which they were called (1 Cor. 7:17, 21a, 23–24), and like all other Christians, in their secular activities they were to give their best in living up to an especially high standard (Philemon 11). Does the abbreviated phrase in 1 Cor. 7:21b perhaps intend to say that if slaves are offered their release, they should seize the opportunity? If this is indeed the case, then this would still represent the exception, not the goal one should generally strive for. A parallel in the formal sense is the idea that as a rule a Christian wife should not leave her non-Christian husband, but if he demands a divorce, she is not to blame for it (1 Cor. 7:12–16). However, the context suggests another, more convincing interpretation of 1 Cor. 7:21b, namely, that slaves who have the chance to gain their freedom should nevertheless remain in their current state (Laub, pp. 64–65). According to this reading, Paul was perhaps mindful of the fact that Christian slaves were frequently much worse off after their release from a non-Christian household than they were before under their master, and that in such cases they then sought to be cared for by the church (as an analogy, see 1 Thess. 4:11; 1 Cor. 9:18). Besides, within a Christian household the relationship between master and slave was in Paul's view no longer a problem (Philemon). In his remarks it is Paul's sole concern that the gospel—through which one had become a new creation and which proclaimed the world to be a thing of the past and its end to be near (1 Cor. 7:23a, 29–31)—not be misunderstood through a way of thinking that belonged to the old creation (7:23b; cf. 7:33); this would mean to take seriously what could no longer be of importance. Modern thinking is inclined to revolt against this very point on humanitarian grounds. Historically, however, one has to say that Paul in no way spared either himself or his churches from suffering.

When making an overall assessment of this internal solution to the question of slavery, certain facts should be taken into account for the sake of comparison. On the contemporary scene only the *therapeutae*, who lived in seclusion, had actually abolished slavery among themselves (Philo *De vita contemplativa* 70ff.), while the Hellenistic mystery religions (such as the Eleusinian mysteries), which are usually so highly praised in this regard, did admit slaves to the rites but failed to translate this at all into the social sphere. The mystery religions admitted only individuals in isolation from the community of their respective households and only addressed the religious needs of the individual. They were therefore fundamentally disinclined to restructure the social life of a household, for example, or to become socially and politically active within the polis. The frequently cited Essenes presumably cannot be used as an example. It is likely that the monastically inclined Qumran community lived without slaves too (Josephus *Antiquitates* 18.21; Philo *Apologia* 4), but it nevertheless handed down and accepted the family-oriented Damascus scroll as a document that was closely akin to its own theological position. The rules contained in this text treat questions of slavery (CD 11.2; 12.6, 10ff.) as a subject for normal legislation. The solution adopted by the Pauline churches can certainly claim a respectable status when seen against this background.

The third and final pair of opposites mentioned in Gal. 3:26–28 is the difference in gender between male and female. In order to understand how the two sexes are related to one another within the church, it is important to take a look first at the general social and cultural situation of that period. The Roman-Hellenistic world was structured patriarchally. This is especially true for public life as a whole, particularly in politics and the judicial system. In the cities, and here again especially within the more privileged circles, women had, with various degrees of success in different regions, created and seized opportunities for shaping their own fate and taking on responsibility. This process took place since the beginning of the Hellenistic era and noticeably since about the time of Augustus. Particularly suited in this respect were such areas as domestic affairs, culture, religion, and economics, that is, areas in which the state had always granted more freedom for a citizen's self-development (see Schneider, 1:78ff.). However, the sources we have will perhaps never allow us to draw a complete picture that is both accurate and sufficiently detailed. It is necessary to stay away from generalizations, and one should certainly avoid the mistake of extrapolating from the conditions at court, which can be identified relatively accurately, to the everyday life of women in the middle and lower classes. The historical search for emancipatory approaches and their at least partial realization does prove successful here and there. However, one should also consider that the unquestioned and unquestionable view at the time was that men are born to rule, and women to obey. Aristotle (*Politeia* 1.1254b) and Seneca (*De constantina sapientis* 1.1) are two witnesses on either end of a long chain of authors holding this view, and the position of these two certainly cannot otherwise be considered hostile to women. Hellenistic Judaism was no exception in this respect. Quite to the contrary, it seems that here the legal and religious subordination of women was particularly evident (Gerstenberger and Schrage, pp. 106–9). Erotic literature saw a notable revival during this period; this was coupled, however, with a renewed misogynistic view of women. Judaism made its contribution in this respect by often blaming the fall primarily on Eve (Sir. 25:24), for example, or by detecting a constitutional tendency towards fornication in women ('*Abot* 2.7; *T. 12 Patr.* passim); pagan women were depicted as trying to seduce the pious Jew with their eroticism, albeit without success (*T. Jos.; Joseph and Aseneth*).

It seems that the subject of male and female generally did not give rise to serious problems within the Pauline churches, which were centered on the household; Corinth was an exception in this regard. Life in the churches was apparently governed by the following, nearly universal consensus: the missionary message—that is, the gospel—addresses all people in the same way. All human beings—that is, all men and women without distinction—stand under the divine wrath (1 Thess. 1:9; Rom. 3:20). The state of unrighteousness, in which all human beings find themselves, is not demonstrated by Eve but by Adam, as the one who defines all of humanity except for Christ (Rom. 5:12ff.; 1 Cor. 15:21–22, 45–49). Male and female are thus equally in need of the gospel, of baptism, and of being created anew. They both receive the Spirit without distinction and are endowed with charismata in the church (Rom. 12:3ff.; 1 Cor. 11:5; 12–14). Nowhere is there even a hint of a gender-specific hierarchy with respect to charismata. It is therefore not surprising that of those mentioned by name in Paul's letters the majority are men, but that women make up an integral part of that list, even and especially in leading positions (Dautzenberg et al., pp. 182ff.). Such a degree of participation is certainly noteworthy when compared to the synagogue and probably also in comparison with the Hellenistic world in general; yet it was presumably typical for the earliest period of Christianity in general. It is likely that in Rom. 16:7 a woman is even awarded the title of apostle. Precisely this general context—that all human beings are equal when it comes to their need for redemption and their participation in the gifts of the Spirit—is implied in the old baptismal tradition in Gal. 3:26–28. It describes unity in Christ—that is, equality before God and within a particular house church, the body of Christ—by saying that, like other differences, the difference between "male and female" (see Gen. 1:27) has lost its significance through baptism.

Of course, Paul and his churches continue to accept the difference between male and female intended by the Creator. This differentiation is not understood as alienation from a formerly androgynous human being, nor is it assumed that the eschatological redemption will lead to the kind of unity that later was chiefly advocated by the Gnostics (*Gos. Thom.* 22). The marital relationship is intended by the Creator (1 Thess. 4:4–5; 1 Cor. 7). With respect to the end of all things it is true that "flesh and blood cannot inherit the kingdom of God" but must be "changed" (1 Cor. 15:50–55). Yet there is no indication that in his depiction of final salvation Paul describes anything other than the relationship of the individual Christians with the Lord (1 Thess. 4:17; 5:10; etc.). The abolition of sexuality is not even an issue for him, even though he considers marriage to be a part of the first creation and the present aeon (1 Cor. 7:25ff.).

One must exercise caution with the suggestion that since Christianity felt a particular responsibility for the weak, it had a strong reason to pay special attention to women, who, among others, were generally considered weak. Christ is certainly the paradigm of all weakness (2 Cor. 13:4), and divine election is understood as the acceptance especially of the weak (1 Cor. 1:18–31). This does indeed lead the church to accept the weak (1 Cor. 8; Rom. 14–15). But these contexts never deal with the weak woman as such. Weakness is not understood to be gender specific. We do not find any such negative characterization of women; instead, they are accepted within the concrete life of the church.

It comes as no surprise that within a patriarchal society statements and practices that depreciate women were still alive in spite of all the efforts to place equal value on the sexes. The typical paraenesis in 1 Thess. 4:3–6 was quite naturally written from a male perspective; the woman is "his vessel." It is the man who is in charge of arranging a marriage; he makes the main decisions and carries the primary responsibility (1 Cor. 7:36–38). The Corinthian slogan that "it is well for a man not to touch a woman" (1 Cor. 7:1) was also formulated from a male perspective. The wearing of a veil, as sign of a woman's lower rank, was standard practice in the churches (1 Cor. 11:16). Paul retains the custom even when faced with a Corinthian dispute over this question (1 Cor. 11:1–16). Unlike the Synoptics, Paul is not aware in 1 Cor. 15:1–11 of any women among the Easter witnesses. It is obvious that with respect to this issue of equality between the sexes, Paul once again does not tackle the legal and public side of the problem. Equality is implemented on a personal, voluntary basis within the church and within Christian marriages. The conventional language and culture also remain practically unchanged. Yet the instruction for women in 1 Cor. 14:34–35 to keep silent during worship must be considered a later addition to Paul's letter; it is untypical for the churches during the time of the apostle. These verses disrupt the flow of the text, as is commonly recognized, on grounds of textual criticism, syntax, and content. They contradict the fact, mentioned in 1 Cor. 11:5, that women spoke in worship as a matter of course. And those women who, like Phoebe and Mary (Rom. 16:1, 6), held positions of leadership in the church could certainly not carry out this task in silence. This passage is rather an indication of a new understanding of church life in the third generation of early Christianity, and of the attitude toward women that finds expression in 1 Tim. 2:8–15. When 1 Cor. 14 was no longer understood as speaking to a particular situation but instead became a binding rule for every corporate worship service, 1 Cor. 14:34–35 was inserted in order to establish a Jewish-Christian tradition as the lasting (but anti-Pauline) norm.

Typical for earliest Christianity, however, was the uncompromising decision in favor of strict monogamy, which was even noticed by Pliny (*Epistulae* 10.96) in the context of interrogating Christians. The Old Testament and Jewish legacy is obvious from the fact that visiting a hierodule, hetaera, or prostitute is identified as fornication and strictly forbidden (e.g., 1 Cor. 6:12–20), a son is not allowed to marry his widowed stepmother (1 Cor.

5:1), and, contrary to Greek custom, homosexuality is considered something totally reprehensible (Rom. 1:26–27; 1 Cor. 6:9). The Jesus tradition
rules out the possibility of a man having several wives (1 Cor. 7:10; 1
Thess. 4:4–5). A divorce is conceivable only in special cases (1 Cor. 7:12–
16), and divorcees are not permitted to remarry. Only when one partner
dies is it possible for the surviving partner to marry again, although such
persons are encouraged to stay widowed (1 Cor. 7:39–40; Rom. 7:2–3).
Sexual love is considered a normal practice within a monogamous marital
relationship. Within that framework there is nothing sinful about sexuality;
rather, it is considered an aspect of the creation God called good (1 Thess.
4:4–5; 1 Cor. 7:2, 5, 38–39). For a man these regulations within the Pauline churches all implied a reduction of his former rights; for a woman they
meant an elevation of her status. In Paul's view, this was not an accidental
by-product but an intended result. For throughout his entire argument in 1
Cor. 7 he takes great care to base Christian marriage on mutuality and to
affirm without exception the equality of husband and wife as Christian
partners. In doing so he consistently links one partner's conduct to the will
of the other (1 Cor. 7:3–5). This is the same pattern he also uses in other
cases (see 1 Cor. 8; Rom. 14–15). Where in antiquity do we find any parallels of people being placed under such a mutual obligation? The obvious
suggestion is to understand this internal restructuring of the marital relationship as a reflection of the church's experience that the charismata were
given to men and women without distinction. Christian worship and everyday life within a Christian marriage are not separated in a dualistic way.
They are related to each other (Rom. 12:1–2).

In Corinth Paul apparently also espoused this view. But here, presumably for the first time in earliest Christianity, a dispute arises over the question whether a general sexual asceticism with the resultant dissolution of
existing marriages, rather than the traditional monogamous marriage,
ought to be the norm for the church as a whole (1 Cor. 7). It is not necessary immediately to assume that this controversy arose out of a Gnostic
contempt for the body, which could express itself in the extremes of a
libertarian sexual conduct (1 Cor. 6:12ff.) or a sexual asceticism (1 Cor.
7:1) because, for his visit to a hetaira, for example, a Greek did not need
Gnostic theory. For him this was a cultural habit that as a Christian he now
had to renounce. Paul's argument is not directed against a dualistic anthro-
pology that dismisses the body; Paul argues rather from the fact that the
body is a part of creation, which makes it impossible for it to be simultaneously in a relationship with a prostitute and with Christ. In support of

the view that 1 Cor. 7 describes a behavior closely related to Gnosticism, it has often been argued recently that the ascetic slogan in 7:1, "It is well for a man not to touch a woman," was based on a specific understanding of the old baptismal tradition in Gal. 3:26–28 (Thyen). According to this understanding, the old creaturely division into male and female is abolished "in Christ," that is, in the church. For in concert with the myth of an androgynous human being, the new creation is thought to include neither male nor female. But this is neither the meaning implied in Gal. 3:26–28 (see above), nor could it have been the opinion held in Corinth. For otherwise Paul could not have written in such a straightforward fashion to the Corinthians, without being misunderstood, that "those who have wives" should "be as though they had none" (7:29); what he had in mind here was certainly not a sexual asceticism (see vs. 3–5, 29–31). In addition, in 7:18–19 he can state as an undisputed fact that in Christ neither circumcision nor uncircumcision is of any avail (cf. Gal. 5:2–6), thus rendering superfluous an operation to reverse circumcision. If the underlying Corinthian premise had been valid, then this very operation would necessarily have made sense.

But constructs of the kind just described are unnecessary since the text itself answers the question of how 7:1 was understood by the Corinthians and by Paul. An examination of the train of thought in 1 Cor. 7 reveals three parts. (1) In 7:1–7 Paul argues on a fundamental level by pointing out both the legitimacy of the Corinthian premise and the error it contains. The Corinthians understand the ascetic principle as a law that is binding for the church. Paul holds the unmarried state in similarly high esteem but regards it as a gift of God's Spirit that is not at our disposal (as in his own case). Only those who have this charisma should remain unmarried. Those who do not ought to marry, for the marital relationship is a divine institution (cf. 1 Cor. 6:16), and a forced asceticism easily leads to fornication. This second category apparently includes most people (for 7:8ff. has a lot to say about marriage; see also what in 1 Thess. 4:4–5 is considered the normal case). (2) In 7:8–24 Paul corrects the results of the Corinthian view with the same rule he generally applies, namely, that each person ought to remain in the state in which he or she was called. For from 7:1 the Corinthians had to draw the conclusion that all marriages should be dissolved. Paul challenges this view. He will only admit that a Christian partner is no longer bound by existing marriage vows if, and only if, the non-Christian partner requests a separation. (3) In a third part (7:25–40) Paul once again takes up his thesis from 7:1–7 that staying unmarried is preferable, although getting married is not a sin. He argues in favor of this thesis by considering the nearness of the end of all things and the tribulation this entails. Faced with this future, unmarried Christians are better able to devote themselves completely to the Lord. For married Christians, besides their focus on the Lord, have the additional concern for their partner. As far as the underlying eschatological expectation is concerned, the apostle is apparently in agreement with the Corinthians (1 Cor. 1:7; 15; 16:22). Yet while this common belief leads the Corinthians to the conclusion that a legalistically understood asceticism is practically an inevitable necessity, Paul supports a graduated and nonlegalistic solution, knowing quite well that most members of the church, including Peter and the other apostles (1 Cor. 9:5), are married, and that only a very few, such as himself and Barnabas (1 Cor. 9:6), are endowed with the charisma of celibacy. As so often (see, e.g., 1 Cor. 6:1ff.; 11:17ff.; 14), Paul advocates a "middle-of-the-road" solution for the life of the church and is opposed to radical demands. But in 7:25ff. the apostle has to demonstrate that the eschatological expectation he shares with the Corinthians (see 1:8) does not conflict with his moderate solution. It therefore seems likely that the Christians in Corinth, who according to 7:1 advocated a legalistic form of asceticism, also justified their position on eschatological grounds. Is it not, after all, also more consistent to hold the position that since the end is near, one should focus totally on the coming Lord, instead of serving the world—in the form of a spouse, for example? Paul concedes this indirectly (7:26, 28, 29, 32, 34). However, since he does not overlook the real world (as the Corinthians did, according to 4:8), Paul seeks practicable solutions. These entail proving oneself within the existing rules (7:17, 24), without taking these rules more seriously than they deserve in the face of the impending end (7:27 and 7:29–31).

The last issue to be discussed is the tension within the churches between poverty and wealth. In typical fashion, the Pauline letters address this issue almost exclusively in indirect ways. Paul's concrete solution to this tension is not based on a social utopia, nor does he derive his guidelines from the part of the Jesus tradition dealing with this matter or from the early Jerusalem church. His starting point is the reality of the Hellenistic cities that was reflected in his churches. Some churches are poor, such as those in Macedonia (2 Cor. 8:2–3), with the exception of a relatively prosperous church in Philippi (inferred from Phil. 4:10–20). Based on clues gleaned from the list of greetings to the church in Rome (provided it is addressed to Rome), this church was evidently not poor at all. The church in Corinth was characterized by a deep division between rich and poor, which gave rise to many tensions (Theissen). Other letters, such as the Letter to the Galatians, do not speak to this issue at all. Paul does not seek to achieve social equality between the various churches (concerning the collection for the Jerusalem church, see above). He generally presupposes a political order that allowed primarily family-oriented, private enterprises to develop freely, and he does not criticize the success of such efforts at all. A denunciation of wealth as such cannot be found in Paul's writings; he does not subscribe to poverty as an ideal! He accepts the differences between rich and poor within the various churches and only provides for a certain equalization within the fellowship on a voluntary, personal basis. The idea that the difference between rich and poor will be abolished in the final judgment (see, e.g., 1 Enoch 92–105) is a notion that is completely foreign to him. He is equally unfamiliar with the idea that the poor churches are supposedly going to be the heirs of the rich of this world, or that the Christian churches would then have an internal structure that would ensure a uniform and equal level of possessions for all. Rather, the difference between rich and poor will then no longer be an issue, since it will have been overcome altogether as a distinguishing feature of the world. This expectation already determines present attitudes toward the question. Social problems of the polis or the province are not an issue for Paul either; instead, he calls on Christians to scrupulously pay the state its share of taxes from the revenues that are generated by private enterprises (Rom. 13:6–7). This was in line with the practice of the Hellenistic synagogue, out of which Paul came. From the synagogue he apparently had learned some other things too, not least of all the general rule that the churches should themselves take care of their own needs (1 Thess. 4:11–12) and their own disputes (1 Cor. 6:1, 4–5), especially when their livelihood and disputes about property are concerned. This principle of independence is important to Paul.

The apostle clearly expressed what he personally thought about this problem, and he also put those views into practice: by working himself, he seeks to remain as independent as possible from the churches (1 Cor. 9). Apart from that he lives according to the rule: "I know what it is to have little, and I know what it is to have plenty. In any and all circumstances I have learned the secret of being well-fed and of going hungry, having plenty and of being in need. I can do all things through him who strengthens me" (Phil. 4:12–13). A formal analogy of this attitude can be found in the Stoic sage (see Epictetus *Dissertationes* 1.18.22). Yet Paul's starting point is completely different; it lies in the fact that he already looks at the world in a critical light because the Lord is near. This starting point is what leads him to demand of Christians that they should, for example, "buy as though they had no possessions, and . . . deal with the world as though they had no dealings with it" (1 Cor. 7:29–31). Because the Lord is near, everyone, rich and poor, is instructed not to worry about anything but rather to bring all worries in prayer before God (Phil. 4:5–6). This is why a Christian is called to be an honest merchant, for example (1 Thess. 4:6). In disputes he should, for the same reason, not enforce his legal rights but rather allow himself to be robbed (1 Cor. 6:7–8), even if Paul is prepared to soften this harsh demand quite considerably with a compromise that favors rightful property claims (1 Cor. 6:4–5). The vices related to property, such as greed, envy, deceit, and robbery, ill befit Christians (Rom. 1:29–30; 1 Cor. 5:11; 6:9–10). The same holds true for the practices of the rich, such as carousing, gluttony, and self-indulgence (Rom. 13:13; Gal. 5:21). It is pagan godlessness that gives rise to such vices as greed, envy, deceit, unkindness, and ruthlessness (Rom. 1:29–30). Christians ought to be zealous in contributing to the needs of the saints, and in practicing hospitality (Rom. 12:13). House owners are also quite naturally expected to volunteer their homes for congregational meetings. But it is also true that compassion has to be coupled with cheerfulness (Rom. 12:8). To give all possessions to the poor is of no avail to the Christian giver unless it is coupled with love (1 Cor. 13:3). It is to the poor Macedonians' credit that they gave abundantly and of their own free will (2 Cor. 8:2–3). It is therefore only natural that the abundance of some should meet the needs of others (2 Cor. 8:14–15; cf. Gal. 6:2). However, wealth is not frowned upon as such. Paul neither issues warnings against it nor teaches poverty as an ideal according to which Christianity and owning possessions are mutually exclusive.

It is clear, therefore, that Paul reordered the relationship between rich and poor in pragmatic and concrete ways, calling for a new internal attitude toward wealth and poverty and seeking to reduce social differences within the churches on a voluntary basis. In so doing, he neither envisioned general social reforms nor could imagine one church being dependent on another. The equalizing measures he initiated within the churches were almost completely devoid of any structural component: he mentions nothing about a common purse nor anything about a regular Sunday collection for the poor of the church; the collection for Jerusalem was apparently an exception in this respect (1 Cor. 16:2). However, it was certainly common for the more affluent members voluntarily to bring food to the Lord's Supper that was intended for general consumption (inferred from 1 Cor. 11:20). This means that Paul did not yet establish an organized welfare system within the churches. In this respect the Hellenistic synagogue, which had become established long ago, was more advanced.

It is in Corinth that serious problems arise within the framework of this overall solution (for the following discussion, see Theissen, *Studien*, part 3). These difficulties demonstrate, on the one hand, the consistency with which Paul would solve problems that arose within the setting we just outlined. On the other hand, they also reveal to some extent the weakness of the Pauline solution, namely, insofar as the "rich" are able to display self-interested behavior, an attitude of strength, and a lack of love, thereby endangering the unity of the church as a whole or the faith of individual members. The first case concerns factions within the church (1 Cor. 1:10–4:21). What is at issue here certainly goes far beyond mere social tensions. However, regardless of how many rival groups one assumes, it is very likely that the champions and spokesmen of these groupings belonged to affluent families, and that Paul received news of this situation from the perspective of those at the bottom of the social scale. House owners (1 Cor. 1:12–17; 16:15–18; Acts 18:8–9; Rom. 16:23) boastfully associate themselves with well known missionaries in order to win prestige in the church. Chloe's people and others take offense at this behavior (1 Cor. 1:11). They are put under pressure to join one of the factions in such a dispute, without really being able or willing to form a faction of their own. Paul tackles this problem by arguing that all belong to Christ in the same way, and that God chooses that which is low (1:18–30). These disputes are therefore a relapse into a pre-Christian way of thinking (3:1–17). All the members are part of that holy temple of God, which is the church as a whole (3:16–17). The missionaries, whom the various factions use to compete with one another, are Christ's servants (4:1–8); they are not instruments for internal disputes within the church.

The second example concerns the problems associated with eating meat offered to idols (1 Cor. 8; 10). At issue is once again a theological problem that also has certain social aspects. The issue of eating meat is the focused, concrete expression of a larger question, namely, to what extent individual Christians should be part of the ancient polis. The "strong" defend their own liberal and broad-minded position with a Christian insight that Paul had also endorsed. It asserts that the Father of Jesus Christ has dethroned the gods (8:1–6). But in so doing, they also pursue a vital personal interest, namely, the option of maintaining certain social contacts that as the "rich" they were either unable or unwilling to sever completely (see *d* above). This attitude, however, led the "weak" into conflicts with their conscience, regardless of whether this was directly intended or merely caused by thought-lessness on the part of the "strong." The Hellenistic synagogue and the first generations of Christians held a position that was unambiguous and uncompromising; according to their view, the consumption of such meat was categorically forbidden. Paul supports a more flexible solution, which did not lose sight of the fact that a break with the non-Christian world was necessary, but it also allowed for limited involvement in the life of the polis. At the same time it ensured that in no case would the church or even a single one of its members be put at risk.

In formulating his solution, the apostle is guided by the following princi-ples: the position of the "strong" is correct as far as theological insight is concerned, but the conduct resulting from this insight must be guided by love (8:1–4) and the welfare of the church as a whole (10:32–33), and it must serve the glory of God (10:31). One's conduct has to take the place of the meal as well as its character into account. It might be a social meal in a temple (8:10; on this issue see, e.g., Plautus *Rudens* 2.2–3), a cultic meal to worship a deity (10:14), a private meal at home (10:25), or a private meal at the home of a non-Christian (10:27). In the first case it is permissi-ble to participate, provided no Christian takes offense. In the second case participation is categorically prohibited. The third possibility is generally permitted if coupled with a precautionary measure: when purchasing meat at the public market, one should not inquire about its origin, in order not to trouble one's conscience. In the last case a similar rule applies; one should only refuse to eat meat during a meal if a non-Christian explicitly points out its cultic character; otherwise one can participate in the meal. This differentiated solution takes into account the wishes of the "strong," that is, mostly the "rich," but it also defines the limits of what is allowed. It also provides for the protection of the "weak," that is, primarily the "poor," by showing consideration for them, based on theological grounds, without leading to social equalization. This solution promotes the separation of public and private life, for within the private sphere the "strong" are given a broadly defined free space in which they can fully live according to their insights and thus cultivate their social relationships, including the formal meals these relationships entail. This demand to show consideration re-duces the underlying antagonism between rich and poor but does not abol-ish it.

A third example is the celebration of the Lord's Supper in Corinth. Here the social differences apparently clashed head-on (1 Cor. 11:17–34). Those who were more affluent were primarily responsible for providing the room and the food. This responsibility they did indeed meet. But the privilege of having time and food freely at their disposal was exploited by this group (perhaps thoughtlessly and as a reflection of cultural practices?) in a way that showed a lack of love. It is likely that congregational meetings (on Sundays?—cf. 1 Cor. 16:2), among other things, did not yet begin at a set time. Those gathered waited until (at least almost) everybody had arrived. Hired laborers and slaves—the "poor"—frequently arrived rather late. There was general agreement to wait for these members before beginning to celebrate the Lord's Supper. But was it not possible to begin earlier with the joint meal for nourishment that had been ready for quite a while (11:21, 33)? As long as one did not begin with the Lord's Supper, was the host not free, in order to foster community, to ask those who had already arrived (mostly the "rich") to begin with the meal? After all, the food had been brought by those present! It is likely that care was taken to leave some food for those who arrived late. Certainly reserved were the bread and wine for the Lord's Supper itself, which was held in particularly high esteem by all members of the Corinthian church, and which theologically constituted the most important part of the gathering. Yet the "poor," who were perhaps in dire need of a meal, felt slighted by this behavior of the "rich." For them the unity of the church had to include both: the meal for nourishment and the Lord's Supper. Paul shares this view: he regards this behavior of the "rich" as a manifestation of contempt for the church of God and as a humiliation for those who arrive late (v. 22b). Yet in typical fashion he allows the more affluent members to continue with their current practice via an alternate avenue. Just as in the case of meat that had been offered to idols, so they are allowed to eat in a private environment before the public meeting. The lack of love that had surfaced in the official church meetings thus no longer exists (1 Cor. 14:18–19). The social differences, however, are not abolished. Paul does not promote their abolition, "for the kingdom of God is not food and drink" (Rom. 14:17); indeed, he himself lives in such a way as to be able to face plenty and hunger, abundance and want (Phil. 4:11–13).

It has become customary to describe this posture of Paul as the early Christian patriarchalism of love (Troeltsch). However, this must not be understood as the first Christian program designed to deal with the social sphere, as this term would seem to suggest linguistically. It is true, the three particular cases just examined indirectly reflect one of Paul's principles, namely, that every person ought to remain in the state in which he or she was called (1 Cor. 7:20, 24). In the specific case of the difference between rich and poor, the apostle softens this principle by calling for the voluntary practice of love; in 1 Cor. 7 he also softens a principle through a compromise, as we have seen. Yet this is only one part of the underlying structure of Paul's line of argument. For Paul is misrepresented if the other principle in 1 Cor. 7, the eschatological devaluation of all worldly values (vs. 29–31), is not immediately added to the picture. Both principles together constitute the typical Paul, that is, the Paul who in the face of the imminent end, the ultimate, still regulates penultimate matters, while no longer considering them to be of decisive importance. Paul's successors will repress the eschatological proviso, and develop the notion of social class in a more emphatic and independent fashion. They, rather than Paul, are thus more aptly characterized by the catchphrase of a patriarchalism of love.

g) Christians and Their Former World

Section *b* outlined how the missionary proclamation that was addressed to Gentiles called for repentance, and how it expected its hearers to cope with a situation of radical change. This meant the total renunciation of all the gods and a turn to the Father of Jesus Christ. It also led them to see the world in a new light, namely, as a creation about to pass away, because the coming of the Lord was imminent. This in turn resulted in a break with the status quo and a critical distance to it. It also led to a strict new morality. Through baptism Christians had become a new creation. The Spirit brought about their sanctification through brotherly love. They could thus consider themselves "children of God without blemish in the midst of a crooked and perverse generation" (Phil. 2:15). Their verdict about the world was decidedly negative (see, e.g., Rom. 1:18–32). At the same time, they consider themselves part of another world (Phil. 3:20–21). This basic outlook will persist beyond Paul's lifetime. Tertullian, for example, can therefore still write in his defense of Christianity: "It [the Christian church] knows that on earth it will remain a foreigner and will easily meet with hostility on the part of those who do not belong to it. However, it also knows that in heaven it will find a home, a place to stay, hope, gratitude, and status." The thinking of these Christians is therefore characterized by the contrast between the former and the present life (1 Cor. 6:9–11). The old life lies in the past, but they still have to deal with it on a daily basis in the form of the non-Christian world, which continues to exist. They are therefore put to the test regarding the extent to which they still give in to the old ways. Paul admonishes them in this respect to wage the battle between "Spirit" and "flesh" (Gal. 5:16–26) through daily renewal (Rom. 12:1–2).

For Gentile Christians this situation of radical change had no parallel. It was standard practice for them to participate in many festivals, processions, and sacrifices for a whole variety of gods. It was desirable to be initiated into several mystery cults. The basic syncretistic tendency of the time promoted a growing similarity of gods and cults and further increased the tolerance, already present throughout the Hellenistic-Roman world, of the various cults toward each other. All that Hellenists and Romans might have known of Judaism was its exclusivistic command to worship only the one God of Israel as the creator of heaven and earth. The Christian message now confronted them with the claim of an exclusive monotheism that left no room for concessions or compromise. This claim resulted in the concrete conviction that the existence of the world was limited to a very brief period of time because of God's impending judgment, and that the world had to be defined in harsh, negative terms. This meant that all the gods that had been worshiped up until then had now become totally irrelevant (1 Cor. 8:4–6; Gal. 4:8–11) for the question of how to achieve the welfare of the polis and of individual human beings; instead, they were now regarded as only an expression of the reprehensible disobedience of the one God (Rom. 1:21–25). The culpable turning away from this God also led to a total perversion of interpersonal relations (Rom. 1:26–32; Phil. 2:15). All of this will receive its sentence from the one true God in the impending final judgment. Outside of Christianity there will be only death and destruction. Of course, all who agree with this all-embracing assessment are faced with the task of radical change in their lives.

One can hardly overestimate the harshness of this break, for a symbiotic unity of religion with culture, politics, family life, and professional life was an unquestioned reality of that age. Whoever made the break with the world of the ancient gods necessarily attracted attention in all areas of life. For there was a decisive difference between Christian monotheism and the tendency toward monotheism nourished by philosophy and syncretism. In spite of some criticism of religion and occasional latent indifference toward the cults, a Greek would not simply dismiss the existence and practices of these cults. A Christian, however, could no longer either serve the gods even with certain reservations (1 Cor. 10:18–22) or take an oath in their name, for example, as was the standard practice in ratifying business transactions and binding agreements (see Plautus *Rudens* 5.2–3). Christians were therefore considered *atheoi*, godless people. Were they therefore not a danger to the polis, whose welfare depended on the gods? If they could not take an oath in the name of Zeus or refused to seal a contract with a sacrifice for Pallas Athena, were they not thereby avoiding proving that they could be trusted? Were they not revealing themselves as unreliable partners? Is it possible to take a Christian woman as a wife if during a meal in one's own house she demonstratively refuses, in front of all the guests, to join in calling on the household gods? Is it possible to continue to cultivate social contacts with another family if that family neither comes to banquets in the temple nor invites others to them?

Even though it was the visible practices in conflict with the current religion and culture that were most likely to attract attention, one can assume that non-Christians also learned about some of the contents of the new faith. In most cases this happened through hearsay and was coupled with a negatively biased assessment. Tacitus (*Annals* 15.44) and Pliny (*Letters* 10.96) presumably repeat a typical and widely held assessment when, based on this kind of information, they call Christianity a *superstitio;* they describe it as a superstition that is pernicious, bizarre, and resembles a pestilence. Those who converted to Christianity constantly had to face such sentiments. Incidentally, Cicero had already characterized the Jewish religion as *superstitio* in his speech for Flaccius (Stern, *Greek and Latin Authors*, vol. 1, no. 68). In this respect Christians received an unwanted legacy.

Hellenistic Judaism, in its rather comparable situation within the Hellenistic-Roman world, was still better able to cope with similar conflicts, since it was generally recognized as a religious anomaly and enjoyed special treatment and status (*collegia licita*). Jews also emphasized their affiliation with a single nation and frequently lived together in their own separate districts. Strabon's opinion about the inhabitants of Cyrene (in Josephus *Antiquitates* 14.115) is typical: "Here four [groups] existed, namely, townspeople and country folk, third, the category of the foreigners, and, fourth, the Jews." In contrast, the author of the *Letter to Diognetus*, who has a Gentile-Christian orientation, describes the church situation initiated by Paul in the following way (ch. 5): "Christians distinguish themselves from other human beings neither by a country nor by a language nor by any customs. For nowhere do they live in cites of their own, nor do they speak an unusual language, nor do they lead a separate life." This remark provides a glimpse of how Christians continued quietly to distinguish themselves from Judaism through the way they lived in the Roman Empire. For a married woman who had become a Christian in Corinth, for example, it was indeed much more difficult to stay with her non-Christian husband and continue to be in charge of the household than to get a divorce and move into a Christian household. Paul, however, supports the more difficult solution, which placed much greater demands on the individual Christians in terms of courage and patience. It also required much more independence and creativity in solving conflicts (1 Cor. 7:12–16; a typical conflict is described by Plautus *Rudens* 4.6).

There can be no doubt that in this difficult and unfamiliar situation it was more tempting to emphasize separation from the world, rather than reshaping existing conditions. One reason for this was certainly the conviction that the end of all things was imminent. But there were also two additional causes that went beyond the concerns of the individual: first, the general attitude of the time toward the social order and social change and, second, the generally typical attitude of young churches as a whole at times toward the old world. We shall discuss both factors in turn.

The political and social order of the Roman Empire was considered part of a comprehensive pattern of order guaranteed by the gods. This general order-generating principle remained practically unquestioned. The individual had not yet become a locus of the experience of truth or, as a consequence, a source of criticism of the general state of affairs. In the strict sense, this development does not begin until the Reformation and is not completed until the European Enlightenment. It is undoubtedly true that it was early Christianity that raised the status of individuals ("believers for whom Christ died"; 1 Cor. 8:11) in an exemplary way, especially since in accepting the Christian message each individual had to believe for himself or herself: no one could take anyone else's place. Yet this did not yet lead to a new rationale for the political and social system or to its fundamental reconstruction. In antiquity individuals lived instead in the positions given them by birth, which allotted them their share of rights and obligations. Apart from a few exceptions, an individual was thus an integral part of a community. An antagonism wrought with tensions between the individual and the community by and large did not yet exist, for antiquity is inconceivable without its hierarchical system of class and position and its graduated participation in rights and obligations. Even the great philosophers approved of this system and provided its theoretical underpinnings.

It is therefore not surprising to find that human rights, for example, were seen in a completely different light compared to today. The rights of individual liberty were not held in high esteem. Slavery, for example, together with its attendant practices of kidnapping and slave trading, was an unquestioned institution. The right to freedom from injury was also almost unknown; Seneca (De ira 3) describes many exemplary cases where rulers and judges were blind to this right. However, he does not criticize the fact that they violated this right, but rather that those who exercised power did not have themselves under control. They should have pronounced their (same) judgments without anger, even if they happened to hand down a death sentence involving the most agonizing death. For the period from Caesar to Domitian, Suetonius (De vita Caesarum) also provides numerous illustrations of how little weight, judged by modern sensitivities, the rights of the individual carried within Roman jurisprudence (see, e.g., the practice of banishment, divers kinds of corporal punishment, and different methods employed for execution). Basic social rights were also enjoyed only in a very graduated form: the law did not consider everyone equal. Roman citizenship, above all, conferred special privileges. In his trial Paul quite naturally uses this fact to his advantage. Unlike the provincial figure Jesus, Paul could not be crucified by the occupying power, for example. Slaves were tortured without any second thoughts (see, e.g., Pliny Letters 10.96); in this regard, free citizens had more rights to protect them from brutal methods of interrogation. Finally, a look at participatory rights reveals a similar picture. A general right to vote did not exist even in classically democratic Athens. Because of the class system, the distribution of political power was very unequal and comparable to the shape of a pyramid. Thus in antiquity we find serious limitations in all three areas of human rights, without these limitations even being considered a problem. Especially in light of the new way of life taking shape within the Pauline churches, it is noteworthy that early Christianity did not discuss, let alone change, these general social conditions.

Antiquity was also bound by tradition in a much more fundamental way than the modern age is. Apart from the written, codified law, life was in a very profound and unquestioned way ruled by the unwritten law, that is, by conventions and customs. It was, of course, mostly the normal social behavior that was based on such conventions. The available sources make it very difficult and all too often impossible to gain a reliable picture of what that normal social behavior was. If a Corinthian woman in Paul's time generally covered her head, was this merely an Oriental custom that had found its way into parts of Corinthian society, or did the apostle in 1 Cor. 11 expect his church to conform to a custom that was considered foreign by at least the Gentile-Christian women in Corinth? Unfortunately, the answers to these questions can only be speculations. Yet as a general rule we can say that Paul and his churches did not seriously consider revising even a single law. With regard to conventions and customs they generally take a conservative stance, as is clear not least of all in the context of the question of wearing a veil.

The question might arise as to where in the Roman Empire average citizens could understand themselves not only as part of a system, as rooted in a network of traditions, or as subjects, but also had opportunities to act in ways that challenged their personal responsibility. Primarily two areas have to be mentioned: the sphere of economics and social welfare, and the realm of philosophy and religion. Once the Roman state had created the political framework (containment of piracy, a network of roads, urban centers, internal stability, a tax system), the economy, left to itself, was able to flourish. It was not restricted by considerations about the social order but was allowed to develop freely. Social welfare was not guaranteed by the state but by the family (and to a very small extent by private associations and cults). Land ownership, coupled with a large number of descendants, provided the greatest security. Within this context Christianity seized its chance to become actively involved in private welfare, utilizing Christian households. In this way it eased social problems such as the large gap in wealth, emergencies caused by external factors, and personal misfortunes.

Because of the political distribution of power, the second area, philosophy and religion, had largely concentrated its focus on the individual search for happiness and immortality. To the extent that political responsibility and influence were limited to a small ruling elite, individuals were increasingly inclined to live according to an individualistic philosophy of life. In this they were supported by the great philosophical schools, most notably the Stoics, the Cynics, and the Epicureans. This trend was also reinforced by the religious syncretism of late antiquity and by the Hellenistic mystery religions. Early Christianity fits once again into the general picture. For it too granted the individual a certain degree of self-development within the Christian church and placed great emphasis on the question of existence after death. Thus, on the whole Christianity acts in conformity with "the system." For, on the one hand, it speaks to Christians about the current situation only in their role as political subjects (Rom. 13) and does not question the political and social order of the Roman Empire. On the other hand, it emphasizes freedom in the structuring of the house church, carries out its partial social equalization on a voluntary basis, and challenges the individual with regard to faith, love, and hope.

After looking at the general convictions of that period, we will now take a look at the characteristics of the young churches; as examples we will primarily use the Pauline churches. The mission congregations of the young churches in the modern age have taught us that the life of the first generation is always thoroughly shaped by its break with the status quo. This sharply felt contrast between the old and the new causes Christians of the first generation to develop a negative ethic that emphasizes behavior that distinguishes them and sets them apart. They are noticeably uncertain about the extent to which they can still be involved with the past without once again becoming dependent on it; therefore they prefer to set themselves apart in all areas. Is it possible for a Christian, for example, to continue to wear a pagan amulet? A Christian of the first generation will generally answer this question in the negative. A Christian of the third generation will more likely be able to treat it as something that has now become a neutral piece of jewelry.

The Pauline churches are no exception in this respect. Although Paul argues firmly in favor of a dialectical relationship of detachment from and involvement in the world in which the church finds itself, there was clearly a danger within the churches of total withdrawal from the world. For Paul must explicitly tell the Corinthians that they misunderstood him if they took his statements in an earlier letter as a call to break off all contacts with "the immoral of this world, or the greedy and robbers, or idolaters" (1 Cor. 5:9–10). But could one not argue that baptism required the termination of such contacts? After all, had baptism not washed away the old sinful existence? Was it not sanctification that transformed the body into a temple of the Spirit? Was it not justification that radically ended a depraved life as a fornicator and idolater, as an adulterer, catamite, and pederast, as a thief, greedy person, drunkard, reviler, and robber (1 Cor. 6:9–11, 19). And did this not naturally preclude any contacts with such friends from the old environment?

If it was no longer permissible to participate in the temple cultus, and if the separation here was total and without exception (1 Cor. 10:14–22), why should the opposition between the old life and the new existence not also lead just as logically to a break in the social relationships connected with the old life? Were contacts with former friends and acquaintances not much too strong a temptation (1 Cor. 10:1–13), provoking a relapse into the sinful existence that had been renounced?

In any case, a strict and undialectical separation of church and world is also advocated in 2 Cor. 6:14–7:2, which clearly continues the views of (part of) the Corinthian church already expressed in 1 Cor. 5:9–10. This passage asserts a radical opposition between church and world, between light and darkness, and, elevating it to the level of dualism and myth, even between Christ and Belial. The church as the temple of God is charged with leaving the world and staying separate from it, in order to attain the holiness brought about by the Spirit. Now, there are many indications that this passage is neither an original part of its present context nor of Pauline origin. One of these indications is that the terminology is dualistic and closely related to Qumran. Further evidence is the fact that the existential-historical correlation of gospel, election, and faith, which is typical for Paul in other contexts, is replaced here by a mythical dualism based on the concept of substance. The third and final indication is Paul's rejection of the Corinthian position in 1 Cor. 5:9–13. This inserted passage is nevertheless an important piece of evidence for the fact that the tendency of the negative ethics of separation resonated with a basic conviction within the churches. Sanctification without compromise was evidently more important to the churches than is generally assumed today.

If Paul did not agree with this approach of breaking off nearly all contacts with the world, then what solution does he recommend to the churches? The standard structure of the Pauline paraenesis can provide the key to answering this question. The exegesis of 1 Thess. 4:1–12 (see *c* above) already revealed that such a standard paraenesis focused primarily on internal relationships within the fellowship (for details see *e* and *f* above). The relationship with the external world is dealt with only briefly at the end of the passage: in the world outside the church nobody should have reason to take offense at individual Christians. It is significant in this regard that in Paul's writings the church as a whole never appears as an active entity in public life. It is apparently not necessary for the church to negotiate with the polis, since, for example, it did not yet need any real estate within the city. Applications for erecting a church building were equally unknown. The church was even less inclined to argue with the local authorities about what might be the most appropriate form of government or to protest publicly against infringements of the law. In this sense the church felt no responsibility at all for the world. The world is not a partner with which the church cooperates; it is exclusively an object of the church's mission, and it will soon perish unless it embraces the Christian faith. The focus on the Christian household provided room enough for several generations to shape the internal life of the community. Even as the near expectation of the Parousia soon weakened, this situation remained unchanged for a while. Thus the church did not strive to follow the synagogue in negotiating for certain privileges within a city, to say nothing of sending delegations to Rome in order to influence political decisions. The relationship to the outside world was thus defined exclusively by individual Christians, for example, in their function as members of a non-Christian household, professionals, citizens of a city, participants at social functions, and taxpayers.

This clear priority of the internal relationships and the secondary role of the relationship of the individual Christian to the outside world are characteristic not only of 1 Thess. 4:1–12. It is the common structure of all paraenetic texts of early Christianity. In 1 Thess. 5:12ff. the relationship to the outside world appears in a brief and thematically confined way: "See that none of you repays evil for evil, but always seek to do good to one another and to all" (v. 15; cf. Phil. 4:5). The lengthy paraenesis in Gal. 5:13–6:10 contains the following statement only in the last verse: "So then, whenever we have an opportunity, let us work for the good of all, and especially for those of the family of faith." The great passage in Rom. 12:1–13:14 also starts out discussing internal relationships. Yet in its middle part it then deals somewhat more extensively than is usual with the relationship to the outside world, mainly by calling for restraint from reacting in a wrathful manner, a peaceable attitude toward all people, forgoing revenge on society (12:14–21), and finally submission to political powers (13:1–7). The numerous problems Paul had to tackle in Corinth are almost exclusively internal problems of the church. True, the relationship to the outside world, contrary to the desire of some Corinthians, is not broken off completely (1 Cor. 5:9–13). But this relationship is then primarily characterized by the prohibition of going to non-Christian courts (6:1–11) and the prohibition of turning to non-Christian women who offer extramarital sexual intercourse (6:12–20). The text's underlying conceptual structure evidently consists of two concentric circles. A strong emphasis is placed on the inner circle, the church. The outer circle receives little attention and is in each case represented only by individual Christians. It is for the same reason that all the discussions about the commandment to love talk primarily about brotherly love (Becker, "Feindesliebe").

After describing the basic aspects of the relationship to the outside world, we can now turn to the specific problems of that relationship. With respect to the relationship to the institutions, there are two topics to be discussed: the attitude towards the pagan cult and that towards the civil authorities. These same two themes, the preservation of their own religion as distinct from the pagan cult and the vitally necessary integration into the non-Christian state and its society, had already played a central and decisive role in the Jewish Diaspora. When developing guidelines for both of these problem areas, Paul, as a Hellenistic Jew, fell back almost automatically on the practice of diaspora Jews in the Hellenistic cities. The same is true for his churches with their Jewish-Christian segment and their contingent of former God-fearers. In their dealings with a foreign environment diaspora Jews had gathered a lot of experience over a long period of time and developed a basic model of conduct. This model allowed them to preserve their religious identity even though they lived as a minority with relatively few rights; to a limited extent it also permitted them to participate in the commercial and social life of the community.

The charter for this model had been for several centuries the letter of Jeremiah to the exiled community in Babylon, who wished nothing more fervently than to return home so as to preserve its religious identity. Taking the view that the Israelites will unquestionably remain faithful to the God of their fathers, Jeremiah recommends to this group that it get settled in the foreign land and be prepared to stay for a long period of time, to seek their own prosperity, and at the same time to have a positive attitude towards the Gentile government: " . . . seek the welfare of the city . . . and pray to the Lord on its behalf, for in its welfare you will find your welfare" (Jer. 29:5–7). It was even possible to provide a theological basis for this attitude of pragmatic conformism and loyalty to the government: Had the belief that there was only one God not already led to the conviction that the Gentile ruler Cyrus had been God's instrument (Isa. 45:1–7)? It seemed obvious to assume, therefore, that the God of Israel and Creator of the world had appointed all governments, irrespective of their particular design (Ezek. 26:7; Dan. 2:37; Wisd. Sol. 6:23; etc.). But this meant that obedience toward the representatives of the state was at the same time obedience toward God. Thus evolved the concept that within the religious sphere one could serve God in separation from the nations, but in the political arena one would serve him in conformity with the Gentiles by displaying loyalty toward foreign governments. This premise forms the basis of practically all the Jewish diaspora literature, including the writings of Philo and Josephus. When working with this model, it was not always possible to describe actual relationships that were free of conflict (as in, e.g., *Joseph and Aseneth*). This model frequently had to prove its worth in situations of conflict, which were regarded as being forced upon the Hellenistic synagogue from the outside. In such cases authors sought to demonstrate how the Jews remained faithful to Yahweh and loyal to the state, even if this led to martyrdom (Dan. 1–6; 3 Maccabees; etc.).

The Pauline churches adopted this model, thereby apparently setting the tone for early Christianity and the ancient church. They were quite obviously an even smaller minority; they also set themselves apart from the Gentile world in religious matters and experienced the various organs of the state from below, practically without sharing any power. This development was promoted by the strong emphasis on internal relationships and the desire to keep the relationship to the outside world as free from conflict as possible. Those who broke with the pagan cultus already had enough cause for conflict with state and society, even if they took Paul's relatively liberal stance toward eating meat that had been offered to idols. For the rejection of the official state cult amounted to an ongoing flagrant disregard for the public order. It therefore seemed natural that in all other respects one would seek to minimize conflict and be a dependable member of the political community. This is why this model, which Christians inherited from Hellenistic Judaism, can be found not only in Paul (Rom. 13) but also in other writings of earliest Christianity (e.g., 1 Peter 2:13–17; 1 Tim. 2:2–3; 1 Clem. 60.4–61.3) and in texts of the ancient church (see, e.g., Tertullian Apologeticum). The dependency on Judaism goes even so far as to adopt the specific tenet that the powers of the state are instituted by God, and that Christians therefore have a special responsibility to obey them (Rom. 13:1–2) out of insight (Rom. 13:5). This call for obedience was unlimited and extended even to the right of the state to impose the death penalty (13:4). This concrete example makes it clear how little interest the church had in becoming engaged in a debate over human rights. The only contribution of the church that was really profoundly critical was to transfer the source of legitimacy both for the power of the state and for earthly welfare from the pagan pantheon to the Christian God. Whatever other concrete measures of political organization the Roman state implemented (Rom. 13:3–7) was subject to the general rule to be obedient. Paul therefore uses Hellenistic administrative language quite deliberately in Rom. 13. This command to obey the authorities was incidentally even adhered to during periods of persecution (1 Peter 4:12–19), in the face of the imminent expectation of the Parousia (Rom. 13:11–12; 1 Peter 4:7) and not least of all while knowing that one is really a citizen of another world (Phil. 3:20–21; 1 Peter 1:1; 2:11). True, concepts such as the imminent expectation of the Parousia relativized the state; that is, they placed a temporal limit on it. Yet while knowing that the state would come to an end, it was imperative until that time to be all the more conscientious in paying taxes (Rom. 13:7 comes before 13:11–12). Here we may also recall 1 Cor.

7:17, 24 as a parallel: Christians should also not prematurely relinquish their role as political subjects. The call for political disobedience in the face of a state that acts diabolically, that is, an apocalyptic understanding of the state (Rev. 13), is something foreign to the Pauline churches.

The relationship to society was another area that continually generated special problems for individual Christians in their everyday lives. If the need to regulate the relationship to the institutions of cult and state was satisfied by drawing on the legacy of the Hellenistic synagogue, the guiding principle Paul and his churches used with regard to the social relationships was the newly found Christian concept of liberty: "For all things are yours, whether . . . the world or life or death or the present or the future—all belong to you, and you belong to Christ, and Christ belongs to God" (1 Cor. 3:21–22). This is why in the case of eating meat that had come in contact with the pagan cult, Paul can in principle give such a liberal response (1 Cor. 8:1–8; 10:25)—in stark contrast to the synagogue. This is why he does not cut off the relationships of individual Christians to non-Christian "sinners" (1 Cor. 5:9–13). This is why he speaks in favor of preserving a marriage with a non-Christian partner (1 Cor. 7:1ff.). This affirmation of contacts with the outside world is coupled with the basic tenet that Christians ought not judge those on the outside, that is, constantly interfere with their lives by evaluating their conduct (1 Cor. 5:12–13). Instead, it is their own exemplary conduct and their concern for outsiders that is to win others over (1 Cor. 10:32–33; also 9:19–20). They are not to flag in doing good to all people, even if this commission applies primarily within the fellowship (Gal. 6:10). A particularly strong emphasis is placed on the notion that Christians ought to set a personal moral example (Phil. 2:14–15; 4:5). This is not defined legalistically but rather left to the responsibility of each individual (Rom. 12:2; Phil. 4:8), even though the church as a whole certainly has a clear sense of right and wrong (Rom. 1:18–32, 12–13; Gal. 5:13–6:10; etc.). This rigorous demand on the individual to lead a moral life also ensured that the church would not become an object for gossip. This is why Christian brothers ought not to carry on disputes in front of pagan judges, for example (1 Cor. 6:5; a fine illustration of the role judges played is found in Plautus *Rudens* 3.4–4.4), and why they should earn their own living (1 Thess. 4:10–12). Whenever conflicts arise in relations with non-Christians, it is always the first duty of Christians to seek peace and refrain from revenge (Rom. 12:17–21). Finally, the worship of the church will also adjust to visiting outsiders (1 Cor. 14:23–25).

In order to complete our survey of the relationship of the churches to the outside world, we must still take a look at the synagogue. Paul and the Pauline churches owed much to the synagogues. They were in most cases the base and starting point for missionary activity. The crucial first group of Christians in a city often included Jewish Christians and especially God-fearers. But this very fact, together with the fact that Paul's mission was not tied to the law, also proved to be the chief cause of ongoing conflict. Judaism naturally and quite rightly sensed this competition and fought against it. As an established institution it had effective means at its disposal to conduct this fight, namely, synagogal punishments, the instigation of unrest, and accusations before municipal courts. Internally—and more accurately—it was usually said that Christians had essentially rejected the law; externally, before Gentile courts, it was normally claimed that Christians instigated unrest and disturbed the public peace. Consequently, Gentile society, which in any event frequently regarded the new Christian churches as offshoots of Judaism, extended its prejudice toward the Jews and its contempt for the synagogue to include Christians also. Thus the relationship between the local synagogue and the Christian mission church was full of tension and loaded with problems.

It is likely that the Pauline churches already saw a link between the persecution of Jesus and that of Stephen, regarding both events as acts of Jewish violence. The churches were aware, according to Gal. 1:23 (cf. 1 Cor. 15:9), that as a Pharisee Paul had once persecuted the Christians in Damascus. In 1 Thess. 2:14–16 we find Paul's harshest statement against the Jews, "who killed both the Lord Jesus and the prophets, and drove us out . . . and oppose everyone by hindering us from speaking to the Gentiles . . . " These statements are phrased in traditional language and are also typical in their content (concerning hostility toward all people, see, e.g., Tacitus *Historia* 5.5.1). They are one more indication of the fact that the churches frequently had to face Jewish hostility. Among his sufferings at the hands of adversaries (1 Cor. 11:23–29) Paul explicitly includes synagogal punishments (vs. 24–25). Even though Acts might describe the notorious hostility of the synagogue in a legendary and stylized form (Acts 13:50; 14:2, 5, 19; 17:5–8, 13; 18:12–17; etc.), these statement are not sheer inventions, as the Pauline texts prove. For even at the time when he takes the collection to Jerusalem (Rom. 15:31), Paul is still afraid of the hostility of the Jews—and with good reason (Acts 21:10ff.). After Paul, it is authors such as Justin (*Dialogos* 17.108, 117), Origen (*Contra Celsum* 6.27), and Tertullian (*Apologeticum* 7.3) who perpetuate this assessment of the Jews.

The first Christians, having just been recruited from the periphery of the synagogue, were almost unable to defend themselves against this hostile attitude of the synagogue. The fact that the Christian church established itself right away outside the synagogue certainly eased the existing confrontation, but it did not end the conflict. When Jews brought charges against Christians, we may assume that the trial did not always end as favorably for the Christians as in Corinth, when Paul was tried before Gallio (Acts 18:12–17). Yet it is notable that Paul never proposes any special rules to the church on how it ought to deal with this ongoing conflict. Christians ought to behave toward Jews in the same way as toward all people outside the church: they should seek peace and refrain from revenge.

Bibliography

(The standard commentaries on the Pauline letters are not listed.)

Alföldy, Géza. *Römische Sozialgeschichte*. 1975.

Becker, Jürgen. *Auferstehung der Toten im Urchristentum*. 1976.

———. "Feindesliebe—Nächstenliebe—Bruderliebe." *ZEE* 25 (1981): 5–17.

Blanks, Robert. *Paul's Idea of Community: The Early House Churches in Their Historical Setting*. 1980.

Bleicken, Jochen. *Verfassungs- und Sozialgeschichte des Römischen Kaiserreiches*. 2nd ed. 2 vols. 1981.

Bolkestein, Hendrik. *Wohltätigkeit und Armenpflege im vorchristlichen Altertum*. 1967.

Crüsemann, Frank, and Hartwig Thyen. *Als Mann und Frau geschaffen*. 1978.

Dautzenberg, Gerhard, Helmut Merklein, and Karlheinz Müller. *Die Frau im Urchristentum*. 1983.

Gerstenberger, Erhard S., and Wolfgang Schrage. *Mann und Frau*. 1980.

Grant, Robert M. *Early Christianity and Society: Seven Studies*. San Francisco: Harper & Row, 1977.

Grimm, Bernhard. "Untersuchungen zur sozialen Stellung der frühen Christen in der römischen Gesellschaft." Diss., Munich, 1975.

Gülzow, Henneke. *Christentum und Sklaverei in den ersten drei Jahrhunderten*. 1969.

———. "Soziale Gegebenheiten der altkirchlichen Mission." In *Kirchengeschichte als Missionsgeschichte*, 1:189–226. 1974.

Harnack, Adolf von. *Die Mission und Ausbreitung des Christentums in den ersten drei Jahrhunderten*. 4th ed. 1924.

Hengel, Martin. "Christologie und neutestamentliche Chronologie." In *Neues Testament und Geschichte*, FS O. Cullmann, 43–67. 1972.

———. *Eigentum und Reightum in der frühen Kirche.* 1973.

———. *Zur urchristlichen Geschichtsschreibung.* 1979.

Judge, Edwin A. *The Social Pattern of Christian Groups in the First Century.* London: Tyndale, 1960.

Kee, Howard Clark. *Christian Origins in Sociological Perspective: Methods and Resources.* Philadelphia: Westminster, 1980.

Kertelge, Karl, ed. *Mission im Neuen Testament.* 1982.

Klauck, Hans-Josef. *Hausgemeinde und Hauskirche im frühen Christentum.* 1981.

Klein, Richard, ed. *Das frühe Christentum im römischen Staat.* Wege der Forschung 267. 1971.

Kuhn, Karl-Georg, and Hartmut Stegemann. S.v. "Proselyten." *Paulys Realencyclopädie der classischen Altertumswissenschaft*, supp. 9, 1248–84. 1962.

Laub, Franz. *Die Begegnung des frühen Christentums mit der antiken Sklaverei.* 1982.

Leipoldt, Johannes, and Walter Grundmann. *Umwelt des Urchristentums.* Vol. 1, 3rd ed., 1971; vol. 2, 3rd ed., 1972; vol. 3, 2nd ed., 1967.

Lüdemann, Gerd. *Paulus, der Heidenapostel.* Vol. 1. 1980.

Meeks, Wayne A., ed. *God's Christ and His People.* 1977.

———. *The First Urban Christians.* 1983.

Ollrog, Wolf-Henning. *Paulus und seine Mitarbeiter.* 1979.

Pekáry, Thomas. *Die Wirtschaft der griechisch-römischen Antike.* 1976.

Rostovtzeff, Michael. *Gesellschafts- und Wirtschaftsgeschichte der hellenistischen Welt.* 3 vols. 1955–56.

Schneider, Carl. *Kulturgeschichte des Hellenismus.* 2 vols. 1967, 1969.

Schrage, Wolfgang. *Die Christen und der Staat nach dem Neuen Testament.* 1971.

Theissen, Gerd. *Studien zur Soziologie des Urchristentums.* 1979.

Weiss, Johannes. *Das Urchristentum.* 1917.

III

The Post-Apostolic Period

5

The Synoptic Evangelists and Their Communities

John K. Riches

The problems attendant on the question how the Synoptic communities and their evangelists stood in relation to the political authorities and to their surrounding culture and economy cannot be underestimated. Where and when, in the first place, are we to locate them? How do we describe their racial, religious, social, and cultural composition? Then, second, how are we to elicit the social and political attitudes, beliefs, and practices of the Synoptic communities and their evangelists? On occasion one may find statements specifically addressed to such issues, but more often we shall have to catch the overtones and attempt to gauge the point or implication of a story or incident. But equally we shall have to listen just as carefully to what are fairly high-level theological statements, which may, however, have important social-ethical and political implications. Our questions, however, are not answered merely by determining the social-ethical and political beliefs actually held by the Synoptic communities. We still have to ask about the interrelation of such groups with their surrounding cultures. How far were the communities that preserved the traditions of Jesus' teaching, works, death, and resurrection innovative in their attempts to build for themselves new communities, new social worlds; how far were they forced back to the religious, social, and political resources of their inherited cultures? And how far was the drive to produce new communities itself a product of the particular constellation of socio-cultural, -economic, and -political factors that made up the world of the different Synoptic communities?

Before proceeding to differentiate between the three communities, something must be said about what they have in common. Most obviously, but quite significantly, what they share is the fact that they all three, in their efforts to construct their own social worlds and communities, produced a gospel. That is to say, they not only saw themselves as preservers of the Jesus tradition (which in any case they appear to have known in interestingly different forms), but by publishing this tradition in written, book form, they were making particular claims about its socio-cultural significance. Thus, while the gospel form may be distinguished formally from various more or less contemporary forms of biography and reminiscence, what it shares with them, specifically with the lives of religious figures (Apollonius), philosophers (Pythagoras), and political leaders (Augustus), is the same intention to secure for those figures and their attitudes and beliefs a public status, some kind of public, if not official, recognition. It has, that is to say, a common social function.

This social function of each Gospel is not limited to its function *ad extra*. Indeed it is possible in certain cases that the intention of a particular evangelist was more to sustain, develop, and structure his own community than to secure a particular place for it within the contemporary world. Clearly one of the effects of codifying a tradition, doubtless also one of the intentions of its codifiers, is to produce it in an authoritative form. Furthermore, while the writer of a Gospel is undoubtedly constrained by what has been received as traditional and therefore authoritative by the community, he is nevertheless free within such constraints to emphasize certain tendencies within the tradition, to place brackets around others. More specifically, the intention of such Gospel writing may be to provide certain written procedures or guidelines for community discipline or to settle doctrinal and ethical disputes.

Of course, the social significance of the Gospels is not exhausted by their various social *functions*. What is being said in the process of recording the tradition about Jesus of Nazareth clearly also carries its own set of social and ethical *meanings*. Here again the Gospels have a great deal in common. They all make high theological claims for one who met his death as a criminal at the hands of the Roman authorities and who advocated certain social and ethical values. They present Jesus as someone who was also at variance with the leaders of the Jewish community at the time and who committed acts which were seen to be contrary to Jewish norms. In this they all represent in varying degrees a challenge to the authorities of the wider communities in which they were set. Thus the manner in which the events of Jesus' life and of his trial and execution are narrated and in which his ethical teaching is presented is clearly of the greatest importance for our inquiry.

a) Mark's Community and Gospel.

(*1*) *Location and date.* Scholarly opinion is sharply divided on the question whether Mark's Gospel is to be located in the West—specifically, perhaps, in Rome—or in Syria. Hard evidence is difficult to come by. Arguments for a Syrian origin are based more on elements in the tradition (e.g., Jewish theological concerns about purity etc.) than on evidence derived from the evangelist's own redaction (which in the specific case of purity draws on the tradition of the Hellenistic catalog of vices to elucidate the sense of Jesus' logion in Mark 7:15). The case for a Roman origin is based partly on the testimony of early church writings and partly on the character of the theological debates in Mark, which seem to come from a principally Hellenistic context (divine-man Christologies). None of this carries overwhelming conviction, and the debate must turn largely on the question of the most appropriate cultural milieu for the evangelist's redaction. For the purposes of this chapter I shall simply assume with Pesch, Gnilka, and others that Mark comes from a Hellenistic context, where the Jewish theological questions that undoubtedly informed Mark's tradition in its early stages were of diminishing significance—indeed, were not always immediately intelligible. This disposes me to place it in the West, possibly even in Rome.

Questions of date turn partly on the question of the literary relationships between the three Synoptic Gospels and partly on the question of the temporal relationship of each Gospel to the fall of Jerusalem. I shall assume the two-document hypothesis and Markan priority, and that Mark's tradition foretold the fall of Jerusalem, which his Gospel predates. Thus a date in the mid-sixties is assumed.

On these assumptions Mark's Gospel must have been written around the time of—probably shortly after—Nero's grotesque persecution and torture of the Christian community in Rome. Whether or not Mark was writing specifically for that community or for other communities in the West, it seems wholly unlikely that an event of such barbarism would not have left a lasting impression on the Christian community of the time and in an important sense have dominated its perceptions of the Roman state. At the same time, it would have raised painful theological questions about the nature of God's care and providence, questions that would have focused sharply around the story of the similarly barbarous death of Jesus at the hands of the Roman authorities in Jerusalem.

(2) The social function of Mark's Gospel. The social function of Mark's Gospel can be inferred in some measure from considerations of its form. Like other questions in this field, this is highly contentious, but I shall follow Theissen's suggestion that the Markan form of the Gospel is the product of a type of overarching construction that is developed out of the miracle story form. Theissen's designation of this as aretalogical may be misleading, insofar as the precise nature of aretalogies is in doubt. The valid point is that the Gospel is held together by the expectation of a full acclamation of Jesus, which, though it is given by the divine voice at the baptism and also made by the demons, is systematically withheld until the confession of the centurion.

The question here is, (a) What is the social function of miracle stories? and (b) How does the Markan Gospel form relate to this function of the miracle story? Miracles—and by extension, miracle stories—may have a variety of roles within society. Broadly, either they may function as supports to society, providing some kind of consolation and encouragement in face of the unpredictable and unmanageable elements in people's experience, or they may act as a means of legitimation and propaganda for marginal groups within society. Given the obvious conflict between the early Christians and both Romans and Jews, it is more than likely that their miracle stories functioned in the latter way. "Primitive Christian miracle stories are the symbolic actions of a religious minority in ancient society that has set out to conquer the whole world" (Theissen, p. 258). But equally there is no doubt that when such stories were incorporated into the story of Jesus' trial and execution, they must have raised fundamental questions about the nature of his power and authority. How could one who performed such mighty works perish himself so miserably—and have subsequently allowed his followers to perish in similarly barbarous ways? Thus the Gospel raises questions about both the nature of Jesus' power and its recognition and acclamation; it also explores the nature of Christian motivation (discipleship), as it confronts questions of failure and tragedy within Christian experience. There is, that is to say, an element of sophistication in the Gospel, which outstrips the intention of the simple miracle story, even though the Gospel may have developed out of it. It still serves the same end insofar as it is designed to act both as propaganda for the Christian group and as encouragement for its members, but its concern with the dark side of the new group's experience would suggest that it is a work more for the members of the group than for the outside world. Nevertheless, the choice of the centurion for the acclamation at the crucifixion indicates that the propagandist function has been kept in sight.

A further question arises when we consider the existence, documented in the Pauline epistles, of rival groupings within the church. To what extent might the miracle stories or the passion narrative have served a certain purpose for a particular group or groups within the church? It has been suggested by some that the tradition of the miracle stories may have been associated with the wandering preachers from Jerusalem who opposed Paul, or that they were associated with a particular form of christological belief—a *theios aner* Christology—which Mark wished to correct. It seems more plausible to suggest, as does Theissen, that the stories preceded the wandering preachers and formed part of the preliminaries of Christian mission with which, in different ways, subsequent groupings within the church had to come to terms, rather than to see them as particularly the property of any specific group. In a similar way it is likely that the passion narrative with its strong eucharistic connections was part of the general property of the worshiping community, rather than specific to any one group. Thus any group had to come to terms with it.

We should also note the views of those like Kee who would see Mark's Gospel as most closely related to various forms of Jewish apocalyptic thought and exegesis. While Kee's evidence does not in itself provide an explanation of how the actual form of Mark's Gospel emerged, it does show the extent to which apocalyptic elements were embedded in Mark's tradition. This, of course, chimes in well with the function of the miracle stories to which we have just pointed: viz., of legitimizing the miracle worker in a situation where he cannot appeal to institutional or rational forms of legitimation. On the other hand, it does less than justice to the way Mark distances himself from the apocalyptic expectations in Mark 13 and should not be taken to determine either the form or the intention of Mark's Gospel. This Gospel is second generation apocalyptic, that is to say, it is concerned with the problems of supporting and strengthening a community whose initial expectations have been tempered by the experience of suffering and persecution. This does not mean simply the abandonment of such expectations or of its missionary zeal, but it does require considerable theological reflection in order to sustain and in a certain measure to reformulate such hopes.

(3) *The political and social ethical practices and beliefs of the Markan community.* There is little explicit teaching about the state and society in Mark's Gospel, and what there is, viz., the saying about taxes to Caesar

(12:13ff.), is relatively ambiguous. What Mark's tradition is concerned with is threefold: the miracles, the teaching, and the passion of Jesus, which leads into his resurrection. These three themes account for most of the material that may be identified as traditional; at the same time they stand in considerable tension with each other. In the first place, there seems to be some confusion about the relative importance of Jesus' teaching and his miracles. Indeed, there is a certain confusion about the very distinction between Jesus' miracles and teaching. (The exorcism in 1:21ff. is greeted with the acclamation: "What is this? A new teaching!" [1:27].) Equally, while Jesus is very often referred to as a teacher, Mark records substantially less of his teaching than do the other two Gospels. More importantly, perhaps, there is a clear tension between the power and authority that Jesus exercises in his miracles of healing, exorcism, and the multiplication of food, on the one hand, and his suffering at the hands of the Jewish and Roman authorities, on the other. How is it that Jesus, who is presented by Mark as having power over all the spiritual and physical forces that threaten men and women (evil spirits, disease, storm, famine) and who is portrayed in the summary in 6:53 as marching in triumph through Galilee and driving out all ill from it, has nevertheless to undergo torture, degradation, and death at the hands of the authorities? The answer, according to Mark, must lie in the true understanding of the nature of the power that informs Jesus' miracles. This is at least strongly suggested by the discussion of the feeding miracles in Mark 8 and by the somewhat cryptic saying in 8:15: "Watch out—beware of the yeast of the Pharisees and the yeast of Herod." The warning, taken in its context in Mark, must refer, first, to the Pharisees' concern with purity—the concern, that is, to oppose and set firm barriers against all that is alien to the group, all that is abominable to God—and, second, to the use of coercive force and violence by Herod against his critic and opponent John the Baptist. The warning is both a rejection of such understandings of power and an injunction to seek an understanding of the power that is at work in Jesus' miracles in quite different terms. This is further developed by the immediately following exchange (3:17–21), in which Jesus points to the multiplication of the broken loaves. The source of Jesus' power lies in the breaking and multiplication of the bread, that is, in costly self-giving.

Such impressions are confirmed by the treatment of the themes of greatness and power in Mark 9–10, where the glorious figure of the Son of man is identified as one who must suffer and where greatness in the kingdom of God is linked to the notion of servanthood. The question that such claims inevitably prompt, however, is, How can such power triumph over the power of the state with its reserves of coercive force? This is the central question that informs Mark's passion narrative, as indeed is signaled by the threefold prophecy of the suffering and death of the Son of man (8:31; 9:31; 10:33–34).

The passion narrative in Mark is constructed as a dual drama. First, there is the conflict between Jesus and men: his followers, the leaders of the Jews, and the Romans. Then there is the drama of Jesus' *agonia* with his Father, which underlies the narrative as a whole and surfaces explicitly in the scenes in the garden and on the cross.

The story of Jesus' dealings with men highlights the peculiar ambiguity of his particular kind of power. Jesus comes to call the unrighteous, the enemies of God, and his people into the kingdom (2:17), to welcome them unconditionally, and in the end it is precisely this kind of openness that proves his undoing. It is from within the circle of his own group that he is betrayed (cf. the designations of Judas in Mark's account: "one of the twelve, one who is dipping bread with me in the bowl"), and he is betrayed with the sign of love and fellowship. Judas provides the bridgehead for the powers of deception and coercion that then engulf Jesus and destroy him. Mark in his account underlines both the duplicity of the Jews and the brutality of the Roman soldiers. But equally in his portrayal of Peter's denial he shows the inner bankruptcy of Peter's discipleship in a series of vignettes that have been properly recognized by Auerbach as marking an important transition in literary self-consciousness. Peter lacks precisely the inner strength that Jesus had argued for in 7:15ff. But equally Peter's failure is presented by Mark systematically through the Gospel as one of understanding, as is most clearly portrayed in his failure to accept Jesus' prediction of his suffering in 8:32. Peter's rejection of Jesus' announcement of the Son of man's divinely ordained way is satanic precisely because it shows his bondage to false notions of power.

If the story of Jesus' crucifixion is thus principally a story of his betrayal and misuse by those he came to save, precisely because of his openness and the unconditional nature of the grace he offers, then at least at the end there is the beginning of a reversal of this process of rejection and misuse. In the centurion's testimony and the *ekstasis* of the women at the tomb there are the dawnings of a recognition of the divine ground of Jesus' life, suffering, and death. Both these events are given a specifically apocalyptic coloring: the rending of the veil of the temple before the centurion's confession and the language of "terror and amazement" in 16:8. Together they represent the acclamation that, as Theissen has argued, the structure of Mark's Gospel demands but which has to this point been withheld. Even so it must be recognized that the acclamation as it stands represents only the beginnings of an understanding on the part of those whose worlds are being turned upside down by the recognition of real power as residing in the One whom they have respectively executed or come to anoint after his death.

The rending of the veil of the temple, however, comes only after the resolution of the struggle between Jesus and his Father. The question of the true nature of the divine power is posed in the sharpest form by Jesus in his prayer: "Abba, Father, for you all things are possible; remove this cup from me; yet, not what I want, but what you want" (14:36). The question how a good father can permit his son to perish miserably is clearly one of significance for Mark's readers, as well as for Jesus. How is it that an omnipotent God can permit the righteous One to suffer? The theme of the righteous One suffering is part of Mark's tradition, but we may reasonably see in Mark's formulation of the prayer his own particularly sharpened form of expressing the problem; certainly both his fellow Synoptic writers change it in such a way as to blunt the edge of his perception of the problem. Jesus' acceptance of the "cup" (is there any need with Gnilka to see this as a reference back to notions of judgment construed in line with notions of penalties for sin?) is an acceptance of his Father's will *contrary to appearances*. His acceptance immediately ushers in the forces of darkness, who carry him away to his fate. Again for Jesus, as indeed for those who perished under Nero, such a fate must at least appear as abandonment by God. And yet it is only in his bearing of the worst that the powers of evil can do to him that he realizes the true nature of the Father to whom he has committed himself, and that he manifests that power and nature to the world. It is what the centurion sees on Jesus' face as he breathes his last that prompts the centurion's confession of Jesus as the Son of God.

Thus Mark's Gospel certainly speaks about power and does so in a way that clearly contrasts its own understanding of power with that of Caesar and of the temple. To this extent we can say that Mark's Gospel lays the basis for the development of a new social world and a new belief system that can provide the means for structuring a new political and social order. The question that now arises is To what extent does this Gospel specifically point to a new political economy distinct from that of Rome or the temple; to what extent does its detachment from the latter at least make room for subsequent generations to develop such an economy?

The first half of the question can be answered without much hesitation.

Mark 13 clearly envisages the passing away of this world along with the world of Rome and the temple. It is also fairly evident that Mark has had to come to terms with the fact that these events have been delayed and that meanwhile his community is suffering. It would be hard to go further than that. There is nothing quite comparable to what we shall see in Luke and Matthew, where belief in the end becomes less the central focus of Christian belief and more the general background against which Christian discipleship is to be exercised, the context, that is, in which the Christian community, and even a new social order, now needs to be developed. Thus Mark is still concerned with the passing of the old order rather than with the practicalities of the new.

Nevertheless, we may still ask to what extent we can detect signs of the form and structure of the Markan community itself. Remarkably little can be inferred from the text about the form of the community. It is true that Jesus exalts children as a model for the community, and he also attempts to redefine greatness in terms of servanthood. There is, however, as yet no indication of how Mark's community would face the consequential problems of community control and discipline, which would subsequently force the church to define its structures more clearly. Again, Mark 6 describes clearly enough the ideals of homelessness and of lack of protection and possessions, which were associated with early Christian wandering preachers. What we do not learn is to what extent such ideals were to be practiced by the whole community, or indeed how—assuming that such ideals were in fact pursued only by a certain group within the community— they were supported by the rest. Moreover, we have to ask how far such ideals ever actually corresponded to the realities of the lives of the community and its leaders.

Lack of such information, however, is not without its significance. It goes a long way toward reinforcing a picture of a community that is still marginal within its society, that can still live with relatively simple structures—possibly, we might surmise, because the pressures from without have bonded it firmly together—and that is still genuinely inspired by notions of servanthood and noncoercive love, even if these have been sorely tested in its recent experience. Where the community develops such notions—for instance, in the commentary on Jesus' saying in Mark 7:15, which is given in terms of a Hellenistic catalog of vices—it clearly draws on elements taken from popular ethical belief. This in itself indicates something about the nature of its confrontation with contemporary culture, namely, that it is not wholly antagonistic but seeks to draw strength from it where it can. Again, as we have seen, the very fact that Mark produced a Gospel is evidence of the community's desire to place itself more firmly on the public map. Thus we may cautiously suggest that Mark's Gospel stands at the very beginning of the process of world-building, which will be prosecuted to a greater extent by the other two Synoptic writers.

(4) *Cultural influences on the Markan community.* A final question concerns the extent to which Mark and his community were influenced by the culture in which they lived, by the socio-economic, ecological, political, and cultural factors of his day. On the one hand, the community and Mark have preserved traditions that are cast in the form of the protest movements of his day: apocalyptic prophecies and miracle stories; on the other, Mark has developed a literary genre, the gospel, which, while it makes use of the miracle story, is nevertheless importantly innovative. Similarly, in his handling of the story of Peter's denial, he produces literary vignettes of a remarkably original kind. Thus at the formal level Mark shows himself to be deeply indebted to the forms of protest, to be writing in the cultural modes of those estranged from the centers of political and economic power, who long passionately for the overthrow of existing authorities. At the same time he creates, in the service of his own inquiry into the nature of power, new literary forms that, above all in the passion narrative, plumb new areas of human sensibility and suggest a significant new understanding of power.

Again, where the actual understanding of power is concerned, Mark shows himself firmly opposed to both groups that dominate his socio-cultural world, the Pharisees and the Herodians, that is, the forms of Judaism that were developing new forms of purity observance and the ruling Roman polity. Such clear opposition and rejection speaks of the extreme marginalization of Mark's community and is not itself evidence of creative interaction with his society. More interesting is what Mark begins to put in its stead. To some extent this too is borrowed from his cultural environment. The use of the Hellenistic catalog of vices in Mark 7 is an evident example. But again, we have suggested that Mark's own concern with the true nature of understanding and with the inwardness of human betrayal and failure draws on a perception of the nature of love and power that is of a deep originality.

b) Matthew's Community and Gospel.

(1) *Location and date.* The generally Jewish ambiance of Matthew's Gospel has led scholars to place it in a Syrian context. For this a number of arguments can be adduced. Matthew's dependence on Q, which is gener-

ally acknowledged to be Syrian in origin, suggests at least connections with the communities that preserved and developed Q. Matthew's critique of Torah within the context of a general concern for upholding the continuity of Christian teaching with Torah suggests links with the Hellenists of Acts 6, some of whom subsequently went to Syrian Antioch. Further links with Antioch are provided by the citations of Matthew in Ignatius of Antioch. It might also be suggested that the questions of Torah observance that Paul relates in Gal. 2 in connection with Antioch would provide an appropriate context for Matthew. Clearly none of this evidence is compelling, either individually or cumulatively. Scholars are indeed divided as to whether Matthew should be seen as emanating from a rural settlement in Syria or from Antioch itself. Again, some would wish to see the Gospel as principally the product of a debate with the Judaism of Jamnia, while others would stress more Matthew's concern with internal tensions within the Christian community as it encounters the practical and theological problems consequent upon its continued existence. Internal evidence (concern with matters of discipline, with questions of the delay of the Parousia and the provision of material goods) inclines me to see Matthew as more concerned with the internal problems of the Christian community and as perhaps more easily read in an urban than a rural context. This does not, of course, exclude the possibility that Matthew was also influenced by developments in Jamnia. A date in the seventies or early eighties seems most likely if we accept Markan priority on the one hand and the close links between Matthew and general Jewish concerns with Torah on the other.

(2) *The social function of Matthew's Gospel.* Formal considerations suggest that Matthew's Gospel is more concerned with providing material for the instruction and edification of his community and even perhaps of those outside it than, as in the case of Mark, principally with arguing the claims of a millenarian prophet.

In the first instance the construction of extended discourses out of originally independent units of discourse material marks a particular preoccupation of Matthew's community with questions of a social, cultural, and even political kind, which are dealt with here within the context of Jewish religious traditions as seen and interpreted by Jesus of Nazareth. It is not easy to characterize the precise nature of the process by which such blocks of material were built up and to know to what extent the Christian community (insofar as it saw itself as distinct from the Jewish community) was guided by scribal techniques of biblical exegesis, but it is reasonable to assume points of contact here and to see the development of the Q tradition as a significant response to the criticisms of infidelity to Torah leveled at the "Hellenists" by Jewish leaders in Jerusalem. Yet over and above that, there are clearly other concerns that motivate the development of such teaching blocks. The issues dealt with by Matt. 18 are in some respects quite similar to those in the *Rule of the Community* of Qumran. Certainly, whether it is to be seen as rule or more as advice, its subject is the operation of the community: how it shall admit members, how and for what offenses it shall discipline them, and under what conditions it might proceed to exclude them. The formulation of such rules or guidelines is of course in no way divorced from considerations of the community's ruling theological assumptions, viz., about God's concern for the lost and the primacy of forgiveness in the community's scale of values. The function of such literary forms within the Gospel is precisely to reinforce community practice by codifying it and providing it with a theological justification. Similar points will be made about Matthew's redaction of his tradition, where the sense of traditional material is on occasion altered to provide support for community legislation, whereas it had been previously associated with the rejection of—traditional—legal norms.

In addition to these matters of community discipline and regulation, however, there are other concerns, notably with the community's place in its wider social setting, which are evidenced by the Gospel's form. Matthew develops Mark's "aretalogical" Gospel into a more nearly biographical form by the inclusion of the birth stories, thus bringing it closer to the contemporary lives of philosophers, rulers, and religious figures. Here, as indeed in some of the pagan lives, there are elements that have a strongly mythological character and serve to highlight the group's distinctive claims. The final scene in Matthew is an enthronement scene, which acclaims Jesus' universal authority and commissions the church to proclaim and seek acknowledgment of that authority throughout the world. The effect, in short, is to show Jesus as someone rooted in this world, whose life can be portrayed in ways similar to the lives of other important religious and indeed political leaders, while at the same time stressing his unique and absolute claim to allegiance and authority: "All authority . . . has been given to me." Whatever Matthew's concern with internal problems of the community's life and growth, his dominant perspective is a missionary one of great confidence.

(3) *The political and social-ethical practices and beliefs of the Matthean community.* Matthew, by contrast with Mark, contains a considerable body of teaching about matters of ethical, social, and political concern. How-

ever, before giving some account of such material and proceeding to make some assessment of the social realities of the community itself, it will be well to say something about the general theological beliefs that form the context of such teaching. Matthew sees Jesus as the fulfiller of the law. He fulfills it both in that he gives a final and authoritative interpretation of God's will, which may in practice contrast with the Mosaic law (antitheses!), and in that he lives a life of perfect obedience to God's will. At the heart of Jesus' interpretation of the law lies his injunction to love one's enemies, which is seen as an imitation of the fatherly goodness of God (Matt. 5:43–48). At the end of the Gospel Jesus is given all authority over the world, and those whom he has called as his disciples are commissioned to go into the world to make all nations his disciples and teach them all that Jesus had commanded them (Matt. 28). Thus the church is seen fundamentally as a teaching community that is charged with the promulgation of God's will and is answerable to Jesus at the final judgment. At the same time Jesus is present with the church in its deliberations and prayer as they acknowledge his authority and sovereignty in their continuing discipleship.

These very general beliefs are developed by Matthew in quite specific and sometimes quite surprising ways. There are, however, very considerable difficulties in the way of the interpreter. Not only do we have to determine where Matthew's own specific contribution to the body of Christian legislation lies, but we also have to assess what his stance was with regard to the material he has taken over. There are clearly elements in the Gospel that are strongly rigorist (e.g., 5:18, 20); others suggest a much more critical stance toward Torah (15:11) or enjoin a forgiving and generous attitude toward miscreants (18:22). The question one has to ask is, Was Matthew attempting to outflank the more rigorist elements in his community by this juxtaposition of different ethical judgments? Or was he himself, though committed to an ethic of forgiveness and reconciliation, being forced by the internal needs of his community to seek support from these more rigorist elements in his attempt to reinforce community discipline and order? The latter seems the more likely explanation.

With these cautions let us turn to a consideration of Matthew's ethical teaching itself. What, first, were the central values that Matthew wished to advocate? Certain texts may reasonably be taken as indicative of Matthew's central concerns by virtue of their placement within the Gospel. Thus the introduction and conclusion to the Sermon on the Mount, the climax of the antitheses within the Sermon itself and the depiction of the judgment scene (25:31ff.) as the conclusion of all Jesus' sayings have clearly been given prominence. What is interesting about these passages is that they (a) stress the continuity between Jesus' teaching and "the law and the prophets," (b) emphasize the virtues of mercy and love, and (c) contain a strikingly universal element (7:12!).

(a) As Trilling has emphasized, Jesus' teaching is seen as fulfilling "the law and the prophets," not just the Mosaic Torah by itself (versus *b. Šabb.* 31a). That is to say, Jesus' teaching is a "fulfillment" of the divine will, not simply an authoritative guide for interpreting the written Torah. As such it is critical of Torah, insofar as it uses one passage of Torah to relegate another to a subordinate position (Matt. 19:3ff.) and also rejects certain aspects of Torah in toto (15:11).

(b) Matthew stresses Jesus' command to his followers to love their enemies. In its original context this probably referred to the enemies of the Jewish peasantry to whom Jesus addressed himself and thus most likely referred to the Roman and Herodian authorities and those who collaborated with them. Here the precise referent(s) is less easy to determine. In the most general sense it must refer to all those who are a threat to the group, whether from within or without. Within the Gospel those who are most frequently attacked are the Pharisees and the Sadducees (cf. Matt. 16:6 and Mark 8:15, where Mark has "Herodians" instead of "Sadducees"). This could well be taken as a reference to the Pharisaic party as it developed in the period after the destruction of the temple with the establishment of the academy at Jamnia. It is true that in this case the addition of the Sadducees would be somewhat odd, though an ironic reference should not be ruled out. An alternative reading would be to take the Pharisees to refer to a particular group within Matthew's community—possibly those whose views are to be found in the special Matthean material—who were rigorists and who perhaps were the forerunners of the Jewish Christianity that subsequently emerged as a separate entity in Syria. On the whole, I would favor the former suggestion, not least because it would seem to me odd that on the one hand Matt. 18 should enter a strong plea for forbearance and patience in community discipline and then proceed to inveigh against those who were a threat to the community, as he does against the Pharisees in chapter 23. It has to be admitted, however, that there are tensions in Matthew between his desire to commend the virtues of forgiveness, forbearance, and love of enemies and the more strident tones he adopts when condemning the enemies of the gospel, as in Matt. 23, and when recounting the fate of the unmerciful servant in 18:23ff.

In any case the sense of 5:43ff. is that the community should be open to the world outside its own (perhaps not too sharply defined) boundaries, and in Matthew this receives its clearest interpretation in terms of the missionary charges of Matt. 10 and 28. The highest service that the Matthean community can perform towards those outside its community is to do what Jesus had done for them, that is, to make disciples of them and teach them to observe all that he had commanded them. (The sharpness of the opposition to the Pharisees might in this context be ascribed precisely to the competition between the Christian community and the Pharisees.) That such work is appropriately referred to as "love of enemies" is also clearly related to the community's experience of persecution and rejection in the course of such work, as is made clear in 10:16ff.

(c) The universal human element in Matthew's teaching is noteworthy. The touchstone of correct behavior is: "In everything do to others as you would have them do to you; for this is the law and the prophets" (7:12). This is clearly related to the formulation of the Golden Rule, which is found in negative form in *b. Šabb.* 31a (though taken there as fulfilling only the law) and is presented there as a form of missionary teaching. In the Gospel it is echoed again in Jesus' summary of the law, which in Matthew is set in a more polemical context—of Sadducean and Pharisaic opposition to Jesus—than in Mark and receives a quite concrete interpretation in the judgment scene in Matt. 25: acts of human kindness to "one of the least of these who are members of my family" are what will decide the issue between those who inherit the kingdom and those who are cast out. This is, of course, not simply an ethic of self-interest. The point is rather that the world that Christians are trying to build through their missionary activity is one where the true measure of ethical value is in the generous and unquestioning act of mercy that sees and responds to universal human need. Such mercy is characteristic both of the God who sends his rain on the just and the unjust and of the person who gives a drink to someone who is thirsty. These are the ones who will be "rewarded" even though they do not act within an agreed covenant with prescribed rules and terms (20:1–16). There is, however, a question as to whether there is not a certain particularism in Matthew's presentation of this matter. Is there a stress in the phrase "just as you did it to one of the least of *these my brothers*" (25:40, literal) on acts of mercy performed towards members of Matthew's community? It is more likely that "these" represents an underlying Semitic superfluous demonstrative and that the reference is therefore quite generally to anyone in need (Hill).

Let us now look at the specific ethical motifs in Matthew. While it is true that Matthew contains a great deal of ethical material, determining what his own particular stance might have been is not always easy. One needs to plot the tradition history very carefully to see exactly where Matthew's own emphases lie. Here we can attempt only to show how in some cases Matthew has handled his tradition in order to meet the particular needs of his community.

(a) *Teaching on cares and providence* (6:25–34). The point of the original unit, vs. 25–26, 28–30, is not so much to advocate a general doctrine of God's care and providence as to use the greater marvel of God's care for the lilies to bring home to Jesus' disciples the reality of God's care for them, which they are already experiencing in their vagrant, mendicant life with Jesus. Similarly, Theissen has suggested that these sayings will have related directly to the earliest Christians' experience of a wandering charismatic existence, without homes and without protection, traveling through the country with no possessions and no occupation. The question is, In what sense were these beliefs modified when they began to be related to the rather different experience of Matthew's community if, as we suppose, they were living an urban life with homes, possessions, occupations, and families?

Here we have to reckon with the possibility of a change in the sense of the original sayings, partly in virtue of additions that may have been made to the complex of sentences, partly in virtue of such sayings being uttered in a different context, where they will have had associations with perhaps very different kinds of experience. Thus if 6:33, "Strive first for the kingdom of God and his righteousness, and all these things will be given to you as well," is redactional, its sense may have been not so much to enjoin a policy of *abandoning* any attempt to make provision for one's physical well-being, so as to be free for the work of the kingdom, as to enjoin a *subordination* of such attempts to the task of missionary endeavor, of establishing the Christian community and preserving its faithfulness to the teaching of Jesus. But equally the traditional sayings in 6:25–34 will have received a different sense by virtue of being uttered in a different, urban context. In such a context, sayings about not caring for the morrow or about not taking food, money, and adequate clothing when embarking on a journey may have evoked associations with the behavior of the Cynic philosophers of the time, who would not have been unfamiliar figures in the towns of Syria. Did Matthew or his community feel the need to distinguish the behavior of its founders from that of the Cynics? Does the reference to taking neither staff nor sandals (vs. Mark) mean that now they wished to characterize the apostles' behavior more as an act of worship than as a refusal to provide for their own physical needs? Does the remark that the laborer deserves his food represent an attempt to present the mode of existence of wandering charismatics as *work*, rather than as a pure act of renunciation for its own sake? Or were these sayings simply taken as referring to the life of essentially itinerant figures and thus no longer felt to apply to the community itself? They might then be taken as sayings primarily with the function of instructing the community about their duties towards Christian wandering charismatics. It is not easy to give definite answers to these questions. If we allow that the Matthean community was genuinely committed to the task of mission and that this was a task that was primarily the concern of apostles and itinerant figures, then this passage will certainly have reminded the community of its obligations towards this class. On the other hand, it does fairly clearly spell out the obligations of the community to "strive first for the kingdom of God and his righteousness" by contrast with the Gentiles' concern with material things. This contrast, familiar enough from Jewish injunctions to remain faithful to the law, suggests that the sense of the injunction is a more general one than that of specifically itinerant mission. What is enjoined is rather a general search for the meaning of Jesus' teaching and obedience to it as the teaching that is to rule the world.

(b) *Teaching about judgment.* Matthew's Gospel contains a great deal of material about judgment. While for Jesus expressions of belief in an imminent end were intended to encourage his hearers to loose their ties with the old ways and to entrust themselves to what was to come, for Matthew their function was more to *explain* certain tensions within the community and to *reinforce* certain patterns of behavior.

Thus in Matt. 13 the parables of the dragnet and weeds among the wheat both emphasize that the process of sorting out the just from the unjust must wait until the process of catching/growth is completed. It is reasonable to suppose that here the intended points are (1) to explain how it is that God can tolerate the unjust within his community of the new age and (2) to enjoin patience on those who would seek to expel the unjust now. Of course, a whole number of things follow from what is said, viz., about the importance of maintaining the rules of the community, but this may not be the intended point or function of the story in its Matthean version. It is obvious, of course, that if we correctly discover its intended function, we shall be in a position to make certain conjectures about the community and indeed about its history.

Similar points might be made in relation to Matthew's redaction of

Mark 13. Mark, in editing his tradition, has tended to insert the experience of the church into the description of the period preceding the end, thereby offering some general explanation of the experience of persecution by portraying it specifically as part of the predicted schema of the end events. Matthew, for his part, has transposed some of Mark's material into the mission charge in Matt. 10, thus no longer restricting the experience of persecution to the time of the end. But in addition to this, the intention of Matt. 24–25 is clearly to enjoin watchfulness and correct observation of the community's norms. Again, this is achieved by the parables inserted between the Mark 13 material and Matthew's own depiction of the judgment scene. Eschatological material that was originally rule-reversing is used here in a manner that is rule-enforcing. At the same time we should notice how the material in Matt. 24–25 is given a very distinctive sense by the final episode of the sheep and goats. It is compassion and love shown "to one of the least of these" that is the norm by which all are to be judged. That is to say, we have here a clear expression of the new social norms that are to provide the basis of the new community.

(c) *Discipline*. Matt. 18 is the chapter that makes the most specific reference to the community (*ekklesia*) and its problems. It is clearly concerned with questions of entry, discipline, community sanctions, and exclusion from the community. The precise sense of what is being advocated, however, is less than clear. Certainly, Matthew affirms the importance of humility as the fundamental requirement for community membership, just as he stresses the need for forgiveness and tireless searching for the lost brother in the community's dealings with offenders. It is less clear what the specific offenses are against which sanctions are appropriate. Indeed, rather than specific classes of offense (e.g., gross acts of immorality; cf. 1 Cor. 5), the fundamental offense seems to be simply "offending one's brother" and then refusing to listen to the church. It is, that is to say, problems of community cohesion that principally preoccupy the writer, as indeed one might expect in a young community beginning to establish itself in a more sedentary pattern of life, while as yet possessing few clearly formulated rules of conduct. Indeed in such a context the general injunctions to forgive make things, if anything, worse, for it is clearly difficult to reconcile exclusion and forgiveness. The problem here is one of moving from a very loosely structured small-scale organization, where most problems can be dealt with as personal problems and where forgiveness and long-suffering may indeed be the most effective means of reconciling conflicting parties, to a larger scale organization, where personal regulation of conflict becomes more difficult and where there is a greater need for structure and agreed norms. Matthew is still clearly at a stage where he believes that the affairs of the community can be regulated by personal discussion and consultation. One may well conjecture, however, that the need to formulate and to codify certain procedures indicates that the time for developing more complex, less informal structures may be near.

(*d*) In this connection we should consider the somewhat cryptic references in the Gospel to forms of leadership. The most obvious and contentious of these is Matt. 16:18 where clearly authority of some sort is conferred on Peter. There seems little good reason to doubt that this refers specifically to Peter himself and that this is conferred in virtue not of his confession but in virtue of the revelation given to him. This makes his position analogous to that of the Teacher of Righteousness and his successors in the Council of the Community whose duty is to administer by legal ruling the revelation that has been entrusted to them. Specifically, Peter is entrusted with the keys of the kingdom of heaven symbolizing the power of loosing and binding. This may refer either to the authority to give legal interpretations or to the power to condemn or acquit. In practice, as legal rulings may entail deciding whether a particular action falls under a particular prescription, this distinction may be less than sharp. In either case, his task is to administer the revelation that has been entrusted to him. What we are not told is how Peter's authority related to the authority of the church as a body. Matt. 18 envisages various steps in disciplinary procedure, first an individual approach, then a meeting with a small group, and finally a meeting of the whole congregation. This latter body is also given authority to bind and loose (18:18). But equally in the next verse the authority of smaller groups of Christians is strongly affirmed. This, along with the rejection of titles and various forms of hierarchy in 23:8–12, suggests that there were as yet no agreed ranks or institutionalized forms of authority in Matthew's church.

(*e*) Matthew's treatment of Jesus' sayings about adultery, marriage, and divorce represents an interesting development of the tradition and also sheds light on his attitude to community structures. On the one hand, Matthew (dependent on his own community traditions?) emphasizes that it is not just the physical act of adultery that is forbidden but the directing of affections outside the marriage bond; on the other, he excepts from the prohibition of divorce those who have been wronged by adultery. If these two passages can be taken as truly consistent with one another—and there must be some doubt—then it would appear that there is indeed a certain consistency in, on the one hand, insisting that marriage, involving as it does a fully personal relationship, is not simply a matter of compliance with certain rules and norms of behavior, such as the avoidance of sexual intercourse outside the marriage bond, and, on the other, conceding that for those whose relationships have been built up on such trust, the actual act of physical adultery can represent a breaking of that trust, which creates an intolerable barrier to the continuance of any relationship at all. This would also be of a piece with what we have seen elsewhere of the tension in Matthew between, on the one hand, a reluctance to regulate the community's affairs by clearly defined boundaries and levels of authority and, on the other, the clearly felt need to draw certain lines and make some definite rulings.

Matthew's statements on adultery, divorce, and marriage, however, show the extraordinary difficulty of pinning down the precise meaning of ethical statements in Matthew. It may equally well be that what we have in Matt. 5 about adultery represents simply a rigorist trait in Matthew's tradition, setting, as it were, a fence around the prohibition of adultery in such a way as to make the actual offense the more severe and therefore the more difficult to tolerate. Yet even if that were the sense in Matthew's tradition—and it seems quite likely that such rigorist strands are represented in the special Matthean material—this does not preclude Matthew's having given them a different sense in his own redaction.

(4) *The Matthean community and culture.* What then was the interaction of Matthew and his community with their surrounding culture? Where the choice of literary forms is concerned, it is clear that Matthew is less innovative than Mark. He, like Luke, develops the gospel form into a more nearly biographical form, and in so doing he brings it closer to the form of contemporary lives. Again, the teaching material in Matthew shows how the communities behind the Gospel had drawn on forms of didactic material that were at least quite closely related to contemporary Jewish forms of exegesis and teaching. In this there is nothing very surprising if, as we have suggested, Matthew is concerned with establishing the Christian community publicly and giving it a place in his contemporary world. Taking over the culture's own forms is precisely an act of acculturation. But it would be mistaken to see this as simply an attempt at cultural assimilation, abandoning the apocalyptic forms of protest in favor of contemporary didactic and exemplary forms. For Matthew stresses the authority and uniqueness of the Christian message by underlining the revealed character of Jesus' message and authority. Not only is Jesus the son of David, but the secret of his birth

and origin is revealed mysteriously to the wise men from the East; and similarly at the last his heavenly origin and authority are revealed to his disciples. The stress upon the arcane nature of Jesus corresponds to a quite widespread tendency in ancient literature of a contra-cultural kind to reinforce its own distinctive cultural claims by appealing to a special divine origin and authority. And Matthew with his very distinctive message of love of enemies had every reason to seek such support in advocating such virtues in his contemporary world.

It is nevertheless true that Matthew's perspective is less apocalyptic than Mark's, that he is less concerned with the passing away of this world than with its conversion. At the same time, as we have seen, he is not merely concerned with converting the world; he is also sharply aware of the need to sustain his own community and to come to terms with the problems of discipline and community bonding inherent in a larger body that is seeking to maintain itself in an urban environment. Here, as it would appear, Matthew and his community have been constrained to make changes in the received tradition and also to develop their own disciplinary procedures. Again, there is in this nothing very surprising. The pattern of behavior is very comparable to that observed in conversionist sects elsewhere: a concern with increasing the membership of the sect by recruiting from without and a concern with keeping the community closely bonded against outside influence and undermining. What is interesting in this is to see how the distinctive message of Matthew's tradition of forgiveness creates problems for him when he deals with the community's needs for greater discipline and specifically for tighter structures and exclusion rules.

c) Luke's Community and His *Doppelwerk*.

(1) *Location and date.* By contrast with the two other Synoptic Gospels, Luke's work raises a fundamental question as to whether we should relate the Gospel and its author to a particular local congregation or indeed to a particular place. The preface, with its address to Theophilus, suggests that in fact it was not addressed to a particular congregation, and though it may well be that some of the traditions special to Luke have a particular local provenance, there is nothing in Luke's presentation of his story to link it with any particular congregation or place. It is true that Jerusalem and Rome are given particular prominence, but this is more as two poles of a story that encompasses large areas of the eastern Mediterranean world. Luke's parish seems to be a wider one than that of either of the other two

Synoptic evangelists, and his concerns are those of the emerging church with its various settlements scattered across the empire. The movement from Jerusalem to Rome is in a sense programmatic for Luke: what he seeks to present and to establish is the story of this church that has emerged from Judaism and is seeking to find its way in the still strange world of the empire. The date is most likely to be around the eighties. There is a sense that persecution is a concern, rather than an immediately threatening eventuality, which indicates a date before Domitian and sometime after Nero. Luke's concern with questions of the split between Jews and Christians equally suggests some such dating, around the time of Gamaliel II's presidency of the academy at Jamnia, when the "Nazarenes" were formally excluded as heretics. This means, too, that it is to be dated at a time when the church had recruited more extensively from the non-Jewish world and when questions of its identity and its relation to Judaism and the Roman world must have been quite pressing.

(2) *The social function of Luke's* Doppelwerk. Like Matthew, Luke's Gospel is biographical in form and is certainly concerned, inter alia, with presenting Jesus as an exemplary figure. Such concern with Jesus as an example to follow is also brought out in the particular form that is characteristic of Luke's Gospel, the exemplary story. But there is more. By linking his Gospel to Acts and by his prefaces, Luke presents himself as a historian in the Hellenistic mode, concerned with sifting and ordering his sources, concerned, perhaps more importantly, with demonstrating Christianity's historical pedigree and marking out its place in the world of the empire. The manner in which this is achieved is interesting. The Lukan birth stories and genealogy certainly place Jesus firmly within the sphere of the Old Covenant, just as the Emmaus story affirms the continuity between Jesus and the Old Testament scriptures. But the really explicit claims about Christianity's Old Testament pedigree come in the speeches in Acts either in a polemical or in a missionary context (a distinction that, interestingly, is not absolute, since the Jews are from the beginning presented as subjects of Christian missionary preaching), where the Old Testament warrants of Christianity are extensively deployed. This suggests at least that the setting within which such arguments became critical was a dual one: either in debate with the Judaism of Jamnia or in the context of the Christian mission in which Luke himself was an active participant. The Acts speeches are probably part of Luke's source material and this suggests that their function in Luke's work need not necessarily have been identical with their original function. For the question here is, To whom was the Lukan work

addressed? Is the Theophilus of the preface a pagan nobleman to whom Luke is offering some kind of Christian apologetic, or is it more the Christian reader who is being addressed in these terms? The latter seems more likely, in view of the extensive use of Jewish materials and arguments, which would hardly be expected in a work of apologetic directed toward non-Jews. If this is right, then it is likely that the concern with Christianity's Jewish antecedents is part of the author's attempt to meet a particular crisis of self-identity within the Christian community occasioned, on the one hand, by its break with and exclusion from the synagogues and, on the other, by the growing numbers of Gentile converts. In this situation it is necessary both to argue that the Christians are the true heirs to the promises of the Old Testament and to show that God is indeed with the church in its development and history. Acts provides the historical as well as the theological proof of Christianity.

(3) *The political and social-ethical practices advocated in Luke-Acts.* We have already suggested that Luke was not concerned with offering some kind of political apologetic by arguing either that Christians should be treated tolerantly by Roman officials or, more specifically, that Christianity should be adopted as a *religio licita.*

The arguments here are relatively strong. In the first place, it is questionable whether there was a recognized legal category of *religio licita.* The one reference to such a term in Tertullian (*Apology* 21.1) is by no means unambiguously a technical use. Moreover, even if such a technical sense had been current, it would presumably have been necessary to argue for the institutional identity or at least continuity between Jews and Christians. Yet this is precisely what Luke does not do. While he stresses the common heritage of Jews and Christians in the promises and prophecies of the Old Testament, at the climax of the work, the Jewish leaders explicitly disown the Christians, claiming only to know of them that they are generally regarded as subversive, while Paul defies the high priest and the Sanhedrin for the third time by going again to the Gentiles.

The more modest claim that Luke was urging tolerance on Roman officials by showing the innocence of Christians, starting with Jesus, and by presenting Roman officialdom in as favorable a light as possible founders principally on the fact that the material in this connection is relatively sparsely scattered throughout the work. Any official whom Luke so wished to impress would have to read a great deal of material very strange to him before he came to passages like Luke 23, which do indeed exonerate Jesus of any political offense. And even if it were claimed that at least where Acts is concerned, there is a good deal of material relating to Roman officialdom and that, moreover, it culminates in the appeal by Paul to Rome, the rejoinder would have to be made that not all Roman officials appear equally well (cf. Acts 16:22ff.; 18:12ff.; 24:26; 25:9ff.) and that the portrayal of Pilate at best excuses him of deliberate malice while showing him to be the victim of weakness and fear. At the same time, while it is true that Paul's appeal to Rome against Jerusalem is clearly a highly significant element in Luke's story and clearly demonstrates respect for the legal authority of Rome, Luke also makes explicit criticisms of all earthly authority (Acts 4–5), though this is not specifically applied in context to Rome. Luke's reservations vis-à-vis Rome are muted; he omits the name of the emperor Nero to whom Paul appealed, as he leaves his readers to draw the implications of Peter's saying that we must obey God not men.

Luke's work then is not specifically directed, for whatever apologetic purpose, toward Roman officials but rather toward the Christian community at large (taking Theophilus to stand for any—Gentile?—Christian). Nevertheless, there is no denying that the material we have been considering does have a particular political slant, and this, along with other material of a more general social-ethical character from the Gospel, deserves consideration. As Maddox puts it: "It is Christians whom Luke is reassuring that the death of Jesus was due not to any fault on his part or that of the disciples, but to Jewish duplicity and the failure of Roman integrity. It is Christians to whom he is emphasizing that Paul, though accused of civil disruption by both Romans and Jews (Acts 16:20; 17:6; 24:5) and the object of violent jealousy on the part of the Greeks (19:26–31), had always behaved with honour and respect towards the state" (p. 96). Maddox suggests that what this means is that Luke is pointing out to Christians that while Jews, Romans, and Greeks have from the beginning been making accusations against Christians, they have never been justified. Christians must expect unfair accusation and indeed persecution (Acts 14:22), but their proper response is to cultivate a sober and inoffensive style of life and an attitude of respect toward the government. Luke, says Maddox, writes not in a context of actual persecution but rather in one where it was a possibility, particularly if Christians should be tempted to provoke the authorities, even to seek martyrdom. All this puts Luke-Acts close to passages like Rom. 13:1–7 and 1 Peter 2:11–17.

Maddox's thesis seems to me to be essentially correct, but certain aspects of it may require modification. Recently, Cassidy has pointed to the elements in Luke's portrait of Jesus that highlight Jesus' attitude toward social and political affairs. In particular, Jesus emerges as the champion of the poor, the hungry, and the oppressed and as advocating values of nonviolence, nonretaliation, and forgiveness, which, it is suggested, run counter to the prevailing values of Roman society. That is to say, while we may indeed see Luke as advocating a nonretaliatory stance toward Roman officials, this goes hand in hand with a strong sense of social justice and a longing for radical change. Mary's song is a clear expression of this revolutionary zeal, as are the Lukan beatitudes and woes about the poor and the rich respectively. On the other hand, we have to note—and this does not seem to me to be brought out nearly clearly enough by Cassidy—that there is a considerable tension between such radical sayings in Luke (coupled with the demand to sell all) and sayings that seem to take a stage further the process we noted in Matthew of adapting the radical ethic of homelessness, lack of possessions, etc. to a more settled environment. Luke's version of the material in Matt. 6:25–34 is prefaced by the parable of the rich fool, which is part of his own special material and which clearly indicates his own particular interpretation of the sayings, namely, that they are concerned not with the radical abandonment of possessions but with detachment from material goods, sharing what one has, and looking for heavenly rewards. Also, in the same way that Matthew, as we suggested, may have seen the way of total abandonment of possessions as the special way of the apostolic leadership of the church, so too for Luke the "love communism" of the Christian community in Jerusalem is something especially restricted to that group and does not feature in the subsequent accounts of the Christian mission. What Luke seems to replace it with is another ethical stance that Cassidy also isolates but does not adequately distinguish from the more radical ethic, namely, one that encourages the rich to share their excess wealth and urges people to care for the weak and the infirm and the outcast. The ethic of the parables of the rich man and Lazarus and the good Samaritan is much closer to a "love patriarchalism" than to the communism of the early chapters of Acts. In making this kind of ethical shift Luke is moving much closer to Roman-Hellenistic forms of social welfare, with its various forms of association and family care and provision, while at the same time providing powerful motivation for such forms of behavior. The same tendency to turn radical zeal into other-worldly patience and self-denial can be seen in Luke's treatment of the discipleship saying about taking up one's cross daily (9:23). What Luke offers is a system of deferred rewards for conduct inspired by the example of the compassion, care, and patience that Jesus himself gave.

If this is right, then it may be that the more radical elements in Luke's ethical material come from those sectors in the church which, according to Maddox, he was precisely concerned to restrain. At the same time, however, we would also need to recognize that in counseling patience and nonretaliation, Luke is not simply advocating a policy of meek submission. The values of care and self-denial that he advocates so powerfully, while by no means unknown in Roman society (Pliny!), were by no means unquestioned or indeed dominant. To suggest simply, as Cassidy does, that they run counter to the values of Roman society and constitute a threat or a danger to it, is in the end seriously misleading. What Luke is doing is to propose an ethic that will provide the means for a rejuvenation of the patriarchal structures of Roman society.

It may be instructive in this context to ask how Luke's understanding of eschatology relates to this kind of general social strategy. Luke, more clearly even than Matthew, adapts the apocalyptic material of Mark 13 to allow a place for the history of the church, which, of course, he portrays in Acts. Luke's handling of the apocalyptic material marks, that is to say, a clear transition from imminent expectation of the end to a periodization of history, which certainly still entertains a vivid expectation of the end, while at the same time seeing it as the boundary of a history that embraces the church and its mission. That is, Luke is far less concerned with overcoming problems of the delay of the Parousia than with setting out a panoramic view of history that allots to the church and its mission a central place. It may thus be more appropriate to see Luke as, above all, a universal historian rather than as simply a salvation historian. True, the two are intimately intertwined for him. The history of the world finds its center and its key in God's dealings with Israel and the church. But to stress too much the element of salvation history in Luke is to overlook the way in which his Gospel attempts to create a—historical—social world for the church as it cuts its moorings in Judaism and emerges as a distinct entity, even with all its Jewish heritage. It is important for Luke to stress the church's rootedness in the Old Testament history and promises, because they in turn are an essential part of the story of God's dealings with humankind back to Adam. But it just as important for Luke to set down the history of the church's mission and expansion as a central act of world history. The warrants for this are theological: the presence of God's Spirit with the Christians in their missionary work, empowering them to work miracles, guiding their decisions, and preserving them in danger and distress, at least until their essential work is accomplished. In this sense we may speak of realized eschatology in Luke. It is not that he sees the real point of Jesus' mission as being realized already in the present; there is no noticeable dimming of the belief in a final resolution of all things. But he does see the life and mission of the church as a central part of the continuing story of world history under God's providence, and thus he sees that life as continuous with God's purposes, which will be ultimately realized in the last judgment.

(4) *Luke's interaction with contemporary culture.* To argue thus is not to slip back into saying that this is effectively a work of apologetic, after all. The addressees are still the Christians of the emergent church; it is for them that Luke writes, in order to shape their perceptions of the world they inhabit in the crisis of self-identity that was caused, we may conjecture, more by exclusion from the synagogues than by the failure of the end to come at the expected time. (Was the time ever so precisely expected? Is there not plenty of evidence of other groups with similar expectations adapting more or less easily to similar "disappointments"?) The urgency of his situation lies, that is, partly in the need to resolve inner uncertainties in the churches, which would have been fueled by those who were most disposed to see Christianity as a direct continuation of Israel. Is it too speculative to see such groups as identifying Israel with the "poor" and seeing the promises of inheritance and the woes against the rich as directed quite specifically against the Romans? Given the polarization of Jewish-Roman conflict in the decades immediately preceding the writing of the Gospel, this is by no means implausible. Luke, however, is concerned with distancing the church from the historical people of Israel while linking it with the divine promises. Here, however, he is on difficult ground in that the promises were made to the people who now appear to have been rejected. Luke's answers to such questions are not wholly clear but seem to reside largely in asserting that even the Jewish rejection and condemnation of Christ is willed by God.

But this internal debate with Jewish Christians only partly accounts for the tensions that we may suppose beset the churches of Luke's day. If they were no longer a part of Judaism, if they had been formally excluded from the Jewish community, then they had no choice but to find, or create, a place for themselves within the Roman world. In so doing they would clearly have to relate in some way to the realities of Roman society. But the main task is to hammer out a self-understanding that will provide the church with a new "sacred canopy." That is to say, the need to create their own social world was forced on them if they were not to lose their identity altogether. On the other hand, the way in which Luke did this is something that has its own very marked individuality. By fusing elements in the tradition that are strongly Jewish and Old Testamental together with ethical teaching of a widely humanitarian kind that could at least find considerable resonances in the more enlightened Latin writers, and by casting the story of the church in the mode of Hellenistic historiography, he shaped a vision of reality that ultimately would fit Christianity to become the religion of the empire.

Bibliography

On Mark

Auerbach, Erich. *Nimesis: Dargestellte Wirklichkeit in der abendländischen Literatur.* Bern, 1946.

Best, Ernest. *The Gospel as Story.* Edinburg, 1983.

Gnilka, Joachim. *Das Evangelium nach Markus.* Zurich, 1978–79.

Kee, Howard. *Community of the New Age: Studies in Mark's Gospel.* London, 1977.

Kelber, Werner. *The Kingdom in Mark: A New Place and a New Time.* Philadelphia, 1974.

Pesch, Rudolf. *Das Markusevangelium.* Freiburg, 1976–77.

Theissen, Gerd. *Urchristliche Wundergeschichten: Ein Beitrag zur formgeschichtlichen Erforschung der synoptischen Evangelien.* Gütersloh, 1974.

Weeden, Theodore J. *Mark: Traditions in Conflict.* Philadelphia, 1971.

Wilson, Bryan. *Magic and the Millennium.* London, 1973.

On Matthew

Brown, Raymond E., and John P. Meier. *Rome and Antioch.* 1986.

Davies, W. D. *The Setting of the Sermon on the Mount.* London, 1962.

Forkman, Göran. *The Limits of the Religious Community.* Lund, 1972.

Garland, David E. *The Intention of Matthew 23.* Leiden, 1979.

Hill, David. *The Gospel of Matthew.* London, 1972.

Schweizer, Eduard. *Matthäus und seine Gemeinde.* Stuttgart, 1974.

Strecker, Georg. *Der Weg der Gerechtigkeit.* Göttingen, 1962.

Thompson, William G., S.J. *Matthew's Advice to a Divided Community: Matth. 17.22–18.35.* Rome, 1970.

Trilling, Wolfgang. *Das wahre Israel: Studien zur Theologie des Matthäusevangeliums.* Leipzig, 1959.

On Luke

Cassidy, Richard J. *Jesus, Politics and Society: A Study of Luke's Gospel.* New York, 1978.

Jervell, Jacob. *Luke and the People of God: A New Look at Luke-Acts.* Minneapolis, 1972.

Kilpatrick, G. D. "The Gentiles and the Strata of Luke." In *Verborum Veritas*, FS for G. Stählin, 373–90. Wuppertal, 1970.

Maddox, Robert. *The Purpose of Luke-Acts.* Göttingen, 1982.

Plümacher, Eckhard. "Lukas als griechischer Historiker." In *Realencyclopädie der classischen Altertumswissenschaft*, supp. 14 (1974): 235–64.

Talbert, Charles H. *What Is a Gospel?* Nashville, 1974.

6

Post-Pauline Christianity and Pagan Society

Peter Lampe and Ulrich Luz

Preliminary remarks. What does "post-Pauline Christianity" mean? Was Gentile Christianity generally "post-Pauline" in the second generation? Or does only a certain part of the church deserve this title, namely, the churches founded by Paul mainly in the Aegean area? We could take the geographical horizon of the pastoral letters, for example, which spans from Rome in the far west to the center of Asia Minor (2 Tim. 3:11: Iconium, Lystra) but not to Galatia and Syria, and from Crete in the south to Nicopolis in Epirus but not to Palestine, for example. Or is even that too extensive? From the central Pauline church area, from Asia Minor, one could hear toward the end of the first century the harsh message of the apocalyptist John, who rejected the eating of meat sacrificed to idols as a practice of false prophets (Rev. 2:20) and who found no room on the foundations of the heavenly Jerusalem for the name of the apostle Paul (Rev. 22:14). There are no indications denying that the churches to which Paul addressed his letters were ones he had directly or indirectly founded. Revelation may be interpreted as an indication that presumably even the dead Paul could not make the churches of his area exclusively "Pauline" in an objective sense. The argument concerning Paul continued after his death. Apart from Paul, there were other influences, for example, Jewish-Christian, anti-Pauline and non-Pauline, "Synoptic," and somewhat later Gnostic. In addition, most witnesses of this time period can be neither localized nor dated with certainty. The so-called post-Pauline time is less known to us than the Pauline, though the former has left us many more literary testimonies. We have many documents and "impressionistic pictures," but we cannot place them in a historical order.

It is quite natural that any historian has to work in such a case with a

242

hypothetical model of a general overview. Also our study cannot do without premises and definitions that are hypothetical. They cannot be discussed here in detail, but they should be mentioned:

(1) By "post-Pauline churches" we mean the Pauline mission area between Rome and Asia Minor during the second half of the first century.

(2) The churches of this area were never exclusively influenced by Paul during post-Pauline times. Instead, the post-Pauline period saw repeated what was already apparent during Pauline times. Just as the (in our view, Jewish-Christian) "false brothers" entered the Pauline churches because these were churches of Jesus Christ and needed "correction," so also after Paul's death Jewish-Christian prophets who had been expelled from Palestine, for example, the apocalyptist John and his circle, entered quite naturally the Gentile-Christian churches in Asia Minor, not *because* they were Pauline churches, but in spite of it. Hence, in these churches there was variety and, at times, dissension.

(3) Also the argument concerning the apostle Paul continued after his death. That is seen by later Jewish-Christian writings, especially the Pseudoclementines. One of the most important defenders of Paul, in our opinion, was Luke. Only if we read the Acts of the Apostles as the acts of Paul with a detailed introduction can one understand Acts. One of the most important purposes, in our view, was to defend Paul as a member of the church at large. In addition, the Lukan scripture shows how a few decades after Paul's death the Synoptic Jesus tradition was known or being made known in Paul's church area as a part of catechetical instruction (Luke 1:4!).

The post-Pauline congregations were thus theologically a little homogeneous, primarily Gentile-Christian church area, in which Paul was one of the determining factors with respect to his letters and his legacy.

The following study will also consider Acts and the deutero-Pauline letters Colossians, Ephesians, 2 Thessalonians, 1 and 2 Timothy, Titus, and 1 and 2 Peter. Tangentially we will consider James, *1 Clement*, and Hebrews. Revelation will be discussed separately in this volume, even though it actually belongs to the post-Pauline churches. Excluded will be Ignatius, Polycarp, and the early Gnostics in Asia Minor. The chronological emphasis, hence, is on the first, not the second century.

The places of origin of most of these writings are completely uncertain. The origin in the "Pauline" area of Greece, the Aegeis, and Asia Minor is possible for all writings and for some even very likely. However, one also has to consider Rome as the place of origin for the pastoral letters and the

Lukan body of scripture, and Syria for the First Letter of Peter and certainly the Letter of James. Hence, our study cannot differentiate on the basis of location. In regard to chronology, a distinction between the New Testament times and the period after the New Testament is not meaningful. Most of the phenomena observed here could also be found in the Apostolic Fathers and, *mutatis mutandis*, also in the apologists and/or the martyr traditions. Only the Christian Gnosis, which can be observed around the turn of the century, opens up new questions.

a) The Composition of the Churches

(1) *Social strata.* How can the sources be evaluated? We do not always find direct social-historical references, for example, notes about the existence of Christian *home owners* (Col. 4:15; 2 Tim. 1:16; 4:19; cf. 1 Tim. 3:4-5, 12; 5:4, 8). Many things have to be concluded indirectly. It is a prior methodological decision to evaluate even paraeneses carefully. If, for example, in 1 Tim. 2:9 (cf. 1 Peter 3:3), the women are admonished not to adorn themselves with pearls and gold, then in our view this appeal makes sense only if among the addressees there were women who could afford jewelry with gold and pearls. Nothing in this situation-specific evaluation is negated by the fact that the paraenesis is a traditional topos: one must explain why post-Pauline authors used certain traditional themes in their letters to congregations.

(a) *Social variety.* The post-Pauline Christian congregations accepted representatives from the most diverse social positions. When looking at a congregational meeting, which has assembled in the private home of a well-to-do member, we discover *poor widows* (1 Tim. 5:3-16) and *slaves* (1 Tim. 6:1-2; Eph. 6:5-8; Col. 3:11, 22-25; 1 Peter 2:18-23). There sits one of these *women* in expensive clothes, adorned with pearls and gold, her hair artfully braided (1 Tim. 2:9; 1 Peter 3:3). She probably belongs to the class of the *decuriones*, since women below the upper class usually wear only agate jewelry, the wife of a craftsman only corals (cf. Thraede, p. 223). The *decuriones* are members of the city council, form the upper class in the provincial cities, and have wealth—usually more than 100,000 sesterces. That some of them were baptized is reported by the legate Pliny concerning Asia Minor during the year 112 (*Ep.* 10.96: "omnis ordinis"). Also Luke indicates indirectly that the *more prominent women* were part of the life of his community: he points out that "not a few of the leading women" had shown an interest in Christianity already during the apostles' days

(Acts 17:4, 12). The more well-to-do women like Lydia, the dealer in purple cloth, had been supposedly influential in the life of the community (16:14; cf. 12:12ff.). In the Rome of the nineties, not only various wealthy people are members of the congregation (*1 Clem.* 38.2) but also the wife of a consul, Flavia Domitilla (Dio Cassius 67.14.1–2; Euseb. *Hist. Eccl.* 3.18.4). Over there someone enters the assembly room who has brought along his *slave* (cf. 1 Tim. 6:2; Eph. 6:5–9). The slave converses with the *master* in a casual manner, calling him "brother"; but when he even slaps the master crudely on the back, the author of 1 Timothy frowns: slaves "who have believing masters must not be disrespectful of them on the ground that they are members of the church; rather they must serve them all the more" (6:2). Another slave has watched the scene longingly, for he lives in the house of a pagan (6:1). Although the Christian congregation has accepted him in a brotherly way, it decided after a few discussions not to buy his freedom (cf. Ign. *Pol.* 4.3). Also with envy a third slave looks on; he is often unjustly reprimanded and threatened by his master, although the latter is a Christian (Eph. 6:9; Col. 4:1). In the very back sits someone who has not been at the congregational meetings for a long time. His *business* seems more important to him, and some brothers worry about his faith (cf. 1 Tim. 6:9–10). They also worry about some of the *wealthier ones*. Many Christians—sometimes involved in *trade* (cf. Rev. 13:17; James 4:13)—lust for property (1 Tim. 6:6–10; cf. 3:3, 8; Titus 1:7; 2 Tim. 3:2; James 4:13). Their goods make them arrogant (1 Tim. 6:17; cf. Rev. 3:17–18; James 4:16). They should, instead, dive into their pockets a little deeper (1 Tim. 6:18–19; Acts 20:35) to help the numerous *poor* in the congregation (Eph. 4:28; Titus 3:14; 1 Tim. 5:3–16; James 2:15–16; 1:9, 27)!

We find different social positions—and at the same time different degrees of Christian zeal. Those who have arrived socially show a tendency to "become worldly," not to be as serious about their membership in the Christian church as their poorer fellow brothers. A few decades later, *Hermas* will clothe this experience in the image of the vine and the elm tree. The poor man with his strong faith prays for the rich man in the congregation; while he is a juicy vine, the rich man is an unfertile elm tree. In order to bear fruit the vine climbs up the elm tree, and the tree supports the vine. In similar fashion the rich man is supposed to help the poor man with the necessities of life. Both the rich and the poor are thus dependent on each other (*Sim.* 2).

(*b*) *More women than men.* When looking around, we discover more women's faces than men's: that female Christians are married to non-believers is more frequently the case than vice versa (1 Peter 3:1–2; 2 Tim. 1:5). Whether the quantitative preponderance of the female element corresponds to the influence of women in the life of the community will have to be examined.

(c) *Different levels of education?* The elements of education in the post-Pauline writings, which we will examine later in detail, show—as must be anticipated—no more than a high-school education on the part of their authors. That one or the other author attended grammar school up to age seventeen sufficiently explains the existing elements. Grammar school followed elementary school and preceded a possible college education with lecturers or philosophers. It could be best compared to the modern preparatory school. Beside subjects like geometry, arithmetics, music, and astronomy, one read classics, above all Homer. It is not necessary to postulate a higher degree of education for our post-Pauline authors.

Things are different with the readers. Since one or the other post-Pauline author at least *claimed,* as we will see later, to write a somewhat elevated "literature," one can assume a corresponding attitude of expectation on the readers' part. However, we do not know whether the author with his grammar-school education could indeed meet the expectations of every one of his readers.

(d) *A city-country gap?* Pauline Christianity was an urban religion. The same is in large part true also in post-Pauline times. The pastoral letters have cities in mind. Still, at least since the beginning of the second century in Asia Minor, one finds also indications of a tentative foothold of Christianity among the rural population: In Asia Minor, the Bithynian governor Pliny (*Ep.* 10.96) encounters Christians also in the country. The First Letter of Peter considers itself a circular letter to entire regions: "Pontus, Galatia, Cappadocia, Asia, Bithynia"; at least Pontus and Bithynia belong to the province governed by Pliny.

(2) *Balance between various social levels? Integration?* How can people of different backgrounds be "integrated" into relatively stable and robust congregations? One way of objectively overcoming the social imbalance is that some members of the congregation leave their original status behind and adapt to another. The Letter of James seems to make such a demand of the rich. The poor are chosen; the Christian is to remain "unstained" by the world; wealth would wither in the end like the flower in the field (cf. 1:9–11, 27; 2:5; 4:4, 13–14; 5:1ff.).

Of course, the Letter of James is an exception. The other writings presuppose that the differences, objectively speaking, will remain; a rich person may remain rich, a master remain a master, and a slave a slave. Especially the "household rules" (to be discussed shortly) presuppose boundaries between classes and do not question them. How, then, does integration take place? The question cannot be completely answered here. From a sociology-of-religion viewpoint, we could point in general to the fact that groups become united by common symbols, convictions, or theological concepts. Instead, however, we would like to focus on three particular points that emerge directly from the post-Pauline sources. (a) One's awareness of being equal in Christ, though not socially, has an integrating effect. The question is how far this early Christian awareness still remains alive. (b) Hierarchical structures also have an integrating effect, if the power of the strong is limited within the hierarchy in a meaningful way, for example, through the duty of justice and love ("patriarchalism of love"). (c) Social welfare needs to be discussed as a particular aspect of an at least partial balancing between rich and poor.

(a) *Awareness of equality in Christ?* James 2:2–4 cautions not to give a better seat at the congregational meeting to someone with a golden ring and fine attire than to the poor person in worn clothes. In similar fashion, Col. 3:11 says in a more programmatic way: "There is no longer Greek and Jew, circumcised and uncircumcised, barbarian, Scythian, slave and free, but Christ is all and in all." The same was proclaimed already by Paul in Gal. 3:28; the Letter to the Colossians is, indeed, the most similar; it was written by a direct disciple of Paul's and perhaps even during the apostle's lifetime by a secretary. Like Paul, the writer realizes that the teaching about Christ, which talks about a reality among believers that has been established in Christ (Col. 3:1ff., 9ff.), is filled with a socially integrating force. The existing differences within the congregation have to be dealt with "as if they were not." For "you have stripped off the old self . . . and clothed yourselves with the new self" (3:9–10). The slaves in particular must like this sort of teaching (cf. above, 1 Tim. 6:2).

The question is how far such an awareness of equality is still seriously cultivated by the majority of post-Pauline Christians. A lot speaks against drawing a too favorable picture of the congregations. James 2:2–4 presents a warning that is apparently necessary because some Christians are still paying attention to the worldly differences of rank within the life of the community and are still giving the elegantly dressed a better seat than the poorly dressed. Also Col. 3:11 stands in a paraenetic context (different than Gal. 3:28!) and shows that the christologically derived program of the author and congregational reality do not always coincide. As a third point, we notice that (apart from James) after the Letter to the Colossians, the statements concerning equality in the post-Pauline writings disappear, as if this topos of early Christianity had already become outdated in the second generation. Much more important to the second and third generations is the concept of a "patriarchalism of love," as can be found especially in the "household rules" of post-Pauline writings.

(b) *Patriarchalism of love.* The so-called household rules (*Haustafeln*) of the New Testament emerge for the first time in the post-Pauline letters. At the same time it is noteworthy that they appear in the post-Pauline writings especially often and are rather rare elsewhere. The most important texts are Col. 3:18–4:1; Eph. 5:22–6:9; 1 Peter 2:18–3:7; 1 Tim. 2:8–15; Titus 2:1–10; Pol. *Phil.* 4.2–6.3 (Polycarp is strongly influenced by Paul). *Did.* 4:9–11; *Barn.* 19:5–7, and *1 Clem.* 21:6–9 correspond to the household rules in only a limited way.

The texts place the paterfamilias at the center, regard him as the husband, father, and master, and demand the submission to his power from the "weaker" ones, the wife, the children, and the slaves. It is a matter of a clear superiority or inferiority, yet in such a way that the power of the paterfamilias is limited by the fact that he is asked in daily life to practice not only justice but also love (e.g., Eph. 5:25).

"Slaves, obey your earthly masters in everything." "Masters, treat your slaves justly and fairly." That is what Col. 3:22 and 4:1 demand only a few verses after the programmatic sentence that "there is no longer . . . slave nor free" (3:11); in the contexts of other household rules, this sentence is significantly missing. Whether equality in Christ is emphasized or not, the social roles of slave and master are, at any rate, maintained. The patriarchal structure remains in force but in such a way that both sides are exhorted to mutual love and respect: the slave to respectful obedience, the master to responsible care. This principle of a "patriarchalism of love" has, without doubt, socially integrating effects on the post-Pauline churches.

The "patriarchalism of love" applies in large part also to the relationship between husband and wife. The Christian wife is supposed to be subject to her husband, not to speak during the congregational meeting, and to busy herself with home and family. That resounds in large parts of the post-Pauline writings, not only in the household rules (Eph. 5:22, 33; Col. 3:18; 1 Tim. 2:11–15; 5:14, 10; Titus 2:4–5; 1 Peter 3:1, 4–6; *1 Clem.* 21.7; cf. 1 Cor. 14:34–35). Women active in the life of the church, as Pauline Christianity knows them in, say, a Prisca or a Phoebe, are found less often.

A bit of "emancipation," as Pauline Christianity seems to have practiced it, is taken back. The Pauline sentence that in Christ there is "no longer male and female" is significantly missing when Gal. 3:28 is adopted by Col. 3:11. Post-Pauline Christianity develops into a religious group that is directed by men and especially influenced by the presbyter-bishop, who is active in doctrine. It is interesting that the decline in women's influence and the greater prominence of offices, now more firmly defined, go hand and hand.

Still, we should not draw a too uniform picture of "post-Pauline Christianity." The passages cited above are paraeneses and may, for that reason, presuppose the opposite cases in reality. Accordingly, 2 Tim. 3:7 attests that among "false teachers" *there are* well-educated women "who are always being instructed and can never arrive at a knowledge of the truth." We have to expect that at least in fringe groups of post-Pauline Christianity, women still play an eminent role. These are primarily fringe groups in which emphasis is placed less on structured offices than on prophetic charisma; Rev. 2:20 complains about the prophetess Jezebel in Thyatira in Asia Minor. Likewise in Asia Minor, in Hierapolis, the four prophetically gifted daughters of the evangelist Philip are teaching (Euseb. *Hist. Eccl.* 3.39.9; 3.31.3–5; cf. Acts 21:8–9). And a few decades later, Asia Minor will see the rise of the Montanist movement, in which again prophetic women play a role, above all a prophetess Maximilla (Euseb. *Hist. Eccl.* 5.16.9, 12ff. etc.). Also in the Marcionite church, as well as in the Gnostic groups of the second century, women are able to take on more active roles than in the church at large.

Why was the position of the woman weakened in the post-Pauline church at large? Were the prohibition to teach and the command to be subject part of a protest against the emancipation that had partially increased during imperial times and could be seen as the demise of tradition and morality? How much "emancipation" was possible in the surrounding world?

First, the negative side should be noted. Concerning public affairs, women are allowed neither to vote nor to hold a public office. In civil law suits they cannot be jury members; they cannot testify in court. They cannot be legal guardians of their own children. In legal matters, the woman is a dependent. If she has married according to the old traditional Roman marriage ceremony, which is rare, she is dependent on her husband *in manu* and is without personal property. If she has married according to the common, free-marriage procedure, the woman retains her personal property yet remains under the *patria potestas* of her father or the guardianship of a *tutor*, who can be, for example, a close relative; the husband has no right of guardianship! In spite of these dependencies, more "emancipation" is possible than appears. In practice these tutors take their duty rather lightly; it is a formality on paper. If a tutor becomes troublesome to the woman, she can go to the administrator and have the tutor replaced by another, more conducive one. She herself decides whom she marries—and when she divorces. She is entitled to inheritance. And according to Augustan law, she receives not only practical but also legal independence and full business sovereignty once she has delivered three to five children (it varies from region to region) or has received the honorary title of a prolific mother. She then controls her own property in total independence. We find many women during imperial times who deal in business affairs; they are often widows who continue to conduct independently the affairs of their husbands. While the Christian woman is to be silent in the congregation and busy herself with house and family, many of her pagan sisters hold their own in the professional world. Naturally, they do not form the majority, who continue to be content with a life at home, but in the cities they grow to a respectable number that is composed not solely of members from the upper classes (for easily accessible evidence, see Thraede, pp. 239–40, 199, 204, 220–24). Here a woman from Ostia is selling game in her own business; there a woman goldsmith opens her store. A beautician and a seamstress hurry to their clientele; a woman doctor is called to a childbirth; a landlady summons the administrator, who takes care of her dockyard, estate, and brickyard. Regardless of class, many women leave their four walls not only to go shopping or to bathe, but also to attend a banquet, a temple, the latest theater performance, or the wagon races—which are perhaps performed by professional women athletes! In summer women drive off in their carriages, without husband or anyone else, to the spa in Bajae, to a reception, to a conference with their lawyer. Women form organized interest groups in order to devote themselves to singing in the choir or to religious practices. Many educated women can keep up with men in challenging discussions on literature. In a Dionysos mystery cult in Tusculum, Pompeia Agrippinilla presides as head priestess over men; they set up a statue for her. Of course, not everybody in society welcomes these developments. Moralists such as Plutarch (*Praec. Coni.* 31–33) or Valerius Maximus (3.8.6) do not appreciate the emancipation of imperial times. Like our post-Pauline writers, they are oriented toward the old subordination tradition and regret the loosening of morals. According to Plutarch, the man has to rule over the woman, of course, not like a despot over possessions but like a soul over the body (33). Plutarch interprets the shell—Aphrodite's symbol!—as the quiet life at home (32). Whoever sees it this way is not pleased with a dressed-up woman (29). Plutarch and the post-Pauline writers see eye to eye on this point (cf. 1 Tim. 2:9). Did the post-Paulines protest then to a certain degree for traditional values against an emancipation that was in part practiced in the world around them? Do they fear the demise of morality? Rev. 2:20 accuses the prophetess Jezebel, who in Thyatira in Asia Minor led a Christian group, of immorality and libertinism. Was that what people were afraid of?

Or did the church at large curtail the women's influence also because it wanted to distinguish itself more from Christian fringe groups? Was the loss of women's influence the price one paid to the polemics against "false teachers"?

Certainly, these answers are only some possibilities among others. Perhaps, we will have more success if we place the decrease of women's emancipation in a larger context. It is interesting to observe how other developments in the church at large ran parallel to the weakened role of the woman, without our having to make immediate causal connections.

Prophecy, the charismatic-ecstatic expressions of faith, an eschatology geared at a near expectation of the end time—these legacies inherited from the first Christian generation were put aside as remnants to be cared for by special groups. Interestingly enough, however, these very legacies were connected with an advanced emancipation of women.

That the legacy of the imminent eschatological expectation had moved in the background makes one wonder. Obviously, a lively end-time expectation has socially integrating power. People anticipating the end view their present social relationships as less relevant and dividing differences as less important. What, however, happens when the expectation fades, as happened in post-Pauline Christianity? Then new, socially integrating concepts have to be introduced. One of these, in our view, was the concept of a "patriarchalism of love," which favored a more fixed, hierarchical ordering yet did not allow it to become completely overbearing, because it appealed to those involved, especially those hierarchically superior, to exercise love. Apart from the slave-master relationship and the role of women, we would like to address a third aspect of the "patriarchalism of love": the increasing formation of hierarchical offices on the congregational level.

A hierarchical ordering of the congregation with firmly instituted offices begins to emerge. We will only indicate the complexity of the problems.

The churches of the pastoral letters have a fixed structure with a collegium of presbyters-bishops at the top. One can apply for the office of a presbyter-bishop; one is paid in this office: from the congregation's treasury, which—in contrast to 1 Cor. 16:2—has become a standing institution. The task of the members of the collegium is primarily teaching but also the supervision of the financial means of the congregation, and for that reason the holders of this office are not supposed to be money-hungry. Subordinated to the presbyters-bishops are the deacons. They distribute welfare from the congregation's funds to the widows and the poor. Applicants for the office of deacon first have to "be tested" before they are admitted to office; someone seeking shameful gain is inappropriate. The members of the congregation show respect to those holding office (cf. 1 Tim. 3:1, 3; 5:16–18; 3:8–13; Acts 6; etc.).

One can regard this fixation of hierarchical structure as a variant of the "patriarchalism of love." Without doubt the fixation exercised a socially integrating function in the post-Pauline congregations. Although the bureaucracy emerging here did not function exclusively, it at least functioned as one instrument among several others that the congregations employed in meeting social-welfare needs. With the growth of the congregations, the demands of welfare for the poor increased. Fixed offices meant an effective response to these demands. They contributed to a balancing—even if a modest one—between poor and rich within the congregations.

(c) *Social welfare in the congregations.* The following scene allows a glimpse of the social-welfare system within the churches:

> Proteus was arrested and thrown into prison. . . . When he was in prison, the Christians considered that an ill fate and tried everything to get him out. Since that was not possible, he was zealously provided for. . . . Early in the morning, one could see old women waiting by the prison, some widows and orphans; their officeholders even slept inside with the inmate, since they had bribed the guards. Then they carried many foods into prison and read aloud the Holy Scripture. . . . Yes, many came even from some cities in Asia Minor, sent by the Christian churches to help defend his case and comfort the man. They show an incredible swiftness when something of that nature hit the congregation. In short, they know no holding back.

That is indeed a fortunate turn of events: from the perspective of a pagan, we observe how Christians take care of an imprisoned brother. We have here before us the earliest pagan testimony of its kind (Lucianus *Peregr.* 11–13). The pagan world catches a glimpse here of the "social net," which the Christian congregations have spread for their members. When someone is imprisoned, the congregation takes care of that person. Even bribe money represents no obstacle if such "filthy lucre" can make friends.

The Christians gathered by the prison bars function in a society where social welfare is primarily a matter of private initiative. The imperial central government does not have a systematic welfare policy. In individual cases, the emperor may do his patron-related duties concerning the residents of the empire, but only when the needy make a plea to him or to his administrative agencies. On its own accord, the imperial hand intervenes only during catastrophes such as earthquakes, famine, and epidemics; Emperor Antonius Pius, for example, works hard rebuilding Asia Minor after it is destroyed by an earthquake. As far as imperial institutionalized benefit programs exist, they apply only to limited groups of people. A pension fund provides for the army veterans. Discounted or free food supplies, such as grain or cooking oil, are distributed by the emperor for the most part only to the population of the capital city. Only children born free can enjoy imperial welfare (*alimentatio*), if they are needy, and for the most part only if living in Italy. Nerva (A.D. 96–98) and Trajan (98–117) established funds for needy girls and boys (e.g., Dio Cassius 68.5.4). All that, however, does not create a "welfare state." Overall, the imperial administration takes little care of the poor. The contemporary may be able to see "Father State" in prison, but not in a public hospital or nursing home.

Private or organizational services on the "grassroots" level are in high demand. Members of the urban lower classes form *collegia tenuiorum*, self-help groups that finance at times better meals and an orderly burial for their members from membership fees and gifts from rich citizens. Abandoned babies are adopted by private citizens and raised in their homes as *alumni.* The elderly, weak and impoverished, give up hope for themselves— unless they receive an inheritance from relatives The sick are provided for by their families; larger private homes employ their own doctors and install their own hospital rooms (*valetudinaria*). As patrons of a clientele, well-to-do private citizens are asked to protect their clients and help them in need; they have gifts sent to them or even provide a daily *sportula*, a kind of private unemployment benefit by which the client can at least purchase everyday meals. The altruism of well-situated private citizens plays an important role. We read frequently about food and money gifts in the inscriptions. In Veii, for example, a woman provides all the women of her hometown with a meal; in Ancyra a citizen gives out oil all day long to anyone coming to him; in Urvinum Mataurense, a senator sponsors an annual banquet for his fellow citizens (CIL 11.3811; IGRR 3.173; CIL 11.6054; etc.). Not the initiative of the state but of private individuals is in high demand. It bestows honor on them and becomes immortalized in inscriptions.

The post-Pauline Christians—in distinction to the Pauline churches (1 Cor. 16:1ff.)—set up fixed treasuries; from them deacons give especially to the widowed (1 Tim. 5:16; cf. Acts 6; 4:34–35). But that does not relieve the Christian families of their responsibilities. On the contrary, individual families are encouraged to provide for their own, especially for their widowed elderly relatives (1 Tim. 5:4), and not to burden the congregation's funds (v. 16). Whoever shirks this responsibility does less than a pagan family (v. 8).

The insistent appeal apparently reflects conditions in which individual responsibilities were preferably transferred to the treasury of the congregation. The paraenesis tries to delimit the circle of those receiving financial support from the congregation: only the widows left without relatives, having behaved in proper fashion and being at least sixty years old, may be supported by the congregation; those under sixty should remarry (1 Tim. 5:4–16)! In addition, 2 Thess. 3:6–12 challenges people not to linger and eat the free food of the congregation, but to be gainfully employed and earn one's own living.

From these admonitions we can see that apparently a good many live off the means of the congregation—by the way, not just the poor but also church functionaries, who are paid (1 Tim. 5:17–18). For that reason, the fund does not always seem sufficient for all (cf. 1 Tim. 5:16; Acts 6), and our sources call for testing the "deserving nature" of one receiving support.

The financial means of the congregation flow from gifts of individuals. These funds are not "membership fees" like those of the pagan *collegia*— there is nothing like this among Christians—but voluntary gifts, which are given according to each person's discretion. Luke assigns the commandment of almsgiving a central place in his ethics. Especially for the rich among his readers, he draws a golden picture of the past apostolic era by generalizing, based on two individual cases reported to him (Acts 4:36–37; 5:1–11). Whenever members of the congregation suffered need during the apostolic era, well-to-do brothers sold part of their property in order to help out (Acts 2:42–47; 4:32–35). This idealized picture of history is intended to prompt Luke's readers to action! And in order for them to become enchanted with the exemplary behavior of the earliest Christians, Luke adds to his picture of the early church a few dots of color from his pot of Greek learning: "All things in common" (2:44) is a slogan of Greek-Hellenistic social utopias and has characterized since Aristotle the meaning of friendship. "No one claimed private ownership of any possessions" (4:32) is reminiscent of formulations by Musonius and Euripides. For Luke the concept of communal property became reality among the earliest Christians in the way Greek literature had dreamed of. But it is not only Greek reminiscences that underline the paraenesis about almsgiving. In 4:34 Luke has the Old Testament injunction resound that no one was to be in need (Deut. 15:4). In his Gospel, finally, Luke emphasizes more than any other evangelist Jesus' command to relinquish one's property (Luke 5:11, 28; 12:33; 14:33; 18:22). For Luke that does not mean everything in each individual case, but at least as much as possible and as much as necessary: The chief tax collector Zaccheus, described to the readers as a role model, gives away half of his property, not all of it (Luke 19:8); John the Baptist calls for sharing (3:11); the women serve Jesus "out of their resources" (8:3). Luke 14:12–14 challenges readers to call those to the table who cannot return such an invitation. Luke recommends keeping a distance from one's own property (12:13ff.). Luke has the departing Paul formulate in his will: "In all this I have given you an example that by such work we must support the weak, remembering the words of the Lord Jesus, for he himself said, 'It is more blessed to give than to receive' " (Acts 20:35). The latter part of the quote reminds Luke's educated readers of a Greek adage (e.g., Thucydides 2.97.4). In a hardly more impressive manner could well-educated and well-to-do readers be stimulated to altruistic behavior than by this configuration of Paul, Jesus, and Greek aphorism.

Other authors besides Luke join in admonition to altruism, service, and hospitality toward fellow Christians (Eph. 4:28; 1 Peter 4:9–10; James 1:27; 2:15–16; Titus 1:8; 3:14; 1 Tim. 6:17–19; 5:10; 3:2; Matt. 6:19–34). Apparently, this kind of paraenesis was repeatedly necessary. But it was also heard, as even the pagan world observed.

b) Society's Animosity

(*1*) *Trials of Christians, persecutions by the state.* In A.D. 112 an anonymous complaint is submitted to the imperial legate Pliny of Bithynia. No one knows where it came from. Many names are listed on it, names of old and young people, of men and women, names of Roman citizens and people of all classes (*omnis ordinis*). The anonymous informer accuses them all of being Christians. The legate is somewhat at a loss. Is the name Christian in itself (*nomen ipsum*) a crime? (*Ep.* 10.96).

Pliny calls the people on the list to a hearing. Some deny outright having had any dealings with the Christian faith, and they make a sacrifice before the picture of the emperor and the gods. They are released.

Others confess to being Christians. The legate offers them an opportunity for "repentance." Under the threat of capital punishment (*supplicium*), they are told to recant their confession. If they continue to insist even during the second and third hearings, they are arrested; obstinate behavior in itself must be punished. Confessors with Roman citizenship are referred to the imperial court in Rome.

Others, finally, who admitted to being Christians, recant and insist that they have relinquished this superstition—some presumably already years ago. They sacrifice to the gods and the emperor, and they curse Christ. The legate is puzzled as to what to do with these "repenters" who are charged with no other crime.

Emperor Trajan (*Ep.* 10.97) decides that they are to be released. Moreover, no anonymous denunciations were to be accepted in the future, and the Christians are not to be spied on. If, however, someone were to be indicted as a Christian by a named accuser and the accused were to confess to it, he or she is to punish even without evidence of any other crime.

These are the major characteristics of a trial of Christians from the viewpoint of the officiating legate. Pliny's puzzled question to the emperor as to what law was to prevail concerning Christians reveals a legal situation that is still completely unresolved in 112.

Factually, Rome is tolerant toward foreign religions, even if they do not have a secured position—like Judaism, for example—as the faith practice of a united people. For particular reasons, one occasionally prohibits a cult that is perceived as especially obscure, for example, in 186 B.C. the Bacchanalian mystery rites, about which horrible rumors circulated. Basically, however, there was tolerance. The subdued peoples retain their religions; Rome respects them.

The first persecution of Christians is local. It occurs under Nero in the year 64 in Rome. It is not directly related to Christianity. Christians are executed on the pretext that they were arsonists; they must play the role of scapegoats. Since the rumors that Nero himself initiated the fire in 64 in Rome do not subside, Nero searches for a group to which he can successfully attribute the "role of arsonist" (Tacitus *Ann.* 15.44). The event presupposes that already a large number of Christians exist, that they are known to the public, and that they have left there an overall negative impression. Only in this way does it become clear why they seem ideal scapegoats to the public in urban Rome. Tacitus, who is convinced of the Christians' innocence in Rome's fire, still does not hesitate to suspect them of all kinds of evil deeds and atrocities; the accusations reach their climax in the famous *Odium humani generis*. Even though this persecution takes place only in the capital and is not directly related to the Christian faith as such, it still has negative consequences. It increases the negative reputation of Christians and marks them as outsiders of society in such a way that their unstable position increases. From now on they are considered potentially dangerous; similar incidents can be repeated at any time.

The state persecutions coming next are unanimously reported to us from the time of Domitian (Revelation; *1 Clem.* 1.1; Melito in Euseb. *Hist. Eccl.* 4.26.9; 3.18.4; Dio Cassius 67.14). The events taking place under Domitian are hard to evaluate. Similar to Caligula and Nero earlier, Domitian increased the Hellenistic tendencies to worship the emperor; politically, his preference of the emperor cult was probably directed against the senate. Suetonius reports that he liked to have people call him "our lord and god" (*Domitian* 13). It is reasonable to assume that under him the emperor cult was generally required, especially in the East where it was tradition. It is also understandable that Christians could not participate in the emperor cult. Revelation allows glances into the conflict resulting from that: whoever refuses to revere the emperor's picture is killed (13:11–18). No one can go freely to market to buy and sell there without giving religious veneration to the emperor's picture (13:17; 19:20). For Christians it gives the signal for a battle they have lost from the very start (13:7). Many of them are arrested and beheaded (20:4; 2:10, 13; 6:9–11; 17:6). The emperor and his officials are perceived by Christians as horrible beasts (12:18–13:18). The Christians see themselves surrounded by "dangers and hardships that have befallen [them] in a sudden and quick succession" (*1 Clem.* 1.1). Still, one should not speak here of organized Christian persecution staged by Domitian; rather, Christians have become the accidental victims of a political program. Everybody, whether Christian or not, who hesitates to worship the emperor's pictures is arrested. Also many pagans fall victim to Domitian's obsession that he is surrounded by disloyalty and offenses against his majesty (e.g., Suetonius *Domitian* 11–12). One should not interpret what was initiated by Domitian as aimed especially at Christians.

The state persecutions coming after that are again local. Only five years at most prior to Pliny's trial in Bithynia (A.D. 112), Christians were persecuted in Syrian Antioch; their bishop, Ignatius, is condemned together with other Christians (Pol. Phil. 1.1; 9.1; 13.2) to fighting with wild beasts during the Roman circus games. But as soon as this shipment of death candidates arrives in Troas, everything in Antioch has quieted down (cf. Ign. Phld. 10.1; Smyrn. 11.1; Pol. 7.1). Locally and chronologically delimited, the conflict flares up—and dies down again.

Unfortunately, the "fire" underlying 1 Peter cannot be chronologically determined. Where does it originate? The retouched Petrine version of 1 Peter could point to Syria as its place of origin, where perhaps even Matthew knew of the letter. On the other hand, 1 Peter sees itself as addressing Asia Minor (1:1) and is also first cited by people from Asia Minor (Polycarp, Papias, Irenaeus; in Rome the letter is unknown even around A.D. 200). Pseudonymous writings of the New Testament often originate where they appear for the first time or in the place to which they are addressed. For that reason one may look for the author of 1 Peter in Asia Minor. More precisely, 1 Peter sees itself as a circular letter to the Christians in "Pontus, Galatia, Cappadocia, Asia, and Bithynia" (1:1). The geographical sequence becomes understandable in an actual circular letter. In the most literal sense of the word, the letter can "circulate": first to Pontus, then south through Galatia to Cappadocia; from there to Asia in the West and back northeast to Bithynia. The start and final destination of the tour are in the province governed by Pliny! For after 64 B.C. Pontus belonged to the Roman province of Bithynia.

The passage 3:14–17 seems to presuppose legal accusations. "Always be ready to make your apologia to anyone who demands from you an accounting for the hope that is in you. . . . Keep your conscience clear." "Do not fear" (4:12–19; cf. 1:6; 2:20; 5:8–10). "Rejoice insofar as you are sharing Christ's sufferings." "Let none of you suffer as a murderer, a thief, a criminal. . . . Yet if any of you suffers as a Christian, do not consider it a disgrace, but glorify God because you bear his name" (4:15–16). Presupposed are trial situations where Christians, though not accused as murderers or thieves, are accused for their Christian name—as under Pliny.

In the geographical sense, these "sufferings" refer to Pontus/Bithynia, Galatia, Cappadocia, and Asia (1:1). Verse 5:9 even suggests that Christians were hard pressed throughout the empire, so that the sufferings in 1 Peter have often been identified as those under Domitian. Yet such an equation is not without problems. (a) Concerning the situation in Revelation, what sense would the directive in 1 Peter make to submit to the emperor and governors in order to silence possible informers? Are the Christians to submit to the forced emperor cult of Domitian? The situation of an obligatory cult is more or less excluded by 1 Peter 2:13–14. (b) According to Revelation, *government institutions* inflict pain by offensively promoting emperor worship as obligatory and by making sure that everybody worships. In 1 Peter, on the other hand, *private informers* are the tormentors (see below); the government institutions are brought in only in second place, namely, when indictments in court take place. The situation resembles much more the one reported under Pliny, although once again the two are not identical: according to 1 Peter 1:1, not only is the area Pontus/Bithynia affected by the "suffering," as under Pliny, but also other areas in Asia Minor: Galatia, Cappadocia, and Asia.

How then is 1 Peter 5:9 to be interpreted? "You know that your brothers and sisters in all the world are undergoing the same kinds of suffering." The only extensive persecution of Christians of which we know during this time period is that of Domitian, but that is hardly meant here. The indication that in the whole Empire Christians are defamed and have to respond in court for their being Christians is intended by 1 Peter as a comfort to those in Asia Minor who find themselves acutely in this situation. The verse does not necessarily mean that throughout the whole empire and at the same time, this suffering is now experienced. Instead, it potentially exists everywhere and is repeatedly rekindled in individual areas that are locally different (Rome, Antioch, Asia Minor) and chronologically different (in Pontus/Bithynia both in 1 Peter and Pliny), and on the whole, suffering is a permanent state throughout the empire.

We encounter another hot spot with "persecutions" and "afflictions" (in Macedonia?) in 2 Thess. 1:4–7. The senders insist here that the situation has not been only pseudepigraphically feigned—in dependence on 1 Thess. 3:3. Among the members of this congregation, several kindle a burning eschatological expectation, which 2 Thessalonians seeks to dampen (2:1–12). Since suffering and an expectation of the imminent end go hand in hand in other passages (Revelation; 1 Peter 4:7, 17; 5:10; James 5:8–11), the situation in 2 Thess. 1:4–5 might not have been completely invented.

Overall, one notices the lack of a concept. The state does not persecute systematically. Instead, the government is repeatedly nudged "by coincidence" to confront the problem of the Christians, be it by private informers on the grassroots level (Pliny) or by special situations (Nero, Domitian).

Also Trajan does not make matters clear. His reply to Pliny lacks conviction. On the one hand, he does not want the government to actively persecute the Christians; also, he is not pleased with the style of anonymous denunciations, since they are not compatible with the spirit of the time. On the other hand, not even he can bring himself to admit that only crimes committed on the basis of one's faith conviction, but not faith in itself, are punishable. Although trials of Christians are to be conducted at low key, the Christian name as such remains legally punishable, so that in the later martyr trials, almost always the confession of Christ will become the sole reason for conviction. Therefore, the practice of the Roman state in dealing with Christianity is different from the way it deals with other religions, but then the relationship of Christianity to other religions also differs (see section 3 below).

(2) *Animosity from society.* One notices in 1 Peter that the biggest problem is not persecution by government officials but the animosity on the part of contemporaries who encounter Christians in everyday life (1 Peter 2:12, 15–16; 3:16; 4:4, 14–15). There are people who denounce Christians as criminals. Also during Pliny's court hearings, such accusations are brought up (*Ep.* 10.96.7): the Christians emphasize that they neither conspire to commit crimes nor commit theft; that they neither commit adultery nor break their word; also, that they do not withhold money they have been entrusted with and are now asked to return. The passage in 1 Peter 4:15 mentions at least two of the same accusations: theft and mismanagement beside murder and misdeed. In desirable concreteness it becomes clear what was imputed by ill-meaning contemporaries.

A further imputation is mentioned in 1 Peter 2:13–15: "Accept the authority of every human institution, whether of the emperor as supreme or of governors, as sent by him. . . . For it is God's will that by doing right you should silence the ignorance of the foolish." The Christians are accused of lacking loyalty. The same suspicion prompts Pliny to place next to the statues of gods, before which Christians are to sacrifice, also a picture of the emperor (*Ep.* 10.96.5–6). The parallels between 1 Peter and Pliny (*Ep.* 10.96) show how persistently almost identical imputations prevail in the same geographical area, here in Pontus/Bithynia. Repeatedly, fellow citizens are prepared to suspect Christians, to circulate rumors about them, and eventually to denounce them in court.

Less acute and probably devoid of court trials and punishment is the situation around A.D. 100 in Luke's community. Yet even Luke senses the hatred that Christians encounter. In Luke 6:22–23, for example, he elaborates on a written text he has before him. His model reflects the experience that at one time the Jews hated the Christians and excluded them from the synagogue. What does Luke do? He adds the generalizing word *people*: "Blessed are you when people hate you." According to Acts 14:22 and Luke 9:23 (cf. 2 Tim. 3:12), a good deal of persecution and taking up one's cross are part of being a Christian from the very start. That can hardly be formulated in such general terms unless it is also confirmed by personal experience. We will see how familiar Luke is with the accusation of lacking loyalty and how well he defends himself against it.

Overall, society tends to despise the Christian faith as a harmful superstition (Suetonius *Nero* 16.2; *Claudius* 25.3; Pliny *Ep.* 10.96; Tacitus *Ann.* 15.44).

(3) *Reasons for the animosity.* The first reason is *the claim to absoluteness and exclusivity of Christianity*: one God and no other; one faith and no cult in addition. A pagan fellow citizen who is used to practicing several cults at the same time and to being initiated into various mystery religions (e.g., Apuleius *Met.* 3.15.2) can only shake his head when there are people who claim to represent the "only true" faith, which cannot be made to agree with other religious practices. The pagan Celsus compares Christians to "frogs sitting around a pond and holding a meeting . . . insisting: 'We are the ones to whom God revealed everything first. . . . There is one God, and after him come we' " (Fr. 4.23)! Christianity's claim to exclusivity and absoluteness has a definite social consequence: isolation. And that, in turn, breeds distrust and suspicions.

Isolation. In 1 Peter 4:3–4 it is formulated clearly: "You have already spent enough time in doing what the Gentiles like to do, living in licentiousness . . . and lawless idolatry. They are surprised that you no longer join them in the same excesses of dissipation, and so they blaspheme." Christians move away from their pagan environment and isolate themselves, thus becoming the target of suspicions. Pliny (*Ep.* 10.96.7) mentions that the Christians have gathered on a Sunday before dawn. Something like that breeds fears: whoever meets at night could conspire to commit crimes! And what do the Christians eat when meeting on Sundays for a second time? Who knows! Some contemporaries think human flesh (cf. Tertullian *Apol.* 7.5). Perhaps, the Christians' behavior is a cover-up for even worse crimes (cf. 1 Peter 2:16)! Withdrawal from society breeds the suspicion of criminal activity.

Another aspect emerges: among pagan contemporaries, the self-isolation evokes the response, "The Christians do not like us." *Odium humani generis,* hatred for human beings—that is how the pagans interpret the isolation (Tacitus *Ann.* 15.44.4).

And in truth, what is found in Christian writings about pagan life? "Unrestrained," "in lust," "with envy and malice," "given to drunkenness," in "despicable idolatry," "ignorant," "in error," "in the world of evil deeds" . . . (e.g., Titus 3:3; 2:12; Eph. 4:17–19, 22; 2:1–3; 2 Thess. 3:2; 1 Peter 4:3–4; 1:14, 18; 2:1, 11; 2 Peter 1:4; 2:18, 20). In addition there is a strong emphasis that a Christian has to live more properly than the rest of society (Eph. 4:17, 22, 25; 5:11; Col. 3:5, 7–9; 1:21; Titus 3:3–4; 2:12, 14; 1 Peter 1:14–15, 18; 2:1, 11; 2 Peter 1:4–5; 2:20). Who then is surprised that the pagans feel "hated" once they find out about such attitudes? But the Christians do not want to offend with these remarks but simply to tell by means of a photo negative, so to speak, something of their own new reality, which they have received in baptism. The change from the old Adam to the new reality of Christ (Eph. 2; 4:22; Col. 21:21–22; cf. the baptismal context in the corresponding passages of 1 Peter) is at the center of such statements, not a tirade against contemporaries.

Misunderstanding predominates. The Christians' distance from their pagan environment, a sphere from which they have escaped by baptism, is interpreted on the part of the "sphere" as a malicious act. The result is a grotesque situation in which both sides bestow on each other the same attributes: the others are full of "hatred" (Titus 3:3—Tacitus *Ann.* 15.44.4) and "godless" besides (Titus 2:12—Dio Cassius 67.14.1–2; Crescens in Justin *Apol.* 2.3[8].2).

Economic reasons may also fuel the hatred for the Christians. Pliny (*Ep.* 10.96.10) shows that the missionary success of Christians in Bithynia empties the temples; sacrificial animals are no longer needed; the profit of the cattle dealers and butchers is reduced. Luke (Acts 19) reports how the mission of Paul in Ephesus affected the sale of devotional emblems around the temple of Diana, so that the jewelers crafting little Diana temples of silver staged an uproar against the Christians. Acts 19 illustrates how entire trades are dependent on the pagan cult; the Christian mission attacks the economic basis of these trades. Also the accusation, encountered twice (Pliny, *Ep.* 10.96.7; 1 Peter 4:15), that Christians do not repay what has been entrusted to them when asked to return it (*depositum appellati agnegare*), points to the assumption that the informers have economic motives. Do some, perhaps, hope for a "profit" when they send Christians to trial and at the same time demand that presumed outstanding debts be paid back?

c) Christian Reactions to Society's Animosity

(1) *Civilized behavior—apologetics through action.* In order to counter-act accusations, Christian sources recommend that Christians display a morally impeccable life-style, that they shine by their civilized and proper behavior (1 Peter 2:12, 15–16; 3:13; 1 Tim. 2:2–4; cf. 1 Peter 3:16–17). Every Christian is to have a regular occupation and under no circum-stances become known as lazy (Eph. 4:28; 2 Thess. 3:10–12, 6). Young widows had better marry and pursue an orderly life-style, "so as to give the adversary no occasion to revile us" (1 Tim. 5:14). Anyone who plans to give up regular work because of an imminent eschatological expectation is completely mistaken (2 Thess. 2:2–3; 3:10–12). Especially a Christian holding a church office is the congregation's billboard to the outside and is exhorted to a morally impeccable life: "He must be well thought of by outsiders, so that he may not fall into disgrace" (1 Tim. 3:7; Titus 2:8).

Christians are advised to be friendly and respectful to everyone (1 Pe-ter 2:17; Titus 3:2, 8); that sounds as if one wants to extinguish the suspi-cion that the Christians hate people. Above all, members of the congregation are to submit to the governmental institutions and thus show their loyalty (1 Peter 2:13–14, 17; Titus 3:1; cf. 1 Tim. 2:1–2).

The apologetic goal of these paraeneses pressing for "civilized behavior" has often been misinterpreted. Not only the delay of the Parousia makes it necessary to "make oneself at home" in the world. Passages such as 1 Pe-ter 2:12–15; 3:13, 16; 1 Tim. 3:7; 5:14; 6:1; and Titus 2:8 show how much apologetics involved when a Christian is supposed to act properly and loy-ally in the world. Areas vulnerable to attack are to be kept to a minimum. We could call this apologetics through action.

(2) *Literary apologetics.* Counteracting slander by exemplary *behavior* is one way. Another is to draw a better picture of Christians through *word* *and deed.* Luke is the first to attempt to "polish the image" in literary form; in the second century the so-called apologists will follow.

(a) Luke presents Christianity as *politically loyal.* Acts portrays the rela-tionship between Christians and the state in friendly colors: the first Gen-tile to be converted was a Roman centurion (Acts 10–11). Paul had his first missionary success with a Roman proconsul (13:4–12). In Athens an Areopagite joined the converted (17:34), and in Ephesus the Asiarchs be-came friends with Paul (19:31). The "first" among the residents of the island of Malta offered him friendly hospitality (28:7–10). During trials of Christians, officials acted usually correct and even kind (18:12–17; 22:25–

29; 23:10, 16–22; 24:24–26; 26:30–32). The trial against Paul revealed that Christianity did not endanger the state and even interested the rulers (24:24; 25:18–19, 25; 26:30–32; 28:18). Even during Jesus' trial Luke emphasizes more clearly than his tradition the difference between Jesus and disruptive elements (Luke 23:25). More than his sources Luke stresses that the Roman Pilate declared Jesus politically innocent and in fact tried (though not very courageously) to prevent his crucifixion (23:4, 14–15, 22). Christians are loyal citizens! "Without hindrance"—thus the last word in Acts—the gospel message takes its course (28:31). For the Roman authorities are, as Luke has them say, not qualified in religious matters (Acts 18:14–15; 23:29).

It is clear that Luke draws here a basically idealized picture. The mutual understanding between Christians and state *could* indeed appear so untroubled if the authorities only wanted it and emulated the "exemplary" officials Festus and Gallio. That is what *could* be: it is not the fault of Christians or their loyalty that it is not. That reality was much rougher in Luke's time has already been seen. Besides, the Lukan redaction cannot completely conceal the fact that even in the "golden" past high officials and procurators acted toward Christians in an unfriendly manner and that those unqualified authorities interfered in the religious squabble between Jews and Christians and even sided with the Jews (16:22; 24:27; 25:9). We sense the tension between the historical material and the Lukan concept. Still, it is impressive how Luke smoothes over the contrast with his literary artistry. In 25:13–26:32 he is quick to insert two extra scenes that soften the ugly sounds. The procurator Festus, who in 25:9 (cf. v. 20) still wanted to surrender Paul to his archenemies in Jerusalem, assumes a friendly expression; Festus himself admits that he is unqualified as a judge because he does not know anything about the religious arguments that Paul's trial involves (25:20; cf. 25:25–26; 26:24). He declines a transfer to Jerusalem. He is basically convinced of Paul's innocence (25:18–19, 25; 28:18); the scene concludes with a quasi-acquittal (26:30–32). The entire text translates Luke's juridical thesis of the incompetence of government authorities into narrated episodes; Luke uses this episode style skillfully also in other places. He "dramatizes" what he has in mind. He "narrates" a thesis instead of presenting it in abstract form.

Whom does he want to convince by this artistic literary style? One could think of three groups of readers, depending on what purpose we attribute to the texts: apologetic, missionary, or paracletic. They are not mutually exclusive.

The texts possibly appeal *apologetically* directly to those supposed to "keep out of matters" according to the Lukan understanding: pagans entrusted with government power, but also contemporaries possibly tempted to denounce Christians before government authorities. Government courts were not qualified, Christianity was no crime, and Christians were loyal.

Of course, the thesis that Luke addressed his writings directly to Gentiles has inherent problems. The addressee to whom both books are directed, Theophilus, has had Christian instruction (Luke 1:4). The discussion of Judaism, the connecting of the church's history to the Old Testament, and the development of Paul's story show that Luke was primarily interested in the internal affairs of the church; much in Acts would be unintelligible to complete outsiders. Besides, the history of influence of Jewish authors shows in the case of Philo or Josephus, for example, how small the chances were that one's literature would be noticed by Gentiles if one was a Jew—or a Christian. Still, it could be possible, of course, that Luke hopes for Gentile readers who chance upon his books in some way. Yet here one has to place first the missionary, not the directly apologetic function.

The Lukan picture of an untroubled relationship between Christianity and government authorities woos, in a *missionary* sense, the one on the fringe of the congregation who hesitates to take the last step and join Christianity. The reasons are apparent. A prominent Gentile may fear that as a Christian he not only has to sever his previous connections in society but also has to operate in the illegal "underground" or at least in a political backwater after his Christian baptism. Wanting to fill a public office as a Christian is indeed a delusion (e.g., Tertullian *Apol.* 21.24). Whoever becomes a Christian can no longer fully participate in pagan society. Doubts are appropriate. Luke tells such doubters that in principle everything is safe. The relationship to the state is ultimately friendly. Many respectable individuals have sympathized with Christianity; some of them have even converted to it. For example, a real king (26:28–29) and a proconsul are interested in Christianity's teachings (13:7; cf., e.g., 28:7ff.). Not only prominent women became believers (17:4, 12, 34; 16:14), but also an Athenian city council member (17:34), prominent Athenian women and men (17:12), an Ethiopian court official (8:27ff.), as well as one who had been brought up with the ruler Herod (13:1). Luke does not tire of mentioning the social "titles" of Christians.

Then we have the *paracletic* function of the Lukan idealized picture. Whoever is already a Christian may have to endure the very *opposite* realities; we saw that "persecutions" are also experienced by the Lukan congregation (cf., e.g., Acts 14:22). Luke's Christian readers gain strength and comfort from his pictures of history. They learn to look at their own past somewhat positively and to gain moments of hope from the positive experiences Acts reports. They also learn which way they themselves will have to steer their lives. For that reason, the Lukan picture of history represents to the congregation a bit of hope-producing direction, and even though it is an idealistic picture, it has the possibility of coming true.

Above all, the last two thrusts of Acts' political apologetics need to be emphasized. Apologetics here has not only one but several functions, depending on the various kinds of potential readers.

(b) We now look at a second aspect of Luke's polishing of the Christian "image." The second impression Luke suggests says that Christianity is not at all babble (Acts 17:18) but something educated, even by pagan standards, something "socially acceptable" in the Hellenistic world of culture.

Again, Luke "dramatizes" this thesis with narrated episodes. In Acts 17 the educated apostle Paul has discussions in the Athens agora with Epicureans and Stoics; on the Areopagus he proclaims to Athenians the gospel as an exposition of what Greek thought always had fathomed *in nuce*. Well-educated, the apostle quotes Aratus; the Athenians and Paul discourse with each other in optatives. At the center of the Greek spirit, Paul offers a cultivated concept of the spirit of Christian thought. Beyond that, indirect reminders of the trial of Socrates move the apostle closer to the great philosophers (v. 18). Even Socrates was accused of bringing up "new concepts about divine matters" (Xenophon *Mem.* 1.1.2). By the motto to obey God more than people (Acts 4:19; 5:29), a second parallel emerges between the apostles at large and Socrates before his judges (Plato *Apol.* 29 D). According to Acts 19:9, Paul teaches in a "lecture hall." Not only the apostle to the Gentiles is educated (22:3; 26:24–25); also the Alexandrian missionary Apollos is an "educated man" (18:24).

The "dramatized" thesis is conveyed by Luke in still another way: by his own artistry as an author. The "episodic style," copied from pagan historiographers, is only one example. Luke is keen on providing his more educated readers with pleasure. He meets the standard literary gusto when transporting the reader in the midst of a tension-filled sea adventure (ch. 27) or into the Ethiopian empire of "the Candace" (8:27). Since Nero's expedition to the Nile source, the literary public craves the Ethiopian "exotic"; authors such as Iambulus and Euhemeros narrate sea adventures. Luke entertains the reader with the proverbial curiosity of the

Athenians (17:21). He quotes Euripides and Thucydides (26:14; 20:35); in several places he crafts an intentionally more advanced Greek (Luke 2:35; Acts 3:20; 24:11; 26:3; etc.). He tries the common method of mimesis when he imitates the style of the Septuagint: the representatives of the earliest congregation in Palestine talk in the solemn style of Bible language (first part of Acts), for in his opinion the beginnings of church history in Palestine deserve a Jewish style. Various patterns of speech are artfully rendered: the Athenians in Acts 17 use the optative, which had become extinct in the vernacular (v. 18; cf. 8:31), but Simon Peter speaks in expressions reminiscent of the Septuagint and in antiquated *theologumena* ("the God of Abraham, the God of Isaac, and the God of Jacob, the God of our ancestors has glorified his servant . . . the Holy and Righteous One. . . . "; 3:13–15, 26, etc.). Here we find the "patina" of earliest Christian times, there the "glamour" of the Greek agora. Like the Greek historiographers, Luke places at the turning points of his historical presentation certain *speeches,* which influence the further course of events, yet he differs from Greek historians when he presents by means of speeches the central point of the events as God's word. Like pagan historiographers and novelists, Luke interpolates documents and letters that are shaped according to a Greek pattern (15:23ff.; 23:25ff.). Like historiographers, he repeatedly dates his material (Luke 2:1ff.; 1:5; 3:1–2; etc.). Finally, the prologue and preamble at the beginning of Luke's two books betray the literary ambitions of the author.

Of course, the limits of Lukan education also become visible. Quotations from Greek literature are frequent, compared to the rest of the New Testament; compared to the later apologists, however, they are rare (Acts 17:28; 26:14; 20:35). The differentiation of style is not always successful; even in 17:22–31 and 26:2–27, where Paul is supposed to speak in an intentionally eminent manner, uneducated Greek language elements appear (cf. Plümacher, pp. 15, 30, 88). Still Julian ridicules Lukan rhetoric (*Ep.* 42). We would hardly be mistaken in seeing Luke graduate from a grammar school at age seventeen—he is familiar with the authors of the textbooks— yet in granting him beyond that no further literary-philosophical or literary-rhetorical education. Between literary endeavor and literary achievement lies a deep gulf. However, it is the intention that is interesting here, because it tells us about the envisioned circle of readers.

Corresponding with a multifaceted forum of readers, Luke's education can serve various purposes. (1) Luke responds *apologetically* to the accusations that the Christians were uneducated (4:13), talked nonsense (26:25;

17:18), and advocated an erroneous superstition (see above Tacitus and others). No, according to Luke, they represent an element of culture of world-historical significance: the Christ event by no means took place off in a corner (26:26; cf. 17:6; 24:5; Luke 2:1ff.; 3:1–2). (2) It is obvious that such theses, presented in an adequate literary form, promote Christianity in a *missionary* sense. Luke wants to win the Hellenistically educated. (3) And those who have already found their way into Christianity are *affirmed* in their decision by Luke.

Hence, the educated standing within or on the periphery of the congregations are to be addressed; they are people who Luke assumes already have an understanding of the Old Testament and among whom he is not afraid to produce raised eyebrows with his imitations of the Septuagint. Those addressed by Luke are, like Theophilus (Luke 1:3–4), already instructed in Christian teachings or, if they are still pagans, are at least "God-fearers" from around the synagogues, who have not decided yet to be either baptized or circumcised, but who sympathize with Christianity or Judaism.

It is methodologically impossible to determine the upper limit of the educated envisioned by Luke. If he wants to address the highly educated also in literary matters, he misses his goal. If he reaches his goal, then merely the (half-) educated of his own caliber sit in the front rows of his audience. The literary taste which Luke satisfies—with his sea adventure, for example—is marked by the elements of entertainment literature, the novel and the *mimus*. The novel is read even by the lower classes; the *mimus* is known to people from theater. In Pompeian graffiti, we find corresponding literary quotations and allusions. When saying that the Lukan readers are concerned with education, we will have to realize that even the lower classes engaged in a certain degree of literary culture.

(c) Overall, we note the following in Luke's literary "image care" in both the political and the cultural aspects. Although it is directed at newly won Christians like Theophilus and pagan contemporaries from around Christian congregations and synagogues, who have already dealt with the inheritance of the Old Testament and Christian tradition and are now to be strengthened even further, it is not expressly addressed beyond that to the pagan public. That is not attempted until the apologetists of the second century, who, besides, surpass Luke in terms of education. In other words, the necessity of a literary address to the part of society that is inimical to Christianity may be sensed in post-Pauline Christianity, but it cannot actually tackle the task. The radius of apologetics remains restricted to the immediate fringe groups of the churches.

(3) *Assimilation as a solution?* Groups that are hated and at times even persecuted by the world around them can react in two different ways. They can withdraw even more from the world and choose the way of asceticism, of the inner withdrawal from the world. They then exist as a conventicle with its own spirituality and its own ethos, which is inimical to the world and is continually reinforced by the world's animosity. Or they can assimilate to the world to a degree and try to weaken the accusations. On one side stands the extreme of a complete negation of the world and asceticism; on the other, the extreme of complete compliance with the world, with a forsaking of the faith as its ultimate consequence. Prime examples of the first way, each in its own fashion, are Johannine Christianity, the world-negating piety of Revelation, and large parts of Christian Gnosticism. The danger of assimilation clearly emerges in the writings influenced by Paul directly or indirectly; they give in to assimilation at times and to certain degrees, but they always warn of its dangers. Post-Pauline Christianity appears somewhere in the middle between world-negation and dangerous worldliness. In that respect it anticipates a path that the churches of all times will repeatedly attempt to walk, a middle way between a world-negating life in a sect and a forsaking of the faith in favor of a worldly existence. The Pauline heritage—the knowledge that the Christian faith represents a commissioning by God for a life *in* the world and that the future resurrection cannot be spurred on by an exodus from the world—may contribute to the fact that post-Pauline Christianity prepares in distinct fashion the middle road that the church will take later.

We encounter in our sources enough post-Pauline Christians who adapt to pagan ways of life and for that reason have to be corrected by post-Pauline authors. Women Christians have to be warned not to decorate themselves with braided hair, gold jewelry, and expensive clothing (1 Tim. 2:9; 1 Peter 3:3); here we already hear the sounds that the church father Tertullian will make loudly (*De culta feminarum* 2.11). Social differences of rank in pagan society are carried into the life of the community when the rich receive better seats than the poor; James 2:2–6, 9 and 1:10–11 protest against such behavior. Several Christians practice a worldly and libertarian life-style while proclaiming freedom slogans (2 Peter 2:19), which are familiar from the Corinthian church (1 Cor. 6:12); 2 Peter pelts these "false teachers" with insults. Other Christians eat meat sacrificed to idols, which—after the gods have received their share—is eaten during a festive meal at the temple or sold in the markets (Rev. 2:14–15, 20). Also Paul has claimed the freedom to do so (1 Cor. 8:4). When the author of

Revelation opposes such liberty in two circular letters to the congregations in the Pauline church area, some of the tension marking "Paul's" congregations after his death becomes apparent. James has to establish a drastic alternative: friendship with the world is hostility against God (4:4). Is that only a traditional topos or does it also reflect some of the current problems in the congregation?

An interesting phenomenon, even if not clearly recognizable, is the so-called *Colossian heresy*. Whatever may be hiding behind the people opposed by Col. 2:8–3:1, the curious formulations concerning "worship of angels" and "dwelling on visions" (2:18) suggest Christians who worship the "elemental spirits of the universe" (2:8, 20) as angelic powers, who are organized like a mystery group, and who understand themselves in analogy to one of antiquity's mystery cults. They assimilate to a degree to the—religious—world, something the author of Colossians opposes. He emphasizes that Christ alone is the image of God, the head of the body, the first to be raised from the dead (1:15–20). The Colossian hymn, which may stem from the worship service of the congregation, becomes an aide here for the congregation's separation from the world. The Christians have managed to escape from the "elemental spirits" (2:20).

One cannot say of *Ephesians*, either, that here the distance to the world is removed, even though this letter incorporates motifs from mystery piety and popular Hellenistic philosophy. Ephesians uses these motifs for a conceptuality that is interested not in closeness to the pagan world but in the church as an autonomous body. The church represents a body that extends in cosmic dimensions to Christ as its heavenly head (1:22–23; 2:19ff.; 4:15–16); it stands on the foundations laid by the apostles and prophets in the past (2:20). The church is the home of God's fellow residents (2:19). These, however, feel out of place in the world (5:16; 6:12; similarly, 1 Peter 1:1, 17; 2:11; 2 Thess. 3:2; James 1:1; 2 Peter 2:18, 20; etc.). The paraenesis, so important in the Letter to the Ephesians, has its starting point in the distinction between the baptized and pagans (4:17–24; cf. 2:1–10).

In Luke's community many Christians live in so worldly a fashion that their faith becomes endangered. They assimilate to society in their outer appearance by striving for "riches and pleasures of life" (Luke 8:14; 21:34–36; 20:33–35; etc.; cf. 16:14–15).

Luke basically accepts the existence the rich in the congregation. However, he propagates modesty (Luke 3:14; 12:15; Acts 20:33–34) and along with it an ethics of almsgiving, which *bursts* the conceptual frame that

Hellenistically minded Christians usually have about altruism. The principle of reciprocity, of *do ut des,* as the pagan knows altruistic dealings with friends, no longer applies; instead, it is a principle of caring behavior toward those who cannot "give in return." In place of an earthly reward—either through a return gift or the benefactor's "honor" eternalized in inscriptions—there is a divine reward in the eschaton: a remarkable social-historical function of eschatology (Luke 6:32–35; 14:12; 16:19). We can see here how Luke tries to fend off the "worldliness" of Christians.

Yet even Luke makes compromises. He allows wealth as such to remain in the congregation. He strives for a peaceful coexistence between church and state. We have seen how he adapts as an intentionally Hellenistic writer to the profane literary taste of his readers; by trying to be a Hellenistic writer, he becomes—in Paul's sense—a Greek to the Greeks. But is his Christianity, therefore, absorbed in the world? We should not forget that Luke also preaches to prominent people the uncomfortable gospel of "justice, self-control, and the coming judgment," so that they are frightened and withdraw (e.g., Acts 24:25). The socially prominent in the congregation are handed ethical norms about which they may shake their heads, because they never heard anything similar in their pagan past. Distance remains even here.

At first sight this distance seems to be smallest in the *pastoral letters.* In form we see here, as in Luke, pagan elements of style, whether in quotes (Titus 1:12, from Epimenides *De oraculis*; 1 Tim. 5:18, of unknown origin), figurative concepts (cf. 1 Tim. 3:34–35, with Sophocles *Antig.* 661–62), terms (e.g., 1 Tim. 6:6, the Stoic "autarky," i.e., self-sufficiency), or advanced formulations; they speak for a more educated author (grammar school?) and for more educated readers in the congregation, who are delighted when the apostle Paul is equipped with "books," "parchments," and the "cloak" of the traveling philosopher (2 Tim. 4:13).

The matter becomes more difficult in terms of content. The Christian faith is "valuable in every way" (1 Tim. 4:8). Coupled with Stoic self-sufficiency (6:6), it leads to a blessed life—first here and then in eternity (4:8). It becomes a useful tool for "great gain" (6:6). Where, then, does the gospel lead the world into crisis? Has the Christian become adapted to the world?

Again, one has to be careful. "Worldly thought patterns" do not mean that the social barriers to pagan neighbor are torn down. For 2 Timothy (1:8, 15–16; 4:10; cf. 2:3, 12), not to be embarrassed over the apostle's chains and suffering along with him are incompatible with loving the world at the same time. Not even a civilized, inconspicuous life-style guarantees (1 Tim. 2:2) that the distance to pagan contemporaries is overcome since, after all, they still walk as "slaves to passions and pleasures . . . malice and envy" (Titus 3:3).

The household rules of the New Testament are often named as chief witnesses when one wants to describe how post-Pauline Christianity adapted to the world in a "civilized" way. They are often considered the prime example of how in post-Pauline times Christian ethics became conformed to the world and conservative and how the original "revolutionary" impetus of Gal. 3:28 ("there is no longer slave or free, there is no longer male and female") was lost. In what way do the household rules represent an assimilation to the world? They do indeed adapt to prevailing pagan structures of the *oikos*. They respect the power or the paterfamilias and demand the submission of wife, children, and slaves to his rule; the call to obedience and the readiness to suffer can even be christologically motivated (1 Peter 2:18–23). On the other hand, the power of the master is limited, since he is urged to show justice and love, again on the basis of Christology (e.g., Eph. 5:25). Pagan authors formulate a similar "patriarchalism of love." Seneca, for example, writes: "I laugh at those who consider it disgraceful to eat with their slave. . . . Live with the lowliest as you want a superior to live with you. . . . Live with the slave in a gentle, friendly way" (*Ep.* 47). The Christian contribution to the patriarchalism of love is to undergird it with Christology. Other than that, the household rules follow the socio-ethical tradition of society; they can be compared to pagan texts that deal with the proper management of the household. Yet it is important to note that in their dependence on this tradition the household rules fall behind what many pagan contemporaries actually practice. We saw that many women can be emancipated in their society and not at all be satisfied with the role of an obedient maid at the stove. In other words, the household rules may follow pagan traditions, but these traditions are often already outdated in everyday life. With their conservative bent, the household rules do not at all intend to adapt Christian life to that of pagans. On the contrary, we have already seen that to a certain degree they protest against the pagan practice of emancipation, together with ancient moralists such as Plutarch.

Also the *structure of offices* that emerges in post-Pauline Christianity has been frequently seen as an "assimilation" to the social forms of the world. The churches of the pastoral letters have developed a firm structure within the congregation with the collegium of presbyters at the top and offices for which one can apply and for which one is paid (1 Tim. 3:1; 5:18). If we compare the structure of the congregation in the pastoral letters with that of the Pauline churches, the similarity of the former to the religious collegium of antiquity and to the religious association with its fixed constitution, fixed offices, orderly meetings, and its own treasury is much greater than in the case of the Pauline churches. But can one call that an assimilation to the world? It is doubtful. By having a treasury, for example, the Christian congregations resemble most other organizations. But by the lack of admission and membership fees, they distinguish themselves from these groups. The fund is indeed there, but during this period its contents are used neither for maintaining buildings nor for the cult nor for buying cemetery lots nor for festive meals, but primarily for supporting the poor. That is something distinctive. It also seems premature here to speak of an assimilation to the world. Although the Christian churches adopt for their organization certain elements of pagan society—for example, the office title *episcopos,* "overseer"—they develop their own characteristic form, which even Tertullian recognizes as autonomous and distinct from the "world" (*Apol.* 39).

Already with Paul the development started that let Christians become a small independent "society" within pagan society. In 1 Cor. 6 Christians are advised not to carry out their legal arguments before pagan judges, but to settle them among themselves. Eph. 2:19 bestows on Christians, terms from the language of politics. They are "citizens"—not in regard to Roman society but in regard to their own small society! Here something develops that does not "adapt" in the least but, the more it consolidates, begins to resemble a "state within a state," causing increased suspicion among the pagans that this "something" is competing with Roman society—a conflict that will not find a solution until Constantine.

In summary, the catchword "assimilation" may only describe in a minor way the changes that can be observed in post-Pauline times in the form of the church and above all within Christian ethics. Also the common slogan that ethics had become "worldly" helps little in our understanding. If we mean by it that the Christian churches began increasingly to settle for a life in the world, building more durable houses and acting in line with ethical principles that in part were also represented in pagan literature, then the ambiguous catchword "worldliness" may remain. But if we mean that Christians increasingly adapted their form to pagan groups and their behavior to their pagan contemporaries, and that they had abandoned the distance to their pagan neighbors, then we ignore the complex reality of the situation.

The increased "worldliness" of Christians, on the one hand, and their continued isolation from pagan society, on the other, stand in a complex relationship with each other. In summary, the following aspects may be important. (1) If isolation breeds wrongful accusations on the part of society, socially proper behavior is supposed to ward off such insinuations; the latter has a somewhat apologetic orientation, even though that is not its only motive. (2) Instead of decreasing isolation, the "worldliness" of the household rules seems to enhance and even strengthen it through their conservative traits, which in many parts of society are already outdated. (3) "Worldliness" in the form of a socially integrating patriarchalism of love stabilizes the life in the Christian congregation, allows for a continuity of tradition ("obedient children"!), and thus strengthens Christianity as an independent social entity: an effect that again does not contribute to decreasing the distance between Christians and their pagan contemporaries.

d) Mission as Basic Behavior Toward the World

(1) *The missionary perspective.* The Christian claim of wanting to reach the entire world with the proclamation of the gospel is expressed in Colossians and Ephesians in a mythological picture in which the church stretches as a cosmic "body" from earth into heaven and to its head, Christ, and in the process—and that is the important part here—"grows with a growth that is from God" (Col. 2:19; Eph. 2:20–22; cf. Col. 1:6, 23, 28; 4:3–6). Growth through proclamation takes place even in the heavenly spheres where "the wisdom of God" is made known to the "rulers and authorities" (Eph. 3:10).

Luke formulates it differently, yet with the same universal claim. Only he does not speculate ecclesiologically; rather, he expresses in narrative fashion something about the nature of the early church. He tells how the gospel spread from Jerusalem, the center of Israel, to Rome, the center of the world. The early church was a mission-oriented church; driven by the Spirit of God, the "witnesses" (e.g., Acts 1:21–22) carried the proclamation "to the ends of the earth" (1:8).

It is striking that these witnesses connect mission at first only with apostolic times. In Acts, Luke looks back on the golden time of the first missionary apostles; Ephesians connects the "growing" church with the person of Paul (cf. 2 Thess. 3:1; 1 Tim. 2:6–7; 2 Tim. 4:17); Col. 1:23 presupposes that even in Paul's time, the gospel "*has been* proclaimed to every creature." The world mission was already accomplished by the original apostles! The missionary commission "you will be my witnesses in Jerusalem, in all Judaea and Samaria, and *to the ends of the earth*" (Acts 1:8; cf. Matt. 28:16–20) was given to the eleven; it was incomprehensible to post-apostolic generations that the eleven original apostles might not have completed their task. The later early church even invents the legend that the apostles had cast lots to distribute the world's circle among themselves and then had gone out, each to his own mission field. If the world was already won by the first apostles—as was the understanding in postapostolic times—the coming generations can only strengthen the network of Christians that already stretches across the world by continually adding new people but no longer by adding new territory. In the missionary self-understanding of postapostolic churches, world-mission programs play no role at all; as world missionaries, the apostles have no successors. Instead, missionary enterprise is directed at nearby individuals and their destinies. Only in this regard is post-Pauline Christianity a mission church. Some examples may illustrate the point.

Concerning Luke one can say that Acts does not simply look back. We sat at two points that Luke himself, at the end of the first century, had a missionary perspective: whenever we see clearly his tendency to present Christianity (1) as politically loyal and educated, and (2) as acceptable even to the prominent in society. Such an apologetic is intended to win converts—especially those of high social status who have still reservations when it comes to deciding for Christianity. Luke even goes so far as to meet these hesitaters at their own doorstep: Christian faith is nothing else but the formulation of what smart Greeks had suspected all along (Acts 17). Christianity is a continuation of Hellenistic *paideia*: concepts of continuity were supposed to make matters easier for the educated.

Concerning the pastoral letters one can say: "For kings and all who are in high positions," the Christians pray during their worship services (1 Tim. 2:2), as the pagans do when they implore the gods in their public prayers to keep the emperor in good health (e.g., Pliny *Ep.* 10.35–36). One finds here the awareness that even as a Christian one is responsible for the pagan society in which one lives. However, we should not misunderstand the matter. The goal of the prayers is not the health of the emperor or the preservation of the Roman state for its own sake. The aim, rather, is that God will direct the powers of the state "so that we may lead a quiet and peaceable life" (v. 2), free of accusations and insinuations, and become liberated for the proclamation of the gospel, for God "desires everyone to be saved and to come to the knowledge of the truth" (vs. 3ff.). The prayer for the authorities simply means: May God give us the freedom necessary to spread the gospel.

Also 1 Peter 2:9 offers a missionary perspective: "You are a chosen race . . . in order that you may proclaim the mighty deeds of him who called you."

(2) *Mission methods.* If we perceive in post-Pauline Christianity the desire to carry the gospel beyond church boundaries but not the concept of systematically winning geographical or social groups, we find that this method of spreading the Christian faith corresponds with that of postapostolic times. The church "grows" in an unprogrammatic fashion: more or less "by chance" and through the personal contacts of individuals. Dialogue with the individual is important (Col. 4:6).

(a) At first this kind of Christian propaganda is local, in the home and at the work place. Christian women are encouraged to win their pagan husbands (1 Peter 3:1–2). Christian slaves, living and working at a pagan *oikos,* are to serve the gospel there (cf. Titus 2:9–10; 1 Tim. 6:1). "In the women's chambers, in the cobbler's shop, in the mill," the gospel spreads; "we have to see how in private homes, wool workers, cobblers, and millers together with the most uneducated and coarse people . . . bring up the strangest things as soon as they know themselves without witnesses and are alone with the children and some uneducated women." Thus complains the pagan Celsus in the second century (*Fr.* 3.55). In the first postapostolic generation, matters are hardly different. The post-Pauline Christians are not to proclaim by words as much as by a winning life-style, by actions without words (1 Peter 3:1–2; cf. Titus 2:9–10). "Conduct yourselves wisely toward outsiders, making the most of the time. Let your speech always be gracious, seasoned with salt, so that you may know how you ought to answer everyone" (Col. 4:5; cf. also Matt. 5:16; 1 Tim. 3:7; Titus 2:9–10; 2 Thess. 1:11–12).

It is hard to say, how many new converts still are recruited from around the synagogue from the circles of the "God-fearers" who felt drawn to a monotheistic Judaism yet did not yet undergo circumcision. When Luke promotes Christianity, we have seen that he presupposes at least some knowledge of the Old Testament. Rev. 2:9 and 3:9 show that by the end of the century congregations in Smyrna and Philadelphia lived in a rather tension-filled relationship with the synagogues: the Jews "defame" the Christians and deny their legitimacy; God does not love the Christians but the Jews (3:9). The texts apparently assume competition in the propaganda practice of both communities of faith.

For a local "growth" of post-Pauline Christianity is also required that parents bring up their children in the faith (Eph. 6:4; 2 Tim. 1:5; cf. Col. 3:20). Thus, a continuity of tradition forms within Christian families. There is special care that Christians with a church office have believing children (Titus 1:6). The woman is "saved through childbearing, provided they continue in faith and love and holiness" (1 Tim. 2:15). Here, in the spread of Christian thought at home, the post-Pauline woman plays all of a sudden an important role. Titus 2:3–4 can even speak of teaching in this connection: "Tell the older women . . . to teach what is good, so that they may encourage the young women to love their husbands, to love their children to be . . . good managers of the household, kind . . . so that the word of God may not be discredited."

(*b*) With the unprogrammatic spread of post-Pauline Christianity also belongs without doubt the travels of Christians. Ephesians, 1 Peter, and the messages of Rev. 2–3 are intended as circular letters; this presupposes corresponding travel activities on the part of Christians, at least within Asia Minor. "The world lives in peace with the Romans, and we fearlessly walk the streets and sail the sea wherever we please" (Irenaeus *Haer.* 4.30.3). Christians mobile in this way—they travel by church commission with letter in hand or on their own as merchants or craftspeople—can possibly win non-Christians through personal contacts during travel stops. The example of Christian merchants on business travel showing great patience during contract closures—even when others try to take advantage of them (Justin *Apol.* 1.16.4)—seems quite convincing. With knowledge of the Greek language, a brother or sister in the faith can manage in any city; that facilitates the growth of the church. Just as helpful is the remarkable infrastructure of the empire—no internal boundaries, a well-constructed network of streets, and assured ship connections.

(c) A special form of Christian propaganda is still alive in post-Pauline times: itinerant Christian preachers travel from place to place, preach in the streets and squares, and are supported by local congregations. Even Origen of the third century still knows them: "Today" as "in the old days, some make it their life's calling to travel not only from city to city but also from village to village and from farm to farm, in order to win also other people for the faith in the Lord. And one cannot say that they do so for a profit, since at times they do not want to take even as much as they need for survival" (Celsus 3.9; cf. *Did.* 11–13; Euseb. *Hist. Eccl.* 3.37.2–3; etc. for the early second century). One cannot determine how much these itinerant preachers contribute to the growth of Christianity in postapostolic times.

Among the Syrian Christians at the beginning of the century, they enjoy a
better reputation than local church officials (*Did.* 15.2). At the same time
the *Didache* warns of traveling Christian prophets peddling Christ (12.5).
Pagans can even accuse traveling Christians as parasitic vagabonds (Lucianus *Peregr.* 16). How great was their missionary success?

The important point about these traveling prophets is that they set out
because of their personal "charisma." They do not go forth because
churches commission them officially but because they feel individually
called. Thus a planned mission "program" cannot be perceived behind
their existence.

(3) *Success and failure.* How difficult, even dangerous, it often is to proclaim the gospel—in word and deed—is seen by the obduracy and failures
in the mission: "For not all have faith" (2 Thess. 3:2; 1:8; 2:10–12; 1 Peter 2:7–8). Characteristically, the same writings also record some of the
accusations coming from society (see above). At times one would prefer
ashamedly to conceal one's Christianity (cf. 2 Tim. 1:8). Not only does the
mission fail at times, but many Christians forsake their faith (1 Tim. 1:19–
20; 5:15; cf. 2 Tim. 1:15; 4:10), which is considered a mortal sin (Heb. 6).
To some their economic advancement is more important than their faith:
"The love of money is a root of all kinds of evil, and in their eagerness to be
rich some have wandered away from the faith" (1 Tim. 6:10). Also, educat-
ing one's own children to become good Christians is not always successful
in practice. One paraenesis makes this clear (Titus 1:6): The person qualified for an office is "someone . . . whose children are believers not accused
of debauchery and not rebellious." There apparently are such "wayward"
cases (cf. 1 Tim. 2:15; 3:4; 2 Tim. 3:2).

On the other hand, there are successes. We find in the congregations
not only families that have been Christians for two or more generations—
at times "inherited" through grandmother and mother (cf. 2 Tim. 1:5;
3:15). We also discover "*newcomers*" (1 Peter 4:31; 2 Peter 2:18, 20).
However, one should not immediately confer an office on these recent converts, for they could become "puffed up" (1 Tim. 3:6)!

What is behind the last warning: fear that congregation's "oldtimers"
will lose their influence? Are there many "newcomers," who counterbal-
ance the failures? Pliny thinks so: "Not only across the cities but also across
villages and the open country, the epidemic of this superstition has
spread," so that the temples begin to look empty. The faith reaches "great
numbers" (*Ep.* 10.96.9)!

We shall summarize. The church "grows" through the activity of individuals without the congregations having "officially" "planned" and "organized." In contrast to the mission of apostolic times—Paul's planned mission activities, for example, were actively supported by the churches—it is a "qualitative leap." The mission-oriented apostolic church has increasingly become a more defensive church, which grows only "by accident." The clergy are occupied with existing congregations, not with planting new ones. Not active "attack" from outside but consolidation within the church and the solving of problems are emphasized in most writings, especially in the pastoral letters, 2 Thessalonians, *1 Clement,* and the Ignatius letters. Controlling "false teachers" becomes more important than tackling the world.

That Christianity still continues to be propagated is the merit of the brother and sister in the faith working at the grassroots level. They guarantee that Christianity does not simply write off the world. With their proclamation they take on responsibility for the society in which they live. Since Christ is Lord and Savior of the world, the Christian owes the world proclamation.

Bibliography

Balsdon, D. *Die Frau in der römischen Antike,* esp. 48–67, 305–14. Munich, 1979.

Colpe, C., et al. S.v. "Genossenschaft." *RAC* 10:83–155. 1978.

Dautzenberg, G., H. Merklein, and K. Müller, eds. *Die Frau im Urchristentum.* QD 95. Freiburg, 1983.

Elliott, J. H. *A Home for the Homeless: A Sociological Exegesis of I Peter.* London, 1981.

Harnack, A. *Die Mission und Ausbreitung des Christentums in den ersten drei Jahrhunderten.* 4th ed. Leipzig, 1924.

Hengel, M. *Eigentum und Reichtum in der frühen Kirche.* Stuttgart, 1973.

Horn, F. W. *Glaube und Handeln in der Theologie des Lukas.* GTA 26. Göttingen, 1983.

Judge, E. A. *The Social Pattern of Christian Groups in the First Century.* London: Tyndale, 1960.

Lampe, P. *Die stadtrömischen Christen in den ersten beiden Jahrhunderten: Untersuchungen zur Sozialgeschichte.* WUNT 2/18. Tübingen, 1987.

Lührmann, D. "Neutestamentliche Haustafeln und antike Ökonomie." *NTS* 27 (1981): 83–97.

Plümacher, E. *Lukas als hellenistischer Schriftsteller.* SUNT 9. Göttingen, 1972.

Schwarz, R. *Bürgerliches Christentum im Neuen Testament? Eine Studie zu Ethik, Amt und Recht in den Pastoralbriefen.* Klosterneuburg, 1983.

Thraede, K. S.v. "Frau." RAC 8:197–269. 1972.

Verner, D. C. *The Household of God: The Social World of the Pastoral Epistles.* SBLDS 71. Baltimore, 1983.

7

Apocalyptic Currents

Ulrich B. Müller

a) Possible Prerequisites of Early Christian Apocalypticism

(1) *Jewish apocalypticism.* One usually assumes that early Christianity was influenced by Jewish apocalypticism in various ways. Concerning the extent and nature of this relationship, however, differing opinions exist. Still, one may say that in both branches, similar—that is, apocalyptic— thought patterns have developed as well as similar literary forms of expression. The assumption of a direct historical relationship emerges to the extent that early Christianity developed as a special Jewish interest group within the framework of multilayered trends in Judaism before A.D. 70. Also acceptable would be the idea of a rather autonomous formation of similar concepts emerging within Jewish and Christian groups under the same historical and sociological conditions in the same geographic and cultural area of Palestine. However, the two possibilities can hardly be distinguished in a clear fashion. It will be seen, nevertheless, that the apocalypticism of early Christianity is indebted to its Jewish counterpart in many ways, especially since the respective Christian groups were active within the world of Judaism or were originally composed of Jews.

When we use in the title of this chapter the phrase *apocalyptic currents* within earliest Christianity, the term *currents* is used in a rather general way. At any rate, we can in only a limited way describe an unbroken line of the development determined by certain groups or circles that are sociologically uniform and have, accordingly, influenced the history of early Christianity. The respective texts point both to prophetically active circles (cf. *a* and *e* below) and to circles functioning more as teachers (cf. *d* below).

281

First of all, however, one needs to raise the question of definition concerning what is meant by Jewish apocalypticism, since no consensus among scholars exists on this point. At first sight, the quite general definition seems sensible: "By the word apocalypticism can be denoted, first, the literary genre of apocalypses, that is, revelatory writings that reveal otherworldly and especially eschatological secrets, and second, the world of ideas resulting from this literature" (Vielhauer, p. 408). However, the real difficulties arise when one tries to categorize the individual writings as typically apocalyptic or certain themes as typical of this genre.

Prevalent here are attempts to determine apocalypticism mainly on the basis of criteria of common content (e.g., dualism of the two-aeon doctrine, hope for a world beyond, determinism of history) since in terms of literary form apocalypticism does not represent a specific genre. Yet in the meantime the opposite approach is suggested (Koch, Collins, Stegemann). A more detailed analysis of the linguistic genre prompts the hope that the moods and thoughts of apocalypticism will emerge more clearly. As a definition for the writings under consideration, one may suggest the following approach, even though it still relies heavily on matters of content. An *apocalypse* is a special genre of revelatory literature with a narrative framework, in which an otherworldly being transmits a revelation to a human receiver; it reveals a transcendent reality, which can be either time-related, provided that it envisions an eschatological salvation, or space-related, provided that it refers to another, supernatural world (Collins 9). According to this definition, the way in which this revelation is transmitted is important (e.g., by a heavenly figure). The transmission of information takes place in visions, auditions, or dialogue with a receiver, who throughout appears as a pseudonymous figure. The focus on exceptional revelatory occurrences allows one to see what the phenomenon of apocalypticism involves in each particular case. "Heavenly knowledge" and "new insight" are to be publicized under the claim of divine authority (Stegemann). The author cannot base his "revelations" on acknowledged authorities such as the Jewish law, since such revelations are not contained in it and in fact even contradict it (cf. the introduction of the sun year in the astronomical book of Ethiopian *Enoch* 72–82). He chooses a pseudonym in order to assume the authority of an ancient figure (Enoch, Daniel, Moses, etc.). Since this person receives new knowledge from a heavenly being, and in an unusual way at that (visions, auditions, travels into heaven), the legitimacy of this knowledge seems assured. Apocalypticism is primarily encountered as a literary phenomenon. New writings emerge claiming special revelation; they require equal if not more respect than "the law" and "the prophets," especially since they sometimes claim that their chronological origin preceded the law of Moses (cf. the collected Enoch books in Ethiopian *Enoch*).

The need to secure authority opens up a second dimension of apocalypticism. The historical place of these revelatory writings is normally both a religious and social problem or crisis situation (K. Müller; Stegemann, pp. 527–28; Brandenburger, pp. 87, 140ff.). The author wants to present a new, divinely sanctioned order at a time when the old appears threatened or lost. He wants to comfort and admonish. In the Jewish branch of apocalypticism, which precedes earliest Christianity or runs parallel to it, one finds that especially two historical changes have stimulated the writing of apocalyptic literature: (a) the threat to Jewish religion by Hellenistic reform efforts under the Syrian emperor Antiochus IV and (b) the demise of the Jewish theocracy together with the temple and the holy city Jerusalem during the Jewish war (A.D. 66–70).

Characteristic of the first period are, for example, the beast vision of *1 Enoch* 85–90 and the book of Daniel. The beast vision sees Israel's history as having reached a drastic low through the "doings of humankind" (90.41b). The twice-repeated intervention of God's past salvific activity with Adam, Noah, and Abraham could not keep a large part of Israel from ending up in apostasy. Yet a certain turning point occurs during the author's lifetime when the Asidaeic repentance movement united with the militant Maccabeans (90.6–12). Their battles with the Seleucide forces represent the beginning of the eschatological drama (90.16–19). Still, the decisive turning point is yet to come. After the destruction of all injustice, God will restore Israel in an altogether new way. The preexisting heavenly Jerusalem ("the new house") replaces the old. All of Israel seems to participate in the phenomenal future salvation (90.30, 23–24). The beast vision already presents a typical characteristic that is to be repeated in other Jewish apocalypses. The view of the past and present has taught the apocalyptist that deliverance and salvation will not come to pass within earthly history. The experience of the present shows only deficiencies: injustice and disaster. Only God can effect change, namely, by a radically new deed.

Even more consistent is the author of the biblical book of Daniel. He can no longer see the military successes of the Maccabeans under Judas's command as something positive, as does the author of the beast vision (*1 Enoch* 90.19). Theocentrism is increased. The extinction of the world power and the establishment of God's rule will take place "not by (human) hands" (Dan. 2:45; 8:25). The reason for that is the author's completely darkened horizon of experience. His main question is articulated in the lament, "How long?" "How long is this vision concerning the regular burnt offering, the transgression that makes desolate and the giving over of the sanctuary and host to be trampled?" (8:13). Accordingly, an angel asks when the promised end is to come at last (12:6). The apocalyptic reply wants to comfort: the days of the world's kingdoms and of destruction are numbered (7:12; 12:7). Earthly history is seen only as a history of disaster. By dividing this history into four consecutive kingdoms (Dan. 7), the author expresses the conviction that God has limited their time and hence determined their end. The division of history into periods, which is commonly called the determinism of apocalypticism, is an attempt to maintain the belief that regardless of one's experience with the world, God has everything under control, especially the end and with it the time of deliverance. An imminent expectation of the end time is an expression of this hope (Dan. 8:13–14; cf. 12:11–12). Overall, a dualistic concept of the world emerges. The negative experience of the world, which tends to count less and less on God's salvific activity within history analogous to God's past salvific activities concerning Israel, is contrasted with the promise of a basically new salvific event at the end of history.

If one wants to find a conceptual common denominator for the peculiarities of early Jewish apocalypticism, one will find the starting point of its thought in the vehement "eschatologization of the understanding of one's history," which in light of Israel's unfortunate history can see salvation as resulting only from a definitive new act of God, who will establish God's power soon (K. Müller, "Ansätze," p. 32 and passim). Such a concept needs special assurance of authority in order to be accepted during the current crisis experience. Such securing of authority is publicized in the "apocalypses" as special revealed knowledge.

This is not the place to discuss the radical theory of Stegemann that "Jewish apocalypticism in its beginnings had nothing to do with prophecy or even with eschatology; instead, it was determined solely by the aspects of 'divine authority' and 'heavenly knowledge' " (Stegemann, p. 507). It is correct that what was probably the first Jewish apocalypse, the "astronomical book" of Enoch literature, as seen in the Qumran finds (third century B.C.), was not yet determined by eschatology but served to secure the heavenly authority of a new cultic order, that is, the introduction of the solar calendar (Stegemann, pp. 505, 507, n. 39). Yet the majority of Jewish apocalypses have an eschatological orientation, because they try to offer a divinely sanctioned reply to the experience of historical failure. A definite exception is found in the writings of Hellenistic diaspora Judaism, which seem familiar with a strongly individualized hope in the beyond (cf. Slavonic and Greek *Enoch*).

One can assume that the so-called Asidaeans of early Maccabean times are the representatives of early Jewish apocalypticism and the authors of such writings as the beast vision (*1 Enoch* 85–90) and of the book of Daniel (cf. also the ten-week apocalypse in *1 Enoch* 93.3–10; 91.12–17). They are mentioned in 1 Macc. 2:31–38; 2:42; 7:13; 2 Macc. 14:6. These "pious" ones, who sought justice and righteousness in light of the religious apostasy of their contemporaries (1 Macc. 2:29), seem to be those the author of the beast vision has in mind when speaking of the "sheep" (i.e., "Israelites") that have "opened their eyes" (*1 Enoch* 90.6, 9–10). The author empathizes with them greatly; therefore, he is probably part of their movement. The same is true for the author of the book of Daniel, only he does not give as much approval to the militant activities of the Maccabeans, with whom the Asidaeans sometimes collaborated. He is probably one of the "wise among the people" who "give understanding to many" (Dan. 11:32–35; 12:3–4). Meant here are eschatological teachers who gained their new message through a particular exegesis of scripture (Dan. 9:2).

This is not the place to present a complete history of early Jewish apocalypticism. At last, only one more writing needs mentioning; it also was written during an extremely critical time of Judaism's internal struggles: 4 Ezra (cf. also 2 *Apoc. Bar.*). Here an attitude of radical skepticism emerges under the impression of the catastrophe in A.D. 70, the destruction of Jerusalem and the temple. For that reason, Ezra complains in his recourse to history in 3:4–36 that the story of God's relationship with humankind is a story of failure. Despite all of God's attempts, which culminate in God's covenant with Abraham and the gift of the law to Israel, the chosen people became prone to an "evil heart" and like Adam fell into sin and guilt. The consequence is the judgment that has come over Israel and the disgraceful delivery into the hands of all other nations. Ezra doubts the possibility of obedience to the law, the only way to salvation. For that reason he must have doubts about the realization of the prophecy given to the chosen people.

In light of that, the angel teaches what must be understood as the actual message of the entire book and what for the purpose of authorization carries the imprint of a new revelation: the conquest of skepticism. The angel develops here a dualistically designed understanding of time: the contrast between this aeon and the one to come (7:10ff.). On the one hand, history appears as the time of humanity's failure before God; therefore, the ways of this aeon have become narrow, painful, and burdensome. On the other hand, history presents itself in a positive way as an offer to people to use the law's instruction for life and to assure themselves of the life in the aeon to come by good deeds and faithfulness (7:10ff., 19ff., 127–31; 9:7ff.).

Like the author of the early apocalypticism of the Asidaeic movement, the author of 4 Ezra is forced to have his writing authorized as divine revelation. For that reason he uses the long-standing traditional forms of both angelic speech and vision. In light of a rampant skepticism, he must again articulate the old Deuteronomic theology of the law. Therefore, he poses under the pseudonym Ezra, who as a second Moses wants to strengthen his people in obedience to the law (14:1ff.). The eschatologization of the picture of history drawn by early apocalyptic thought is characteristic also of 4 Ezra, especially in the construction of the dualistic view of time, which expects the fulfillment of salvation only in the future aeon, while the present aeon represents a time of struggle and perseverance in the law.

Apparently, the two themes belong together and could be called more than any other the constitutive elements of Jewish apocalyptic thought. In light of the depressing experience of the present, which can be at best viewed as a time of perseverance and struggle, the decisive orientation toward the eschaton emerges, which alone promises salvation. Nevertheless, the thereby necessitated instruction concerning the salvific end time requires heavenly authorization in order to be able to stand as a valid new message next to the "law and the prophets." One will have to ask whether these two foci of Jewish apocalypticism can also be found in early Christianity.

(2) *John the Baptist and Jesus of Nazareth.* Among the prerequisites of early Christian development are John the Baptist and, foremost, Jesus of Nazareth. These two Jewish figures are often assigned to apocalypticism; it is a point that needs to be examined, though one can do so only in brief. Basically, one could be tempted to consider the matter already settled, since Jewish apocalypticism is correctly regarded as essentially literary movement, and John and Jesus were not at all active in producing literature. Still, it seems reasonable to compare their world of ideas and their understanding of faith with Jewish apocalyptists, since the result will have

significance for the development of early Christianity. If Jesus was an apocalyptist, it would certainly have had consequences for the Christian community after Easter. His appearance as an apocalyptist would lead us to expect corresponding dimensions in the early churches.

It is similar with John the Baptist. His importance for the early church may not be as apparent as that of Jesus. Still, he has at least indirect significance, since it is clear that Jesus' religious heritage is directly related to the Baptist movement (Becker). Jesus had himself baptized by John (Mark 1:9–11), and he probably attested thereby that he was among John's disciples. Certain characteristics of the Baptist's proclamation could warrant assigning him to apocalypticism (Matt. 3:7–12 par.). His judgment sermon to all of Israel presupposes that the day of judgment is soon to come ("the wrath to come"), since all of Israel has fallen into sin. By the Israelites' consistent ungodliness, they have lost the salvation connected with their kinship to Abraham, so that now only baptism as a sign of one's willingness to repent offers the possibility of salvation. The eschatologization of thought in an exclusive orientation toward the "wrath to come" could remind us of Jewish apocalypticism, since this wrath corresponds to the downgrading of Israel's entire history as a history of disaster. Likewise, the future-related statement concerning the "one to come" or the "one who is more powerful" (Mark 1:7; Matt. 3:11; Luke 3:16)—who will baptize by fire, that is, by destroying all the godless—has traits that point to apocalypticism. However, we must be careful here. The harshness of the Baptist's announcement concerning judgment day is more reminiscent of the prophecies of Jeremiah (7:1–15) and especially of Amos (9:1–4, 7–10) when the latter completely smashes Israel's certainty of salvation and only vaguely indicates the possibility of salvation. In contrast, the apocalyptic announcement concerning the doom of the godless is only like a photo negative, which allows the bliss of the just to shine all the more. Another point that warns of too quickly assigning the Baptist to apocalypticism is the fact that any allusion to a periodic concept of history is missing, for this generation of Israel is facing immediate judgment day.

The decision on how to categorize John the Baptist is made on the basis of his increased claim to authority, which distinguishes him from any other apocalyptist and even seems to place him above the prophets of the Old Testament. While the apocalyptic author has to use a pseudonym, authorizing his message as the new heavenly revelation by means of visionary reports, travels to heaven, and formulas of oath and reenforcement, John has no perceptible desire for legitimization. The Baptist talks authoritatively in the first person ("for I tell you"; Matt. 3:9), which ultimately addresses the listeners and confronts them with the immediately impending end. One can recognize in the Baptist the type of a final prophet sent by God, who in contrast to Israel's claim to salvation exercises an ultimate function as salvific mediator (Becker).

One will have to judge similarly in the case of Jesus of Nazareth. As with the Baptist, any need for legitimization is missing in Jesus. He is able to give authoritative injunctions in the first person and use a form of speech that claims to proclaim the immediate will of God (cf. "but I say to you" in the so-called primary antitheses in Matt. 5:21-21, 27-28). It may be true that the enforcement formula "Amen, I tell you" has its parallels in apocalyptic oath formulas, where the apocalyptist vows to write down only what he has seen on heavenly tablets; still, it is characteristic of Jesus that the recourse to extraordinary revelatory formulas is missing. An apparent exception is the vision report in Luke 10:18: "I watched Satan fall from heaven like a flash of lightning" (meaning "be cast down"). Yet the isolated character of these words in Jesus' proclamation should warn us already not to see in them an immediate analogy with the numerous vision reports in apocalyptic writings. Instead, Luke 10:18 corresponds to the vision reports that give a basic tenor to the prophet's message (Amos 8:1-2; Isa. 6; Jer. 1:13-14). Just as the prophets of the Old Testament on the basis of visions reached the conviction that God intends to do ultimate things even in the present, so also Jesus, on the basis of the vision in Luke 10:18, probably came to the conviction that even events of the present can proclaim God's rule (U. B. Müller).

This point also touches on the aspect of content that distinguishes Jesus from all apocalyptists and also from John the Baptist: the dominance of salvation already at the present time. It is certain that Jesus shares the Baptist's view that all of Israel is condemned because of its sin (Luke 13:1-5; Mark 8:12). Here he goes even beyond the apocalyptic conviction that sin and disaster prevail at the present, since no group in Israel is exempt from it. Still, Jesus dares to announce the salvific rule of God to disaster-ridden Israel: "If it is by the finger of God that I cast out demons, then the kingdom of God has come to you" (Luke 11:20). The Beatitudes proclaim salvation for those who are now poor, hungry, and in tears (Luke 6:20b-21). God's rule breaks in already in the here and now. The present becomes the "place" of the future. Thus, any apocalyptic view of history is superseded. Past and present no longer have to be divided into periods of increasing doom that sharply contrast with the salvific future. The perfection of God's rule is yet to come in a chronological sense; however, it is quite certain to arrive because of its dynamic character. When Jesus uses individual apocalyptic concepts in his announcement of judgment (e.g., Luke 17:22ff.: the expectation of the Son of man), then these are of only limited importance. They are available means of expression to demonstrate the fierceness of the eschatological disaster. Both John the Baptist and Jesus are influenced by apocalyptic ideas, since they were in the air back then; however, neither is a representative of Jewish apocalypticism, since their messages are determined differently and not marked by the need for legitimation.

b) The Early Period of Primitive Christianity

(1) *The early Palestinian church after Easter.* Ernst Käsemann has advocated the thesis of a twofold discontinuity, first, in the relationship of John the Baptist to Jesus, and then, of Jesus to the primitive church. Jesus used as a point of departure the apocalyptically tinted message of the Baptist, yet his own preaching was not defined by apocalypticism but, instead, announced the immediacy of the God who is near. Easter and the gift of the Spirit prompted early Christianity to respond to Jesus' message of a near God in apocalyptic fashion and to replace it to a certain degree (Käsemann, pp. 99–100, 108–10). The twofold break in the historical development and the exceptional position that Jesus assumes in this view actually seem as unlikely as possible, especially since Käsemann's concept of apocalypticism is not verified along religious-historical lines. Based on another view of apocalypticism, one needs to distinguish John and Jesus from Jewish apocalypticism. That is also true for the early Palestinian church.

In distinction to Käsemann, one should view Easter and the gift of the Spirit as precisely the kind of congregational experiences that determined the congregation's continuity with Jesus and thus the nonapocalyptic orientation of the early church. Probably the oldest interpretation of Easter (Becker) is found in the participial construction: "[God] who raised Jesus from the dead" (Rom. 4:24b; 8:11; 2 Cor. 4:14; Gal. 1:1; Eph. 1:20; Col. 2:12; 1 Peter 1:21). This formula characteristically interprets what is extraordinary of Jesus' destiny. God has newly legitimized this Jesus, who proclaimed in the name of his God the already present arrival of God's rule, yet who failed at the cross, and by legitimizing Jesus anew, God also confirmed Jesus' message in an ultimate way. Thereby, God also substantiates the disciples' understanding of their commission after Easter, and they, in turn, see themselves authorized to proclaim the arrival of God's rule (Luke 10:9 par.). The community is enabled to experience the present as the arrival of salvation, which prevents a single-minded orientation toward the future, in the sense of Jewish apocalyptic thought. In addition, the disciples do not interpret Jesus' resurrection at first as the beginning of a general resurrection of the dead (cf., however, 1 Cor. 15:20; Col. 1:18; 1 Peter 1:3; Rev. 1:5) and hence do not view it along the lines of apocalyptic future expectations.

One can make corresponding observations concerning the experience of the post-Easter gift of the Spirit (Acts 2). Even though we find in the Synoptic tradition only a few direct statements concerning the Spirit that could inform us of the self-understanding of the Palestinian congregation (Luke 3:16; 12:10, 12 par.), one might still say that especially Luke 12:12 points to the fact that Jesus' post-Easter messengers ministered with the certainty that they were aided by the Spirit. Here, however, we see two things that only reinforce the observations concerning the above-mentioned oldest interpretation of Easter. The early church did not perceive the present primarily as a time of its Lord's depressing absence but as an opportunity for the ultimate salvific perfection, which was to take place in the near future, provided Jesus' messengers were welcomed. Furthermore, one no longer needed to authorize one's own message in apocalyptic fashion (cf. the reference to visions or insight into heavenly mysteries). God legitimized Jesus' proclamation of the kingdom through his resurrection and thus sent his disciples to announce this proclamation with renewed authority. Even in the possibly later stratum of redaction, in the so-called sayings source Q, which originated in the Palestinian tradition, one can recognize the special awareness of authority on the part of the Q reporters. According to Luke 10:21-22, the "Father" has revealed everything to "infants," that is, to the Q group, through the "Son." At first, the structure of this exclusive event of revelation may point to an apocalyptic tradition. However, the revelatory activity of the "Son" occurs—in contrast to the existing tradition (cf. 1 Enoch 46.3; 62.7)—in the present. The "infants" are identical with the messengers sent by Jesus (cf. the connection of Luke 10:21-22 with the preceding commissioning speech). Based on the decisive christological realization, the church knows that Jesus' claim and his message do not cease with his death. The church can pass his words on without a separate apocalyptic authorization of its message. After all, the mere Easter event is the basis for the Son's revelatory activity in the present, as described in Luke 10:21-22.

The understanding of history of the Q community has a certain correlation with apocalyptic thought in that the eschatological tribulations have begun with the appearance of John (Matt. 11:12–13). The days in this world are experienced as a possible threat, as a danger by which one might become enticed to "fall asleep" or "become drunk"; for that reason the appeal to watchfulness is issued, since the time for the return of the Son of man is unknown (Luke 12:36–38; Matt. 24:45–51 par.). If one were to see here already an apocalyptic horizon of experience, one still notes how vague the situation appears in which the appeal for watchfulness is issued. The general reference (sleep, drunkenness) is enough, since a danger is discussed here that does not yet need to be fundamentally questioned. Overall, the Q source is certain of the return of the Son of man, even though one ponders the delay of his Parousia and does not know its exact date. That distinguishes the Q redactors from the mentality of early Christian apocalyptists, who want to proclaim as new revelation within their group what has become in the meantime uncertain or questionable in a crisis situation, namely, that God has already prepared the time of salvation and that its nearness can be discovered in certain signs (cf. Mark 13:14–20, 24–27).

(2) *Paul.* We encounter in Paul a representative of Hellenistic Jewish Christianity outside the narrow region of Palestine. His early function as part of the five-member leadership committee of the Antiochene congregation, to which belonged "prophets" and "teachers" (Acts 13:1), as well as his high esteem for prophecy noticeable also later (1 Cor. 14), imply that he felt obliged to this congregational charisma from the very beginning of his Christian phase. Prophetic forms of expression were probably the so-called statements of holy justice (Sätze heiligen Rechts), which can be found in pure form only in Paul (1 Cor. 3:17; 1 Cor. 14:38; 16:22; Gal. 1:9). In distinction to comparable sayings in the Synoptic tradition (e.g., Matt. 19:28–29; Luke 12:8–9), they not only pronounce eschatological instruction but also belong in the area of blessing or curse, which takes effect even in the present (cf. the present tense in the added remarks of 1 Cor. 14:38; 16:22; Gal. 1:9). Paul acts with an awareness of authority (cf. also 1 Cor. 5:3–5), which links the divine destiny of the audience with his own word of proclamation (1 Cor. 1:18; 2 Cor. 2:15–16; Rom. 1:16–17). This pronounced authority is certainly not found among Jewish apocalyptists, but only in early Christian prophecy, for which the possession of the Spirit is constitutive.

According to Käsemann, the apostolic self-confidence of the apostle is primarily based on apocalypticism, which, furthermore, is also the mother of his theology. One cannot sufficiently analyze the problem at this point. We will have to limit ourselves to applying to Paul, in a few strokes, the understanding of apocalyptic thought so far presupposed.

The apostle mentions his basic calling as missionary to the Gentiles in analogy to accounts of prophetic call experiences (Gal. 1:15–16; cf. Isa. 49:1; Jer. 1:5). His call represents a unique act of revelation in the past, which also contains a visionary aspect (seeing the risen Lord; 1 Cor. 9:1; 1 Cor. 15:8). Vision and audition are the means of revelation not only in prophecy but also in apocalypticism. If one were now to correlate the Pauline understanding of calling with the one of Jewish apocalyptists, one would certainly have to observe a reduction in the apocalyptic phenomena. The revelatory process as such is only alluded to, not developed. The sole emphasis is on the fact of the divine calling.

The vision or audition involved in the calling has a different function from that in apocalypticism. It demonstrates a fundamental turn in the life and work of Paul, which changes him from a zealot of the Jewish law to the proclaimer of the gospel that is freed of the law (Gal. 1:13ff.; Phil. 3:4ff.). The fundamental uniqueness of this call experience thereby attributes both vision and audition to prophecy rather than to apocalypticism, since the prophet can receive the basic tenor of his message in a commissioning vision (Isa. 6; Jer. 1:13–14), while the repeated visionary reception of revelation is typical for the apocalyptist, if not an arbitrary literary stylistic device. Moreover, Paul underlines the legitimacy of his apostolate with his divine calling as such, not by special phenomena of revelation, which receive only marginal note. Nowhere do reports of visions or auditions become the actual means of legitimizing his new message.

Characteristic for Paul is the mention of his personal "visions and revelations of the Lord" (2 Cor. 12:1), which he had in addition to his call experience. Paul boasts about these privileges only by necessity, because his opponents refer to similar experiences on their part. However, these references do not serve to legitimize his message, which is solely based on his unique calling by God. Apparent also is the reticent manner in which Paul speaks of such visionary experiences. Despite the plural form in 2 Cor. 12:1, he mentions factually only one such experience; the event is largely divested of its visionary elements. Only the word of the Lord is important (2 Cor. 12:9), and it interprets for him his apostolic existence. All these observations caution us against calling Paul an apocalyptist, even though he may be influenced by apocalyptic ideas.

With the foregoing we have thematized the Pauline reception of Jewish or early Christian apocalyptic thought. One is most likely to agree with the common thesis that Paul has critically absorbed the apocalyptic two-aeon view; for the apostle can be connected with this concept by his qualitative distinction between the time of doom and the time of salvation, as well as his characterization of the time preceding the last judgment as a time of decision. However, the underlying concept seems radically reformulated. "If with the Christ event the fullness of time (Gal. 4:4) and the end of the law (Rom. 10:4) have arrived, then 'time' is constituted here in a new way and (eternal) life is no longer seen as postmortal but as something already realized in the present. The radicalism of a break with the apocalypticism of later Israel culminates in the fact that justification is not a matter of God's eschatological judgment, but of a God who gives and of faith in Jesus Christ (Rom. 1:16–17; 3:24–26), even if the connection between justification and judgment is not dissolved by Paul" (Baumgarten, p. 234). This addresses the Pauline dialectic of a salvation that is already present, which began with the sending of the Son of God but still places the believer on probation. The traditional aeon concept has fundamentally changed in light of the Christ event. On the question whether Paul is an apocalyptist, scholars have mainly turned to these eschatological passages: 1 Thess. 4:13–18; 5:1–11; 1 Cor. 15, especially vs. 20–28; 2 Cor. 5:1–9; Rom. 8:18ff.; 11:25–26.

In view of the hopelessness over the death of church members, the apostle wants to comfort by affirming the resurrection of the dead; everyone, even those who have already died, will be with the "Lord" (1 Thess. 4:13ff.). The afflictions of the present time do not count when keeping focused on the future glory, because the latter even encompasses the rest of creation apart from human beings (Rom. 8:18ff.). Accordingly, Paul applies apocalyptic traditions so as to express faith as hope through a reinterpretation of apocalypticism. The need for this eschatological comfort is provoked by individually different situations in the congregation and does not correspond to an apocalyptic overall concept that the apostle conveys as a special revelation that is divinely authorized. This fact is supported especially by the reduction of apocalyptic thought to one central truth (cf. 1 Thess. 4:17: "And so we will be with the Lord forever"). It might, nevertheless, be possible here to see the starting point for early Christian apocalypticism: in an unusual crisis situation that requires a special identity affirmation. In 1 Thess. 4:13ff. the above-mentioned hopelessness of the congregation prompts Paul to make for the first time a future-related statement about the destiny of Christians who have died before the Parousia;

for this purpose he actualizes the Jewish apocalyptic concept of the resurrection of the just with regard to the deceased members of the congregation. That Paul is aware that he is conveying a new revelation is seen by the legitimation of his message as the "word of the Lord" (4:15). In Rom. 11:25–26, the apostle can proclaim the eschatological salvation of all Israel. That is the reply to the question forced on him as to whether God has forsaken God's people (Rom. 9:1ff.; 10:1ff.; 11:1). This time it requires authorization as a "mystery" (Rom. 11:25). Like other apocalyptists, Paul refers here to his special insight into God's eschatological plan for history (also 1 Cor. 15:51–52). The occasional crisis situation prompts Paul to proclaim new eschatological truth in the manner of an apocalyptic prophet without this actually making him an apocalyptist. Whether this alone supplies the basic prerequisite for apocalyptic thought in early Christianity is a question to be examined in the following section.

As already in the case of the Palestinian church, one is also prompted in Paul's case to conclude that apocalyptic concepts were absorbed in a Christian way, but that this absorption does not represent an ultimately determinative influence, since the prevalence of the already present experience of salvation prevents it. Neither based on an awareness of their authority nor in view of their basic theological concept can the early Christians be characterized as apocalyptists. This conclusion is ultimately substantiated by the simple fact that the first Christians wrote no apocalypses.

(3) *The apocalyptic starting point in Palestinian Christianity.* The first clear testimonies of early Christian apocalypticism can be found in the literary source of the Synoptic apocalypse of Mark 13, as well as in the Revelation to John. As will be seen, the basic outline of Mark 13 was written during the turmoil of the Jewish war in A.D. 66–70, and Revelation about 95. How can one explain the turn to apocalyptic thought? Where is the starting point for such a development that early Christianity did not yet know, but which has its parallels in contemporary Judaism?

The early church was convinced of the nearness of God's rule (Luke 10:9 par.). Here it was following Jesus' message, which was newly legitimized by the Easter experience. A clear sign of the original imminent expectation is the Aramaic prayer exclamation *Marana tha*, "Our Lord, come!" (1 Cor. 16:22; Rev. 22:20). It presupposes that based on his resurrection and exaltation by God, Jesus is "Lord," that is, an eschatological salvific figure. A Christology oriented on the Son of man is probably implied here. The congregation expects in Jesus the future Son of man, who guarantees salvation in the eschaton. The origin of the prayerful exclamation "Our Lord, come!" in (ecstatic) Spirit-related utterances of the worshiping congregation suggests regarding it as a plea for Jesus' return; that plea is expressed, however, with the comforting awareness that his Parousia is near, because God has exalted him as Lord and judge. The experience of a salvation already present is otherwise found mainly in the sayings source Q (see *b*, 3 above). Hence, Jesus' Beatitudes, for example, continue to be valid for the Christians (Luke 6:20–22); deliverance from earthly hardships is within the scope of Jesus' proclamation.

Such indications of a present salvific certainty were called into question, however, as the external situation of the Palestinian church became more and more threatening. For this there are historical reasons. In the fifties and sixties of the first century the religious and political opposition between Judaism and the Roman rule deepened. The Zealot party, which opposed foreign occupation by Rome, gained ground. The distress of Palestinian Christianity increased, the more Judaism sought to secure its own religious identity in distinction to Rome. The result was the persecution of Christians, even though one has to remember that Christians were under the pressure of persecution from the very start. The longer this situation lasted, the more the question was raised about the end of this calamity. The experience of the present certainty of salvation reached a crisis. Faith in the nearness of God's rule longed for verification of this hope. This basic mood has its analogy in the awareness of doom, a concept that emerged in early Jewish apocalypticism. In light of the darkening horizon of experience, a pressing question emerged: When would God finally intervene and bring about the decisive turn of events? For the pious, earthly history was merely a time of disaster; only the expectation of a complete change in the eschatological future could sustain the believer. There are indications that a similar basic attitude developed among Christian groups.

The point of departure is supposed to be the relatively early logion of Matt. 10:23: "When they persecute you in one town, flee to the next; for truly I tell you, you will not have gone through all the towns of Israel before the Son of Man comes." The saying anticipates the difficulties that Christian groups encountered during their mission efforts in Israel. In light of threatening persecutions the delay of the Son of man, Jesus, becomes a problem. A date is mentioned in order to comfort. Despite the apparent delay, the hard pressed congregation needs to know that the Son of man will come soon. The reference to the short time until the end comes is still sufficient to strengthen the troubled disciples; apocalyptic reassurance is not yet needed, and thus the saying does not extensively adopt apocalyptic ideas.

A similar case is Luke 18:7-8. The original parable of the godless judge in verses 2-5 is followed by the possibly secondary usage in verses 6-8a, which have received a Lukan redaction in verse 8b. For our context only the saying in verses 7-8a is important: "And will not God grant justice to his chosen ones who cry to him day and night? Will he [as it seems] delay long in helping them? I tell you, he will quickly grant justice to them."

The structure of the entire passage is significant. The first sentence contains a rhetorical question, which probably reiterates the complaints of distressed people longing for the realization of God's justice. The response is a salvific announcement, emphasizing the nearness of God's intervention. We have already seen something similar in the question of Dan. 8:13 (repeated in 12:6) and in the apocalyptist's reply that the days of the world's empires are numbered. In 1 Enoch 47:2 the saints in heaven ask that they be judged and that the execution of judgment not last forever for them. Then 47:3-4 describes the imminent execution of judgment. Under discussion, accordingly, is the carrying out of divine justice, which the pious do without in this age and which, therefore, needs special affirmation. Redemption can only be expected in the salvific future. Luke 18:7-8 has the same thought structure as the apocalyptic parallels. The longing cry for justice, which is promised to the "chosen ones" on the basis of their election, indicates that their salvific awareness is in crisis. Their present life is marked by affliction, so that their eyes are turned to the future and divine justification.

Nevertheless, two aspects distinguish Luke 18:7-8 from the apocalyptic parallels. The announcement of salvation has the form of a Jesus saying, introduced by the emphatic "I tell you." It seems that an early Christian prophet is speaking here who can make these promises of salvation by identifying with the exalted Lord. Aware of Jesus' salvific activity that is effective in the here and now in his congregation (cf. Luke 10:21-22), the author can proclaim Jesus' comforting message—as his messenger, who sees himself authorized by the exalted Lord. For that reason the saying in Luke 18:7-8 does not have the problem of legitimation found in apocalyptic writings. It is also interesting to note that there is no coloration of the future salvation by adopting apocalyptic ideas; the affirmation that God's judgment is near suffices. Still, Luke 18:7-8 is able to indicate the point of departure for early Christian apocalyptic thought: in the experience that the realization of divine justice is missing in the present and can be expected only in the future. After all, this basic feature unites the prophetic saying with apocalyptic parallels.

A basic aspect may be added here. The search for the triggering factors of early Christian apocalypticism has to remember that the necessity of coping with certain crisis situations is, of course, not always
sufficient to explain the typically apocalyptic solution to a problem.
The Gospel of John, the Letter to the Hebrews, and also some Gnostic texts show a different way of coping with such crisis situations.
"Hence, one needs as a necessary condition also the specific historical influence of problems that are overcome, yet always by individually different theological solutions. Already the viewpoint of a
problematic situation and one's attitude to it are different from case
to case, depending on the theological and historical horizon in the
various circles" (Brandenburger, p. 143). In the texts in question, the
(in)direct relationship to Jewish apocalypticism in the Palestinian
area is more or less clear.

c) Apocalyptic Prophecy in the Synoptic Apocalypse of Mark 13

(1) *Determining the literary source.* In Mark 13 one encounters for the
first time a Christian text that justly carries the label "apocalyptic." This
text leads into the crisis times of the Jewish war (A.D. 66–70), which also for
the Christian churches in Palestine represented an extremely threatening
situation. Before characterizing the text on the basis of content, however,
one needs to clarify literary problems. For scholarship has observed that
content-related tensions exist between the basic tendency of the evangelist
Mark and the individual statements in Mark 13. For Mark, the beginning of
God's rule has already taken place with Jesus' ministry (1:15). Mark interprets the entire post-Easter situation of the church from the viewpoint of
eschatology. The persecutions of the church are seen in this context; therefore, Christians are to be attentive and to cling to the eschatological hope
with constant readiness (13:33–34). Since the arrival of God's rule is not
connected with particular historical events that are yet to come but has
already come with Jesus' ministry, the evangelist is forced to correct the
imminent expectation of the end, which is oriented toward earthly events
that could be interpreted as signs of the end because of their terrifying
characteristics. As will be seen, the original meaning of verses 14ff. is the
expected manifestation of the "desolating sacrilege" in the Jerusalem temple as the beginning of the last and ultimate tribulation and hence as a
symbol that signals the imminent consummation (vs. 24–27). But not for

Mark. For him, the events of verses 14–22 are already things of the past, as can be gleaned from his comment in verse 23, which definitely looks back. He probably wrote after Jerusalem and the temple were destroyed, thus fulfilling the prophecy of verse 14 in a certain way. However, the arrival of the Son of man has not yet taken place. A new orientation is necessary. Mark dissolves the connection between hope and certain historical phenomena (verse 14 in particular). "The sign solely indicative of the end time consists of cosmic appearances from heaven that precede his coming [i.e., the Son of man's]" (Brandenburger, p. 103). Connected with forsaking the eschatological interpretation of the sign in verse 14 and the sobering effects of the delay of the Son of man is a certain reduction of the imminent expectation, even though it is not the actual goal of Markan redaction, as is always suggested. After all, "this generation" is supposed to experience the time of salvation (v. 30).

Different is the primary tendency in the eschatological speech of Mark 13. This speech is essentially determined by the passages in verses 7–8, 14–20, and 24–27, which describe events preceding or accompanying the Parousia of the Son of man. The readers are supposed to draw certain conclusions from the perception of earthly phenomena concerning their behavior in the end time ("when you hear . . . ": verse 7; "when you see . . . ": verse 14). Verses 24–27 have to be interpreted separately, since they describe the consummation, in light of which a renewed admonition for proper behavior is not needed.

The statements in verses 7–8 and 14–20 are marked by an acute expectation of the imminent end. One can recognize a series of historical events leading up to the end. Even though "wars and rumors of wars" are not yet the end (v. 7), they still appear in clear connection with the latter as the "beginning of the birthpangs" (v. 8). The visible "desolating sacrilege" (v. 14) marks then an escalation of horror, which describes this period as an affliction "such as has not been from the beginning of the creation" (v. 19). However, God has shortened these days for the sake of rescuing the elect so that deliverance is near (v. 20). "In those days," that is, immediately thereafter, the change of times takes place, which is the revelation of the Son of man initiated by cosmic signs. Since verses 7–8 illustrate the "beginning of the birthpangs" and verses 14–20 show these pangs as a time of extreme hardship, which soon leads to deliverance because of God's shortening the days (vs. 24–27), the last period in particular shows the nearness of the end. The "desolating sacrilege" (v. 14) initiating this time becomes the sign of the impending rescue of the "elect."

One can draw a preliminary conclusion from what has been said: In verses 7–8, 14–20, and 24–27, one seems to encounter a coherent eschatological "speech," which is governed by an immediate expectation of the end and oriented toward certain historical happenings. This speech is rounded off at the end, because verses 24–27 represent a sensible conclusion, one where with the appearance of the Son of man a complete reversal of the situation occurs and the "chosen ones" are redeemed from the previous period of greatest affliction. This "speech" might have been part of the evangelist's source, but he interprets it in the course of his eschatological reorientation, which rejects determining the time of salvation on the basis of historical signs (cf. v. 32). One still has to ask whether further statements within verses 5–27 were part of Mark's source. The present beginning of the "speech," verses 5–6, may come from the evangelist, since the outline of chronologically escalating periods, typical of the source, does not begin until verse 7. Verses 21–23 betray the same origin, since according to the original, still recognizable plan of the "speech," the mentioning of pseudoprophets lags behind here. They belong most logically to verses 7–8, or at least not to the assurance that the days of affliction are shortened by God (v. 20), since this assurance leads *directly* into verses 24–27 in light of the expectation that salvation is near.

It is different with verses 9–13. Verses 9 and 11–13 appear to be part of the source mainly because verse 10, which represents the initial Markan reduction of the imminent expectation, disrupts the train of thought. The introduction of verse 11, "and when," connects across verse 10 to verse 9. The concrete expression "the gospel" is typical of the evangelist (1:15; 8:35; 10:29; 14:9). In addition, there is a further consideration. In the source's original conception, verses 7–8 refer to the present time of the author, while verses 14ff. contain the actual prophecy. It would contradict the way of presentation of similar—apocalyptic—descriptions of history to mention the sufferings of the present time only in passing and then turn immediately to the future. After all, it is from the present sufferings that the look into the future results. Only the sayings in verses 9 and 11–13 concerning the persecutions actually make clear the nature of the congregation's crisis situation. If one wants to presuppose a source, for which there are good reasons, one will be forced to attribute also verses 9, 11–13 to this source.

Redactionally we find throughout the present form of the speech the accompanying "See!" (NRSV: "Beware"). That is true for verse 5 because of the overall redactional character of verses 5–6. One will likewise have to

assume the same for verse 9a, for it interrupts the otherwise good connection of verse 8 with verse 9b. It is similar with verse 23, which one can
wholly attribute to Markan redaction, as is commonly assumed. It remains
to be seen whether in verse 24 the time indication is doubled by the phrase
"after that suffering" in the typically Markan manner.

In summary one can say from this analysis that the pre-Markan
"speech" comprises verses 7–8, 9b, 11–13, 14–10, and 24–27. Concerning
its characteristics, the following points can be made:

(a) The Parousia speech is already of Christian origin, which can be
clearly seen by verses 9b and 11–13. A limitation of the pre-Markan source
to verses 7–8, 12, and 14–27 (without small Christian additions), which
could constitute an originally Jewish apocalyptic writing (Bultmann), is
difficult. Besides that, one will see that the idea of the Son of man in
verses 24–27 is Christian rather than Jewish.

(b) The source shows an acute expectation of the imminent end, which
is oriented toward earthly signs of the time of salvation yet does not correlate with the Markan purpose (cf. vs. 10, 32).

(c) As in other apocalyptic writings (Dan. 9:23, 25; Rev. 13:9, 18;
17:9), there is an interpolated instruction to the reader to interpret the
secret statement in the correct way: "Let the reader understand!" (v. 14).
The source contained probably the entire "speech." According to these
preliminary literary observations, one has to ask how far the Parousia
speech of the source is apocalyptic. Thereby, it is not enough to establish
the infusion of the Jewish-apocalyptic idea of the Son of man especially in
verses 24–27. The apocalyptic character is not sufficiently demonstrated by
the mere usage of corresponding tradition material but primarily by the
basic attitude underlying the entire "speech," which has provoked the
adoption of apocalyptic ides.

(2) *The apocalyptic character of the original Parousia speech.* We have
already seen that the time indications in verse 7 ("when you hear"),
verse 14 ("when you see"), and verse 24 ("but in those days") are clearly
structuring signals in the "speech." Accordingly, the first part comprises
verses 7–8, 9b, and 11–13; the second, verses 14–20; and the third,
verses 24–27. With the time indications, the three parts follow a chronological order. At the center of the first part, verses 7–13 (without additions), one finds two admonitions (v. 7 and v. 11) that are urgent in view of
the acute dangers.

(a) One already hears of "wars and rumors of wars," which apparently
affect geographically distant areas yet still disconcert the Christians, so that

the warning "do not be alarmed" becomes necessary (v. 7). One may have to imagine a situation during the Jewish war (A.D. 66–70) when the battles concentrated on Galilee while the churches in Judea were not immediately affected. If that is true, then verse 7 reflects the concern of the addressees that the war might spill over from Galilee into Judea (Brandenburger, p. 46). At any rate, the churches in Judea are being addressed, as the request in verse 14 reveals. Verse 8 explains, by means of a global prophecy, the eschatological necessity of the terror mentioned in verse 7 and thus shows that everything happens according to God's plan (as the "beginning of the birthpangs").

(b) In a next step of the argument, another prophecy is issued to the congregations, which reflects factually their entire experience of persecution up to this point (v. 9b). In a futuristic prophetic manner—after all, the entire speech is styled as one given by the earthly Jesus—the text enumerates the threats against Christians, which go beyond the present situation in their comprehensiveness and are in part already traditional (cf. the Q tradition in Matt. 10:19–20 par. Luke 12:11–12). On account of Jesus, the Christians are delivered up to Jewish courts or made to defend themselves before governors and kings. Yet they are admonished by the still valid, comforting admonition: "Do not worry beforehand"; for the Spirit will tell them how to answer in each court situation (v. 11).

In verses 9b and 11 one finds the application of an already existing sayings tradition, as can be seen by the independent Q tradition of Matt. 10:19–20 par. Luke 12:11–12. The Q tradition also shows that verse 10 is interpolated (probably by Mark), since Q does not have anything corresponding to verse 10.

Then verse 12 places the threat to the Christians in the larger context of eschatological afflictions, which have to proceed according to divine predestination and will culminate in a general hatred of the surrounding world (v. 13a). In verse 13a there may be hints of the extensive persecution of Christians in Rome under Nero (A.D. 64). Despite the encouraging words in verse 11, the present situation of the congregations appears dark and threatening, especially since it is interpreted as the "beginning of the birthpangs."

Verses 7–13 (without additions) mention the acute dangers for the addressees, which necessitate a warning in each particular case (vs. 7, 11). However, verses 8 and 12 expand these dangers to extreme apocalyptic dimensions—without precise indications that can be historically verified. That is so because the perception of the present involves a certain interpretation of it. It is noteworthy that individual words reflecting the visually comprehensible experiences of Christians (vs. 7, 11) are directly connected with statements going far beyond the present horizon of experience. In verse 8 the series of horrible happenings takes on worldwide cosmic dimensions; these events are part of the repertoire of Jewish and Christian apocalypticism (4 Ezra 13:30–32; 2 Apoc. Bar. 70.8; Rev. 6:1ff.). Likewise, in verse 12 the anticipated general discord within families as a sign of the end points to apocalypticism (Jub. 23.19; 1 Enoch 100.1–2; 4 Ezra 5:9; 6:24). The author has interpreted his own experiences or those of his congregations as a part of these extensive catastrophes mentioned, even as an indication of the imminent end (v. 7). Thus the extremely negative experience of trying to cope with the world leads to an eschatologization of the general thought, which is also constitutive of early Jewish apocalypticism. The only hope lies in a patient endurance to the end. The word of promise stimulating this hope (v. 13) finds its parallels in the sayings on overcoming in Rev. 2–3, as well as in Jewish apocalypticism (Dan. 12:12; 4 Ezra 6:25).

With the new beginning of verse 14, the author transcends the present, a step that can already be observed in the preceding promise of verse 13. He points to the manifestation of a secret entity, of the "desolating sacrilege," in light of which the Christians in Judea are to flee not into the fortified city Jerusalem but into the mountains. At the same time, the author characterizes "those days" as an affliction "such as has not been from the beginning of the creation" (v. 19). Here the future aspect of the events introduced by verse 14 becomes clear. These are events leading to the eschatological consummation (vs. 24–27). This time of ultimate affliction represents to the Christians ("the chosen ones") a threat they would not have endured if God had not shortened these days.

If one interprets verses 14ff. against the background of the catastrophic experience of the present, which is apparent in verses 7ff., the meaning of these verses becomes clear. The sufferings of the present provoke the expectation of a final time of horror. Here the imagination of the author absorbs ideas that had already been coined in Jewish apocalypticism a long time ago because of similar experiences. (1) The appearance of the "desolating sacrilege" is stimulated by Dan. 12:11 (cf. 9:27; 11:31) and probably denotes a renewed desecration of the temple in Jerusalem, since the intentionally mysterious expression "he stands where he should not" (Luther; NRSV: "set up where it ought not to be") refers most likely to the temple. The identification by means of the masculine form (in Luther's translation; also possible in the Greek) is ultimately aimed at a person taking a seat in the temple and thus stepping in God's place. Apart from the reminiscence of Daniel, also the remembrance of the blasphemous attempt of the emperor Caligula may play a role here; he wanted to have his own statue erected in the temple (A.D. 39/40). Then the sinister person would be the Roman emperor as the ultimate tyrant. (2) The idea of an unprecedented affliction stems from Dan. 12:1 (cf. *Jub.* 16.8; *As. Mos.* 8.1; Rev. 16:18). The reassurance that God has shortened the days (cf. 4 Ezra 4:26; *2 Apoc. Bar.* 20.1) serves as a comfort for the elect, since it means that the final affliction will last only for a limited time. The description of the ultimate time of salvation stands in intentional contrast to the earthly time of doom (vs. 24–27). The apocalyptic opposition between this and the coming aeon finds expression here.

The time of salvation (vs. 24–27) is introduced by cosmic signs (cf. Isa. 13:10; 34:4; Joel 2:10–11; 3:4; 4:15–16; Rev. 6:12ff.). The Son of man holds judgment over the godless people; however, verse 26 only alludes to that—in contrast to comparable Jewish apocalyptic texts, which find satisfaction in the punishment of the godless. At the center of the passage stands the salvation of the "elect" (v. 27) as the decisive response to their present danger (vs. 7ff.) but especially in response to their affliction in the last days (vs. 14ff.).

In the contrast between verses 7ff., 14ff. and verses 24–27, one finds basically a thought similar to Luke 18:7ff., where the cry of the hard pressed "elect" is followed by a salvific announcement promising them their eschatological justice. In contrast to Luke 18:7–8, the source of Mark 13 structures the time before the ultimate perfection in an apocalyptic way, namely, according to periods (the present: vs. 7ff.; affliction; vs. 14ff.). In it we see what has already been indicated. (1) The horizon of experience of the addressed has so greatly darkened that a final period of horror is conceived in analogy with Jewish apocalypticism. (2) In contrast to Jewish apocalypticism, however, the author affirms that God is in control of the eschatological development (cf. "this must take place"; v. 7—phrased negatively in v. 14). God has shortened the last days of horror (v. 20).

Overall, the adoption of apocalyptic themes serves to draw a specific picture of history that interprets the situation of the persecuted churches. The negative perception of their environment is resolved by the construction of an eschatological schema in which God will soon enact his salvific plan for the "elect."

The overview up to this point has shown that the historical picture of the source in Mark 13 has apocalyptic overtones. The author wants to convey to his churches an eschatological message that has a revelatory character because it provides insight into the divine eschatological plan. By what authority does he do this? Does one find here an attempt, similar to that of Jewish apocalyptists, to legitimize what is said as new revelation? One can answer this question only under certain aspects. The entire source is styled as a Jesus speech and claims the authority of the earthly Jesus. Here the author seems to choose a pseudonym, and even though it is a Christian one, it still finds its analogy to a certain degree in Jewish apocalypses. However, one finds numerous "spurious" Jesus sayings with eschatological content also in the Synoptic tradition (e.g., Matt. 10:23; Luke 18:7–8; see above), where they enlist Jesus' authority and where it would not be justified to question such authority, since these sayings originated probably with remarks of early Christian prophets identifying in the Spirit with the risen One. It is somewhat different with Mark 13, which is the *literary* combination of such sayings and other material into an "apocalyptic speech." The challenge "let the *reader* understand" (v. 14), originally part of the source, can show it quite clearly (cf. the interpolated instruction to the reader in Rev. 13:9, 18; 17:9; also Dan. 9:23, 25). In this case, Jesus is used so to speak as a literary pseudonym (Vielhauer, p. 429) in order to guarantee the entire "speech" as revelation, a method that has its analogies in Jewish apocalypses. Yet this is only one noteworthy aspect here. It is important that it is Jesus who is chosen as a pseudonym, not a figure from the distant past who has authority just by reason of age (Enoch, Moses, Ezra, etc.). The author uses the earthly Jesus as legitimation because of the conviction that Jesus was exalted by God and now assists his church as its present Lord. The heavenly origin of revelation and the human mediator are to a certain extent identical here. The problem of authority is not the same as in Jewish apocalypses and thus is solved differently. The source's "speech" in Mark 13 does not have the form typical of Jewish apocalypses (cf. the definition on page 282). Even though the revelation is conveyed by an "otherworldly" being (the subsequently exalted Jesus), the characteristic revelatory procedures such as visual and auditory reports from a human recipient are missing. Nevertheless, the apocalyptic character of the "speech" is preserved, since the view of history is apocalyptically determined.

Finally, one has to examine the question, To which circles did the author of the apocalyptic speech belong? It is likely that he is addressing Palestinian churches (especially in Judea; v. 14) that are hard pressed by the tumults of the Jewish war. Being handed over to local Jewish courts and synagogues plays an ominous role (v. 9). The author himself was no doubt active in this very area. He is probably close to such Jewish prophets as Agabus, who predicted a great hunger spreading across the entire globe (Acts 11:27–28; cf. 21:10ff.). Basically, Christian prophets prophesied in oral form, for example, during worship services. If we find here a "speech" that existed before Mark in written form, we have to interpret it as a rare exception, which nonetheless has a significant parallel in the later book of Revelation (chs. 2–3). The "speech" should reach several churches in Judea; thus a written form becomes necessary. When the author addresses his readers as the "elect" (vs. 20, 27), he regards them as a limited circle, as a particular group that is opposed by the entire world (vs. 7–8, 9b, 11–13). Especially during the time of salvation, the readers are clearly distinguished from all others, since only they will experience salvation by the Son of man (v. 27). They have a "curious middle position" in the Jewish environment in which they live (Brandenburger, pp. 68ff.). They share with Judaism, on the one hand, the positive view of the temple in Jerusalem, since they consider the temple's desecration as a "desolating sacrilege." On the other hand, they differ from Judaism in that they attach to the temple no salvific expectations—for example, that it would be miraculously preserved from all attacks or that God would one day restore it. All hope is directed toward the coming of the Son of man from heaven (vs. 24–27). This view matches the assumption that the original "speech" is of Jewish-Christian origin. The Christian characteristic can be seen especially in the description of the Son of man. This figure assumes traits of a theophany (cf. *1 Enoch* 1.3–9; *As. Mos.* 10.3ff.), which show that the Son of man has taken over God's governing function. This aspect speaks for the idea that the Son-of-man concept is formulated here from a Christian perspective, which results from the conviction that God has enthroned Jesus as the Son of man so that the latter, as judge of the world, can effect the time of salvation.

　　In the case of Mark 13, apocalyptic prophecy is found in the central area of Palestine. However, the treatment of the "speech" by the Gospel of Mark shows that during the time of his writing, such tradition material was widespread beyond the area of Palestine. For the Gospel of Mark, Greek-speaking Syria seems to be the most likely place.

　　Finally, one needs to address the redactional work of the evangelist since one finds also in his work apocalyptic forms of speech and thought. Mark is probably writing after the catastrophe of the year 70, as can be seen from the retrospective remark in verse 23, which presupposes that the "desolating sacrilege" has meanwhile come to pass (v. 14). Basically, this prophecy was fulfilled with the destruction of the temple. "But as a sign, as a reliable indicator of the imminent time of salvation, it had failed." The Son of man had not come yet. "A new problem situation had arisen" (Brandenburger, p. 93). The sobering effects of the delay of the Son of man had to lead to a reformulation of the eschatological expectation. In the form of a lecture or instructional discourse, which has its parallels especially in 4 Ezra, one asks again the questions, based on the disciples' question in verses 3–4, When will the end come? and What will be the true sign of its arrival? These questions are answered in two steps (vs. 5–27 and vs. 28–32). Jesus acts here as an apocalyptic teacher who has been initiated into the mysteries of the end-time events and conveys them to the esoteric circle of disciples. The sign for the time of salvation is no longer the "desolating sacrilege" but instead: "when you see *these things* taking place, you know that he is near, at the very gates" (v. 29). "These things" refers to what in the context is the most obvious, namely, what can be interpreted as a "sign" for the coming of the Son of man. These are the cosmic phenomena in verses 24–25, which, set off from verse 26 ("then"), lead up to the appearance of the salvific figure. Hence, Mark severs the connection between hope and the earthly historical phenomena ("the desolating sacrilege"), which have proved deceptive. However, he remains within the horizon of apocalyptic eschatology when he sees history and the time of salvation within the time frame predestined by God, in which the time of salvation announces itself by certain signs. In light of the crisis situation that results from the delay of the Parousia, he wants to give the disillusioned churches a new hope that is based on the revelation of the only valid sign of the Parousia.

d) Apocalyptic Instruction in 2 Thessalonians

One can see also in 2 Thessalonians that the apocalyptic material of tradition has taken root outside the Palestinian churches a long time ago. That is not surprising, since Paul had already used apocalyptic ideas within his eschatological explanations simply to illustrate a point. However, one may leave it open at this point how much 2 Thessalonians, not as a "genuine" letter of the apostle but as a pseudonymous writing of an unknown author, owes in its apocalyptic reception to Pauline tradition. One has to consider the possibility that especially after the events of the Jewish war and the further spread of Jewish-Christian circles beyond the Palestinian area, there was a particular incorporation of apocalyptic ideas in the Greek churches of the former Pauline missionary area.

Meanwhile, scholarship has clearly observed that in genre-critical terms 2 Thessalonians is not a "letter" but a "writing of instruction and admonition" that claims apostolic authority (Trilling, *Der zweite Brief,* p. 161). The pseudonymous author has appropriated the model of a "Pauline letter" in order to succeed in presenting those of his personal thoughts that in a particular crisis situation are especially close to his heart. The occasion is eschatological in nature. During the author's time a wave of enthusiasm has caught the Christian churches, and they announced: "The day of the Lord is already here" in the sense of "it is imminent" (2:2). One refers to prophetic utterances of the Spirit, and especially to a letter of Paul's that apparently says that the Parousia is near. This letter is probably 1 Thessalonians (more specifically 5:2; cf. 4:15, 17). In order to counter the possible misunderstanding of 1 Thessalonians, which has caused confusion and fear among the Christians, the author writes a new "Letter to the Thessalonians," in order to correct people's wrong opinion through his instruction.

Utterances of the Spirit like those in 1 Thessalonians were arguments set forth by Parousia enthusiasts. But what was the concrete historical occasion for the formation of eschatological enthusiasm? It is not all that easy to determine the motives. "Is the backdrop the 'afflictions' (1:4), which as an initiating experience prompted one to expect the immediate arrival of the Lord? Is it the 'high pressure' that was caused by the 'delay' of the Parousia and has now found this outlet? Or is it both a prophetic and a charismatic new beginning, which arose from the dissatisfaction of a congregation that had already become lukewarm and tired?" (Trilling, *Der zweite Brief,* pp. 113–14). Most likely, it was the persecutions and afflictions the congregations had to endure, which the author of 2 Thessalonians also had in mind when describing the end time (1:4–5): they are "evidence of the right judgment of God." The enthusiasts interpret these persecutions and afflictions as eschatological birthpangs, signaling the imminence of the Parousia. One can assume that these enthusiasts were familiar with common apocalyptic thought patterns, which helped interpret the present experience of persecution and lead to a comforting solution: it is time; the day of the Lord is about to come (2:2). It is certainly not unthinkable that the persecutions were experienced as especially threatening because of the delay of the Parousia and that these persecutions provoked, in turn, a reactivation of the expectation that the end was near (cf. Luke 18:7–8; Rev. 6:9–11). Then 1 Thessalonians would have provided stimulation with its imminent expectation.

One generally assumes that this eschatological enthusiasm is connected with the particular mentality of some members of the congregation, which the author criticizes: "For we hear that some of you are living in idleness, mere busybodies not doing any work" (3:11; cf. 3:6). If that is true, one will have to imagine the conditions similar to those surrounding a later event in Pontus, descriptively related by Hippolytus (Commentary on Daniel 4.19). Like a prophet, a bishop announced the coming of the last judgment within one year. His followers, however, upon hearing that the day of the Lord was near, "pleaded with the Lord under cries and woes, since night and day they thought of nothing but the approaching day of judgment. And it caused such fear and contrition among the brothers that they left their farms and land unworked, and most of them sold their possessions."

The author of 2 Thessalonians tries now to settle the confusion that had arisen in the congregation by subduing the intense expectation of the end. This expectation used thoroughly apocalyptic ideas when characterizing the present as the beginning of the end time. One observes that 2 Thessalonians, in turn, employs apocalyptic thought patterns for argumentative purposes: Apocalypticism is, so to speak, fought by apocalypticism. The author sketches a chronological pattern of time periods, which postpones the end.

At first, the author wants to recall a familiar tradition (2:5) when saying that before the Parousia, the "rebellion" must take place and the "lawless one," "one destined for destruction," must be revealed (2:3). Both entities stem from the negative picture of history that apocalypticism has. The catastrophic experience of the present provokes the expectation of a general demise of morality at the end of days, humanity's universal "rebellion" (cf. 1 Enoch 91.7; 4 Ezra 5:1-12). This includes the "lawless one," who becomes the representative of all that is opposed to the divine (2:4), and in whom historical experience (Dan. 9:26-27; 11:31-39; 12:11) is condensed to a mythical entity depending on the situation (cf. already Mark 13:14). Besides the function of God's archenemy, this opponent assumes the role of the last great seducer and pseudoprophet (2:8ff.). In Rev. 13 these two traits are distributed between two figures, the first and the second beast.

By the reference to "rebellion" and the "lawless one," the author appeals to traditions familiar to the church (2:5). With 2:6-7 the author comes to his actually intended point, which characterizes him clearly as an apocalyptic teacher. The new stage of reflection reached in 2:6-7 results from the contrast of the earlier instruction ("when I was still with you," referring to verses 3-4) with the present one (v. 6). This state reveals a view that paints the present in intensely negative colors. The opponent hostile to God, the Antichrist, has not yet revealed himself; yet he already has his effect on the present through the "mystery" (v. 7a). At the moment a preventive power is still at work and restrains the appearance of this opponent (2:6). Who or what this power is remains unclear, yet it seems to operate according to the will of God, who is still preventing the open outbreak of evil. The present becomes thereby a time of battle and opposition against the dark powers (Trilling). Up to this point, neither the Antichrist nor God, or Christ, appears openly.

Only with the disappearance of the preventive power, the coming of rebellion, and the appearance of the Antichrist make possible the Parousia of Christ, who will destroy the "evil one."

One generally assumes that with this periodic "timetable," by which the author represses the acute expectation of the imminent end, the influence of apocalyptic ideas in 2 Thessalonians is made apparent. That is correct yet does not clearly qualify the author as apocalyptist. For it could mean that he uses such apocalyptic thought patterns only for argumentative purposes without being directly influenced by a corresponding horizon of experience. The actual eschatological reflection, which the author wants especially emphasized, is contained in verses 2:6–7 (distinguished from the context by verse 5). This reflection betrays a view of the present that in its dark outlook corresponds to other apocalyptists. Even now the "mystery of lawlessness" is at work. The consequences are persecution and affliction. For that reason the relationship to the environment is marked by dualism. The believers are the afflicted, and the rest of society causes the affliction (1:6–7). A positive view in state and society is not apparent. Accordingly, salvation is uniformly placed in the future. The Christian church prepares itself through perseverance and faith (1:4; cf. Rev. 13:10). It is comforted by considering the future judgment of its tormentors (1:6ff.; cf. 2 *Apoc. Bar.* 82.1ff.). With the last judgment, a decisive reversal of conditions takes place: those causing affliction become the afflicted, and those now afflicted find peace (1:6ff.). Accordingly, the image of Christ is primarily determined by his function as judge and punisher and absorbs mainly traits that are attributed to God in Jewish-apocalyptic tradition (on 1:7–8, cf. *1 Enoch* 1.4).

After these observations, one sees that the view of history conveyed by 2 Thessalonians is in its origin apocalyptic. Can one say that also about the corresponding need for legitimation, which causes the apocalyptist to authorize his new revelation in a special way? One should first recall the pseudonymity that the author of 2 Thessalonians uses in order to lend his writing apostolic authority. For that reason he claims in 2:5 that Paul himself held the expectation of the Antichrist and that it, therefore, was part of the church's tradition. Pseudonymity as such, however, does not necessarily point to apocalypticism, as the other pseudo-Pauline letters show. However, because of the otherwise apocalyptic orientation of the author, the pseudonymity found in 2 Thessalonians gains some importance. It is not unimportant here that the author describes his key statement about the character of the present time as "mystery" when speaking of the "mystery of lawlessness," which is effective already at this time (2:7). The possession of secret knowledge characterizes the author in an apocalyptic way as the bearer of special knowledge. This fact is not negated simply because the instruction in 2:6–7 is to appear as knowledge of the church at large: "And you know what is now restraining . . . " The readers are supposed to be indirectly stimulated by this to pay attention and reflect in order to find the deeper meaning of the instruction. At first, however, such knowledge is supposed to characterize only the author. Despite such indications of a proximity to apocalypticism, many important traits of Jewish apocalypses are missing. Concerning his revelation, the author does not refer to a heavenly being who validates the author's messages. The visual and auditory reports that are so typical of apocalypses are missing. Only with Revelation is a literary form of the apocalypse achieved of early Christianity. The kinship of the author to early Christian apocalypticism does not help in assigning him to otherwise known groups. Such groups are nowhere discernible in 2 Thessalonians. The author knows 1 Thessalonians and tries to imitate it; he tries literarily to use Paul as established authority. Other than that, however, nothing characterizes him as a representative of genuine Pauline tradition. In contrast to Colossians, Ephesians, and even the pastoral letters, one finds no further development of Pauline ideas. What is called valid Pauline tradition (2:5) is in reality invalid and stems, instead, from anonymous tradition that belongs to the larger area of early Christian apocalypticism (cf. Mark 13:14; Rev. 13). The insistence on the "traditions that you were taught," allegedly Pauline in nature (2:15), shows only the language usage of a later period, in which the faith had become a tradition that could be taught (Jude 3; 2 Peter 2:21), yet without any perceivable relation to Pauline tradition. The instructive correction of an exaggerated expectation of the end has certain parallels with Mark 13, as well as, in a completely different way, with Luke's historical work, in which corresponding slogans are almost branded as false teachings (Luke 21:8–9;

cf. also 17:20–21, 23; 19:11; Acts 1:6–7). Accordingly, 2 Thessalonians belongs with the church dispute that was to erupt because of the "apocalyptic fever" in the second half of the first century.

It would be interesting to clarify for which church(es) 2 Thessalonians was written. At first, of course, one thinks of the church in Thessalonica. Yet this addressing could merely result from literary fiction, whereby the author had to write an epistle to the Thessalonians, because the Parousia enthusiasts refer to statements made in 1 Thessalonians, and he now wants to correct this particular interpretation. Otherwise, speaking against Thessalonica is the fact that the letter could have been easily recognized there as non-Pauline. Based on general observations, Asia Minor could be suggested. The persecutions that the church has to endure recall 1 Peter 4:12ff. Besides that, Revelation is a certain testimony of persecution measures in the province of Asia, as well as a corresponding imminent expectation of the end.

e) Apocalyptic Prophecy in the Revelation to John

(1) *The historical situation in Revelation.* With Revelation one encounters in early Christian history a work whose literary form shows the greatest closeness to Jewish apocalypses. According to ancient church tradition (Irenaeus *Adv. Haer.* 5.30.3), it was written toward the end of the emperor Domitian's reign (A.D. 81–96). This chronological assessment is confirmed by Revelation. The propagation of the emperor cult—the requirement that everyone worship the living emperor as a divine being—can be clearly recognized in Revelation as the background of existing problems. This propagation finds its clear expression in the horror of worshiping the "beast" and its image, which are manifestations of the Antichrist (ch. 13). One may not be able to prove a centralized emperor worship under Domitian and, therefore, also no systematically staged persecution of the Christians who refused emperor worship. Still, the province of Asia with its capital Ephesus is an area where emperor worship finds a particular resonance among the pagan population. Ephesus built a new temple to the emperor with an impressive cultic picture of Domitian and, hence, responded willingly to the intentions of this emperor, who demanded for himself the address "our lord and god." The worship of Caesar, however, is not only a religious act but an expression of political loyalty toward the Roman power. The refusal to worship the emperor or his image can for that reason appear to be an act of political disobedience. Locally based persecu-

tions are the consequence. In the city of Pergamon a case of martyrdom took place that is explicitly mentioned by name (2:13; in the person of Anitpas). For the congregation in Smyrna, the author of Revelation, John, anticipates prison and death. He himself is banned to the island Patmos "because of the word of God and the testimony of Jesus" (1:9). These experiences of the present direct attention to the past when the Roman congregation had to endure massive persecution under the emperor Nero. It is possible that the outcry of the souls that had been killed as martyrs and are now calling for God's intervention (6:9–11) presupposes these persecutions. To the seer John, Rome, appearing under the pseudonymous name "Babylon," is drunk with the blood of the saints (17:6). At the center of discussion is the conflict between state and church, because the totalitarian state with its requirement of religious worship demands the entire person. John can see here only seduction and pressure to idol worship, which leads the church to the final rebellion against God.

This conflict does involve not only the concrete situation of acknowledging one's faith in instances where Christians were possibly supposed to deny Jesus' name in court (2:13, 3:8) but also normal everyday life. Suspicion is drawn toward anyone who does not adapt to the social customs of the pagan environment, anyone who during private as well as public feasts does not eat meat that in John carries the label "meat sacrificed to idols" because it could have been sacrificed to a deity. This person is hit by economic boycott, since those without the mark of the "beast" as a sign of loyalty toward state and society can no longer buy or sell (13:17). That means, practically, that "Christians are discovered when they do not buy sacrificial meat in the market, when they neither participate in the celebration of public feasts nor swear by the name of the emperor" (Lampe, p. 94).

As in Jewish and early Christian apocalypticism, this historical experience provokes a negative view of the world in general, which calls for a speedy, all-encompassing change by God, even for a "new heaven" and a "new earth" (21:1ff.). After all, this world is stained; it is ruled by Rome, "the mother of whores and of earth's abominations" (17:5). The view of the present is completely darkened. In the activities of the state and the ancient society influenced by the state, this view sees only the agitation of Satan himself, who after falling out of heaven wreaks havoc on the earth (12:12ff.; 13). The persecution of the church, which opposes the satanic seduction to emperor worship, is the concrete climax of the crisis. The dark mood and the longing for the end go together. This fact is clearly expressed in the relationship of the martyrs' cries with the heavenly reply in 6:9–11.

"Sovereign Lord, holy and true one, how long will it be before you judge and avenge our blood on the inhabitants of the earth? They were each given a white robe and told to rest [only] a little while longer. . . . "

Accordingly, the "prayers of all the saints" who had to endure persecution on earth ascend into heaven in order to move God to intervene (8:3–5). Like the heavenly reply in 6:9–11, the seer John himself now proclaims: "The time is near" (1:3). The heavenly Christ promises: "I am coming soon" (3:11; 22:7, 12, 20). This word of comfort is to strengthen the earthly churches and encourage them to persevere patiently until the imminent end. The acute expectation of the end results, as in Jewish apocalypses, from the unavoidable question of the time of salvation, since the present and the past lack the justice the believers hope to receive from God.

(2) *The literary form of the Revelation of John.* John's message serves to proclaim the imminent end, the deliverance from suffering, hardship, and death. In light of the immense superiority of the Roman Empire, which through its actual representatives provokes the sufferings of the Christian churches, this message is not in the least bit obvious but had to deal with doubt, skepticism, and even rejection. In any case, the everyday experience of Christians in a society completely dominated by pagans spoke against believing this message. For that reason John has to legitimize his proclamation in a certain way in order to count on acceptance by the churches. One has to remember here that John himself shares the suffering of his companions in misfortune (1:9) and desperately longs for deliverance. Yet he has received the heavenly revelation that Christ, the Lamb, has received the authority to realize God's historical plan for the end time and to bring the desired time of salvation (5:5). John wants to pass this revelation on to the Christian churches; he has to legitimize it as heavenly truth and for this purpose uses the stylistic means available to him from his background, and they point to Jewish and early Christian apocalypticism: visual and auditory reports, the words of Christ or an angel, and the description of a transport into heaven. This procedure presupposes, to be sure, that a certain resonance existed in the churches of Asia Minor—a familiarity with apocalyptic forms of presentation that would lead one to expect understanding. Nevertheless, one observes that as a Christian apocalypse Revelation is curiously structured, since apart from the mentioned literary forms, elements appear that reveal a different origin.

Conspicuous at first is the lack of pseudonymity. John writes not under the name and borrowed authority of a great figure of the past but under his own. He is the one known by the churches of the province Asia as John

(1:4). He introduces himself as their brother and companion in the misfortune of their affliction (1:9). This characteristic signals a self-confidence that differs from that of Jewish apocalyptists. John is first of all a prophet. He may not say so explicitly. Still, he calls his book "the words of the prophecy" (or foretelling; 1:3; 22:7, 10, 18–19). He considers other prophets his brothers (22:9). Hence, he possesses a special charismatic authority. As a prophet, he writes to the churches known to him, since because of his geographical separation from them, he must tell them by letter what he actually would want to tell them orally. For that reason, his book takes on the form of a letter, which has hardly any parallels in Jewish apocalypticism (cf., however, 2 Apoc. Bar. 78–87). His work has the structure of a letter. Included are a preface (1:4–5)—which names the author and the addressed, the seven churches in Asia—and at the end of his book the traditional final greeting of New Testament letters (22:21). Also among Revelation's characteristics as a letter is the fact that seven writings, or letters, to the churches (chs. 2–3) precede the apocalyptic main part (4:1–22:5).

John expects his book to be read during congregational meetings (cf. 1:3: "Blessed is the one who reads aloud the words of the prophecy and blessed are those who hear"). It directly recalls the practice of reading apostolic letters during worship (1 Thess. 5:27). The conclusion is obvious: an apocalypse styled as letter is most likely to be read during the congregational meeting. At any rate, it was the explicit purpose of the author (1:3).

Hence, Revelation presents a twofold face when one looks at its literary form. For one, it is outwardly designed as a letter, which has as its author the John whom the churches of Asia Minor know and who probably was active as a prophet among them. The author's lack of pseudonymity is thereby explained. For another, this writing shows apocalyptic elements of style such as visual and auditory reports, which serve to authorize the new revelation. These literary forms dominate the apocalyptic main part of 4:1–22:5, which develops the author's eschatological message. Despite the prophet's authority, which allows him to write under his own name, John feels compelled to legitimize the content of his prophecy in an apocalyptic manner.

(3) *The eschatological message.* The apocalyptic main part of 4:1–22:5 deals with the ultimate stage of history and presents as revelation "what must soon take place" (1:1; 4:1; 22:6). This period comprises the time between Jesus' exaltation (12:1–5) and the world consummation (21:1–22:5). The interim consists of a period of struggle between God and Satan,

of conflict between believers and the godless residents of the earth. John develops this eschatological drama by presenting the struggle of God's accession to power in ever new acts, even in ever new approaches. As already indicated, this message is a reply to the problem—so crucial for the author—that the satanic ungodliness on earth (Rome) has the upper hand, and God's judgment of the world threatens to be delayed (6:9–11). The emphasized orientation toward the eschatological end, provoked by a catastrophic experience of the present, is typically apocalyptic. In contrast to Jewish apocalypses, however, Revelation no longer characterizes the history of the world, which is increasingly inclined to evil, as a succession of world empires (cf. Dan. 2; 7) that come to an end with the arrival of God's kingdom. With the exaltation of Christ (12:1–5), the historical past is already finished. Of sole interest now is the final stage, the rule of God that has already begun with Christ's exaltation (11:15; 12:10ff.). This Christian reformulation of apocalyptic thought is, of course, aware of the negative character of the earthly present; still, it is also aware that in heavenly reality it has already been decided what is yet to become a victorious reality on earth. By a visionary glimpse into the heavenly world, which the apocalyptist John manages, he can grasp the nature of God's salvific plan for the end time. As a comfort for the afflicted churches, this plan is unchangeably fixed. It comprises "what *must* soon take place" (1:1; 22:6). This apocalyptic determinism of history finds a further clear expression in the concept of the seven-seal scroll (ch. 5). Christ receives this scroll, comprising the entire plan of God concerning the end time as it is described from chapter 6 on, so that by breaking the seals, the eschatological event can begin. In ever new approaches, visions of trumpets and bowls describe how God's rule is implemented (8:2–11:19; 15–16).

This positive outcome corresponds to the negative view of earthly historical events, which is limited to descriptions of doom. The residents of the earth insist on their idol worship (9:20–21) and persecute the Christian church. The divine response is the punishment of the godless, which the author describes in cycles of torment, involving trumpet and bowl visions.

In comparison to earlier Christian apocalypticism, the present horizon of experience has become even darker. Second Thess. 2:3–4 already anticipates the appearance of the Antichrist, even though his silhouette still remains mysterious. In Rev. 13, the experience of the already existing situation of persecution is intensified by the figure of two satanic "beasts." The first "beast" assumes the face of Nero redivivus, who is assisted by his likeness, the second "beast," as the propaganda agent of Nero's supremacy.

By the effects of this supremacy, a worldwide persecution of the church (13:11–17) emerges, the concrete features of which are a result of the general application and expansion of already existing measures of persecution. In relation to earlier Christian apocalyptic concepts, an increased dualism governs the underlying thought. The Christian church and the pagan world power are diametrically opposed; this corresponds to the battle between Christ and Satan, which is brought to mind here. This world has to pass away in order to make room for the reality of a "new heaven" and a "new earth." Such an antagonism is the poignant expression of the present negative experience, which finds that for the present salvation can take place only in heaven, but otherwise awaits the future as salvation. The present salvific experience, which Christians can have during the worship service (sacrament and prophetic utterances of the Spirit), cannot relieve the dominating mood of doom.

During the cosmic struggle between God/Christ and Satan, which the apocalyptic perspective would interpret as the underlying conflict between Roman world power and the afflicted Christians, the Christians remain, at first sight, passive. They are given the request to endure patiently until the end (13:10; 14:12; cf. already Mark 13:13). The sayings in the circular letters about overcoming promise eschatological reward to those who stand firm. Their victory consists in their martyrdom, which allows them by the power of Christ's blood to ultimately demonstrate their Christian identity (12:11). Christ appears in the symbolic figure of the Lamb that is slaughtered (5:6; 7:17; 13:8). The sufferers can identify with this Lamb: "To the one who conquers I will give a place with me on my throne, *just as I myself conquered* and sat down with my Father on his throne" (3:21). The Christians can understand and accept their own perseverance when looking up to the exalted Lamb who has been slaughtered.

This attitude includes the renunciation of any active resistance to Roman state power. In the conviction that God and his Christ have begun their battle against the satanic power of Rome, Christians accept the necessary suffering. In this destiny of theirs, they are to see the final decree of God (13:10): "If you are to be taken captive, into captivity you go; if you kill with the sword, with the sword you must be killed. Here is a call for the endurance and faith of the saints." This attitude of nonviolence finds its parallel in apocalypticism. The author of Daniel sees in the military activities of the Maccabeans only "a little help" (Dan. 11:34). Only God can be successful without any human help (8:25; 2:34–35). In the economic area, one sees in John a rather indirect protest against prevailing conditions. In

Rev. 6:5–6 an anticipated immense price increase in the province is mentioned: "A quart of wheat for a day's pay, and three quarts of barley for a
day's pay." That is eight to sixteen times as much as the regular price,
depending on which comparable ancient measures one applies. For the
simple people, it means the threat of famine. In Rome, however, people live
in luxury (18:12, 16). Merchants and shipmasters take advantage of the
city's cravings for luxury items (18:3, 15, 19). The protest uttered in light
of this paradox remains powerless. A change of this situation as well as any
removal of doom at all are reserved for the "new earth" and the "new
Jerusalem," where God "will wipe away every tear from their eyes" (7:16–
17; 21:4).

(4) *The origin of the apocalyptic prophet John.* John considers himself a
prophet as indicated in 22:9, which talks about his "brothers," the
prophets. The latter appear here as a special group in John's environment,
since John distinguishes between his "brothers" the prophets and those
preserving the "words of this book." The verse of 22:16 confirms this assumption: "It is I, Jesus, who sent my angel to you with this testimony for
the churches." After that, the revelation of the book is directed to a first
circle of addressees ("you"), which is different from the churches. The final
part of 22:6ff. has the function in the overall context of the work to confirm
it as a heavenly revelatory writing. Jesus himself appears in 22:16 as the
source of the revelation. The legitimation may be required, since all church
members hear the words of this prophecy, also including, for example, the
opponents within the churches whom John attacks in the circular letter of
chapters 2 and 3. Still, 22:16 has at first a particular circle in mind ("you"),
which is most likely identical with the circle of prophets that are colleagues
of John. It is for them that John wants to legitimize his writing. One does
not receive any further information in Revelation about the existence and
activity of this prophetic circle, unless one establishes a connection between John's apocalyptic prophecy and that of his "brothers"—which is
probably justified. The prophetess "Jezebel" (2:20–22) is certainly not
among the members of this circle, since she is condemned by John as a
propagator of libertinism.

In this context, a great problem arises. As contemporary writings of the
church area in Asia Minor demonstrate, the churches there have long since
grown into communities with an institutionalized discipline and fixed offices, such as those of bishop, elder, and deacon (Acts, pastoral letters,
1 Peter, the letters of Ignatius and Polycarp). A charismatic congregational
order, as was still common in Paul's days, is probably a matter of the past

(cf. 1 Cor. 14). The conclusion is obvious: "The place where the congregational form represented by Revelation was maintained may be found in
particular Jewish-Christian conventicles" (Bornkamm). One will have to
think of a certain circle of prophets, over which John probably presided.

Can anything be said about this circle's origin? John was not the leading
member of only one of the addressed churches. He seems to have been
active in some or all of them. His intimate knowledge of each of their
particular situations is probably not based simply on hearsay but is rooted
in his personal visits with the congregations. The fixed congregational offices were given to people in residence, and they tied these people to the
church. For that reason it is best to imagine John as an itinerant prophet
who every so often preached in this or that church. Certain behavioral
patterns, especially his tendency toward asceticism, can be best explained
by his participation in itinerant prophetic activity. In 14:1–5 he draws the
picture of the perfected church on Mount Zion. About the perfected members he says: "It is these who have not defiled themselves with women, for
they are virgins; these follow the Lamb wherever he goes." One inevitably
gains the impression here that John characterizes the perfected church in
terms typical of his own life-style. The ideal of sexual abstinence results
from his description of the ascetic as the type that represents the true
Christian. Moreover, it is possible that the activity of following the lamb,
which applies to perfected Christians, reflects his own itinerant work,
which he understands as following the Lord. On this basis we can also
explain the distance to and even rejection of libertine practices in the addressed churches. In each instance he discusses the conflict between the
liberal practices of ancient urban culture and an ascetic attitude with its
origins in itinerant charismatics, who ministered primarily in the rural culturally less developed areas of Palestine and Syria. That can be shown in
detail. The church in Laodicea is considered materially rich but spiritually
poor (3:17). The wealth of leading members in the congregation suggests a
certain degree of education, implying, as among the "strong" in Corinth, a
certain "knowledge" that allows them to participate without harm in the
social life of the city (cf. 1 Cor. 8). Part of that is the custom to move about
naked in the gymnasiums ("the shame of your nakedness"; Rev. 3:18). The
same can be expected in the cases of Pergamon, Thyatira, and Sardis. The
accusation of eating meat sacrificed to idols and of engaging in immorality
could be addressed to the richer Christians, whose sustained contacts with
the pagan environment results in their unconsidered meat consumption
during banquets and feasts and in their participation in libertine sexual

practices. Since they feel, they can see through the "deep things of Satan" (2:24), so that for them the power of Satan and idols no longer exists (cf. 1 Cor. 8:4), they can in good conscience adapt to the rules of urban culture and life-style. One finds here a form of enthusiasm that claims to have life already in the present (3:1), and which spiritualizes the final redemption. This understanding of perfection contrasts with John's apocalyptic concept of the future, which, in view of the still remaining power of Satan, expects the ultimate manifestation of God's rule in the future.

The Christian itinerant prophecy that is most likely to correspond with John's can be found in the Palestinian-Syrian church area, where the Gospel of Matthew and the *Didache* originated. Like Revelation, both writings view prophets as God's servants and count on their effectiveness in the churches. Based on Matt. 10:41 and 23:34, one can show that these prophets act as itinerant prophets (Matt. 10:41) and represent a contemporary phenomenon (however, *Did.* 11.7–12 and 13.1 show that prophets do not have to travel and can also settle down). Among the behavioral patterns of itinerant prophets and itinerant apostles are homelessness and material need (Matt. 10:41; cf. 8:20; *Did.* 11.4–6, 12). One also finds an ascetic tendency such as John's in these circles (*Did.* 11.11; Matt. 19:12). Both writings are rooted in the Jewish-Christian tradition that conveys traditional material of Palestinian origin. That is also true for Revelation. The apocalyptic idea of the Son of man, which plays an important role especially in the Gospel of Matthew and in *Did.* 16, is employed by John in his eschatology. On the one hand, the seer beholds the Son of man, Jesus, as the present Lord of the churches (Rev. 1:12ff.), on the other, as the one who will come soon to judge and destroy the godless (14:14ff.; 19:11ff.). Also speaking for the Palestinian origin of John is the strongly Semitic style, which has no parallel in the other writings of the New Testament.

As far as one can tell by Revelation, John was active in the churches of the Roman province of Asia. If one assumes John's Palestinian origin, he must have migrated to what used to be the Pauline mission field. His original activity as an itinerant prophet could thus be explained. More important, however, is the fact that John is no exception since after the Jewish war (A.D. 66–70) many Jewish Christians left Palestine to go to Asia Minor: "Philip, the evangelist, who had already left Jerusalem because of Stephen's persecution [Acts 8:1ff.] and then had settled in Caesarea by the sea, where we still find him in A.D. 60 [Acts 21:8–9], moved to Hierapolis . . . and brought with him his prophesying daughters. The 'old' John, the Lord's disciple, probably exchanged Jerusalem for Ephesus" (Bauer, p. 90).

Asia Minor becomes a church region where Jewish-Christian tradition can continue to develop under favorable conditions. That is also true for the chiliastic tradition, which finds rich expression here.

(5) *Apocalyptic chiliasm in John and the so-called presbyters.* A special expression of an apocalyptic future hope is found in the expectation of a kingdom lasting a thousand years (chiliasm), which in John forms one element in the chain of eschatological events. Prior to the appearance of the new heaven and the new earth (Rev. 21:1–22:5), prior to the destruction of Satan (20:7–10), there is supposed to be a limited salvific period on this earth when the Christian martyrs will rule together with Christ (20:4–6). For this purpose they will experience a premature awakening, one prior to the general resurrection of the dead (20:11–15). The expectation of a kingdom lasting for a thousand years prior to the actual end of the world finds its parallels in Jewish apocalyptic literature. According to 4 Ezra 7:28, the Messiah will reveal himself, and a four-hundred-year period of peace will begin.

To John, the promise of a thousand-year reign is of particular importance. It serves to honor the Christian martyrs. Before the arrival of the new aeon, they will see realized on this earth especially for them what the salvific death of Christ as such has effected for all believers, namely, that they are destined to rule and to become priests on God's behalf (1:5–6). Those who are not martyrs among the Christians will enjoy this privilege only in the new aeon (22:5).

In the description of this salvific time, John remains extremely reticent; the enumeration of particular salvific phenomena is reserved for the presentation of the new world (21:1–22:5). The promise of the martyrs' thousand-year rule is a concrete salvific affirmation to the persecuted Christians and a particular stimulus to resist temptation to the end. That is seen by the beatitude that comments on the resurrection of those that will participate in the reign (20:6): "Blessed and holy are those who share in the first resurrection. Over these the second death has no power, but they will be priests of God and of Christ, and they will reign with him a thousand years."

It is different with the tradition about the so-called presbyters (or elders), which is preserved in Irenaeus (*Adv. Haer.* 5.33.3–4). It describes in bright colors the "times of the reign . . . when the just, raised from the dead, will rule"; it does so by declaring the ten-thousand-fold fruitfulness of this reign. One finds here an advanced form of this expectation. It tends more to satisfy a speculative imagination, by borrowing from traditional ideas (cf. *1 Enoch* 10.19; *2 Apoc. Bar.* 29.5), than to give new hope to afflicted Christians. Chiliasm becomes an imaginatively formulated teaching that serves the idea of vindication (of the just):

There will be days when vines will grow, each of which will have ten thousand branches, and on one branch ten thousand twigs, and actually on one twig will be ten thousand tendrils, and on every single tendril ten thousand grapes, and every grape will have ten thousand berries, and every pressed berry will make twenty-five measures of wine. And when one of the saints touches a grape, another grape will call: I am better; take me; praise the Lord with me!

It is interesting to examine the circle of tradition bearers from which this form of chiliasm stems. The circle reveals a sociological kinship with John, the author of Revelation, although differences exist. At any rate, the so-called presbyters are representatives of Jewish-Christian currents that have gained influence in Asia Minor. Irenaeus (*Adv. Haer.* 5.33.3–4) makes it clear that his information concerning this reign's hope is based on the oral tradition of the so-called presbyters, and that this information, in turn, was recorded in written form by Papias, bishop of Hierapolis, during the first quarter of the second century.

A similar conclusion is drawn from the Papias tradition recorded in Eusebius (*Hist. Eccl.* 3.39.11–12). In Bishop Papias' case, the special informant for the orally reported tradition is, apart from the other "presbyters," the "presbyter" John, whom he especially singles out. Although Papias does not explicitly say this in respect to the millennium concept, it can be inferred from the general information about the origin of his teachings (Euseb. *Hist. Eccl.* 3.39.4; Körtner): "But when someone came who had followed the presbyters, I used to inquire about the words of the presbyters, what Andrew or what Peter *said* . . . or what John or Matthew or anyone else of the Lord's disciples (*said*); also, what Aristion and the presbyter John, disciple of the Lord, *are saying.*" According to this text, Papias has inquired among people who followed the "presbyters" as to what they had heard from the "Lord's disciples." Hence, the "presbyters" have to be distinguished from the "Lord's disciples." Hereby, a pupil-teacher relationship seems to exist between Papias' informants and those they followed after, the "presbyters," just like that between the "presbyters" and the "Lord's disciples." The informants report what they heard from the "presbyters," and the latter what they heard from the "Lord's disciples." One has to imagine an itinerant group of teachers in this context. The stationary bishop Papias of Hierapolis inquires among those who stop by and have on their part followed the "presbyters," which indicates the itinerant situation of the "presbyters." Who then are the "presbyters"? The term *presbyter* or *elder* corresponds to the Jewish *father* and is the honorary title for a teacher. That means concretely concerning the people mentioned by Papias (as well as by Irenaeus *Adv. Haer.* 5.33.3) that they are early Christian itinerant teachers, who are considered pupils of the Lord's disciples, or the apostles, and who pass on their ancient tradition.

Aristion and the "presbyter" John, who are mentioned last in the above quote, play a particular role for Papias. While the first-mentioned "Lord's disciples" constitute an entity from the past (Papias inquires "what Andrew or Peter *said*"), Aristion and John are apparently still alive (Papias is interested in what "they *are saying*"). Papias also calls them "Lord's disciples," since he probably considers them personal disciples of Jesus, which they were probably not in the historical sense. However, this classification may at least indicate that they were from Palestine and for that reason were Jewish Christians (Körtner, pp. 126–27, 186–87).

Overall, one can say that the "presbyters" were active as itinerant teachers in Asia Minor. Their honorary title, which corresponds to Jewish language usage, and their function as transmitters of very early Christian tradition (of the "Lord's disciples") show that at least some of them are Palestinian Jewish Christians. Both criteria move the "presbyters" close to the apocalyptic prophet John, the author of Revelation, although no identity is thereby declared between the "presbyter" John in Papias and the author of Revelation. Eusebius (*Hist. Eccl.* 3.39.6 and modern scholarship) may hazard such an identification because of Papias's information. However, Papias himself does not say so. Also, an equation of the two Johns is not very likely, because the "presbyter" John, as well as the other "presbyters," is a transmitter of oral tradition; they are early Christian teachers, not charismatic prophetic figures like John, the author of Revelation. Also different is the formulation of chiliastic hope. In John it takes on the character of actual comfort; apocalypticism serves for prophetic comfort during the crisis situation of persecuted churches. By contrast, the presbyter tradition in Irenaeus (*Adv. Haer.* 5.33.3–4) has the same apocalyptic teaching become a speculative doctrine. One finds that apocalyptic thought material is rather popular in the churches of Asia Minor, although in different forms: as apocalyptic prophecy in John and as old—that is, authoritatively valid—teaching among the so-called presbyters, for whom an apocalyptic experience of the world is no longer recognizable and the related securing of authority has become superfluous.

f) The Changed Character of Apocalyptic Thought at the Turn of the First Century

Originated during the later reign of the emperor Domitian and provoked by the persecutions of Christians especially in the province of Asia, Revelation has become the most important document of early Christian apocalypticism. From about the same time is 1 Peter. This letter is probably characterized by the same acute eschatological expectation (4:7). Suffering and persecution mark the situation of the church. Christians are suspected and apparently indicted in court on the basis of their Christianity (4:14, 16). Suffering is considered a "fiery ordeal that is taking place among you to test you" (4:12). The crisis situation of the church seems to have assumed worldwide dimensions, which lead to apocalyptic interpretations: "The time has come for judgment to begin with the household of God" (4:17). According to God's plan, suffering is the sign that the eschatological hour has come, and this suffering has reached such dimensions that it indicates the beginning of the last judgment. Apocalyptic thought is also influential in the sense that Rome, as in Revelation, is given the secret name "Babylon" (5:13; cf. Rev. 14:8; 16–18).

Despite the great similarities with early Christian apocalypticism, 1 Peter did not become an apocalyptic writing. Missing are important literary criteria that would clearly point to apocalypticism. Despite the serious threat to the church, the focus of the pseudonymous author is not directed one-sidedly to the future, which alone promises deliverance. Instead, the letter begins with rejoicing over the fact that the congregation has been reborn into a living hope, which allows its members to endure the brief period of tribulation (1:3ff.). The rebirth experienced by baptism (cf. also 1:22–23) provides the members with the certainty of their ultimate election as saved people (2:9–10). An apocalyptic assurance of identity does not seem necessary. Nevertheless, one can see that 1 Peter originated within the area of influence of strong apocalyptic currents, even though they had no ultimate influence.

Things are different in the *Didache* (the teaching of the apostles), which is not part of the New Testament canon but is counted among the writings of the so-called Apostolic Fathers. They represent probably the oldest known church order. The end of the book provides an eschatological outlook, at times also called the "small apocalypse" (ch. 16). This name is not warranted. In the literary sense one cannot find an element of style typical of apocalypticism that could serve to legitimize new revelation. That is also unnecessary. For the eschatological instruction is passed on as tradition long since known; the instruction is to make urgent and obligatory the previously given admonitions and ordinances. Eschatology becomes an autonomous "instructional device about the last things," an "appendix of ethics" (Wengst).

The sequence of events described in *Did.* 16 could certainly be found in an apocalypse. The schema calls Mark 13, Matt. 24, and 2 Thess. 2. Verses 3 and 4a describe the increase of lawlessness, the appearance of pseudoprophets and instigators of corruption, and the hatred of all against all. Verse 4b mentions the world seducer acting as the Antichrist. The last trial of endurance (v. 5) is succeeded by the "signs of truth," three traditional apocalyptic acts (vs. 6–7) with their climax in the Parousia of the Lord and the last judgment (v. 8).

It is important, however, to note that the eschatological events beginning with verse 4 do not at all concern the present. Verse 2 shows that the last days are still far away. The "last days" (3ff.) are clearly distinguished from the present (v. 2). In genuine apocalyptic texts, statements like those in verses 3 and 4a are a painful expression of concrete experience, and the present seems to be headed for a catastrophe that will have to bring the end and hence the time of salvation. But that is not the case in *Did.* 16, where the expectation of eschatological horrors has become a mere element of tradition. "That points . . . to a time when one no longer anticipated the imminent end of the world," since the expectation of the end was no longer prompted by persecutions (Vielhauer). A role may be played by the fact that the *Didache* is written in a region (rural areas of Syria) where persecutions do not present an acute danger. One has to remember in this context that the *Didache* presupposes certain circles in the churches (itinerant prophets in 11:7ff.; 13), which show behavioral patterns and ideas similar to those of John, the author of Revelation. Still, a corresponding apocalyptic form of expression does not develop, since the real historical situation of the churches does not necessitate an actualization of apocalyptic ideas.

In two later writings of the New Testament, Jude and 2 Peter, apocalyptic concepts have likewise become mere tradition that one uses in argumentative fashion in battles against the heretical teachers of Gnosticism. These teachers are to appear as phenomena of the end time, the arrival of which the "Lord's apostles" have already predicted: "In the last time there will be scoffers, indulging their own ungodly lusts" (Jude 18; cf. 2 Peter 3:2-3). Here a common apocalyptic idea is used to brand opponents; according to this idea there will be apostasy and false teaching in the last days (*As. Mos.* 7; Mark 13:6, 22; *Did.* 16.3; cf. also 1 Tim. 4:1; 2 Tim. 3:1ff.).

Apart from that, the Letter of Jude is interesting because it shows knowledge of Jewish apocalyptic writings (vs. 6, 9, 11) and even mentions them explicitly (vs. 14-15). These cited writings are those collected in Ethiopian *Enoch*, as well as the *Ascension of Moses* (cf. Jude 9), mentioned in the documents of the ancient church; the latter could be identical with the fragmentarily preserved *Assumption of Moses*. The author of Jude considers the book of *Enoch* inspired and canonical, since he quotes *1 Enoch* 1.9 in verses 14-15 (cf. the similarity with *Barn.* 4.3; 16.5-6): "It was also about these [i.e., the false teachers] that Enoch, in the seventh generation from Adam, prophesied, saying, 'See, the Lord is coming with ten thousands of his holy ones, to execute judgment on all. . . . ' "

The author of 2 Peter fights against the rejection of the future hope, especially of Christ's Parousia. Mockers emerge from the congregation asking: "Where is the promise of his coming? For ever since our ancestors died, all things continue as they were from the beginning of creation!" (3:4). The opponents may be identical with the libertine Gnostics attacked in 2:10, 18, even though the argument for the Parousia's rejection does not sound Gnostic. More important, however, is another aspect. The defense of eschatology uses apocalyptic ideas in order to clarify the dangers involved at the end of the world, especially for opponents. Emphasized are the suddenness of the world's end (3:10a), as well as the horrors connected with the cosmic conflagration (3:10b). The pious, however, are to accelerate the world's end by their holy life-style (3:11-12). The aim is the extinction of the godless (3:7) and the creation of a new world in which only the just will live (3:13). Factually, however, the end is now very far off, since with the Lord one day is like a thousand years (3:8).

Apocalyptic eschatology has become a "teaching of the last things," which is supposed to guarantee vengeance on the godless. However, it is no longer a reply prompted by a crisis or one of comfort in response to a present that is perceived as a catastrophe and requires a strengthening of faith in God's justice. This observation is also true, in its own particular way, for the chronologically earlier Lukan historical works (the Gospel of Luke and Acts), in which the eschatological perspective merely serves to substantiate paraenetic encouragement. Here lies the mainstream of the early Christian development of tradition around the turn of the first century. It corresponds to the theology of later centuries more than to the apocalypticism kindled by hard times here and there among groups hit by a distressing identity crisis.

Finally, one needs to mention the *Shepherd of Hermas* (third or fourth decade of the second century), which has clearly preserved the form of an apocalypse, especially in the first part, the book of visions (*Herm. Vis.* 1–4). The author is aware of proclaiming a new message, namely, the possibility of a second chance of repentance after conversion and baptism. Here he clearly differs from rigorous older views that did not allow for a second repentance (*Herm. Man.* 4.3; cf. Heb. 6:4ff.). The newness of the message has to be divinely sanctioned if it is to have authority in the church: "A break of the radical command is . . . generally only possible when God explicitly prompts it" (Dibelius, p. 511). For that reason, Hermas uses the form of a heavenly letter (*Herm. Vis.* 2), as well as the role of a "[revelatory] angel of repentance." The form of an apocalypse lends the book a revelatory character, "an authority that the author alone could not claim and for which he cannot refer to any tradition" (Vielhauer, *Literatur*, p. 522; also Hellholm, p. 191). The writing does not describe eschatological future events; wherever originally eschatological horror figures emerge (*Herm. Vis.* 4), they are divested of their eschatological character. It is therefore a question of definition whether one should call the *Shepherd of Hermas* a pseudoapocalypse (Vielhauer). If one focuses in particular on aspects of content, that is, genre-specific themes (e.g., eschatology), the term *pseudoapocalypse* might be justified (however, see Hellholm). Still, the *Shepherd of Hermas* proves to be a genuine apocalyptic writing in that it refers to a religious crisis situation during the second century, in which the rigorous prohibition of a second repentance, which is doomed in light of the factual reality of the church, is met with a new solution. This solution then requires—as is typical of apocalypticism—divine legitimation. At any rate, the author was familiar with the conceptual world of traditional Jewish-Christian apocalypticism. He knows this world's literary means of presentation and their function. He is a late witness of apocalyptic currents in early Christianity without being able to share their basic eschatological outlook. That is true in similar fashion for the so-called *Apocalypse of Peter* (perhaps around A.D. 135). Concerning other, much later apocalypses of the ancient church (cf. Weinel), it seems likely that they "no longer arose from actual occasions" and do not represent "resistance literature" but reflect "only the expectations of more or less speculative groups" (Vielhauer, *Literatur*, p. 528).

Bibliography

On part a:

Becker, Jürgen. *Johannes der Täufer und Jesus von Nazareth.* BibS(N) 63. 1972.

Brandenburger, Egon. *Markus 13 und die Apokalyptik.* FRLANT 134. 1984.

Collins, John J. "Towards the Morphology of a Genre." In *Apocalypse: The Morphology of a Genre,* edited by John J. Collins, 1–20. Semeia 14. Missoula, Mt., 1979.

Hellholm, David, ed. *Apocalypticism in the Mediterranean World and the Near East.* 1983.

Hengel, Martin. *Judentum und Hellenismus.* WUNT 10. 2nd ed. 1973.

Koch, Klaus. *Ratlos vor der Apokalyptik.* 1970.

Müller, Karlheinz. "Die Ansätze der Apokalyptik." In *Literatur und Religion des Frühjudentums,* edited by Johann Maier and Josef Schreiner, 31–42. 1973.

———. S.v. "Apokalyptik/Apokalypsen 3." *TRE* 3:202–51. 1978.

Müller, Ulrich B. "Vision und Botschaft: Erwägungen zur prophetischen Struktur der Verkündigung Jesu." *ZTK* 74 (1977): 416–48.

Stegemann, Hartmut. "Die Bedeutung der Qumranfunde für die Erforschung der Apokalyptik." In *Apocalypticism in the Mediterranean World and the Near East,* edited by David Hellholm, 495–530. 1983.

Vielhauer, Philipp. "Apokalypsen und Verwandtes." In *Neutestamentliche Apokryphen,* edited by Edgar Hennecke and Wilhelm Schneemelcher, 2:405–54. 3rd ed. 1964.

On part b:

Baumgartner, Jörg. *Paulus und die Apokalyptik.* WMANT 44. 1975.

Becker, Jürgen. *Auferstehung der Toten im Urchristentum.* SBS 82. 1976.

Brandenburger, Egon. *Markus 13 und die Apokalyptik.* FRLANT 134. 1984.

Grässer, Erich. *Das Problem der Parusieverzögerung in den synoptischen Evangelien und in der Apostelgeschichte.* BZNW 22. 3rd ed. 1977.

Hoffmann, Paul. *Studien zur Theologie der Logienquelle.* NTA 8. 1972.

Käsemann, Ernst. *Exegetische Versuche und Besinnungen.* Vol. 2. 3rd ed. 1970.

On part c:

Brandenburger, Egon. *Markus 13 und die Apokalyptik.* FRLANT 134. 1984.

Bultmann, Rudolf. *Die Geschichte der synoptischen Tradition.* FRLANT 29. 8th ed. 1970.

Hahn, Ferdinand. "Die Rede von der Parusie des Menschensohnes Markus 13." In *Jesus und der Menschensohn,* FS for A. Vögtle, 240–66. 1975.

Pesch, Rudolf. *Naherwartungen: Tradition und Redaktion in Mk 13.* KBANT. 1968.

———. *Das Markusevangelium.* Vol. 2. HTKNT 2/2. 1980.

Vielhauer, Philipp. "Apokalypsen und Verwandtes." In *Neutestamentliche Apokryphen,* edited by Edgar Hennecke and Wilhelm Schneemelcher, 2:405–54, esp. 434–37. 3rd ed. 1964.

On part d:

Trilling, Wolfgang. *Untersuchungen zum 2. Thessalonicherbrief.* ETS 27. 1972.

———. *Der zweite Brief an die Thessalonicher.* EKKNT 14. 1980.

Vielhauer, Philipp. "Apokalypsen und Verwandtes." In *Neutestamentliche Apokryphen,* edited by Edgar Hennecke and Wilhelm Schneemelcher, 2:405–54, esp. 430–34. 3rd ed. 1964.

———. *Geschichte der urchristlichen Literatur,* 89–103. 1975. Reprint. 1978.

On part e:

Bauer, Walter. *Rechtgläubigkeit und Ketzerei im ältesten Christentum.* BHTH 10. 2nd ed. 1964.

Bousset, Wilhelm. *Die Offenbarung Johannis.* MeyerK. 6th ed. 1906.

Körtner, Ulrich H. J. *Papias von Hierapolis.* FRLANT 133. 1983.

Kraft, Heinrich. *Die Offenbarung des Johannes.* HNT 16a. 1974.

Lambrecht, Jan, ed. *L'Apocalypse johannique et l'Apocalyptique dans le Nouveau Testament.* BETL 53. 1980.

Lampe, Peter. "Die Apokalyptiker—ihre Situation und ihr Handeln." In *Eschatologie und Friedenshandeln,* 50–114. SBS 101. 1981.

Lohse, Eduard. *Die Offenbarung des Johannes.* NTD 11. 12th ed. 1979.

Müller, Ulrich B. *Zur frühchristlichen Theologiegeschichte: Judenchristentum und Paulinismus in Kleinasien an der Wende vom ersten zum zweiten Jahrhundert n. Chr.* 1976.

———. *Die Offenbarung des Johannes.* ÖTK 19. 1984.

On part f:

Dibelius, Martin. *Der Hirt des Hermas.* HNT supp.: Die Apostolischen Väter. Vol. 4. 1923.

Hellholm, David. *Das Visionsbuch des Hermas als Apokalypse.* Vol. 1. ConBNT 13:1. 1980.

Schrage, Wolfgang. *Der erste Petrusbrief; Der zweite Petrusbrief; Der Judasbrief,* 59–117, 118–49, 217–32. NTD 10. 1973.

Vielhauer, Philipp. "Apokalypsen und Verwandtes." In *Neutestamentliche Apokryphen,* edited by Edgar Hennecke and Wilhelm Schneemelcher, 2:405–54, esp. 442–44 on the Didache. 3rd ed. 1964.

———. *Geschichte der urchristlichen Literatur.* 1975.

Weinel, Heinrich. "Die spätere christliche Apokalyptik." In *Eucharisterion,* Festschrift for Hermann Gunkel, 141–73. FRLANT n.s. 19. 1923.

Wengst, Klaus. "Didache" (Apostolic Teachings) etc. Part 2 of *Schriften des Urchristentums,* 1–100. 1984.

Windisch, Hans. *Die katholischen Briefe.* HNT 15. 3rd ed. 1951.

8

Johannine Christianity

C. K. Barrett

a) The Basic Problem

Nowhere is it easy to describe the relation of early New Testament Christianity with the society that surrounded it. The reason for this difficulty is evident. Not one New Testament author had as his goal the comparing or contrasting of the new group of which he was a member with other groups and with the population at large or of working out their mutual interaction.[1] This fact is generally true for all early writers of history, though in various degrees. Social history is a modern invention, and little of it can be observed in antiquity: very little in Thucydides, for example; more in Herodotus, basically because Herodotus was in a way a less serious historian than Thucydides. Herodotus stops and reminisces once in a while, thus from time to time relaying to us pieces of information that, though not necessarily required for his reporting, are in fact of great interest to us. In Plutarch's *Moralia* we find more social history than in his biographies; the latter deal with history that, when it is not strictly biographical, is largely military and political. The *Moralia*, on the other hand, or at least parts of them, convey a large amount of information about people's life-style and the structure of their society.

It is possible to make a similar observation in the comparison of Paul's letters with Acts, all of which at least appear to refer to the same period and to a great extent to the same people. In its own way, Acts is history, yet it provides little information (it would be wrong to say that it provides no information) on the personal and social life of the average Christian and his or her Jewish or pagan contemporaries. Although the letters are certainly theological, they provide the reader who is willing and able to read between the lines a great deal of information about social matters.[2] Yet even so, one does not find much. Social history (and to an even higher degree sociology as a science), which is undoubtedly of interest to the twentieth century, was of no interest to the first century, and perhaps least of all was it of interest to the Christians of the first century. It is surprising that we even have Acts as a "history of the church." Up to the end of the first century, it was not expected that the following generations would continue to pass on history to their readers. The author was much more concerned to proclaim the gospel in his own way and to impress upon his readers the gospel's goals and consequences than to describe the past, especially in its individual and social details.

If we turn to the writings of John, the characteristics of the New Testament that have just been described become even clearer for two reasons. The first arises out of John's theological purpose. It is not necessary to show here in detail that this is a subject that has been discussed at great length by many authors.[3] For example, it has been considered proved that the Fourth Gospel is a Palestinian Jewish work originating in Palestine on the basis of Palestinian traditions of the life of Jesus and written for Palestinian readers who would fully understand the Gospel's allusions to the Torah and to the circumstances of Palestinian life. It has also however been taken as proved that the Gospel's background is Hellenistic, that it was written for the Hellenistic world, a process in which the original terms and language used by the historical Jesus were translated into a new, Greek, more or less philosophical form. A view related to this is that the Gospel rests on a Gnostic basis and thus presents the reader with the historicizing and Christianizing of a Gnostic myth. Then again it has been argued that the Gospel of John was indeed a Jewish work but was intended for readers in the Diaspora rather than for Palestinian Judaism. Palestinian Judaism had rejected Jesus; speeches and signs were now interwoven in a new way in the hope that the Jews outside Palestine would not repeat the terrible mistake of their brothers living in the land of Israel. In this view the Gospel is a work of Judaism in the Diaspora and has to be understood in connection with debates in the diaspora synagogue.

This vast diversity of opinions contributes greatly to what may be considered a better understanding of John's theological intention. "When we turn from this study of the Synoptic Gospels to John, we may occasionally find that John has adapted traditional material to yet another historical setting; but much oftener we find that John has liberated his material from particular settings to give it universal applicability."[4] John employs a multi-

tude of theological concepts and expressions. It is also true that he writes
with such simplicity that common people throughout the Christian centuries have accepted the Gospel and understood it by no means badly,
though they knew nothing about Palestinian or diaspora Judaism, or about
Hellenistic religious and philosophical concepts or about gnosis. If John
did not intend to give his work universal appeal, he was the victim (or the
beneficiary) of a uniquely happy coincidence. So far as these observations
are true, one will have to conclude that only an extremely limited amount
of information concerning John's environment can be expected. It was precisely not his intention to make his Gospel conform to a particular form of
society. The more completely people are placed and considered *coram Deo*,
the less they will differ from each other. A person described thus appears
primarily as non-God; as created, not as creator; as mortal, not as immor-
tal; as changeable, not as unchangeable; as sinful, not holy. And this person appears, unless at second glance, not as Jew or non-Jew, male or female,
old or young, civilized or barbarian.

The second reason why John—and he more than the other authors of
the New Testament—is of little help to the social historian is that his
theology prompts him to speak in a special way of the "cosmos," which is
portrayed as almost completely evil. The cosmos was created by the Word;
yet when the Word appeared in it, the cosmos would not acknowledge it
(John 1:10). The world lies wholly in the evil one (1 John 5:19). One could
add many other passages, especially that the world will hate believers as it
hated Jesus (John 15:18; 1 John 3:13). This means that John and his congregation believed that for their part they were different and separate from
the world. Only those who never truly belonged to "us" go out into the
world, speak of the world, and are heard by the world (1 John 4:5). It can
therefore hardly be expected that John would give information about the
world, about life in the world, and about the way the world presents itself.
The world is a creature that has turned its back on the Creator. It may be of
marginal interest to examine the reasons for this decline, but it is not really
important to describe them: the world passes away together with its desires
(1 John 2:17). It is therefore of no lasting interest. It corresponds to this
that the Christian community can have only negative relations with the
world and cannot accept the world's life-style or worldly social patterns. Of
course, it is possible that the community nonetheless does accept them
unconsciously.

Accordingly, the Johannine literature (from which, for the purpose of
the present discussion, Revelation is excluded) is hardly a promising field

for an examination of "Christianity and society." It would be misleading to begin such an examination without explicitly acknowledging this fact. The prospect, however, is not quite as unfavorable as it may at first appear. Few great theological works have been written in complete isolation from the things of this world. Augustine's *City of God* is unintelligible without some knowledge of the breakup of the Roman Empire. For Calvin's *Institutio* one must be aware of the attempt to transform Geneva into a city of God. Barth's theology presupposes not only familiarity with the history of liberal Protestantism in the nineteenth century but also awareness of the Great War of 1914–1918 and the Third Reich. There is no reason to assume that John alone lived in an ivory tower and remained untouched by his environment. It is his greatness that he viewed contemporary events under theological rather than sociological aspects; it is our misfortune (as far as the present study is concerned) that theology may be drawn directly from the text but social history only by means of hints and inferences. Even the world has a theological meaning, and a positive one at that. However much it may revolt against God, the world is still the object of his love (John 3:16). Jesus does not pray for the world (17:9), and it cannot receive or understand the Holy Spirit (14:17); that, however, does not mean that it is without hope, but the hope consists only in its ceasing to be what it is.

Up to this point I have used the name John as if the entire Johannine corpus had been written by only one author. This is in fact most improbable. This essay is not the place to discuss the question of authorship; I shall presuppose that we are dealing with at least four authors, who wrote, respectively, John 1–20, John 21, 1 John, and 2 and 3 John.[5] In addition, there may have been those who interpolated and edited the texts. It is impossible at this point to probe into this question in detail, though it will be mentioned occasionally. The question of authorship is, however, important; references already made in this discussion to the Johannine understanding of the cosmos may suggest that a distinction exists between the Gospel and the letters. A distinction, however, exists not only in this respect but also in regard to the interest shown in the Christian society and the behavior of Christians in the world.

Naturally, such distinctions would be unavoidable even if there were no question of differing authorship. Prima facie, the Gospel tells the story of the words and deeds of Jesus of Nazareth. So far as the story is historically correct, these date from the time before the existence of any Christian congregation. So far as it is based on old tradition, their background is that of Palestinian Judaism. It is a matter of debate how far these presuppositions are correct. Even if, however, the Gospel were completely fictional, it would still be true that the evangelist uses the form of a story played out in Galilee, Judea, and Jerusalem. Certainly, the Gospel writer wrote for his contemporaries, but the writer of the letters wrote to his contemporaries, and what he wrote had to relate to the conditions under which they lived if it was to be of any value to them. From this it follows that we shall do well to begin by gathering data from the letters, and first from the two shorter ones.

b) The Situation in the Johannine Letters

The second and third letters of John offer a picture of a precisely delimited and strictly disciplined Christian community. They are of special importance since they observe this community from two points of view; better, perhaps, they describe this community as divided into two parts, each of which could be described as the mirror image of the other. Each letter claims to have been written by someone who describes himself as "the elder" (2 John 1; 3 John 1). The second letter is addressed to a church (that is the most likely meaning of "the elect lady"; 2 John 1), the third to a person named Gaius (3 John 1). In addition, the third letter refers with great disapproval to another person, Diotrephes, who is accused of defaming the elder, of wanting to be in first place in his group, and of attempting to exclude those whom the group wants to include (3 John 9-10). Gaius, on the other hand, has helped these brothers on their way. These are said to have ventured out "for the sake of the name" without accepting anything from those who stood outside the congregation ("They went out 'for the name' [i.e., for Christ], without accepting anything from the Gentiles"; 3 John 6-7). The brothers are evidently traveling Christians, that is, not Christians traveling on their own business but Christians doing the business of the church, of Christ. They are missionaries and depend on the support of Christian congregations, which they find and try to turn into their base of operations. They are not simply wandering prophets (like those mentioned in Didache 11-13), for such travelers could not have made claims on the "Gentiles." They are rather evangelists, itinerant preachers, who as such have dealings with non-Christians yet are not willing to be supported by them, lest they should undermine their own purpose by making it appear as if they worked for personal gain. There are other Christian travelers.

The elder hopes to meet Gaius soon (3 John 14). Who it is that will visit the other is not mentioned explicitly; perhaps the intention was to meet halfway. Why did Diotrephes oppose the elder, and why did he refuse to accommodate the Christian travelers? The third letter of John gives no answer to that question. Since no reasonable explanation for the refusal exists, one gains the impression, which the elder certainly sought to create, that Diotrephes was motivated by baseness and jealousy. He wished to be in first place and therefore did not want to accept the authority of the elder (whether as an equal or possibly as an ecclesiastical official who was responsible for an area that included Diotrephes's district); he did not want to grant support to the itinerant preachers because they were from the elder's church and not his own.

For further information we turn to the Second Letter of John, where a similar situation appears. Here no one is mentioned by name. The reason for this may be that the leading man of the church with which the letter deals is Diotrephes himself, and that the only way to address the church is to circumvent him (3 John 9: "I have written something to the church; but Diotrephes, who likes to put himself first, does not acknowledge our authority"). Perhaps. But it is more probable that another church is meant here, since the "elect lady" and her children are commended for their good behavior and are warned not to accommodate traveling missionaries—perhaps from the heretical church headed by Diotrephes? This time a reason is given for the refusal of recognition: it is doctrinal. "Do not receive into the house or welcome anyone who comes to you and does not bring this teaching" (2 John 10). Whoever does so makes himself a partner in his evil deeds (his false doctrine is an evil work; 2 John 11). Of course, it might be that Diotrephes, if given a chance to explain, would have given a reason for rejecting the preachers similar to that recommended by the elder. It is possible that the unfriendly remarks he made about the elder were based on the same identification of heresy and moral baseness.

In the second letter of John the elder suggests two tests for wholesome orthodox Christianity by which one could identify the antichrists and deceivers. Deceivers do not confess Jesus Christ as coming in the flesh (2 John 7). Second, it is required of Christians that they love one another. Love is defined as walking in agreement with the commands of God, and walking in agreement with God's commands appears to lead back to the confession of faith mentioned earlier (2 John 5–7). In this confession of faith there has been a long debate on the meaning of the present participle "coming";[6] either an aorist or a future tense would have been much more readily intelligible. The words of the elder as they stand sound like a slogan or catchword in which the time scheme is of no importance, as one might say (without using a verb), "Jesus Christ in the flesh," meaning that this is how he came (in the incarnation) and how he will come (at his return). Catchwords in theology are always dangerous. They prevent thought, and behind the second and third letters of John there are few indications of active theological thinking. One finds here, however, at least an endeavor to maintain a theological position and a strict order. This is important for any attempt to discover what the respective Christian congregations were like.

In a remarkable essay E. Käsemann[7] contends that Diotrephes was an early bishop who believed that he was acting wholly in the interests of the Catholic church, while the elder presided over a group of enthusiasts who still lived the Christian life-style that can be discovered in early passages in the New Testament. The one maintained a formal discipline based on what one could almost call canon law. The other considered a certain kind of spiritual experience to be an unconditional requirement for membership in the church. This distinction does not seem to match the observations we have made up to this point. Both congregations, or at least their leaders, the elder and Diotrephes, appear to act in similar ways. We know (for he tells us) that the elder practiced excommunication on the basis of doctrine and behavior. Diotrephes does not have a chance to speak for himself, so that if one of the two acted on the basis of enthusiastic criteria, it must have been he. It is more likely, however, that he too expected doctrinal and ethical conformity.

Both congregations are surrounded by "Gentiles," a word we can understand in the sense of "outsiders." Its origin, however, is important. The word does not signify non-Jews in the ethnic sense; it has etymological overtones (cf. Matt. 18:17) that suggest the relation between the Jewish and the non-Jewish world. From this we might conclude that both congregations stood in some danger not only of living in an isolated fashion but also of becoming inwardly directed. It is not that the synagogue always or necessarily directed its vision inward, but that congregations in this situation are always inclined to develop in this direction. We are certainly not dealing here with an extreme tendency, for it seems that the congregations had sent out missionaries whose purpose must have been to convert "Gentiles" and to bring them into the communities as new members. But conversion in itself presupposes the existence of a clearly recognizable borderline, which the converted have to pass in order to leave the old life and enter into the new. And "loving one another" (2 John 5) is a rule of behavior that can be easily understood in a delimiting sense if one looks inwardly. Thus the phrase "loving one's neighbor" (before Christianity and within Christianity) has often led to hating one's enemies. That the two congregations formed a closed front toward the world around them is most convincingly confirmed by the fact that they also formed a closed front against each other. It is bad enough not to confess "that Jesus Christ has come in the flesh" in the interest of some heretical view, but the total rejection of Jesus Christ is worse.

It seems impossible to say much about the inner structure of these two closed groups. Both seem to have been monarchical. Diotrephes wants "to put himself first" and seems to have been a person capable of acting with authority, since those of whom he disapproves he excludes from the church (3 John 9–10). The elder writes in a way that indicates that he has equal or even greater authority. This is the general style of his letters, and it becomes especially clear in his threat to put Diotrephes in his place (3 John 10). That could mean that the elder exercised jurisdiction over a fairly large region that included the area over which Diotrephes presided. Or they may have been rivals in neighboring cities. The elder, like Diotrephes, could exclude those whom he did not wish to welcome "into the house." *House* could mean a house owned by a single member of the congregation or a place used by the church itself, or perhaps, to judge from Paul's letters (Rom. 16:5; 1 Cor. 16:19; Philemon 2; cf. Col. 4:15), the house of a church member where the congregation met. It is not important whether Diotrephes and the elder were termed *bishops*. There are many indications[8] that suggest that the two terms *elder* (or *presbyter*) and *bishop* had the same meaning and that the monarchical episcopate grew out of the college of presbyters.[9] The term *presbyter* is perhaps not used in a fully technical sense. On the one hand, there are passages in the New Testament (1 Tim. 5:1, 17, 19; Titus 2:2; 1 Peter 5:1–5) that make it fairly clear that presbyters, or elders, were originally older members of the congregation. This term remained in use (advanced by the Jewish example) even when it became clear that not all older men possessed in notable measure the appropriate gifts. On the other hand, one finds indications among the authors of the second century[10] that "presbyter" was a term that did not identify men who held a particular office but men of high standing in the earlier days of the church. It seems as if the churches in question moved towards a monarchical form of congregation leadership, whatever the term may have been that was used to denote it.

When we turn to the first letter it becomes clear that we are still in the same general environment. This emerges from the basic doctrinal affirmation of Jesus Christ's incarnation (1 John 4:2) and the basic Christian commandment to walk in love and to keep the commandments (2:3, 7, 10 and passim). It is almost as clear that we have moved back in time. Both doctrine and commandments appear in a less strict and schematized fashion. Ecclesiastical reprimands have not yet assumed such a clear and drastic form. The writer is evidently someone who has, or assumes that he has, authority among those whom he addresses. He addresses fathers, young men, and little children (2:12–14) always in the same commanding way and can speak to an entire congregation as his little children (2:1, 18), reminding, admonishing, directing, with no trace of any lack of self-confidence. He does not write, however, as elder or with the application of any other title. We may suppose that his authority was of a personal rather than an institutional kind. He can expect attention and obedience simply on the ground that he is known to be who he is.

In some matters the longest—and probably earliest—letter gives us fuller information, which nevertheless is in full agreement with the general picture that we were able to form from the second and third letters. Three things in particular call for mention here. First, it is clear that the author was confronted with the problem of sin in the church. Exegetes have always found difficulty in his observations on this theme, but this is not the place for a detailed discussion. It seems that there were members of the church who asserted that they were free from sin. The author evidently questions the validity of their assertion. "If we say that we have no sin, we deceive ourselves, and the truth is not in us" (1 John 1:8). "If we say that we have not sinned, we make him a liar, and his word is not in us" (1:10). Sinlessness means righteousness and perfect love (4:7–12). Were these people, who asserted of themselves that they were without sin, Käsemann's enthusiasts, people filled with religious ecstasy and incapable of applying serious criticism to their own behavior and of distinguishing between excitement and moral perfection?

The author's critical discussion is complicated and obscures the fact that he is compelled to admit that these enthusiasts are in a sense right. "He was revealed to take away sins. . . . The Son of God was revealed for this purpose, to destroy the works of the devil" (1 John 3:5, 8). "If anyone does sin, we have an advocate with the Father . . . and he is the atoning sacrifice for our sins" (2:1–2; cf. 4:10). These are theological assertions. One could argue that they do not go beyond the Pauline doctrine of justification. "In Christ" the believer is without sin since he or she receives the righteousness of Christ. It is, however, difficult not to accept that there are also passages that go beyond this. "Those who have been born of God do not sin, because God's seed abides in them; they cannot sin because they have been born of God" (3:9; cf. 5:18). John seems to expect not only a forensic but also a moral freedom from sin.

Fortunately it is not our task in this study to tackle the theologically difficult problem of amalgamating these remarks into a theological unity. Our task is to grasp that upon the author was laid a heavy practical responsibility in that he was obliged to deal with those who wrongly claimed to be without sin (wrongly, for they did not love their brothers, 3:10), without at the same time invalidating the fundamental Christian conviction that Christ died to put an end to sin, and that there was a Christian obligation to love. Were those who caused the difficulty enthusiasts? Along with the assertion, "We are without sin," we should note also the assertion, "I have come to know God" (2:4). For this one can hardly find another term than gnosis, although gnosis of a primitive, undeveloped kind. Gnosis is not the same as enthusiasm, though it may be connected with it.

Second, we can better understand enthusiasm if we note that the author of 1 John had to deal with the phenomenon of inspiration and accordingly was forced to insist on the church's duty to test the spirits so as to determine whether they came from God (4:1). But here also we again encounter an intellectual, dogmatic element, since the test the prophets have to undergo is a doctrinal one. "By this you know the Spirit of God: every Spirit that confesses that Jesus Christ has come in the flesh is from God, and every spirit that does not confess Jesus is not from God" (4:2–3). No other test is proposed. No attempt is made to measure the degree of inspiration or ecstasy. And here one finds again a connection with gnosis, for the false prophets or antichrists are presumably Docetists. When it is said that they do not confess Jesus, what is meant is that they do not confess that he has come in the flesh. Had they surrendered all interest in Jesus, they would not have claimed to be Christians, as they evidently did. Again, John responds to the Gnostic claim with the counterclaim that he and his friends are the true Gnostics because they keep God's commandments. "Now by this way we can be sure that we know him, if we obey his commandments. Whoever says, 'I have come to know him,' but does not obey his commandments, is a liar" (2:3–4). "I write to you, not because you do not know the truth, but because you know it" (2:21). The truth or insight that the Christians possess is due to an anointing (*chrisma*) that they have received. "I write these things to you concerning those who would deceive you. As for you, the anointing that you received from him abides in you, and so you do not need anyone to teach you. But as his anointing teaches you about all things, and is true and is not a lie, and just as it [or: he (Christ)] has taught you, abide in him" (2:26–27).

Thus we see rival groups, both claiming and striving to be without sin, but in different ways. Both claim to be enlightened, but each by its own gnosis. Both concentrate, but in different ways and in terms of their own understanding, on the person of Jesus. This leads to the third point that we have to consider. John relates his opponents to the cosmos. In the first reference to antichrists the word cosmos is not used: "They went out from us, but they did not belong to us; for if they had belonged to us, they would have remained with us. But by going out they made it plain that none of them belongs to us" (1 John 2:19). There is no doubt, however, that we are dealing here with the same group that is referred to in 4:1, 5–6: "Many false prophets have gone out into the world. . . . They are from the world; therefore what they say is from the world, and the world listens to them. We are from God. Whoever knows God listens to us, and whoever is not from God does not listen to us."

It is true that John theologizes the meaning of the cosmos and that to him worldliness is not a matter of wine, women, and song but of that which had the appearance of a highly spiritual gnosis. It is possible, however, and in the present context even necessary, to take his word in both a historical and a theological sense and thereby to see a congregation from which members set out to acquaint themselves with the world and especially with the philosophical and religious language of the world, which they then use with some success. The world listens to them. Theologically speaking, they may have been antichrists, but it is not necessary to question their motives, unless this is justified by such pictures as John offers in 1 John 3:17: "How does God's love abide in anyone who has the world's goods and sees a brother or sister in need and yet refuses to help?" In fact it may not only be generous but completely correct to suppose that their intention was to offer to the world what they held to be the Christian message, and that it was their method to learn and use the language of the world. This, however, was the language of gnosis, and the result was that they adopted a Docetic Christology. From what they learned from the world, they may also have drawn the conclusion that since all matter was essentially evil, the ethical or unethical actions of their physical lives were of no significance, so that no moral value was inherent in loving one's neighbor or Christian brother. About such people the author of 1 John can only sadly shake his head and say: They never really belong to us. This is a more favorable attitude than that of the elder or of Diotrephes, but one can hardly call it positive.

In addition to its Gnostic language and theology, the author of 1 John seems to know of the world outside the church only that it is connected with "desire" and "pride" (2:16–17). He is much too good a theologian to assume that "the desire of the flesh" is the only kind of desire there is. He points to the basic characteristics of life in the world: selfishness and boastful clamor. Both belong to the cosmos, not to God. But does not the cosmos itself belong to God? I cannot find that the author seriously examines this question. That must mean that in the end he had no theology of society, or perhaps we should say that in this letter he did not intend to develop one. He leaves us a picture of this world no more than he leaves us with a theology of it.

c) The Gospel of John and the Past Social World of Jesus

We now turn to the Gospel and must recall that in our treatment of "Christianity and society" at least two societies are involved: that of Palestine in or about A.D. 30 (for whatever our estimate of the historical value of the Gospel may be, its story is set in this framework) and that of the region and time in which the Gospel was written.

Gospel passages about the social and religious conditions in Palestine before the fall of Jerusalem (and about the kind of Judaism that existed after the catastrophe) have often been gathered. To enumerate and describe them in detail is not necessary. Jesus is depicted as one who existed within the religious framework of Jewish life, even though he does not always observe its regulations. His contemporaries complain that he does not keep the Sabbath (John 5:9–16; 9:14–16). He replies not only in theological pronouncements (5:17), which need not be discussed here, but also by referring to the well-known argument in which the Sabbath law and the law of circumcision were weighted against each other (7:22–23). He keeps the Jewish feasts, though it may be doubtful whether he will go to the Passover feast in Jerusalem (11:56). He chooses not to go to the feast of Booths at the usual time (7:14). He does, however, celebrate the relatively unimportant feast of Temple Dedication (10:22). He interprets the Old Testament by rabbinic methods; for this we can cite especially the *'al-tiqre'* interpretation of Ps. 78:24 in John 6. It is not surprising that the sermon of this chapter is placed in the synagogue in Capernaum (6:59), an appropriate place for a sermon in this form. Jesus can make use of a recognized legal basis of proof: the testimony of two persons is valid (8:17).

Some of the statements made in the Gospel are of dubious correctness. The statement in 11:49 (cf. 18:13) that Caiaphas was high priest "that year" has been used on both sides. Here it is sufficient to say that should John have had the impression that the office of high priest was one that changed hands every year, he was mistaken. It is, of course, possible that he meant only that Caiaphas was high priest in the year of the crucifixion. More questionable is the statement in 18:28 that the Jewish officials were unwilling to enter the Praetorium, so as not to be defiled and thereby prevented from participating in the Passover feast. Whether that was so is disputable. Questionable in another sense is the remark in 4:9: "Jews do not share things in common with the Samaritans." There is manuscript evidence for the omission of this phrase,[11] so that we may be dealing here with a late redactional interpolation (but this is unlikely). It is also disputed whether the meaning is only that "Jews have nothing to do with Samaritans" (which would require only superficial knowledge of Palestinian conditions), or that "Jews do not use dishes with Samaritans" (which would require familiarity with the opinion that Samaritan women had to be considered as menstruating from birth [Niddah 4.1] and therefore always unclean). There is much more material of this kind to be found in commentaries.

All of this forms a picture, nebulous and blurred in some details, of Jesus as a Palestinian Jew who lived within, yet in tension with, the structure of Palestinian Jewish society. In the end the tension becomes strong enough to result in Jesus' complete rejection ("It is better for you to have one man die for the people than to have the whole nation destroyed" [11:50]), in his being handed over to the Roman judiciary ("Your own nation and the chief priests have handed you over to me. What have you done?" [18:35]), and in his crucifixion.

This leads to a second element in Palestinian society: the Roman prefect Pontius Pilate and his assistants in the provincial government. We may note that Galilee under its ruler Herod Antipas, who plays an important part in the Synoptic Gospels, remains in the Fourth Gospel relatively insignificant and does not at this point call for special consideration. In fact Pilate too appears only at the end of the story in the only place where, according to John, Jesus has any dealings with secular, political society. It is important here to make a distinction. The exactness of the historical material reported by John is extremely questionable. In John's narrative of Jesus' arrest (18:1–11) a cohort of soldiers is accompanied by a band of retainers from the high priest and the Pharisees, the entire group being apparently under the command of a military tribune (18:12). Yet the Roman part of this surprisingly mixed group is ready to permit Jesus to be taken immediately to Annas, not to the Roman governor. Throughout the entire story Pilate appears favorably inclined toward Jesus and much less inclined toward shedding blood than other indications would suggest. He permits the Jews to address him with incredible impudence. "What accusation do you bring against this man?" "If this man were not a criminal, we would not have handed him over to you" (18:29, 30). After deciding that Jesus is innocent, Pilate nevertheless has him flogged (19:1) and permits his soldiers to ridicule him (19:2, 3). He seems to expect that the Jews will carry out the crucifixion (19:16). The Johannine passion story thus contains little material that can be considered to be of great historical value.

To be distinguished, however, from this lack of historical information are two dialogues between Jesus and Pilate (18:33–38; 19:9–11) and also some of the conversations between Pilate and the Jews (esp. 18:31–32, 38b–40; 19:6–8, 12–13). These passages are not of importance because of their historical value, which is in fact nil—who was in a position to report what private conversations (if indeed there were any) took place between the prefect and his prisoner? They are, however, of great importance for the Johannine understanding of authority and the theological significance of the state. Moreover, this combination of historical worthlessness and weighty theological content means that this material must be regarded as shedding light on John's relationship with the second society or environment with which his book is concerned, that is, the environment that surrounded John as author. We shall return to this later.

The Johannine relationship to history is curious. The fact that a historical Jesus existed, of whom one could know at least certain things, was a central and indispensable element in his thought. To tell the story of this Jesus, the incarnate Word of God, to tell it with exact and verifiable details, was a task that for John had no theological or other significance. Had Jesus been other than he was, John could not have written as he did. His main concern, however, was to describe Jesus as he is, or rather, perhaps, to tell the consequences resulting *now* from what he was *then*. All that we should at present conclude from this is that we should not be surprised if the Gospel has little to tell us about the relationship between Jesus and the religious and political groups of his day. What we may hope to find in the Gospel is an implicit representation of the Johannine reaction (a theological rather than a sociological reaction) to John's own environment. It is this reaction that we shall examine now.

d) The Environment of the Fourth Evangelist

It would lead far beyond the limits of this study if more than brief reference were made to one of the essential elements in the background of the Fourth Gospel: I refer to gnosis. In an investigation of "Christianity and society" it must be left almost completely out of account. This is not because gnosis is unimportant but because in the first century it did not represent a society. In fact, it was hardly a sharply defined religious or philosophical form of thought, though it became that later, and in the second century it became a society, a kind of church. In John's time it resembled rather an atmosphere that one inhaled than a clearly distinguishable entity or even a formulated myth. For this reason it need not be considered here, important as it is for an assessment of Johannine theology.

Judaism, on the other hand, offers an almost exact opposite. Within Judaism theology is very various. The author (or authors) of Enoch did not think in the same way as Philo. Yet Judaism is above all the embodiment of an institution, of a firmly established and strictly organized society with no essential confession apart from the monotheism of the Shema, with a disciplined life regulated by the precepts of the Torah, at least of the written Torah, for many expanded and explained by the additional precepts of the oral Torah. John shows that he is aware of precisely this kind of institutional Judaism. He is an heir of the Old Testament and makes it his own, since Moses wrote of Christ (John 5:46), Isaiah saw his glory (12:41), and Abraham rejoiced to see his day (8:56).

As many generations of commentators have pointed out, John tends to refer to "the Jews" in general. This is unlike the Synoptic Gospels, which prefer to speak of certain groups or classes among the Jews: Pharisees, Sadducees, Herodians, teachers of the law, priests. Various reasons have been suggested to explain why the Johannine treatment differs. Most of them have at least some validity. Especially important is the fact that John wrote (in all probability) at a time when earlier distinctions had disappeared with the disaster of A.D. 70. Most important of all, however, is the fact that the expression "the Jews" points to Judaism as an institution—one that had rejected Jesus and now stood over against the church in apparently irreconcilable detachment. John writes (9:22; 12:42; 16:2) with knowledge of the Benediction[12] that had the effect of excluding Jewish Christians from the synagogue. At the first mention of this action it is attributed to "the Jews": "For the Jews had already agreed that anyone who confessed Jesus to be the Messiah would be put out of the synagogue" (9:22).

The phrase *the Jews* is characteristic of the Gospel as a whole. "The Jews" had sent to John the Baptist (1:19); the feasts are feasts of "the Jews" (e.g., 2:13); "the Jews" were intent on killing Jesus (e.g., 5:18); "the Jews" who believed are in an insecure and dangerous situation (8:31: " . . . if you continue in my word"); and so on. John is fully aware that the entire story of Jesus took place within Judaism, up to the point when he was buried "according to the burial custom of the Jews" (19:40). Yet, finally, by the end of the first century, the Jews had separated themselves from the Christians. For John, salvation comes from the Jews (4:22). But this is in the first instance a historical statement. Salvation was to come out of Judaism and had been predicted by the prophets, but from that point onward Christianity no longer needed Judaism. When modern authors search for signs of anti-Semitism, or rather of anti-Judaism, in the New Testament, they begin quite naturally with John. There is no indication in the Gospel that the evangelist and his companions were aware of a continuing special mission to Israel. John has no parallel to the terrible sentence in Matthew, "His blood be on us and on our children" (Matt. 27:25), but "We have no king but the emperor" (John 19:15) is in many respects an even clearer proclamation that those who speak thus reject their position as the people of the one king, God. For the Johannine church the synagogue represents a threat and a warning. The synagogue is not a sister nor even a mission field.

The last paragraph referred to Johannine statements concerning the Jews in general—"the Jews"; some remarks about the Pharisees could be taken in the same way. Are there exceptions? Are there Jewish groups who were exempt from the process by which John distanced himself from his compatriots? Before the military catastrophe of the year 70 Judaism was a manifold religious phenomenon. The universal applicability of the Torah to the whole of Judaism inevitably produced a certain measure of uniformity, as I have already indicated. But the Torah had to be interpreted. The interpretations differed, and they differed more in the earlier time than in the later. We know today that the term "normative Judaism" is an expression that must be used, if at all, with great caution, and that sectarian groups existed with their own interpretations and customs, a situation in which each viewed itself not as sectarian but as the central group, as the only soldier within the troop who kept step. Early Christianity must have appeared as such a sectarian group within Judaism at large. Did Christianity then have in those early days, and did it continue to have later, a special kind of relation with any other sectarian group?

Since the discovery of the Dead Sea Scrolls a relationship of this kind between Johannine Christianity and the Qumran sect has often been maintained. On the whole, however, this relationship has over the years come to seem increasingly improbable. A few superficial similarities are misleading. The sect shows antipathy to the temple; John declares that the Father will be worshiped "neither on this mountain nor in Jerusalem" (4:21). The two attitudes, however, differ substantially. Essentially the sect had nothing against the temple; it would have used the temple had it been allowed to do so in its own way, which differed from what the sect considered the temple's desecration by the officiating priests. The Johannine rejection of the temple resulted from the conviction that the temple had been fulfilled and thus abolished by Jesus, since he had taken its place and now served himself as the link between God and humanity. Much has been made of the modified dualism that, as has been repeatedly claimed, can be found in both John and the Qumran literature. In its essential features, however, this modified dualism can be found also in the Old Testament.

The differences between *Qumran* and the Gospel are fundamental. The Qumran community had its own understanding and interpretation of the Torah, but it insisted with extreme rigidity that the Torah, thus understood and interpreted, should be strictly kept. That was the foundation of the community's piety. For John the law had at best a subordinate status ("The law indeed was given through Moses; grace and truth came through Jesus Christ"; John 1:17). Moses is important because "he wrote about me" (5:46). Jesus does not keep the Sabbath law in a literal sense (5:16; 9:16). Qumran is not sufficient to explain the Gnostic traits of the Gospel.

We know far too little of the variety, the subdivisions, and the cross-currents in the Judaism of the first century to be able to affirm that no contacts ever existed between the traditions that eventually found their way respectively into the Fourth Gospel and into the Qumran sect and its writings. We can probably accept that the first Christian group displayed in many respects parallels and similarities with the groups that settled by the Dead Sea. Further than that we cannot go, unless it is in more detailed similarities between the organization of the Johannine communities (which are described more clearly in the letters than in the Gospel) and the organization of the sect. The parallel between the group of twelve disciples in the Gospel and the twelve merciful judges of Qumran (1QS 8.1)[13] is neither remarkable in itself nor specifically Johannine. At best it could indicate an early contact of Christians with Qumran, but no particularly Johannine interest lies there. The fact that the letters show an increasingly monarchical structure (as pointed out above) is no special parallel with the Teacher of Righteousness or any other Qumran figure.

There is another group of Jewish origin that deserves brief mention. It has often been taken as proved that one of the motives that contributed to the fact that the Gospel was written down was the necessity felt by the Christians to counter the claims made in their master's name by the *disciples of John the Baptist,* who continued to exist as a group after the deaths of both John and Jesus. This was done (it is held) by integrating these claims into the demands made for Jesus. Some who believe that behind the extant Prologue to the Gospel (John 1:1–18) there lies an *Urprolog* are of the opinion that it originated in Baptist circles.[14] Here, however, there is a danger of building one hypothesis upon another.[15] Still, it is correctly observed that the Gospel contains a number of passages that, though ranking John the Baptist highly, assert emphatically that he is inferior to Jesus. Thus he himself declares that he is not the Christ or Elijah or the prophet (1:20–23). The disciples leave him in order to follow Jesus (1:37). He welcomes the greater success that Jesus has and compares himself to the friend of the bridegroom—an important but secondary figure: "He must increase, but I must decrease" (3:26–30; cf. 4:1). The Baptist is an important witness to Jesus but not the most important (5:33–36). The difficulty we encounter here lies in the lack of concrete evidence for the existence of a Baptist sect.[16] For such evidence it is natural to point to the narratives in Acts that deal with Apollos (Acts 18:24–28), who knew "only the baptism of John," and with the disciples (19:1–7) who had been baptized "into John's baptism." It is not possible at this point to appraise the historical value of these two reports. Nor would it be wise to make too much of them or of whatever may be hidden behind the infancy narratives in Luke 1–2. It is certainly correct to argue that the fourth evangelist would not have written in such a pointedly negative way about the Baptist had he not known some who made equally pointed positive assertions about him. It is probable therefore that such people existed and certain that if they existed, John the evangelist could not have agreed with them, and it is likely that he would express his lack of agreement. We cannot, however, on the basis of this lack of agreement draw any conclusions about the social structure of the two groups, the one following John the Baptist and the other gathered about John the evangelist. Here as elsewhere John's interests lie more in the theological than the sociological realm.

The Fourth Gospel shows without doubt an interest in *Samaria and the Samaritans*. Not only are the important words about the water of life spoken in Samaria (John 4–5) and directed in the course of conversation to a Samaritan woman. The passage also concludes with the statement that Jesus was accepted by many Samaritans as "the Savior of the world" (4:39–42). There is perhaps more to be learned from this chapter. After the woman's departure the disciples return to Jesus and invite him to eat some of the provisions they have brought. He replies, "I have food to eat that you do not know about." When the disciples take this literally (a typically Johannine development, which shows that we have here Johannine rather than traditional material), he explains that his food is to do the will of him who sent him and to accomplish his work. This in turn leads to a series of sayings about the work of sowing and reaping and finally to the statement: "I sent you to reap that for which you did not labor. Others have labored, and you have entered into their labor" (4:38). Taken in the light of Acts 8, this passage has been understood to mean that Samaria was converted to Christianity by the Hellenists and had subsequently been taken over as a mission field by the church's nucleus, the Twelve.[17] This in turn has led to the conclusion that there was a connection between the Gospel and the Hellenists. The connection, however, is too hypothetical and problematic to mean much to us. It is exegetically uncertain. In 4:38 the mention of "others" may be a concealed reference to Jesus himself.[18] It was he who began the work of evangelizing in Samaria; now it is up to his disciples to bring in the harvest. The word *Samaritan* appears once more in the Gospel (8:48), where it is used as a Jewish accusation against Jesus: "Are we not right in saying that you are a Samaritan and have a demon?"

Where do these references to the Samaritans lead? There can be no doubt that John, or the Johannine tradition, was aware that the Samaritans formed a group that was related to the Jews but repudiated by them. The Samaritans worship the same God but in a different place (4:20). The Samaritans expect the coming of a Messiah, a prophetic and teaching Messiah ("He will proclaim all things to us"—4:25; " . . . a man who told me everything I have ever done! He cannot be the Messiah, can he?"—4:29), and Jesus can say with reference to the Samaritan expectation, "I am he" (4:26). This seems to indicate a greater willingness on John's part than on that of some Jews to accept the Samaritans as part of God's people. One can hardly claim, however, that it proves more than that. There is a prophetic component (based on Deut. 18) in at least the Qumran form of Judaism (1QS 9.11; 4QTestim 5–8) and in early non-Johannine messianism (Acts 3:22). One may reasonably suppose that the Johannine Christians had at a certain stage come into sufficiently close contact with Samaritans to have an interest in and sympathy for them. There is nothing in John 4 that could not have taken place (from the standpoint of the narrative) in Galilee, for example. It may very well be significant also that in John the Samaritans are the first to hail Jesus as the Savior of the world, even though significance may lie in the fact that other representatives of the world outside Judaism are hardly mentioned in the Gospel and that there is some appropriateness in having this truth proclaimed by the despised and undervalued. Contacts between the Johannine community and the Samaritans could have led to the rejection of Jesus as a Samaritan (8:48). The insinuation that Jesus was born out of wedlock (8:41, in the same context) is an accusation that was made at a later time, possibly as late as when the Fourth Gospel was written, and that may be true of the Samaritan accusation too. But John makes no comment on it. Only the criticism that Jesus has a demon (8:49) receives a reply. The most that can be said is that a number of doors open up to speculations regarding the social environment of Johannine Christianity; valid proofs hardly exist.

The Samaritans have led us a step outside Judaism. It remains to consider John in relation to *Roman society*. We have already seen that Rome plays only a relatively small part in the story told in the Gospel. Fear of Rome is represented as contributing to the Jewish decision to get rid of Jesus (John 11:48). Pilate proves to be a partner in the conspiracy, though a reluctant one, so that eventually, in spite of his assertions of Jesus' innocence (18:38; 19:4, 6, 12), Pilate hands him over to be crucified (19:16). John himself, however—whether he wrote in Ephesus, Antioch, or Alexandria—wrote under the law of the empire. He must have known, though there is no evidence for it in the letters, that he had his own local Pilate, an authority to which he and the church to which he belonged were inevitably bound, whether in a positive or a negative sense. This means that the conversations reported in chapters 18 and 19 must be considered, regardless of their historical origin, as expressing his opinions about the relationship between his church and the state and in particular about his understanding of the state's authority.

The main thought in John 18:29–32 (we ignore here many particular problems and additional statements) is that the Jews have decided on Jesus' death for their own reasons. They demand nothing less than his death; that is why they hand the case over to Rome. Pilate has Jesus called before him and asks immediately, "Are you the King of the Jews?" (18:33).

From the fact that the death sentence was demanded we are perhaps expected to infer that it had already been stated that Jesus had declared himself king, but it is much more likely that John is simply borrowing from the source he used, shortening it by omitting this feature. Jesus' evasive reply (18:34 and esp. 18:37) is strongly reminiscent of the Synoptic narrative (e.g., Mark 15:2).

What follows is a discussion about the nature of kingship. Jesus insists that he possesses a kingdom but proves that his kingship is not of this world by pointing out that his followers are not fighting in order to prevent his falling into the hands of the Jews. It is a natural characteristic of a this-worldly kingdom that its followers fight for it, but for Jesus' kingdom his followers do not fight. This argument overlooks the fact that the true reason why the disciples are not fighting is not that they understand Jesus' kingship but that they have run away out of cowardice. Or is it hinted that had they been encouraged by Jesus, they would have been brave enough to fight? At any rate, Jesus confirms that his kingship is not rooted in this world (it is not "from here"; John 18:36). By his words Jesus in fact admits that he is a king. "So you are a king?" (18:37). The "you" may be emphatic: you, wretched man, a king! The reply, "You say that I am a king," is not a renunciation of kingship but probably means that kingship was not the word that Jesus would have chosen. Politicians like Pilate may use it, but Jesus prefers to speak of the "truth." The meaning of his life is to be a witness to the truth. Pilate can only reply by another question: "What is truth?" (18:37–38). This seems to mean that a conversation between Jesus (and those whom he represents, who also represent him, namely, the Christian community) and Pilate (and the society he represents) can only lapse into silence, since the two parties speak different languages. The language Pilate chooses is that of political dominion. Christians will use his language only if they are allowed to turn its meaning upside down. To Pilate, kingship is only a matter of this world and of power understood in terms of this world. For Jesus, however, kingship is precisely *not* of this world and carries in itself a repudiation of this-worldly power. Jesus is concerned with the truth, but that is a word that Pilate does not understand.

The next conversation begins when the Jews inform Pilate that Jesus claims to be the Son of God. The assertion that Jesus is of supernatural origin puts fear into Pilate. He asks, "Where are you from?" (19:9), a question that shows that we are dealing here with a typical Johannine development of traditional material, for it originates in Pilate's discovery, reported in the Synoptics (Luke 23:6ff.), that Jesus is from Galilee and can therefore be remitted to Herod. But the matter is no longer a question of Jesus' country of origin, and there is no reply. Jesus' silence prompts Pilate to a further question, intended to make the prisoner talk. Is he not aware that Pilate has the power to set him free or to crucify him (John 19:10)? This claim to power is true in so far as Pilate's decision, whatever it may be, will be carried out. The rights that Pilate has as Roman governor, however, are not something that he possesses in himself. He has power only because it has been given him from God ("from above"; cf. 3:3). It follows that Pilate cannot be considered an entirely free agent. In regard to Jesus' death he has less guilt on his shoulders than "the one who handed me over to you" (commentators disagree on the question, here irrelevant, whether the phrase refers to Judas, Caiaphas, or the Jewish people as a whole). From this point onward (19:12) Pilate tries to release Jesus, partly because he is now convinced of the supernatural (if not divine) origin of his prisoner. But he is overruled by the political threat: "If you release this man, you are no friend of the emperor. Everyone who claims to be a king sets himself against the emperor."

The primary Johannine interest in these conversations is theological and especially christological. John asserts that Jesus will die as an innocent man, for he does not claim for himself kingship, and thus power, as the world knows it. Rather, he sees it as his task in the world to bear witness to the truth. He also dies as a divine being who rules a kingdom that is not of this world, and he thus has a power that Pilate does not share. At the same time it is admitted that earthly rulers like Pilate have a measure of power that has been granted them by God. This is depicted in the form of a record of Jesus' historical confrontation with Pilate. Since, however, this report is clearly a Johannine addition to the passion narrative, it must be understood as containing also John's commentary on his own situation, in which he and the congregation to which he belonged found themselves confronted with the Roman state. John 16:2 indeed points primarily to resistance from the Jewish side. That becomes clear in the reference to expulsion from the synagogue and also in the death threat, for those who "kill you" and believe that "by doing so they are offering worship to God" can only be Jews. It is doubtful, however, whether at the time at which John wrote, Jews often had the opportunity to execute Christians. Probably John's train of thought is intended only to indicate the general dislike that Christians experienced (15:18). With this in mind, John uses the confrontation between Jesus and Pilate, on the one hand, for its own sake (in order to bear witness to the truth about Jesus, that is, about Christology) and, on the other, as a prime example of the relationship between church and state.

It is of the highest importance, and absolutely characteristic, that John views this confrontation much more from the standpoint of theology than from that of sociology. Social and political relations have a theological basis in so far as the power exercised by the state and applied in part in persecutions is given to it by God. This takes the matter one step beyond Rom. 13:1–7, where the state suppresses baseness and vice, rewards virtue, and is thus quite naturally regarded as God's servant, empowered and approved by God. For John the state is the persecuting power[19] with undisputed authority to acquit or to crucify. Yet this power, too, which includes the power to do evil and to oppose the work of God, is based on an authority of command that comes from God. It is a different version of the doctrine of the two swords, in which the one can be turned against the other. Presumably, John does not mean that it is God's will that the state should attack the church, but that the power given to the state by God is given without any conditions attached to the gift. The power may be abused as well as used for good. This attitude was adopted by the early church. "We respect in the emperors the ordinance of God, who has set them over the nations. We know that there is that in them which God has willed; and to what God has willed we desire all safety, and we account an oath by it a great oath" (Tertullian *Apology* 32). It is important to recognize that in the beginning this attitude was based mainly on theological grounds rather than on grounds of expediency. We have already pointed to John 15:18 at an earlier point: "If the world hates you, be aware that it hated me before it hated you." With that we may compare 1 John 3:13: "Do not be astonished, brothers and sisters, that the world hates you." As we have seen above, the *world*, the *cosmos*, is a fundamental theological theme in the Johannine literature, especially in the Gospel and in the first letter (cf. also 2 John 7). The theological theme has two historical, social forms of expression. One appears in the Gospel in the frequently used term *the Jews*. This term is not used in the Prologue, but the idea is present. "He was in the world, and the world came into being through him, yet the world did not know him; he came to what was his own, and his own people did not receive him" (John 1:10–11). The world is God's creation, which has used the freedom given to it to rebel against its creator. To the world has been given the power to release or to crucify, and it chooses to crucify. According to the Johannine view, the Jews are the best example of this abuse of power; the words of 19:11 must be understood in this way. The Jews deserve more reproach than the Romans, for while Pilate can only ask, "What is truth?" (18:38), the Jews are supposed to know the truth. Israel's teacher should understand what is said to him (3:10). Salvation comes from the life and traditions of the Jews (4:22). The most painful rebellion against God is that of the pious. In addition, however, there is also the rebellion of the worldly power, which also abuses what has been entrusted to it. Although John exonerates the governor rather than the Jews in his passion story— mainly for theological reasons but in part also perhaps out of prudence— he cannot avoid the conclusion that Pilate handed Jesus over to be crucified (19:16). Jesus was *crucifixus sub Pontio Pilato*. In this clause the cosmos is written into the confession of faith. This observation is true only for the Gospel. Strangely enough, the cosmos seems to assume another meaning in the first letter. The state disappears, and *cosmos* becomes a word belonging to the realm of thought rather than to that of political action and power. People leave the church and go out into the world (1 John 2:19; 4:5). They go out in order to speak the world's language in such a way that the world may listen to them, as it was not listening to John and his associates. The world has now become not the source of persecution but the fount of unbelief and heresy. This theme has been discussed earlier and now leads to the last question to be raised in this study.

e) Tensions in the Johannine Community

We have examined the Christian congregation or congregations as they are set forth in the Johannine literature in relation to various groups in their environment: Jews and Romans, Samaritans, Qumran sectarians, and disciples of John the Baptist. We must now examine the Christian group in relation to itself, that is, in relation to claims and tensions that were caused not by external but by internal pressure. To a certain degree this topic also has already been dealt with. The letters clearly show that there were those who went out into "the world" and learned to speak as the world speaks and no doubt to live as the world lives, at least to the degree that they separated themselves from the circle of Christian love. So it appeared at least to the authors of the letters. Those who went out, however, would describe what they did in a different way.

The Gospel also shows traces of controversy and schism. At this point we should note the passages that Bultmann and others have attributed to an ecclesiastical redactor, who believed that the Gospel in its original version was unsatisfactory in regard to eschatological doctrines and sacramental practice and accordingly inserted passages such as John 3:5 (with its clear reference to baptism) and 6:51–58 (with its allusion to eating and drinking at the Eucharist), as well as references to the "last day" (6:39–40, 44, 54). The possibility must not be excluded that these passages belonged to the many-sided dialectical theology of the evangelist.[20] If however they are correctly considered to be insertions, they testify to sacramental and nonsacramental elements in the congregation and to rival convictions regarding whether eschatology was or was not to be completely transposed into the present. In any case, it must be emphasized that the Gospel as it stands testifies to a theology and a practice that were able to accommodate both a futuristic and an already realized eschatology, as well as an adoption of baptism and Eucharist as critical as that which can be seen in Paul's writings.

Less problematic is another group of passages, which tell explicitly of dissensions among the disciples. Such passages are found in John 6:60–71 ("When many of his disciples heard it, they said, 'This teaching is difficult; who can accept it?' But Jesus, being aware that his disciples were complaining about it, said to them, 'Does this offend you? . . . But among you there are some who do not believe.' For Jesus knew from the first who were the ones that did not believe, and who was the one that would betray him. . . . Because of this many of his disciples turned back and no longer went about with him. So Jesus asked the twelve, 'Do you also wish to go away?' "). In addition one may point to the following passages: 7:5 ("Not even his brothers believed in him"); 8:30–59 ("As he was saying these things, many believed in him. Then Jesus said to the Jews who had believed in him, 'If you continue in my word, you are truly my disciples. . . . You are trying to kill me. . . . You are from your father the devil' "); 10:1–16 ("Anyone who does not enter by the gate into the sheepfold but climbs in another way is a thief and a bandit. . . . All who came before me are thieves and bandits"); 12:42ff. ("Nevertheless many, even of the authorities, believed in him. But because of the Pharisees they did not confess it, for fear that they would be put out of the synagogue; for they loved human glory more than the glory that comes from God"); 13:11 ("Not all of you are clean"); 13:30 ("After receiving the piece of bread, he immediately went out"); 15:1–10 ("He removes every branch in me that bears no fruit. . . . Whoever does not abide in me is thrown away like a branch and withers; such branches are gathered, thrown into the fire, and burned"); 16:32 ("The hour is coming, indeed it has come, when you will be scattered, each one to his home, and you will leave me"); 18:17 ("[Peter] said, "I am not' "); 18:25–27 ("He denied it and said, 'I am not.' . . . Again Peter denied it").

If we are unwilling to accept the view that John included all this material in his Gospel only in order to preserve the memory of some interesting past events, which is highly unlikely, we have to conclude that the material reflected divisions in the post-Easter congregation, divisions John believed to have been prefigured in events that took place during the course of Jesus' life or are presented as if they had taken place there. The texts listed above do not simply deal with the unbelieving. If they did, they would belong to a different category, one that has already been examined. In the passages cited here we encounter, rather, those who did believe, but out of fear did not confess their faith, and those who did believe but abandoned their faith either for doctrinal reasons (they find Jesus' teaching "difficult") or succumbed to moral temptation (as, for example, in the case of Judas, to the love of money); also we have those who deny their faith when under pressure, like Peter, even though one cannot say that they have actually given up their faith; finally, there are those who in truth were never really branches of the vine. It is not difficult to speculate on the circumstances in a Christian congregation in the first century in which things of this kind could occur, if only because they occur in every generation of Christian history. Because of the lack of clues, however, it is impossible to lay one's finger on particular events in the history of the Johannine congregation that could be brought into relation with the foreshadowings so cleverly described in the Gospel. Rather, we see in the Gospel only in general terms the reflection of a congregation in which such events took place. There was persecution. (No one in the England of the twentieth century could have written such a sentence as John 16:2, for in England people are not killed because they are Christians.) Some broke down under persecution. For some, temptation proved too strong. Doctrinal disagreements existed, possibly in connection with the sacraments, more probably in regard to Christology. Not all who separated from the Johannine church believed that they thereby ceased to be Christians. At least some probably believed most profoundly that they were maintaining the faith in its purity over against Johannine corruptions.

This leads us almost back to the point from which we started. In the letters also one observes this turning away from the Johannine church, and in them it appears to be treated with increasing harshness. It is not, however, that the evangelist discusses such matters only superficially; rather, he discusses them theologically.[21] The authors of the letters, on the other hand—especially the author of the second and third letters—view such matters from an institutional point of view. It may be possible to make conjectures about this historical variation; it may simply have happened with the lapse of time: theological insight disappeared as the church became increasingly institutionalized. It may be, however, that there is a clue in John 21, if it is correct to consider this chapter an addition to the Gospel in its original form. It is often thought, and probably rightly, that John 21:23 reflects the death of the disciple whom Jesus loved, and that one motive for writing the chapter was not only to point out that Jesus had not predicted that this disciple would live to see Jesus' return but also to point out the different though complementary roles that he and Peter would play in the life of the church: Peter would be the shepherd; the beloved disciple the witness. It is unlikely that the chapter would have been added to the Gospel if the beloved disciple had not been connected in some way with the writing of it as its link to the earliest beginnings (or unless it was believed, or alleged, that he had been so connected with it). His death, accordingly, denoted the end of an era: an era in which the current of theological thought flowed strongly and the church could cope with a high degree of elasticity in form and discipline. In the new era strict discipline replaced creative theological thought. To weather the storm the church battened down the hatches and left no doubt that the end of freedom had arrived. "Do not receive into the house or welcome anyone who comes to you and does not bring this teaching; for to welcome is to participate in the evil deeds of such a person" (2 John 10–11).

Bibliography

In addition to the commentaries on the Johannine writings and works on the social history of the New Testament generally (e.g., those by H. C. Kee, A. J. Malherbe, and G. Theissen), the following may be mentioned.

Boismard, Marie Emile, and Arnoud Lamouille. L'Évangile de Jean, Synopse des quatre Évangiles. Vol. 3. 1977.
Brown, R. E. The Community of the Beloved Disciple. 1979.
Cullmann, Oscar. The Johannine Circle. 1976.
Culpepper, Richard Allan. The Johannine School. 1975.
Lieu, Judith. The Second and Third Epistles of John: History and Background. 1986.
Malherbe, A. J. "The Inhospitality of Diotrephes." In God's Christ and his

People, FS for N. A. Dahl, edited by J. Jervell and W. Meeks, 222–32. 1977.

Martyn, J. Louis. *History and Theology in the Fourth Gospel.* 1968, rev. ed. 1979.

———. *The Gospel of John in Christian History.* 1978.

Meeks, Wayne A. "The Man from Heaven in Johannine Sectarianism." *JBL* 91 (1972): 44–72.

Painter, John. "The Farewell Discourses and the History of Johannine Christianity." *NTS* 27 (1980/81): 525–43.

———. *The Quest for the Messiah: The History, Literature and Theology of the Johannine Community.* 1991.

Purvis, James D. "The Fourth Gospel and the Samaritans." *NovT* 17 (1975): 161–98.

Robinson, John A. T. "The Destination and Purpose of the Johannine Epistles." *NTS* 7 (1960/61): 56–65.

Smith, D. Moody. *Johannine Christianity*, esp. 1–36. 1984.

Thyen, Hartwig. "Entwicklungen innerhalb der johanneischen Theologie und Kirche im Spiegel von Joh. 21 und der Lieblingsjüngertexte des Evangeliums." In *L'Évangile de Jean*, edited by M. de Jonge, 259–99. 1977.

Notes

1. To say this does not mean to deny the value of an attempt to write the social history of early Christianity. But it is important to recognize the difficulty of such an undertaking and to point out that the success of the undertaking is bound to be limited.

2. Cf. (in addition to other essays in this volume) the bibliographical listing by Robin Scroggs, "The Sociological Interpretation of the New Testament: The Present State of Research," *NTS* 26 (1979/80): 164–79.

3. Cf., e.g., C. K. Barrett, *The Gospel According to St John* (1978), 96–99, 139–44; *The Gospel of John and Judaism* (1975), 1–19.

4. C. K. Barrett, *Essays on John* (1982), 131.

5. Barrett, *St John*, 59–62, 133ff.

6. Cf. the recent discussion by R. E. Brown, *The Epistles of John* (1983), 669ff.; also J. Lieu, *The Second and Third Epistles of John* (1986).

7. E. Käsemann, "Ketzer und Zeuge," in *Exegetische Versuche und Besinnungen* (1960), 1:168–87.

8. Acts 20:17, 27; Titus 1:5, 7.

9. The classical account of his view is found in J. B. Lightfoot, "The Christian Ministry," a dissertation appended to his commentary on Philippians (1st ed., 1868), 181–269.

10. See the material collected by Günther Bornkamm in *TWNT* 6:676–80.

11. Omitted by the manuscripts D a b e j.

12. See Barrett, *St John*, 362; *Judaism*, 47ff.

13. It is uncertain whether the group consisted of twelve all told, of whom three had to be priests, or of twelve Israelites together with three priests. CD 10:4–6 requires a group of ten judges.

14. Cf. especially R. Bultmann, *The Gospel of John* (1971), 13–18.

15. Cf. C. K. Barret, *St John*, 149–51; *New Testament Essays* (1972), 27–48.

16. Cf. John H. Hughes, "Disciples of John the Baptist" (Durham University thesis, 1969).

17. O. Cullmann, *The Johannine Circle* (1976).

18. E.g., Barrett, *St John*, 243.

19. It would be appropriate, though it would go beyond the appointed limits of this study, to consider in this context the role of the state in the Johannine Apocalypse. Even when the state has given itself over to evil, its power is from God.

20. See Barrett, *New Testament Essays*, 49–69; also *Essays on John*, 128–30.

21. In John 8 we can perhaps observe the evangelist at work as he rethe-ologizes accusations that are merely insulting. The Jews insist that their freedom and ancestry stem from Abraham (v. 33) and on that basis accuse Jesus of being illegitimate (v. 41). John, in turn, insists that freedom and ancestry have to be interpreted in a theological sense. There is no true freedom unless it is freedom from sin; ancestry manifests itself in behavior.

Contributors

C. K. Barrett	Professor Emeritus of New Testament, Durham (England)
Jürgen Becker	Professor of New Testament, Kiel
Christoph Burchard	Professor of New Testament, Heidelberg
Carsten Colpe	Professor of Religious Studies, Berlin
Peter Lampe	Assistant Professor of New Testament, Berne
Karl Löning	Professor of New Testament, Münster
Ulrich Luz	Professor of New Testament, Berne
Ulrich B. Müller	Professor of New Testament, Saarbrücken
John K. Riches	Professor of New Testament, Glasow